HERITAGE MATTERS

THE BEAR: CULTURE, NATURE, HERITAGE

HERITAGE MATTERS

ISSN 1756-4832

The field of heritage studies is increasingly important as the environment and society face global, national, and local challenges. The study of heritage overlaps with well-established fields such as Museology, Public History, Uses of the Past, Historical Consciousness, Archaeology, Ecology, Nature Conservation, and Memory Studies; it is practised by scholars from multiple disciplines. Heritage Matters is a series of edited and single-authored volumes that address the whole range of issues that confront the heritage sector. The series follows the ethos of Newcastle University Centre of Research Excellence in Heritage, where these issues are seen as part of an integrated whole, an inclusive platform that avoids disciplinary and field compartmentalisation. The series aims to address the most critical and pressing questions about our relations with all forms of heritage – cultural, natural, and intangible.

Previous volumes are listed at the back of this book.

The Bear: Culture, Nature, Heritage

Edited by

Owen Nevin, Ian Convery and Peter Davis

THE BOYDELL PRESS

First published 2019
The Boydell Press, Woodbridge
Paperback edition 2025

ISBN 978-1-78327-460-4 hardback
ISBN 978-1-83765-265-5 paperback

The Boydell Press is an imprint of Boydell & Brewer Ltd
PO Box 9, Woodbridge, Suffolk IP12 3DF, UK
and of Boydell & Brewer Inc.
668 Mt Hope Avenue, Rochester, NY 14620–2731, USA
website: www.boydellandbrewer.com

Our Authorised Representative for product safety in the EU is Easy Access System Europe -
Mustamäe tee 50, 10621 Tallinn, Estonia, gpsr.requests@easproject.com

The publisher has no responsibility for the continued existence or accuracy of URLs for external or
third-party internet websites referred to in this book, and does not guarantee that any content on
such websites is, or will remain, accurate or appropriate

A CIP record for this book is available
from the British Library

Contents

Illustrations

The editors, contributors and publisher are grateful to all the institutions and persons listed for permission to reproduce the materials in which they hold copyright. Every effort has been made to trace the copyright holders; apologies are offered for any omission, and the publisher will be pleased to add any necessary acknowledgement in subsequent editions.

TABLES

Acknowledgments

This book had its origins during work for an earlier volume in the Heritage Matters series, *Changing Perceptions of Nature*. From discussions about ideas of wilderness, and how our approach to landscapes, geology, plants and animals have changed over time, our thoughts began to focus on those animals that people had engaged with, been scared by, utilised, or adored, for centuries. Of all these iconic animals – including wolves, whales and elephants – one animal in particular stood out: the bear. We knew that there was a rich seam of information to mine here – not only on the biology of bears, but more importantly on the human-bear relationship and how this has been expressed in folklore, in first nations' societies, in childhood stories and toys. We wanted also to discuss how our perception of bears is influenced by the manner in which they are revealed to the public in the wild, in museums and galleries, and to give a message about just how threatened some species are, and why, and the efforts being made to conserve them. We also wanted to reflect on what our long association with bears says about *us*; to borrow from Shakespeare, we wanted to hold, as *'twere, the mirror up to* [bears], *to show virtue her own feature, scorn her own image, and the very age and body of the time his form and pressure.'* The reflected image is contradictory, complex and at times frankly disturbing.

To achieve these wide-ranging aims we have been fortunate to bring together a distinguished field of authors, all of whom have addressed bear species from different standpoints. To all of them we are extremely grateful for their time, expertise and patience, but especially so to the two doyens of bear studies: Barrie Gilbert and Lynn Rogers who have kindly provided the Foreword and Afterword for this book. Special thanks are due to Caroline Palmer at Boydell, who has been extremely patient with the Editors, keeping us on track, delighted and sane by her ability to barely contain herself with ursine puns and jokes. We are indebted to Caroline and her team, especially Emily Champion and Elizabeth McDonald, for all their support during the long gestation (and occasional hibernation) of this book. This volume marks a departure in cover design for the Heritage Matters Series and we are especially grateful to Nick Bingham at Boydell for his assistance and patience as we considered various alternative designs – needless to say, the Editors are delighted with the result. Ian would like to thank Kate, Maille, Freya and Ceara; and special thanks to Elspeth Lees, who once again has accommodated his bear obsession when he really should have been doing other things.

Owen Nevin (Central Queensland University)
Ian Convery (University of Cumbria)
Peter Davis (Newcastle University)

Abbreviations

AGS	Anal Gland Secretion
ANWR	Arctic National Wildlife Refuge
API	American Petroleum Institute
BBC	British Broadcasting Corporation
BC	British Columbia
BCE	Before Common Era
CBC	Canadian Broadcasting Corporation
CE	Common Era
COSEWIC	Committee on the Status of Endangered Wildlife in Canada
DNA	Deoxyribonucleic acid
EU	European Union
FG	Forest Guardian
FLIR	Forward Looking Infra-Red
GPS	Global Positioning System
GRR	Grizzly Research in the Rockies
HDW	Human Dimensions of Wildlife
IGBC	Interagency Grizzly Bear Committee
IUCN	International Union for the Conservation of Nature
KIL	Knight Inlet Lodge
LIFE	L'Instrument Financier pour l'Environnement
masl	metres above sea level
NABC	North American Bear Center
NGO	Non-Governmental Organisation
NOAA	National Oceanographic and Atmospheric Administration
OH&S	Occupational Health and Safety
PNALM	Parco Nazionale d'Abruzzo, Lazio e Molise
SBC	Spectacled Bear Conservation Society
SDZG	San Diego Zoo Global
SEAS	Supporting Emerging Aboriginal Stewards
USFWS	United States Fish and Wildlife Service
VOC	Volatile Organic Compound
WWF	World Wide Fund for Nature
XML	eXtensible Markup Language
YNP	Yellowstone National Park
ZSL	Zoological Society of London

Foreword

The Bear: A Cultural and Natural Heritage

Barrie K. Gilbert

Few animals evoke such a range of attitudes in people as bears do. As large iconic predators capable of competing with humans far back in time, their stature and behaviour places them as an alien culture, often in conflict with people's endeavours. The wonderfully exact drawings of bears in the Chauvet Caves of France suggest that worship and respect for bears goes back at least 30,000 years. While indigenous people in North America have co-existed with brown bears for millennia, the proprietorial mindset of trappers, settlers and colonists from Europe succeeded in almost extinguishing the species everywhere settlement occurred. Only in national parks and remote wilderness do grizzlies survive in the contiguous United States and Canada; even there, the ebb and flow of legal battles rages on.

Among the many regions on earth where the diminishing numbers of the eight species struggle to survive, bear habitat is being lost due to the activities of billions of humans. Even where wild country is adequate for the survival of residual populations, those formerly wilderness areas suffer from human intrusion. When, because of habitat loss, bears move out into human-occupied zones there is always the potential to create conflicts. Negative impacts can also be indirect on bears in remote areas, as with polar bears, where toxic chemicals in ocean and air currents are sterilising bears and global warming continues to shrink their habitat and seal diet.

The organisers of this volume invited authors to deliver topics that will appeal to a wide international audience. Unlike many proceedings of scientific conferences and symposia on specialised aspects of bear ecology, behaviour and management, the author-editors have mapped new avenues to advance solutions. It is a most propitious time to have scholars with broad experience contribute current results from many parts of the world. The reader cannot fail to recognise how many of the threats and conflicts in human-wildlife relations are similar around the globe. Concomitant benefits from this revelation of ideas for management applications are policies that preserve bears, such as engaging local people and integrating their needs along with those of the threatened bears. This is especially well done in the cooperative work in Peru for Andean or spectacled bears. The results are heartening, indeed.

Other work shows how forest destruction for firewood by indigenous people can be reduced, their health improved and labour saved by improvements in cooking methods such as adoption of simple efficient stoves that funnel smoke outside living spaces. This is an example of the breadth of scope of this volume and its attention to the growing acceptance of the human dimensions in bear conservation efforts. Bear biologists frequently lament that human-bear management is too often directed at victimised bears and too little at human behaviour management. This appears to be changing, but as we currently observe in North America, often good science and factual evidence are overruled by misinformation and raw political power from special interests. In many ways, this compilation of expert scholarship stands as a call for rescue action.

A very rewarding part of my scientific career has been in field ethological studies of North America's three bear species, especially where human safety and disturbance impacts on bears were primary concerns. These studies varied from detection and deterrent techniques for polar bears in Churchill, Manitoba, aversion techniques to reduce black bear damage to Alberta bee-yards and later cooperative research in Yosemite National Park with my student, Bruce Hastings, which resulted in successful tests of a bear-resistant canister to deter food conditioning in bears. More recent and long-term studies with graduate students took us to bear viewing sites in Alaska and coastal British Columbia. Studying bears daily on salmon streams is very different from remote tracking of radio-collared bears, especially in learning about bear behaviour. Not only can observers identify individuals, but close observation of habituated animals leads to an appreciation of the differences in the temperaments of bears, their subtle communication and how their responses to people varies over time when longitudinal records are assembled. The perceptive field naturalist Charlie Russell[1] remarked that it is a matter of hearing what the bear has to say.

My experience with grizzly bears began over 40 years ago with a life-threatening encounter deep in the high-mountain backcountry of Yellowstone National Park, described in early chapters of my recent book *One of Us: A Biologist's Walk among Bears*. Despite this experience, I returned to what some might call an obsession with grizzlies, to see how we can improve our relationship with these animals. Oddly, I bore no ill will towards grizzlies after I realised my error in invading the bear's personal space in an area that I assumed bears rarely visited. In the back of my mind, at that time, was a Craighead brothers'[2] conclusion that only one in a million visitors to YNP is injured. But I had failed to factor in that most visitors to YNP never move beyond a few dozen feet from a road. If you are tracking grizzlies to study them, the statistics aren't as good, as I learned too late the hard way. Nevertheless, I had a determination to solve problems through close observation of bears.

Surviving a grizzly bear defensive attack caused me to focus on our need to understand what triggers such behaviour in an animal that generally prefers to avoid humans if given the opportunity. Our perception of grizzlies could be changed, it seemed to me, if we understood how our invasion of their personal space, defence of cubs or carcass ownership trigger aggression. Even now, with personal defence using capsaicin spray available, hiking safely in brown bear country requires special alertness. A surprised grizzly is an angry grizzly and an angry grizzly is a dangerous grizzly. It is still scary to stand and face a bear with spray at the ready, but it remains the best tactic in the experience of all the grizzly gurus that I know.

This multi-authored book has scholarly contributions ranging from valuable syntheses invoking human dimensions in bear management to a comprehensive treatment of worldwide accounts of man-bears variously referred to as Yeti, Sasquatch or forest people depending on the region. Initially I wondered how that bizarre topic could possibly relate to bears, as it might be perceived as a rhetorical conspiracy theory. However, the trenchant analysis of human-like tracks and sightings struck me as a wonderfully suitable case for any college course stressing critical thinking and hypothesis testing, even for law and medical students.

1 Andrew Charles Russell (1941–2018) Canadian naturalist, guide and author known for his studies of grizzly bears, particularly his work in Kamchatka
2 Frank Cooper Craighead and John Johnson Craighead were twin brothers, American conservationists and naturalists who made important contributions to the study of grizzly bear biology.

Another chapter suggests changing our attitudes to bears by promoting public understanding and conservation of bear habitats in museums. Peter Davis recommends the adoption of new interpretive techniques to capitalise on modern technologies and social media to promote the need for bear habitat conservation. The number of museums in the UK alone featuring almost all of the world's extant bears as well as skulls of extinct species like cave bears is truly impressive and lends credence to Davis's optimism for enlightening the public. I was inspired to cross the pond to visit as many as I could.

How our attitudes about bears develop as children are described comprehensively with reference to some obvious sources: children's literature, toys, games and books, but the authors delve into intriguing issues of parent-child interactions in attitude formation. Further insights are given about the public's changing values with accounts of the role of ancient and aboriginal storytelling with bear lore in a central role. Another chapter explores more modern relationships of humans toward bears kept in captivity, highlighting the evolution from medieval bear-baiting and European bear gardens to circus acts, zoos and finally to more natural and humane captive collections stressing biology and conservation issues.

Much recent research on brown bears on salmon streams has verified the importance of bears to ecosystems. They are uniquely and irreplaceably important links in ecosystem function and biodiverse productivity. If we continue to lose parts out of nature's machinery both bears and humans will suffer in a wounded world. If we relate well to large carnivores so too can we revitalise our relationship to the remaining wild places on our blue planet.

Introduction: What is a Bear?

OWEN T. NEVIN, IAN CONVERY, PETER DAVIS, JOHN KITCHIN AND MELANIE CLAPHAM

Bears are iconic animals; they are totemic of the non-human world, symbols of multiple human-cultural manifestations of nature. In human culture, bears have played a number of roles; gods, monsters, kings, fools, brothers, lovers, dancers, medicine, food and pest. They are seen as protectors of the forest; symbols of masculinity; the strength of a fighter, football team or army; a comfort for our children; political bargaining chips; an economic indicator; the first casualty/poster boy of global warming; symbols for conservation; worthy adversaries for a hunter's rifle; prize photography subjects for nature tourists or the last bastion of wilderness. Bears offer a unique insight into a multiplicity of paradigms that explore human-non-human animal relationships. Bear totems reinforce and maintain our connection to the natural world.

Bears and humans have shared a similar geographic journey; as we colonised the world from Africa, bears did so from Europe (albeit a few thousand years earlier), with the brown bear being found most frequently where our species also found hospitable conditions. The ecology of (early) *Homo sapiens* and *Ursus arctos* (brown bear) are matched closely: dietary requirements, habitat choice and environmental tolerances. There are many stories that permeate from the past describing our ancestral eaves-dropping on bear foods (and medicines). There are stories of cultures that gathered berries in the same fields as bears and fished on the same rivers: a time when bears and people respected one another's personal space. This is true of some cultures to the present day.

Myths, legends and folklore have informed generations of our and bears' place in the world. Oral histories passed through generations and through ever-changing norms of communication. From imagined fireside tales to blue-chip documentaries in the 21st century, bears have always been good for us to reflect upon; to ponder our lives in relation to their world, to define our own world, one seemingly at odds to the lives of the other. Bears interweave with many of our cultures.

Cave paintings, sculptures, stories of half-men and monsters, how we perceive bear species can have a huge impact on their survival. Our attitudes towards animals, people and places will shape the face of our planet, our climate and our survival. These attitudes are driven by cultural values, which in turn are shaped by a constant and ever-changing rhetoric – led increasingly by visual media but also by religion, tradition, art, politics and science. Bears feed our deepest fears of the 'natural world' while giving us hope for the survival of the wilderness areas we see them inhabiting. They encapsulate a number of paradigms relating to our attitudes to all non-humans, polarising attitudes and often stirring an emotional response.

Bears have played an important role in mediating the human-nature relationship for thousands of years; their significance has been challenged and reshaped over millennia but bears still play an important part in many lives symbolically and materially. Exploring these relationships and attitudes can give us insight into the changing face of species survival and the significance of conservation engagement in the 21st century: all through one very familiar and charismatic group of animals, bears.

In this book, we look at the world of bears through the lens of human cultures and societies, encompassing history, folk stories, art and literature alongside science and conservation. This is a reasonably novel approach to take, but one that we think is long overdue. Bears transcend both natural and disciplinary boundaries. In the following introductory sections, we focus on one species of bear, the brown bear *Ursus arctos*; it is only at this point in the book where we discuss bear biology, behaviour and ecology as a way of introducing these extraordinary animals. Whilst we recognise that 'other species of bear are available', we would argue that the brown bear in particular holds a special place in human emotions, and to a greater or lesser extent the story we tell below can also be applied to other bears, in other places, at other points in time.

SOME EVOLUTIONARY, BIOLOGICAL AND BEHAVIOURAL PERSPECTIVES

Only those able to see the pageant of evolution can be expected to value its theatre, the wilderness, or its outstanding achievement, the grizzly – Aldo Leopold (1970)

The Ursinae line, and the genus *Ursus*, first appears in the fossil record in Europe during the Astian (upper Pliocene) as the Auvergne bear, *Ursus minimus*. This small bear anatomically resembled the black bears and persisted until the early Villafranchian (lower Pleistocene) when it was gradually replaced by *Ursus etruscus*, the Etruscan bear. Early forms of this bear were also small, black bear-sized; however they subsequently increased in size, later approaching the size of a brown bear. It is likely that, much like its antecedent the Auvergne bear, the Etruscan bear was forest-adapted. The Etruscan bear probably gave rise to the brown bear, black bears and the extinct cave bears, *Ursus spelaeus* (Wozencraft 1989).

Ursus maritimus, the polar bear, is the most recent bear in the fossil record and appears to have evolved from a coastal brown bear population which specialised for life on the sea ice margins of the far north (Kurtén 1964). Whilst the brown bears are commonly recognised as one species widely distributed in the Palaearctic and Nearctic (Rausch 1963; Couturier 1954; Kurtén 1968), local populations in Europe, Asia and North America may be somewhat distinct.

While we are considering the evolution and classification of bears, there has been significant debate about the 'are pandas bears?' question. When morphology alone was considered, there was much discussion on skull structure and dentition, which can be summarised as 'they share some features with Ursids (bears) and others with Procyonids (raccoons etc)', and so some chose to place them in Procyonidae and others placed them in Ursidae. Additionally, some people placed the Ailuropods (giant pandas and their extinct relatives) in a separate family within the sub-order which used to be referred to as Fissipedia and is now Caniformia (Delisle and Strobeck 2005).

For our purposes, and in line with current taxonomy, let us assume that family Ursidae contains three sub-families: Ursinae (the bears [although all the sub-families are bears, just to make things more confusing!]), Tremarctinae (the short-faced bears [all extinct except for the spectacled bear]) and Ailuropodinae (pandas but not the red panda [all extinct except the giant panda]) (Peng *et al* 2007).

Back now to brown bears and our question of what – biologically, behaviourally and culturally – constitutes a brown bear? We might first consider this question from a biological and behavioural perspective. Brown bears are one of eight extant species of bear that belong to the family Ursidae, within the order Carnivora (Stirling and Derocher 1990). Their distribution is the most widespread of all bear species, occurring in Europe, Asia and North America, and inhabiting a range of habitats from Arctic tundra to dry desert (Servheen 1990). They are a predominantly solitary species, with a hierarchical social structure, influenced by the distribution of resources as well as inter- and intra-specific competition (Stirling and Derocher 1990). Their mating strategy is promiscuous and they display sex-biased dispersal where males disperse further from the natal range and females exhibit a kin-related spatial structure that may form multigenerational matrilineal assemblages (Stringham 1983; Craighead *et al* 1995a; McLellan and Hovey 2001; Støen *et al* 2005). Brown bears are not strictly territorial but have home ranges that overlap both inter- and intra-sexually (Craighead *et al* 1995a; McLellan and Hovey 2001). The breeding season lasts for approximately two months from late May until mid/late July (Curry-Lindahl 1972; Dahle and Swenson 2003; Nevin and Gilbert 2005b, c), during which the home range sizes of different age-sex classes differ significantly. Both breeding males and oestrous females expand their ranges and roam widely, presumably to increase the likelihood of finding a mate (Dahle and Swenson 2003). Female brown bears experience embryonic diapause (delayed implantation) whereby fertilised eggs lays dormant in the uterus until fat-stores have increased later in the year (Blanc *et al* 2014). Females give birth in dens to usually one to three cubs, but larger litters have been documented (Gonzalez *et al* 2012). Both sexes are known to den during winter months of reduced food availability. Dens sites vary by geographic area but can include caves and high-altitude terrain (Eriksen *et al* 2018; Chirichella *et al* 2019). Brown bears enter a hibernation-state while denning, reducing their heartrate, body temperature and other energetically expensive processes and relying on reserves of fat and lean mass to support them (López-Alfaro *et al* 2013).

Having briefly established biologically, ecologically and behaviourally what bears are, we next consider how we co-exist with them within these contexts. As mentioned above, humans have lived alongside bears for centuries and have co-existed in a variety of different habitats. As those habitats continue to shrink and change due to overexploitation and climate change, pressure on bear populations will increase and co-existence could become more difficult.

Carnivore conflict is a complex and often emotive issue with deeply held social values overlaid on economic, ecological and political reality. Whilst a single incident of conflict between human land-users and a resident carnivore may be reduced to some fairly prosaic measures of economic loss, these are rarely the measures which form the centre of mass of any debate around which conflict management circulates; this is especially true when human injury results from the conflict, as is often the case in widely publicised but rare 'bear attacks'. Globally, incidence and awareness of carnivore conflicts are on the rise, driven by a number of factors.

First, where conservation programmes have been successful and predator control measures have been largely or completely removed (eg the western United States or southern Europe) carnivore populations are expanding and beginning to re-occupy peri-urban (and even deeply urban) settings – consider as an extreme example the presence of healthy mountain lions and coyote populations in Griffith Park in downtown Los Angeles or black bears in back yards in the leafy and affluent suburbs where the city presses up against the Angeles Mountains. In this context, unlike Scandinavia or Alaska, residents are often ill-prepared or unaware of the potential for conflict often catalysed by easily controlled, and some would suggest common sense, measures around managing pets, pet foods, bird feeders and back yard fruit trees. Even where carnivore encounter is more of a 'fact of life', human behaviour in per-urban developments like winter deer feeding can draw mountain lions into neighbourhoods where people are unprepared for encounter.

Second, extreme sports, adventure- and eco-tourism are bringing increasing numbers of people into remote backcountry areas worldwide. The number of people visiting wilderness areas is set to continue to increase and represents one of the fastest growing sectors in the $3.5 trillion global annual tourism market (see Nevin *et al* 2014). Human-powered backcountry recreation has changed substantially in the last decade in the rapidity with which people move through, and the depth of incursion into, remote and wilderness areas – compare the heavily laden back-packer to the agile extreme runner or mountain biker. This is another human behavioural change which increases encounter rate and the potential severity of encounter as carnivores are unused to such rapid movement through the landscape. This changing recreational dynamic also demands a response from recreation managers who must recognise in their protocols that day users will regularly penetrate many tens of kilometres into the backcountry and prime carnivore habitat. This is addressed by Elmeligi *et al* within this volume.

Third, changing agricultural practices driven by both land abandonment and climate change are leaving livestock exposed to depredation risk for longer periods and so increasing the inci-dence of conflict. This can also combine with 'cultural amnesia' of best pastoral practice where carnivores have recently returned.

In each of these cases, education and behavioural change for humans can have a large impact in reducing and mitigating potential conflict. As bear populations expanded in the Greater Yellowstone Ecosystem, the city of Jackson, Wyoming, pre-emptively installed bear-proof garbage containers, a significant investment for a community, with the outcome that as populations reached and passed their town, bears did not become a problem. When this is compared to communities which did not prepare, or could not for economic reasons, the difference is stark.

These are not, however, the issues debated by policy-makers globally when we discuss carni-vore conflict. Unfortunately, much of the debate is not around compromise or mitigation but the dark 'other' of the wild wood. Framed in this context, the response is invariably to limit or curtail the 'other' and emphasis is too frequently placed on carnivore control or aversive conditioning and too infrequently on modifying and managing human behaviour. In the following section we explore some of these issues further, describe some examples of human-bear interactions and contemplate ways that peaceful co-existence could be managed.

HUMAN-BEAR CO-EXISTENCE

Although currently listed as a species of least concern by the IUCN Red List, brown bears occupy an extremely reduced geographic range compared to just 500 years ago (see, for example, Elgmork 1994). The causes of this decline are familiar – habitat loss and fragmen-tation, over-exploitation, persecution through hunting and conflict; in short, human agency, and whilst the term Anthropocene is contested, there is general agreement that we are living through a time in earth's history when humanity has the greatest impact on climate, envi-ronment and, ultimately, species survival. The species that survive this sixth great extinction event (see Briggs 2017) will need to be resilient, adaptive and of value to humans. Brown bears have historically adapted to changing environmental conditions, but the rapidity of current climate-related environmental change, together with ongoing human persecution, presents a unique set of challenges for their survival.

Taken in context, brown bear population decline is a relatively recent phenomenon. It is only 500 years since the last bear walked the British Isles and 200 years or less since the bears in the contiguous United States of America were all, but a few, eradicated. As humans are the main cause of fewer brown bears in the world today, both directly and indirectly, it is important to consider how (or indeed if) we co-existed with bears in the past; what caused the shift in attitudes that appears to inform our contemporary perception of brown bears? Have we ever been able to live alongside bears? This knowledge could help to identify strategies to conserve a species with an uncertain future.

Genetic, evolutionary and archaeological evidence suggests that modern humans first appeared in Africa around 200,000 years ago. We spread out across the globe through the Middle East, eventually arriving in Europe around 40,000 YBP and arguably reaching North America 15,000 years YBP. The timing of this journey is important when considering the temporal and spatial dimensions of human/bear co-existence. We know that bears were once found in North Africa and across a broad range of ecotypes throughout the Northern Hemisphere. This meant that, as humans found new places to live and expanded into new territories, we would have interacted with brown bears on a regular basis. Brown bears also have a very similar omnivorous diet to that of humans. Bears may have even – perhaps unwittingly – led our ancestors to sources of food. We know that through careful observation one species is able to learn from another. Did our species learn from bears: what to eat and where to find it? What else may we have learned from them?

There is archaeological evidence, largely from the late Pleistocene, of humans and bears co-existing. For example, the network of caves in Chouvet, France, offers some of the best-preserved (and celebrated) examples of early cave art. As with most cave art from this period, there is a focus on the role of animals in human lifescapes. Indeed, most paintings in the caves are representations of animal forms: bison, deer and lions; predators and prey. Often painted over the top of each other, they form hard-to-decipher images of animal forms, layers of information built up over time, indicating a social and perhaps spiritual need to record animal images; it is likely that our need to communicate about animals was linked closely to our survival and the formation of our social groups and structures. Multiple species are illustrated together, but in such groups, bears never feature. Instead, bear paintings feature in very distinct places, separate from other animal images. One interpretation of this is that bears were in some way special to our ancestors, although evidence of this is lacking.

Beyond the rather abstract and ambiguous interpretations of bears in cave paintings, there is more recent evidence that brown bears were important to a number of different cultures across various spatial and temporal contexts. As Kolosova *et al* (2017) state, bear worship has been common all over the circumpolar area. Some peoples regarded bears as their ancestors, and in Slavonic folk tales a bear is often a human transformed into a beast as punishment for some transgression. Small and geographically distinct hunter-gatherer communities across the range of the brown bear developed strikingly similar cultural representations, including stories, legends, in the names of places and constellations, mythologies and physical representations of bears in pictographs, sculpture and carvings. Bear worship has been practised by several ethnic groups, including the Sami, Nivkh, Ainu and pre-Christian Finns and Basques. It would appear that human understanding of bears and how to navigate a bear-rich environment was built on interpretations of bear ecology linked to spiritual belief systems and cultural understandings.

In the past, the key to human-bear co-existence appears to have been some notion of shared resources and space. Accepting this was, for many cultures, simply part of everyday life, based in part on some indigenous peoples' cosmologies where humans are on an equal level with bears and all other species, who are simply non-human persons (Clark and Slocombe 2009). For millennia humans and bears have had very close links in some societies. It is beyond the scope of this chapter to cover these human-bear relationships comprehensively, and there is a good deal of literature to explore on this topic (see, for example, Clark and Slocombe (2009) for an overview of aboriginal co-existence with bears; and Hallowell's seminal 1926 paper Bear Ceremonialism in the Northern Hemisphere; this is further explored by Shepard 1993 [republished in 2007]; whilst the bear in myth and ritual often crosses between two worlds, Black (1998) literally straddles two worlds bringing an insightful anthropological discourse to the literature of mainstream bear science and management).

However, a good example of the cultural significance of bears is provided by the Ainu people of the Japanese archipelago, who refer to the Ussuri brown bear (*Ursus arctos*) as 'kamuy' in their language, which translates as 'god'. Not only that, but whilst other animals may also be gods, the brown bear is the head of the gods. In Ainu culture orphaned bears were suckled by Ainu mothers and raised as one of the family (Kindaichi and Yoshida 1949). Loved and played with by the children, it was a great honour to have a bear in your household, even if the life of the bear was destined to be short. The bear was fattened and, at the age of about two years, paraded through every home in the village before a ritual sacrifice and consumption of the meat. The bear was sent to the afterlife with offerings and prayers to the gods for a bountiful year. The human mother of the bear would often grieve her loss as though a child were taken from her (Kindaichi and Yoshida 1949). In Älvdalen, in the Swedish province Dalecarlia, a fiancée was called 'she-bear', and bears are connected with the rituals and traditions before a wedding (Kolosova *et al* 2017).

For the Abenaki people of north-eastern North America, there was a custom of calling bears 'cousin' (partly because a skinned bear looks very much like a human), and when hunters found bear tracks in the woods they would say 'these are our cousin's tracks' (Hallowell 1926). According to Thornton (1992, 32), for the Tlingit people of the Pacific north-west coast, certain rituals and behaviours were required before a bear hunt. Men bathed, fasted and abstained from sexual activity in order to cleanse and purify themselves for the hunt. Family members were expected to eat little, remain quiet and not to move excessively. If they fought or became angry, it was thought that the bear would do the same to the hunter. Elsewhere, the Ainu of Japan invited the bear from the den as a willing sacrifice during hard winters; the bear chose to die or not and was killed with a short spear at close range (Hallowell 1926). Perhaps more fundamentally, Brightman (1993) suggested that of all the hunted animals, the bear was the only one capable of turning the tables and hunting humans.

'A bear is wiser than a man because a man does not know how to live all winter without eating anything' (Hallowell 1926). Bears can leave the world in the winter when food is scarce: for many cultures, their sudden disappearance marked the time when bears would return to the underworld, to the gods, where they would barter for food. These 'messengers' returned in the spring when food became plentiful again. If bears were messengers of the gods, creatures of the underworld, then they needed to be treated with care and respect. Serra (2003, 76) cites the cultural historian Michel Pastoureau, who links the association of black and the devil with the bear. The bear's 'dark fur and anthropomorphic appearance made it a formidable creature, good to hunt but attributed with wicked behaviour' in Roman times. In medieval times, its dark colour became the main feature of the diabolical beast: 'Like Satan, the bear was dark and hairy; like him it was cruel and harmful; like him it loved dark, secret Places' (Pastoureau 2008). Direct reference to bears became taboo in some cultures; they were given a number of names that followed similar themes; old man of the forest, king of the forest, brother and father. Speaking of a bear was bad luck. 'One of the most constant and distinctive practices associated with bears is the custom of referring or speaking to the animal by some other term than the generic name for it. In many instances, in fact, there seems to be a specific prohibition upon the use of the proper name of the beast, especially upon certain occasions' (Hallowell 1926, 43). Clark and Slocombe (2009) report that there are two interrelated ways of speaking about bears that can be considered practices of respect. The first is to avoid speaking about them directly, that is, to avoid saying 'bear' in English or any indigenous languages and not saying anything that implies human superiority over bears. The second is to use some form of circumlocution in place of 'bear', often an honorific term denoting some form of kinship. According to Kolosova *et al* (2017), the Russian literary and common name for bear is also a euphemism literally meaning 'honey eater', and in the Germanic languages bear/björn/bjørn/Bär literally mean 'the brown one'. All of these terms are used instead of the old Indo-European name *r̥kso that has apparently been tabooed for many centuries. Amongst the Blackfoot in North America, there are important substitutions for 'bear', for example, when there are medicine bundles hanging up in a tipi. Guests must then refer to the bear as the 'unmentionable one' or 'that big hairy', or when referring to a specific bear 'sticky mouth' (Hallowell 1926).

In some areas of North America, both bears and humans would use the same fishing areas. People would learn to recognise individual bears by sight, they understood enough about bear population dynamics to leave the dominant bears alone. They also knew that bears could become more predictable the longer they spent time around people, habituation was key to the mutual use of space without conflict. For example, Clarke and Slocombe (2009, 14) describe interactions of people and bears during salmon runs in the Tatshenshini River system of south-west Yukon, where salmon are an important food resource for both people and bears. There appeared to be two main sharing strategies – fishing in shifts; 'everybody left the river by the afternoon 'cause the morning was the people time and the afternoon and evening was the bear's turn to fish'; and recognising the role of 'good bears' (usually older male or female bears) in mediating the behaviour of potentially more troublesome younger bears. This practice in particular reflects a sophisticated, experience-based understanding of bears and their behaviour.

Today, for many people, wild animals and places are experienced through the medium of film and photography. For people who live outside the range of bears, it is likely their first bear was seen catching salmon on a television natural history documentary or else perhaps attacking an unwitting protagonist in the forest of a Hollywood movie. We think we know about bears because we have seen them in action from the safety of our homes or the local cinema; is this really an accurate representation of these species? Wilderness-based tourism (ecotourism) is a popular and growing industry globally, and it is changing the shape of human-bear interactions (Nevin and Gilbert 2005a, c; Nevin *et al* 2014). The goal for many ecotourists is to capture images of their own. Thanks to the ubiquity of smartphones and digital images we are all photographers, we are all able to tell our stories of wildlife through images and circumstance that are in essence 'easy' to achieve. There are now countless stories of interactions between people and bears on YouTube and similar media platforms. However, even though there exists a plethora of information on how to react and stay safe during encounters, many of the videos are framed in the idea of bear attacks, bluff charges and survival against the odds when encountering an 'unpredictable and dangerous' animal.

Further associations between bears and people are discussed in detail in this volume, from the relationship of indigenous societies with bears to modern day interactions via ecotourism and concerns for the conservation of bear populations and their habitat. We have divided the book into three sections: Bear-People interactions; Bears in the public gaze; Bear biology, management and conservation.

In the wide-ranging first section Gareth Longstaff addresses the ways in which the image of the bear has been utilised in gay culture; Mike Jeffries describes how the Teddy Bear evolved and became such a feature of human childhood. Philip Charles has worked closely with indigenous communities in Canada and his chapter describes their relationship with an all-white variant of the American black bear known as the spirit bear. Keeping bears in captivity occurs in Laos and Cambodia, where their use in human medicine is discussed by Elizabeth Davis and Jenny Anne Glikman. Jeff Meldrum provides an insight into the discourse about, and identification of, Sasquatch, Yetis and Wildmen and the role played by bears. Bears have always featured strongly in children's storybooks and Tracy Hayes, Heather Prince and Ian Convery discuss the bear illustrations in the stories and how they affect our perceptions of this iconic animal.

The second section explores the ways in which bears are presented to the public through exhibitions in zoological gardens, museums, contemporary art installations and folklore narratives. Koen Cuyten and Ian Convery explore how bears have been kept captive throughout history, as dancing bears and as 'medicine bears'. Peter Davis describes the ways in which bears have been collected and exhibited in museums and how they have the potential to inform the public and promote environmental understanding. Henry McGhie continues this theme by referring to museum exhibits of polar bears in relation to one specific environmental issue, climate change. Mark Wilson and Bryndis Snaebjörnsdóttir reflect on their cooperative work as artists who are deeply concerned with the interactions between people, environment and wildlife, especially in the Arctic, where their recent work relates to polar bears. This species of bear is also the focus for Kristinn Schram and Jón Jónsson, who explore how narratives from folklore have impacted on the social and cultural history of polar bears in Iceland and the northern Atlantic.

The book's final section is devoted to the management and conservation of bears and their habitats. Jenny Anne Glikman and Beatrice Frank assess how attitudes to brown bear conservation in the Apennines are influenced by local folklore and memories. Identifying individual bears – and how that can aid research – is the theme for Owen Nevin and Ian Convery as they describe their work which heavily relies on the identification and knowledge of individuals within a bear population. Miha Krofel looks at how people in Europe co-exist with bears and the approaches taken to ameliorate potential conflict. Managing bear populations is difficult and reducing uncertainty is the focus for Sarah Elmeligi, Owen Nevin and Ian Convery. In the following chapter these three authors also discuss how citizen science can provide information that aids successful conservation initiatives. Samantha Young, Russ Van Horn and Jenny Anne Glikman describe how community-based initiatives support the conservation of Andean bears in north-west Peru. In the afterword, Lynn Rogers closes the book by exploring his journey from fearful teenager to experienced scientist, bear advocate and sometimes lightning-rod for controversy, walking in communion with bears in the woods of Minnesota, a journey which has both enlightened and enraged many and is emblematic of our complex relationship with these magnificent bears.

Bibliography and references

Black, L T, 1998 Bear in human imagination and in ritual, *Ursus* 10, 343–7

Blanc, S, Fleissner, G, Arnemo, J M, Evans, A L, Swenson, J E, Brunberg, S, Zedrosser, A and Friebe, A, 2014 Factors Affecting Date of Implantation, Parturition, and Den Entry Estimated from Activity and Body Temperature in Free-Ranging Brown Bears, *PLoS One* 9, e101410

Briggs, J C, 2017 Emergence of a sixth mass extinction? *Biological Journal of the Linnean Society* 122 (2), 243–8

Brightman, R A, 1993 *Grateful prey: Rock Cree human-animal relationships*, University of California Press, Berkeley, California, USA

Chirichella, R, Mustoni, A, Zibordi, F, Armanini, M, Caliari, A and Apollonio, M, 2019 Rent a room in the Alps: winter den site preferences of native and reintroduced brown bears, *Mammal Research* 64, 213–22

Clark, D A and Slocombe, D S, 2009 Respect for Grizzly Bears: An Aboriginal Approach for Co-existence and Resilience, *Ecology and Society* 14 (1), 42–60

Couturier, M A J, 1954 *L'ours brun, Ursus arctos L.* Marcel Couturier, Grenoble, Isere, France, 905

Craighead, J J, Sumner, J S and Mitchell, J A, 1995 *The Grizzly Bears of Yellowstone: Their Ecology in the Yellowstone Ecosystem, 1959–1992*, Island Press, Washington DC

Curry-Lindahl, K, 1972 The brown bear (*Ursus arctos*) in Europe: decline, present distribution, biology and ecology, *Bears: Their Biology and Management* 2, 74–80

Dahle, B and Swenson, J E, 2003 Seasonal range size in relation to reproductive strategies in brown bears *Ursus arctos*, *Journal of Animal Ecology* 72, 660–7

Delisle, I and Strobeck, C, 2005 A phylogeny of the Caniformia (order Carnivora) based on 12 complete protein-coding mitochondrial genes, *Molecular Phylogenetics and Evolution* 37 (1), 192–201

Elgmork, K, 1994 The decline of the brown bear *Ursus arctos* L. population in central South Norway, *Biological Conservation* 69 (2), 123–9

Eriksen, A, Wabakken, P, Maartmann, E and Zimmermann, B, 2018 Den site selection by male brown bears at the population's expansion front, *PLoS One* 13, e0202653

Gonzalez, O, Zedrosser, A, Pelletier, F, Swenson, J E and Festa-Bianchet, M, 2012 Litter reductions reveal a trade-off between offspring size and number in brown bears, *Behavioural Ecology and Sociobiology* 66: 1025–32

Hallowell A, 1926 Bear ceremonialism in the Northern Hemisphere, *American Anthropologist* 28, 1–175

Kindaichi, K and Yoshida, M, 1949 The Concepts behind the Ainu Bear Festival (Kumamatsuri), *Southwestern Journal of Anthropology* 5 (4), 345–50

Kolosova, V, Svanberg, I, Kalle, R *et al* 2017 The bear in Eurasian plant names: motivations and models, *Journal of Ethnobiology Ethnomedicine* 13 (14), https://doi.org/10.1186/s13002-016-0132-9

Kurtén, B, 1964 The evolution of the polar bear, Ursus maritimus Phipps, *Acta Zoologica Fennica* 108, 1–30

——, 1968 *Pleistocene mammals of Europe*, The World Naturalist Series, Weidenfeld and Nicolson, London, 317

Leopold, A S, 1970 Weaning grizzly bears, *Natural History* 79 (1), 94–101.

López-Alfaro, C, Robbins, C T, Zedrosser, A and Nielsen, S E, 2013 Energetics of hibernation and reproductive trade-offs in brown bears, *Ecological Modelling* 270, 1–10

McLellan, B N and Hovey, F W, 2001 Natal dispersal of grizzly bears, *Canadian Journal of Zoolog*, 79, 838–44

Nevin, O T and Gilbert, B K, 2005a Measuring the cost of risk avoidance in brown bears: further evidence of positive impacts of ecotourism, *Biological Conservation* 123, 453–60

———, 2005b Observations of autumn courtship and breeding in Brown Bears, Ursus arctos, from coastal British Columbia, *Canadian Field-Naturalist* 119 (3), 449–50

———, 2005c Perceived risk, displacement and refuging in brown bears: Positive impacts of ecotourism? *Biological Conservation* 121, 611–22

Nevin, O T, Swain, P and Convery I, 2014 Bears, place-making, and authenticity in British Columbia, *Natural Areas Journal* 34 (2), 216–21

Pastoureau, M, 2008 *Black: The History of a Color* (trans Jody Gladding), Princeton

Peng, R, Zeng, B, Meng, X X, Yue, B S, Zhang, Z H, Zou, F D, 2007 The complete mitochondrial genome and phylogenetic analysis of the giant panda (Ailuropoda melanoleuca), *Gene* 397 (1–2), 76–83

Rausch, R L, 1963 Geographic variation in size in North American brown bears, Ursus arctos L., as indicated by condylobasal length, *Canadian Journal of Zoology* 41, 33–45

Serra, I, 2013 On Men and Bears: A Forgotten Migration in Nineteenth-Century Italy, *History Workshop Journal* 76 (1), 57–84

Servheen, C, 1990 The status and conservation of the bears of the world, *International Conference on Bear Research and Management, Monograph Series* 2, 32

Shepard, P, 2007 The Biological Bases of Bear Mythology and Ceremonialism, *The Trumpeter* 23 (2), 74–80

Stirling, I and Derocher, A E, 1990 Factors affecting the evolution and behavioral ecology of the modern bears, *Bears: Their Biology and Management* 8, 189–204

Støen, O G, Bellemain, E, Sæbø, S and Swenson, J E, 2005 Kin-related spatial structure in brown bears Ursus arctos, *Behavioral Ecology and Sociobiology* 59, 191–7

Stringham, S F, 1983 Roles of adult males in grizzly bear population biology, *Bears: Their Biology and Management* 5, 140–151

Thornton, T F, 1992 Subsistence Use of Brown Bear in Southeast Alaska, Technical Paper No 214, Alaska Department of Fish and Game Division of Subsistence, Juneau, Alaska

Turner, N J, Ignace, M B and Ignace, R, 2000 Traditional ecological knowledge and wisdom

of aboriginal peoples, *Ecological Applications* 10 (5), 1275–87

Turner N J, 2014 *Ancient Pathways – Ancestral Knowledge Ethnobotany and Ecological Wisdom of Indigenous Peoples of Northwestern North America*, McGill-Queen's University Press, Montreal

Wozencraft, W C, 1989 The phylogeny of the recent Carnivora, in *Carnivore behavior, ecology, and evolution* (ed J L Gittleman), 495-535, Comstock Publishing Associates, Ithaca, NY

Bear-People Interactions

1

The Spirit Bear

Philip Charles

The Spirit Bear is a sub-species of black bear found in the British Columbia area and on a small number of islands near Alaska. It is an all-white bear known as the Kermode Bear *(Ursus americanus kermodei)*, but for First Nations people it is the Spirit Bear. Described in 1905 by William Hornaday, the scientific name recognizes the contribution made by his co-researcher Francis Kermode. During the early decades of the 21st century sightings remain scarce, principally due to the small cryptic populations being found in rather inaccessible locations combined with the secrecy of the aboriginal peoples for whom the bear is held so dearly. This chapter aims to provide an understanding of Canada's First Nations peoples, their relationship with the Spirit Bear and their role in a dynamic conservation setting through collaborative research and ecotourism ventures. It is based on my personal experiences of living and working with the Kitasoo and Xai'xais nations between 2011 and 2016.

The Coastal First Nations

To understand the sociocultural importance of the Spirit Bear, it is essential to better understand the First Nations peoples in whose traditional territories the bear resides. The presence of humans on the central and northern coast of British Columbia dates to 11,000 BC, which coincides with the glacial retreat of the last ice age, providing the beginnings of an intimate relationship humans in this region enjoy with nature, a connection that continues to flourish today. These men and women were warriors, hunters, traders and expert custodians of their lands and waters, to whom 'conservation', informed by rich ecological knowledge, has always been a natural way of life (Clarke and Slocombe 2009; Hallowell 1926; Turner *et al* 2000). For example, the harvesting traditions of the Kitasoo and Xai'xais nations demand that you must always leave the first four of anything you gather; for example, when picking berries, upon reaching a bush the first four berries you pick will be thrown over your shoulder. Coastal communities are still highly dependent on ocean and forest resources for both food and medicine. Species such as devil's club *(Oplopanax horridus)* and poison root *(Veratrum viride)* are still used medicinally on a daily basis. Elders teach that the medicinal properties of these plants increase in strength the farther from the community that they are gathered, thus providing suggestion of a conservation-oriented culture. Such practices ensure local resources are not overexploited and subsequently the harvest of these resources becomes less spatially intensive. As Turner *et al* (2000, 1271) note (in relation to the indigenous peoples of British Columbia), understanding the 'life cycles of different species; seasonal signals such as position and size of snow patches on the mountains, or the arrival of the first snow in the fall; relative numbers of particular birds in a given location; flowering of certain plants; and productivity of certain berries: all provide indicators for people to know when to expect a salmon run, when the clams are ready to be dug, or when particular roots are ready for harvesting.'

Much of the coastal harvest is shared between the people and the resident ursid species, and perhaps surprisingly this is not a diet based exclusively on salmon and berries. In springtime, it is common to see grizzly bears digging for roots on the estuaries; aerating the soil with every excavation, they are referred to as the gardeners of these landscapes. Despite a poor archaeological record, ethnobotanists now understand the extent that people also cultivated the land over centuries as managed, highly productive estuarine root gardens (Deur *et al 2005*). Springbank clover (*Trifolium wormskioldii*), Pacific silverweed (*Argentina pacifica*) and northern rice root (*Fritillaria camschatcensis*) were commonly managed, all of which are also key to the coastal grizzly diet.

The fact that little is accurately known of these First Nation societies pre 1778, the date of first European contact in British Columbia, is due to the lack of any written evidence. Native peoples documented events through songs and stories, many of which have survived and are used still to this day. Petroglyphs and pictographs are also still present, each of which pre-date living memory and whose meanings often remain a mystery. Many customs, protocols and traditions have survived despite persistent cultural persecution by European settlers who were attempting to assimilate the 'savages' into modern Euro-Canadian society. Up to 150,000 First Nations children were forcibly removed from their communities and sent to residential schools where they were to strictly follow the rules set by the schoolmaster (Onciul 2014). These children were not permitted to speak their native tongue, practice native customs or traditions; their songs, dances and clothing were all outlawed. In many respects their experience is not unique; similar cultural genocide practices were also used against the Sami people of northern Scandinavia, American (USA) first peoples and aboriginal people of Australia (see, for example, Minton 2016). A campaign of physical, mental and sexual abuse against many of the children has resulted in a chain of broken generations of First Nation peoples that is still visible. Having overcome so much, today's First Nations are strong and have a new-found resilience. With each new generation, the weight of the past seems to be slightly lifted, but not forgotten. In 2008 the Canadian government apologised for its role in the residential school system.[1] Reconciliation between First Nations and the government of Canada is ongoing and is particularly difficult with regard to rights and title over traditional territories. Indeed, First Nation society as a whole has gone through a cultural bottleneck and certainly aspects of their cultural identity have been lost. Fortunately, by piecing together work by anthropologists and ethnobotanists (often researched in collaboration with First Nation communities) we are able to better understand some of the historic relationship of the Nations with nature, and with bears in particular (see, for example, Boas 2002; Bolt 1992; Turner 2014).

Collectively, across all Canadian provinces, these nations are referred to as the First Nations Peoples. Each First Nation is distinctively different to each other. Neighbouring communities, despite their close geographical proximity to one another, will often have a different language, hereditary chief structure, clan system, ceremonial protocol and traditional colours. On the central coast of British Columbia there are four nations that share habitat with the Spirit Bear – the community of Hartley Bay of the Gitga'at nation, the Bella Bella community of the Heiltsuk

---

[1] See https://www.aadnc-aandc.gc.ca/DAM/DAM-INTER-HQ/STAGING/texte-text/rqpi_apo_pdf_1322167347706_eng.pdf

nation and the community of Klemtu, where peoples of the Kitasoo and Xai'xais nations live together. All of these isolated island communities have small human populations, approximately 150, 1500 and 350 respectively.

I am an adopted member of the Kitasoo/Xai'xais nation of Klemtu, culturally adopted in 2012 by Chief Haimas Nismuutk; Charlie Mason is his given English name. Upon my adoption I was given the traditional name of Gvim, 'the one who swims with whales', but literally translated as humpback whale. I was also now a member of the Raven clan, one of four clans that remain extant in Klemtu along with the Wolf, Eagle and Black Fish (double-finned killer whale). Families are associated with a particular totem animal, or clan, and there were once many clans in this region, including the Frog, Black Bear, Grizzly Bear and Mountain Goat, all of which are now extinct due to entire families dying during smallpox epidemics. Clans are assigned maternally, so as my adopted mother is of the Raven clan, I am too. This remains a huge honour and during the many years I have spent in Klemtu I have always been accepted as a member of the community and able to learn so much from my adopted father, elders and the community as a whole. This adoption, coupled with the sensitive work I was undertaking, has allowed me fascinating insights into the modern relationship between the Kitasoo/Xai'xais people and the lands and waters of their traditional territory.

Formed in the late 19th century, Klemtu saw two different nations unite in order to maximise trade opportunities with visiting European vessels. It was at this time that the tradition of living in mobile camps within the territory (3939 square kilometres) and harvesting traditional foods started to dwindle. Community elders would tell me that this was when the people's relationship with the animal inhabitants of the forest started to change; rather than moving from one camp to another they settled in one central locale. Soon after I arrived onto Kitasoo/Xai'xais territory I was introduced to Violet Neasloss, a matriarch of the community, who at 97 years of age was its oldest member. Violet spoke in Sgüüx̣s, a local dialect of the Tsimshian language, and English. I was enthralled to hear her stories of childhood spent in traditional camps that were temporary and portable, allowing people to move accordingly with the harvest. 'In late spring we would be in Poison Cove', she would tell me, 'that's where the eulachon [an anadromous fish] would run, and the berries were good too.' I would ask her about her families' relationship with bears growing up and she would speak of tolerance and mutual respect, remembering only one occasion that a bear had to be killed for the safety of the community. Violet passed away two years later in 2013, aged 99; the Sgüüx̣s language became extinct as she was the last person to speak it. Although efforts were made to save this language, Violet was the only remaining speaker and as a consequence the lack of meaningful dialogue resulted in the language not being documented. Such events act as a reminder of continued cultural loss within these communities and drives members forward to preserve, document and share traditional practices.

In the early decades of the 20th century, Klemtu and other similar coastal communities enjoyed a period of high employment as trade opportunities with Europeans increased. A salmon canning factory was opened in Klemtu, but it closed in 1954 and the community was left with minimal employment. This situation changed in the 1990s when the community agreed to allow Marine Harvest[2] to operate salmon fish farms in the territory, with a processing plant established

---

[2] Marine Harvest [renamed Mowi in January 2019] is a major international seafood producer employing over 13,000 people and operating in more than 20 countries. The approach pioneered in Klemtu is still known internationally within the industry as the 'Kitasoo model of community engagement'.

in the community on the site of the old cannery. Agreements remain in place to ensure that at least 50 per cent of the employees are from Klemtu.

The Spirit Bear

The Kermode bear remains an exceptionally rare subspecies of the American black bear *(Ursus americanus)* found almost exclusively on the central and northern coasts of British Columbia, Canada. Long revered by the First Nations people who live in this sparsely populated region of dense temperate rainforest, they refer to this cream-coloured bear as moskgm'ol, which translates as the 'white bear'. Internationally known and commonly recognized as the Spirit Bear, it is the provincial mammal of British Columbia, and commonly regarded as the rarest bear on the planet. The cryptic and relatively isolated population remains a poorly studied species for which there are no accurate population estimates, yet an accepted figure of up to 400^3 white-phase individuals across the central coast region remains (Marshall *et al* 2002). Recent observations from local people and tourism operators suggest this figure is inaccurate, indicating the population of white-phase Spirit Bears is now in decline.

The mutant MC1R gene facilitates the remarkable and visually striking white-phase Kermode bear (Ritland *et al* 2001*)*. When two copies of this recessive gene are present, melanin is not produced. A single copy of the MC1R gene results in a black-phase Kermode that visually looks and behaves in an identical manner to a true American black bear. However, carrying the recessive gene means that breeding with another black-phase Kermode or indeed a white-phase Kermode can produce white-phase offspring. The highest concentrations of Spirit Bears are found on two islands in the Great Bear Rainforest, namely Gribbell Island in Gitga'at traditional territory and Princess Royal Island, which overlaps both Gitga'at and Kitasoo territories. The latter, the second largest island in British Columbia after Vancouver Island, is often referred to as the home of the Spirit Bear. It is believed that up to one in ten black bears on this island are white-phase Kermodes; this coincides with the Xai'xais creation myth whereby the Creator turned every one in ten black bears white to serve as a reminder of the ice age. It is a sad irony that the Spirit Bear is just one of the species facing climate change and extinction. Even today, increased water temperatures in salmon spawning streams are seen to be negatively impacting on the spawning success of Pacific salmon.

The Great Bear Rainforest, roughly the size of Switzerland, is an intricate tapestry of wilderness and conservation hope; it is home to the black bear, Spirit Bear and grizzly bear *(Ursus arctos horribilis)* as well as many other iconic species such as the coastal gray wolf (*Canis lupus*), North American beaver (*Castor canadensis*) and cougar (*Puma concolor*). The combined efforts of NGOs and coastal communities resulted in the formation of the Great Bear Rainforest in 1997 and it is afforded greater protection from non-sustainable extractive industries such as logging and mining (Howlett *et al* 2009). Since 2017, hunting of grizzly bears in this region, by both trophy hunters and residents, is banned by provincial law. The mountainous landscape is dominated by glacier-

---

[3]   This figure is based on non-scientific observations (mostly tourism) between the two major bear viewing managers Tim McGrady of SBL and Marven Robinson of Hartley Bay. Throughout our viewing seasons (1 July–10 October) we cover all major and most minor river systems in the region and between us see on average a total of ten different white bears across the season. Local people used to see more than this, leading to local suggestions that perhaps the number has dropped to below 100.

carved ocean-flooded fjordland and it is the forest's relationship and proximity to these coastal waters that truly defines its place and purpose. These cool nutrient-rich waters attract and support many cetacean and pinniped species and arguably the rainforest's most notable non-ursid resident, Pacific salmon (*Oncorhynchus spp*); the five species return to their natal spawning grounds each year. Vernon Brown, marine planning coordinator for the Kitasoo/Xai'xais First Nation, would often tell visitors to the territory that 'Once you have tasted the salmon here you are part of the cycle, a part of this coast.'

Many species depend on the reliable return of salmon each year; the bears most famously but the wolves of this area are arguably equally dependent on this vital energy resource. Coastal gray wolves, 30 per cent smaller than their mainland conspecifics, face increased difficulty in finding preferred ungulate prey in these steep mountainous forests and as such have become some of the only wolves to actively hunt and consume fish. Cryptic, even more so than the bears, and often nocturnal, these wolves are not commonly seen, but evidence reveals such hunting activity. I once counted 87 dead coho salmon *(Oncorhynchus kisutch)* neatly piled adjacent to a salmon river, each as intact as you'd expect to see for sale at the local fishmongers, with the exception of the omega-3-rich brain having been consumed. It is thought these wolves do not consume the rest of the salmon due to either parasite avoidance or for simple nutritional reasons (Darimont *et al* 2003). Many predators catch salmon from the rivers and then consume them away from the river. Bears are no exception, often taking salmon into the forest, back to their day beds where they can feed without the dangers of interference from other river inhabitants. Core testing of trees near to salmon-bearing rivers shows that they have acquired nutrients that are only found in marine environments (Ben-David *et al* 1998), a remarkable example of how far-stretching the relationship of salmon is to the plants, animals and ecosystem as a whole in this region.

Eco-Tourism

There is a long history of bear-viewing in British Columbia and the province remains a top destination for this activity. Due to its cryptic nature, low population density, minimal media coverage and difficult access to its habitat, the Spirit Bear has long avoided too much attention. However, a recent combination of factors, including the popularity of sharing images on the internet with a global audience, the increased attractiveness of seeing rare mega-fauna in the wild and a 2011 front page *National Geographic* (Barcott 2011) story has created increased demand to see the Spirit Bear.

Klemtu owns and operates the Spirit Bear Lodge that opened fully in 2011. The importance of this lodge to the community and to the local conservation efforts cannot be understated. The hereditary chiefs and the elected council of Klemtu have decided to create a conservation-based economy that shifts focus away from extractive industry and a dependency on employment from fish farms. The creation of the Spirit Bear Lodge, owned and operated by the community, is a large step towards this goal. The lodge has become an internationally recognized leader in the aboriginal eco-tourism field and employs and trains local chefs, guides, boat operators, crew members and housekeepers. However, a key role is to educate visitors about the wildlife of the region. Only those members of the community with access to a boat are able to venture into the territory as the island community has no roads outside the village boundary. The lodge uses a fleet of five small passenger vessels to take tourists to various locations in order to view bears; these boats are also essential for the work undertaken by staff and community members. This new-found connection to the territory has reignited a conservation interest and concern amongst many members of the community across all ages. There are 52 salmon-bearing rivers in the Kitasoo/Xai'xais territory, nearly all of which are utilised in order to minimise potential impact on certain river systems.

There are also a number of boat-based tourism operators in the region. These are limited in number by the Kitasoo/Xai'xais nation in order to reduce any potential impact. The community works closely with these operators, sharing observations and concerns. A dedicated and popular Spirit Bear viewing operation is based in Hartley Bay, where they access just one river system known to be occupied by white-phase individuals.

THREATS TO THE SPIRIT BEAR

Two types of bear hunt occur in British Columbia: the trophy bear hunt and the resident bear hunt. The trophy hunt sees individuals from outside British Columbia pay large sums of money to shoot both grizzly and black bears for trophy purposes. It is common to have a photograph taken with the 'trophy' and take the head, pelt and/or paws where permitted. The resident hunt is for residents of British Columbia only and is conducted for sport or food purposes. The provincial government controls and monitors both forms of hunting and a set number of hunting tags is issued each year. This has for a long time been the accepted norm for British Columbians but in recent years there has been a shift in perception of the hunt following large and effective campaigns fronted by First Nations communities in the Great Bear Rainforest. Nine coastal communities banned all trophy hunting of bears on their lands in 2012, but ongoing disputes with the province over sovereignty of land meant nothing changed; the provincial government continues to issue licenses for the region. The nations had to push further and began targeting the trophy hunt with a strategic combination of the social, cultural and economic arguments against the hunt. Public opinion shifted dramatically and 2017 saw the trophy hunting of grizzly bears banned across all of British Columbia; as mentioned above, resident and trophy hunting of them is banned in the Great Bear Rainforest. Grizzly bear populations are far smaller than those of black bears across British Columbia and they produce fewer offspring over a lifetime. However positive this result, the hunting of black bears is still permitted, and this stimulates a concern amongst many for the dwindling population of Spirit Bears. Although the hunting of the Spirit Bear in any capacity is already illegal, carrying a fine of up to $100,000 CAD, this is only applicable to white-phase individuals. The hunting of black bears is still allowed, which includes the black-phase Kermode bears as they are visually identical. The lack of ability to distinguish between the two will inevitably lead to the killing of black-phase individuals that are able to produce white-phase offspring.

GRIZZLY BEAR DISPERSAL

Wild Pacific salmon, on which the bears of the region depend, face many pressures and are in steady decline. Studies indicate that in recent years grizzly bears have dispersed from their traditional mainland habitat of sedge-rich estuaries and are establishing viable populations on the adjacent islands that are the preferred habitat of black bear species (Service *et al* 2014). Whilst a sympatric relationship has long been observed between the species (Holm *et al* 1999), the grizzly bear will often spatially and temporally outcompete the black bear, taking the dominant share of vital resources. I have witnessed myself this very phenomenon where a very reliable and busy island black bear river system is now occupied by one or more grizzly bears and this forces the blacks to shift their behaviour patterns quite dramatically. Temporal observations show these black bears now access the river more at night, and for much shorter periods of time. Spatially, the bears feed on secondary or tertiary locations on the river due to the increased difficulty in accessing the energy-rich salmon areas. Occurrences such as this act as a catalyst for debate within the community of Klemtu, for which the Spirit Bear is so revered. If a grizzly bear has been seen to move into Spirit Bear habitat should action be taken to remove the grizzly bear? Amongst community members the answer is yes. However, perhaps research is needed to discover why the grizzly bears are dispersing in the first place, rather than removing individuals that have already chosen to do so.

Such a distinct behavioural shift is having a negative impact on tourism operations in the region. Whereas in previous years guests were often rewarded with reliable Spirit Bear viewing on the islands during day time, they are now often greeted with an over-indulgent and dominant grizzly bear without a black or white bear in sight. This could lead to financial implications for those tourism operations who all pay into and support local conservation-based initiatives, including local bear research led by the Spirit Bear Research Foundation.[4]

CONCLUSION

Despite not all residents of Klemtu being convinced by a community decision to open the doors of the territory to the wider world, tourism is visibly stimulating a cultural resurgence that is favoured by most. For many years, local people would not talk of the Spirit Bear so as not to advertise its presence, especially during years of trapping and the fur trade. However, it is now common for journalists from film and print to be seen in Klemtu, documenting the region for all to see. A full-feature IMAX documentary focused on the Spirit Bear and the Great Bear Rainforest, due for release in 2019, will only increase global appetite to visit the region. However, the voices of concern about this exposure are currently outweighed by voices of support. Local artists now have a customer base to whom they can directly sell their wares and regular cultural performances are seen in the traditional big house[5]; although presented for the tourists they are an essential component to maintaining culture. These performances are planned and presented by the Súa Youth Cultural Group, a summer project funded by the Spirit Bear Lodge which is accessible to all youth in the village. Tourism dollars also help facilitate the Coastal Guardian Watchmen programme, locally employing four community members. Watchmen undertake daily boat-based patrols across the territory with a focus on estuaries and river systems that are known to have a higher tourism footprint and increased risk of illegal resource extraction. With limited enforcement powers and unable to issue fines, these watchmen prefer to see their roles as educators rather than enforcers, offering visitors to the area guidance in acceptable practices in the territory.

---

4   This foundation was set up in 2014 through a partnership of the University of Victoria, Raincoast Conservation and central coast communities. It is committed to applied conservation research investigating the interrelationships of bears, salmon and people of the region.
5   A big house, also known as a long house, is the most important structure within a First Nation community. Ceremonial protocols must take place here, including passing of chief names, marriages, tombstone feasts and coming of age ceremonies.

Figure 1.1 Klemtu SEAS interns created this first pictograph in local living memory in 2016. It depicts animals in a canoe with a series of hands beneath it, all done in dark-coloured ochre. It acts as a marker of identity, ensuring contact with the local flora and fauna.

As healing from past events continues within the Kitasoo/Xai'xais community, so does the focus on future generations. Douglas Neasloss, elected Chief Councillor[6] of Klemtu and holder of the Spirit Bear traditional name, is adamant that the youth are the next chiefs and matriarchs, the next policy-makers and stewards for the territory. In a community as small as Klemtu this could not be more true. In 2012, the Klemtu Supporting Emerging Aboriginal Stewards (SEAS) programme was formed; initially an annual eight-week summer internship for four community youth members, it has now extended to be part of the school syllabus. The programme expertly blends theory and practical elements with a focus on what is happening locally, including scientific research, tourism, language preservation, indigenous law and re-connecting with the lands and waters of their territory. In 2016, the Klemtu SEAS interns created the first pictograph in local living memory, animals in a canoe with a series of hands beneath it, all done in dark-coloured ochre (Fig 1). Many feared such a feat would never be achieved. The importance of maintaining such markers of identity is critical for the preservation of culture, but also as a means of ensuring contact with the local flora and fauna. It is the First Nations' instinctive nature to protect and preserve; hence taking young people out into the landscape, championing culture whilst spending time with the wildlife of their territory, creates an unrivalled sense of understanding and

---

6   There are two governance structures in most First Nation communities. The hereditary chief structure where names and rank are passed within families, and the elected council structure whereby a chief and council are formally elected by community members (currently every two years in Klemtu).

ownership. This is vital in the ongoing process of treaty talks between the Canadian government and individual First Nations communities.

An ongoing dispute over land claims and access to resources continues between coastal communities, but a united approach to scientific research and conservation is continually gaining strength. The Central Coast First Nations Bear Working Group is a partnership between four nations whose collaborative effort of scientists, elected council members and stewardship staff was instrumental in the recent success regarding banning the trophy hunting of grizzly bears in their respective territories. Collaborative bear research between these nations continues, as well as the continued sharing of knowledge and resources. Such an alliance of the coastal nations will certainly serve to protect the cultural legacy as well as the biodiversity of the region. The future of the regions' biodiversity, and indeed the Spirit Bear, rests with these young leaders, and I feel confident that the intricate complexity of life in the region will remain abundant for many years to come under the expert guidance of the First Nations peoples.

BIBLIOGRAPHY AND REFERENCES

Barcott, B, 2011 Land of the Spirit Bear, *National Geographic*, 220 (2), 34–65

Ben-David, M, Hanley, T A, Schell, D M, 1998 Fertilization of terrestrial vegetation by spawning Pacific salmon: the role of flooding and predator activity, *Oikos* 83, 47–55

Boas, F (edited and annotated by Bouchard, R, Kennedy, D), 2002 *Indian Myths and Legends from the North Pacific Coast of America*, Talonbooks, Vancouver

Bolt, C, 1992 *Thomas Crosby and the Tsimshian, Small Shoes for Feet Too Large*, University of British Columbia Press, Vancouver

Clark, D A, and Slocombe, D S, 2009 Respect for Grizzly Bears: an Aboriginal Approach for Co-existence and Resilience, *Ecology and Society* 14 (1), 42–60

Darimont, C T, Reimchen, T E, and Paquet, P C, 2003 Foraging behaviour by gray wolves on salmon streams in coastal British Columbia, *Canadian Journal of Zoology* 81 (2), 349–53

Deur, D, Turner, N J, Dick, A, Sewid-Smith, D, and Recalma-Clutsei, K, 2013 Subsistence and resistance on the British Columbia Coast: Kingcome village's estuarine gardens as contested space, *BC Studies* 179, 13–37

Hallowell A, 1926 Bear ceremonialism in the Northern Hemisphere, *American Anthropologist* 28, 1–175

Holm, G, Lindzey, F, and Moody, D, 1999 Interactions of Sympatric Black and Grizzly Bears in Northwest Wyoming, *Ursus* 11, 99–108

Howlett, M, Rayner, J, and Tollefson, C, 2009 From government to governance in forest planning? Lessons from the case of the British Columbia Great Bear Rainforest Initiative, *Forest Policy and Economics* 11, 383–91

Marshall, H D, and Ritland, K, 2002 Genetic diversity and differentiation of Kermode bear populations, *Molecular Ecology* 11: 685–97

Mcllwraith, T F, 1948 (Reissued 1992) *The Bella Coola Indians*, The University of Toronto Press, Toronto

Minton, S J, 2016 Educational Systems and Cultural Genocide, in *Marginalisation and Aggression from Bullying to Genocide. Innovations and Controversies: Interrogating Educational Change*, SensePublishers, Rotterdam

Onciul, B A, 2014 Revitalizing Blackfoot heritage and addressing residential school trauma, in *Displaced Heritage: Responses to Disaster, Trauma, and Loss* (eds I Convery, G Corsane and P Davis), Boydell and Brewer, Woodbridge, Suffolk

Ritland, K, Newton, C and Marshall, H D, 2001 Inheritance and population structure of the white-phased "Kermode" black bear, *Current Biology* 11, 1468–72

Service, C N, Adams, M S, Artelle, K A, Paquet, P, Grant, L V, and Darimont, C T, 2014 Indigenous Knowledge and Science Unite to Reveal Spatial and Temporal Dimensions of Distributional Shift in Wildlife of Conservation Concern, *PLoS ONE* 9 (7), e101595, doi:10.1371/journal.pone.0101595

Turner, N J, Ignace, M B, and Ignace, R, 2000 Traditional ecological knowledge and wisdom of aboriginal peoples, *Ecological Applications* 10 (5), 1275–87

Turner, N J, 2014 *Ancient Pathways – Ancestral Knowledge Ethnobotany and Ecological Wisdom of Indigenous Peoples of Northwestern North America*, McGill-Queen's University Press, Montreal

2

Out of the Wild Wood and into our Beds: The Evolutionary History of Teddy Bears and the Natural Selection of Deadly Cuteness

MIKE JEFFRIES

The teddy bear, *Brunus edwardii* (Blackmore and Young 1972), has been a toy throughout western Europe and North America since at least 1903. The popularity of teddy bears has ensured their continued survival whilst other cuddly toys have become extinct (eg Billy Possum), or waned in popularity and/or cultural acceptance (eg golliwogs, whose popularity declined sharply from the 1960s onwards because of the perceived racism in the representation, Pilgrim 2012), or have been associated with short-lived fads, including the Tellytubbies. Teddy bears are dispropor-tionately important in North American and European culture; 'they concern our most intimate and deep-going feelings and experiences' (Caldas-Coulthard and van Leeuwen 2003, 26). They are intended to be played with and, perhaps even more importantly, cuddled and loved (see Hayes *et al*, this volume; Jones 2018). Teddy bears are commonly portrayed as very important in the emotional lives of children, both as a significant resource to cuddle but also a consolation when adults do not give children sufficient time: they are seen as 'commoditised sentimentality' (Sutton-Smith 1986; Vargas 2009a). Teddies are an important, but poorly researched, signifier in childhood studies (Nieuwenhuys 2011). Given their significance, the ecology of their interaction with humans reveals some remarkable natural history.

A striking feature of teddy bears are the changes to the predominant anatomical characteristics of manufactured bears throughout the roughly 110 years of their existence. The longevity of the teddy taxon, combined with their collectability, has preserved a wealth of detail about teddy bear morphology. There have been recorded changes to diversity and success, based on overall numbers (White 1971; Picot 1988) along with shifts in the frequency of anatomical forms (Picot 1988; Morris *et al* 1995; Nieuwenhuys 2011). Hinde and Barden (1985) presented evidence of changes in measurable morphology and suggested that these changes mimicked biological evolution. The changes to teddies are primarily a reduction in wild adult bear features (long limbs, long snouts, small heads) and an increase in juvenile bear and human baby characters (eg disproportionately large heads and short limbs), so called neotenic, or infantile, anatomy. Similar evolutionary selec-tion has been described for other children's toys, including Mickey Mouse and Donald Duck (Gould 1980), and action figures where increased muscularity conforms to male body stereotypes (Pope *et al* 1999). There is a widespread consensus that the anatomy of the majority of manufac-tured teddy bears has become more akin to juvenile humans in form, generally cuter. Whilst the trend is well documented the actual process has not been interrogated. There is often a simple assumption that cuter bears will be chosen over wilder looking brethren.

To understand the process, I explore the evolutionary history of the teddy bear as a taxon and its ecological interaction with humans. Teddy bears provide a remarkable analogy to the complex origins and histories of many real fossil lineages. Their ecological interactions with humans provide a surprise, which some might see as disturbing, if not downright nasty.

THE ORIGINS AND PALEOECOLOGY OF TEDDY BEARS

Teddy bears appear in the fossil record of toys apparently abruptly and in large numbers in 1903, in North America and Europe. The dominant narrative for their origin is that President 'Teddy' Roosevelt of the USA refused to shoot a bear cub during a hunting trip in 1902. Publicity for this sentimental act led to Roosevelt's adoption of the cub as an electioneering symbol, coincident with the sudden availability of toy bears from German (Steiff) and American (Michtom) manufacturers. However, this widely accepted version of teddy bear origins is deceptive. The full story is more complex and there are consequences for the subsequent evolution of teddy bears. In particular teddies benefitted from a particular social and cultural opportunity as attitudes to nature and wildness changed during the 19th and into the early 20th century.

Varga (2009a, 2009b) explores the teddy bear's origins in detail. Roosevelt's merciful encounter with a bear cub is a myth. The bear he refused to shoot was an adult female, which had already been captured and bound to a tree; it was subsequently killed by another member of the hunting party. This event is therefore a strong indication that bears were (and remain) a symbol of the wild (Ray 2014). Such wild places were to be dominated and bears hunted down. Public reaction to Roosevelt's action was informed by a cartoon on the front page of the *Washington Post*, drawn by Clifford Berryman. In the original the bear is adult size and fearful of its captors, perhaps a critique of Roosevelt, in particular the ambiguity of his nature conservation credentials given his fondness for hunting (Varga 2009b). Between 1903 and 1906 Berryman redrew the cartoon, now depicting the bear as a vulnerable cub and beginning to acquire childlike characteristics, even a name, 'Bruin' (Varga 2009c).

Roosevelt's hunt and the advent of Bruin coincided with the completion of a transitional period when wilderness in Europe and North America changed from archetypal threat to a romanticised idyll, pristine and innocent even when dangerous (Varga 2009c). Whilst Varga specifically links the advent of the teddy to a timely opportunity created by changing attitudes to wilderness, our perceptions of wild nature have a deeper, richer and complex history. Wilderness is a potent and ambiguous idea, in particular for developed Western cultures (Nash 1967) and their settler emigrants, eg in the USA (Castree 2005). In Europe prior to c. 1700 wilderness was, at least, disliked and often feared. The shift to admiration (that 'wildness pleases', Thomas 1983, 260) was driven by romanticism, the rise of the sublime in art and some clerical reinterpretation of nature (Thomas 1983). One outcome is that the wilderness, with its core attributes of naturalness and pristine landscape, is an artificial cultural construct (Castree 2005). Whilst modern environmentalism routinely eulogises this wild nature, the American wilderness has retained some menace, for example in the backwoods rural gothic of films and television (Murphy 2013). However, where once the wildlife was to be feared the dangers are now other people and we cling to our teddies for comfort. Simultaneously there was an increasing recognition of childhood as a special stage in life, evident in Europe with the introduction of widespread public schooling and taking children out of the labour market. Children's behaviour and actions were characterised as natural and innocent, echoing the intrinsic virtues of wildness, even wild play, 'a natural kinship between animal and children' (Varga 2009, 197; Nieuwenhuys 2011. Jenks, 2005, neatly summarises the tensions in our wider representation of childhood in the West as a natural but distinct stage, the distinction potentially one of savagery). This was substantially gendered for boys' play and the teddy bear may have originally been seen as an appropriate cuddly toy for boys, an alternative to girls' dolls (Caldas-Coulthard and van Leeuwen 2003). This combination of innocent and naughty is still evident in representations of teddy bears and their mischievous behaviour in many children's stories, eg Paddington Bear. Naughty, risky play is expected in boys, partly an outcome of social construction (eg Morrongiello and Hogg 2004). Teddies retain a mix of child and wild (fur, snout) characteristics and this may reflect adult ambivalence to small children, who require training (or taming). For example, Philo (2018) and Caldas-Coulthard and van Leeuwen (2003) suggest the teddy has an important role as a transitional object, helping children explore the differentiation of the objective and subjective world.

Changing attitudes to nature, wild animals and children created an ecological opportunity for teddy bears, their rise to dominance unleashed by the serendipity of Roosevelt's hunt. Steiff had started manufacturing stuffed toys from 1880, with at least 13 species in 1890 including elephants and horses. These animals were cuddly but still essentially wild. The teddy bear was just one taxon out of several, its eventual dominance perhaps not obvious in advance, possessing teeth, claws and a humped back. Its success was contingent on the environment, only flourishing by association with Roosevelt and, in the UK, King Edward VII. There are echoes here of the rise of real taxa, eg the emergence of the dinosaurs as the successful groups from amongst several diverse lineages in the Triassic and the difficulties of anticipating nature's winners and losers in advance, perhaps most famously Stephen Jay Gould's take on the Burgess Shale Fauna (Gould 1989). Teddies faced competition from other taxa, notably Billy the Possum (Mullins 1986), therefore pitching a toy placental mammal, the teddy, against a marsupial, Billy, in an odd echo of clashes between actual mammalian dynasties. Billy Possum, who appeared in 1909, was also associated with political events in the USA, having been adopted as a symbol by Roosevelt's successor, William Taft. Postcards even depict Teddy handing on the role to Billy Possum. Billy was heavily promoted by manufacturers; however, the public did not take to Billy (nor to William Taft) and Billy became extinct.

At a White House banquet in 1906 tables were decorated with toy bears made by Steiff, which were christened 'Teddy Bears'. Steiff bears had been on sale since 1903 but largely ignored by the public. Their breakthrough is credited to the American Michtom Toy Company, which produced a version for the New York Toy Fair in 1903, co-incident with Roosevelt's adoption of the motif, and, after 1906, they became a commercial success. Significantly the Michtom bears had been unwilded: gone were the stiff Steiff limbs. Changes to the proportions of head and body created a more infantile bear. Manufactured bear toys had been available since at least 1894 (Hebbs 1988) but it was these cuddly teddies which were the success.

Teddy bears rapidly became the predominant companion toy for children, although, vitally, this role was mediated by adults with important consequences for teddy evolution. By the 1920s teddies were no longer the wild creatures of Steiff's early fauna. They had been sentimentalised, creating an opportunity for gifting emotional support to children (Varga 2009a). The 1930s saw the widespread adoption of teddy bears as children's story characters and according to Caldas-Coulthard and van Leeuwen (2003) they are at the heart of the nuclear family in North America and Europe. Note that the teddy bear does have biogeographical limits. The primary range lies within North America, Europe and Australasia 'where the upbringing of children places most stress on restraining the emotions' (Caldas-Coulthard and van Leeuwen 2003, 23). Nieuwenhuys (2011) provides examples of the teddy bears' contested and vulnerable iconography outside their normal geographical range.

The key role of adults and the emotional pressures that drive teddy bear acquisition are important to understand evolutionary selection processes at work on teddy bears:

(1) Adults are the providers of teddies to young children. In general children do not choose their own teddies, though shops and websites such as Build a Bear (according to its 2017 annual report, Build a Bear has grown to 361 stores globally since starting in 1997) and The Bear Works do allow children to make their own bears, albeit from a limited set of options.

(2) The role of the teddy as a powerful and significant gift providing emotional support. Such support is a resource every bit as important as more concrete needs such as food or shelter, the familiar stuff of natural selection, especially in societies where the basics of food and shelter are available but in which parents worry that they are not giving sufficient time to their children (Caldas-Coulthard and van Leeuwen 2003).

In summary, changes to the morphology of teddy anatomy since their origin have been widely reported. The main changes are an infantilisation of bears from their wild origins by an increase in body proportions associated with human babies. The data presented here document anatomical change throughout the fossil record of teddy bears and provide a causal explanation of natural selection underpinning teddy-human ecology.

THE TEDDY BEAR FOSSIL DATA

I have built up a teddy fossil data set since the 1980s. Data have been collected primarily at public events, eg British Science Festival, Newcastle Science Festival and also undergraduate workshops run in the style of teddy bears' picnics encouraging people to bring along their teddy bears. Some older bear data comes from visiting museum collections where the bears are on display.

To be included in the data set bears had to meet several criteria.

1. They had to be manufactured and not home-made, so that there must have been some selecting of the toy from a source pool.
2. Bears must have had an owner.
3. Bears were omitted if their core design was dominated by an additional purpose, eg mechanical acrobats or musicians.
4. Ages had to be available, at least to the nearest five years, although the majority could be aged to a specific year.

CHARACTERISING MORPHOLOGY

Three features of bear anatomy were recorded for the data set, all three based on relative proportions that can be seen and do not require precise measurement. No bears were harmed during the data collection. Three morphological characteristics were recorded: the size of snout relative to the whole head, the size of head relative to the torso and length of forearms relative to the length of torso, each characteristic divided into three categories a, b and c as follows.

Relative size of snout. (a) Long snout, longer than the head is deep when viewed from the side, with distinct break of slope between forehead and snout; (b) Medium snout, distinct with a break of slope from forehead but less than half depth of the head; (c) No distinct snout, often just a button, flat patch or coloured area.

Relative size of head. (a) Small head, the height < half the length of the torso; (b) larger head, greater than half the length of but not longer than the torso; (c) head height bigger than length of torso.

Forelimb length. (a) Forelimbs longer than the torso; (b) forelimbs shorter than the torso but at least half the length; (c) forelimbs less than half the length of the torso.

These simple categories worked well at public events, proving replicable and relatively easy. The characters do not vary in any systematic way across different sizes of bear except for very small bears (less than 10cm total height) which tended to have larger heads regardless of other characteristics. Each bear in the data set is therefore represented by a triplet of characters always given in the sequence snout length, head size, forelimb length, eg 'a,a,a' meaning big snout, small head, long limbs, along with an age of purchase usually to year but occasionally five-year span.

A total of 596 teddy bears has been recorded.

The Evolutionary History of the Teddy Bear

The fossil data base and morphological records (Fig 2.1) provide striking evidence of variations to overall bear diversity, periods of radiation and extinction and a significant shift in dominant morphological characteristics (Fig 2.2). The varying fortunes of teddies are similar to patterns shown by many fossil groups, in particular low points associated with environmental change akin to mass extinctions and diversification to exploit new environments. Both world wars represent low points, but the lowest ebb of the teddy was the 1960s, perhaps the result of competition with the new plastic toys such as Barbie and Action Man. There are conspicuous booms too, notably the post-war baby boom and the 1980s Care Bear fad. There are some distinct artefacts, notably the relatively large number of old bears resulting from their collectable status and also the over-representation of recent bears resulting from data collection at teddy bear events held over the last two decades. Nonetheless the changes to the frequency of morphological types suggest some form of natural selection. If so, this requires an interrogation of the teddy bear-human interaction and the underlying biology of their relationship.

The Natural Selection of Cuteness and the Teddy-Human Interaction

There is a consensus that the changing frequency of teddy bear morphological types over the last century represents selection for cuteness. 'Cute' is associated with the body proportions of human and mammal babies, notably heads that are large relative to the whole body but with relatively short faces, most obvious as small, button noses and short limbs. Cuteness is, according to Morreall (1991), 'an unsubtle property', akin to kitsch, not a characteristic of high culture, not something that needs to be learned, but it is a cue to which we respond quickly, thoughtlessly even. More positively Bradshaw and Paul (2010) suggest that our response to cuteness, especially in adolescent girls, may be a valuable evolved trait, helping to drive nurturing behaviours. Cuteness manipulates us irresistibly. A study of African-American chief executive officers in the USA demonstrated that cute, baby-facedness was associated with higher ranking black executives, although the reverse is true for white CEOs (Livingstone and Pearce 2014). The conclusion made by these authors was that cuteness disarms threatening stereotypes. Cute features are obvious in

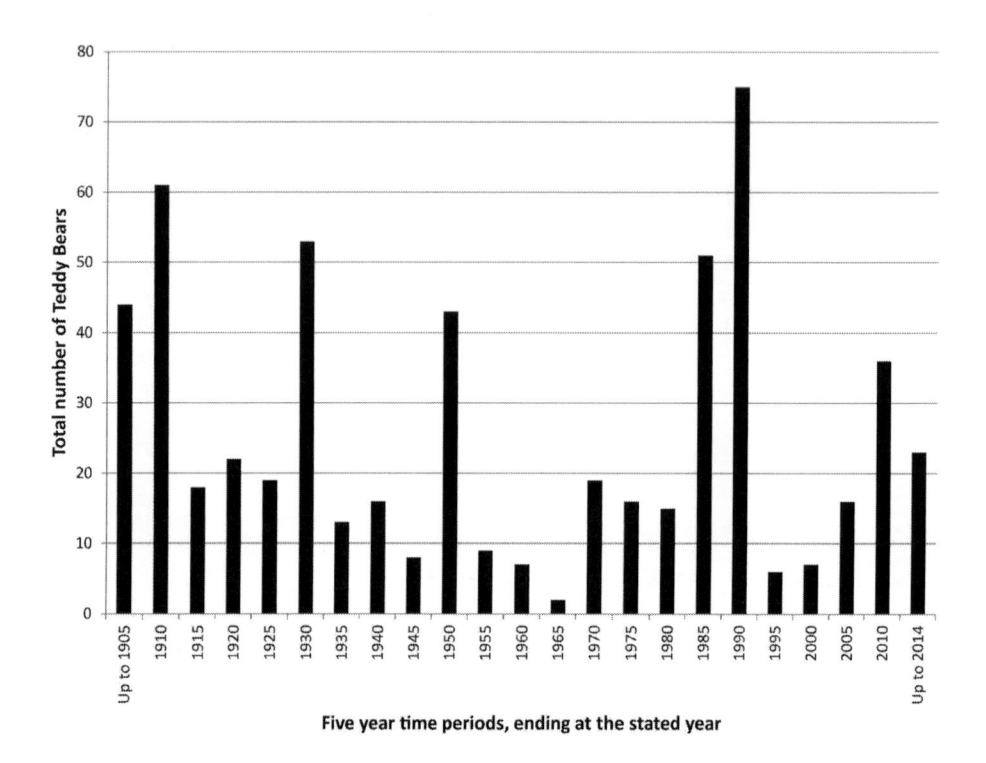

Figure 2.1 Total numbers of Teddy Bears in the Fossil Teddy Database. Data are combined into five yearly periods starting from 1901 to 1905. The final category is up to 2014.

many breeds of domestic animals kept for their companion role, eg toy dogs. The selection for cuteness is therefore a selection of juvenile, babyish characteristics. An innate, powerful reaction to cuteness is likely to be a significant form of selection pressure.

Whilst previous studies have identified the selection for cuteness in teddy bears, they have not attempted to identify the selection pressures which drive this process. It is superficially easy to suggest that a cute teddy is more likely to be bought than a more naturalistic bear toy, but this is simplistic. To understand the nature of the selection requires an understanding of the teddy-human relationship.

I have explored the teddy-human interaction at every teddy bears' picnic data collection by outlining the variety of species interactions familiar from ecological theory, and also suggesting how these interactions might work for teddy bears and people and asking for audiences to vote. The interactions are:

1. **Inter-specific competition**. Species competing for the same limiting resource, either by active aggression through fights or display, or 'scramble' competition monopolising the resource faster than other species. Teddies might be competitors with humans, for example, by using space in our homes.

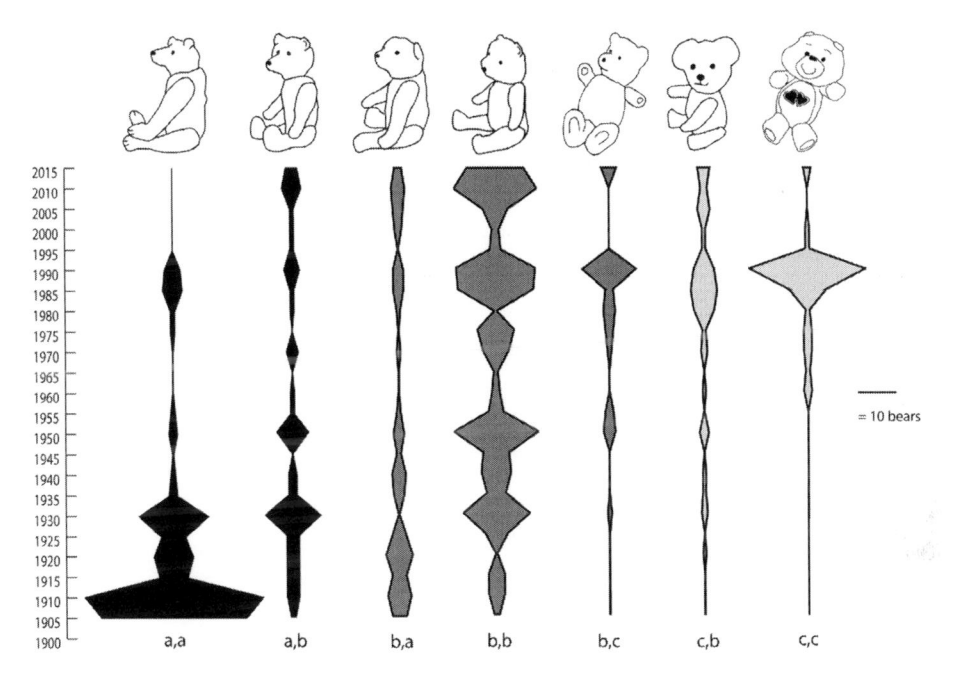

FIGURE 2.2 VARIATIONS TO THE FREQUENCY OF TEDDY BEAR MORPHOLOGY THROUGH THEIR EVOLUTIONARY HISTORY. THE KITE DIAGRAM DEPICTS THE NUMBERS OF TEDDY BEARS FOR THE SEVEN NUMERICALLY DOMINANT MORPHOLOGICAL TYPES IN THE FOSSIL DATABASE. THE DRAWINGS SHOW EXEMPLARS FOR EACH MORPHOLOGICAL TYPE.

2. **Exploitation**. Trophic interactions, with one species benefitting at the expense of the other which is the food source. These interactions include predation, parasitism and parasitoid attacks, herbivory and disease. Teddies rely on us to reproduce them so could be seen as parasites, although the teddy manufacturers and their staff benefit when the teddies are bought, a form of mutualism.

3. **Mutualisms**. Interactions where the two species involved both benefit. The benefits can be nutritional, (eg Zooxanthellae algae in coral polyps), transport (eg seed dispersal by fruit-eating birds) or protection (eg acacia ants, *Pseudomyrmex ferruginea*, on acacia trees).

4. **Other categories**, eg Commensalism (one sided mutualism where there is a clear beneficiary but the gains to the other species involved are unclear) or ecological engineers, which are species that create and alter habitats significantly, eg beavers building dams. Note that Blackmore and Young (1995) in their study surveying diseases and injuries to teddy bears characterised the teddy-human interactions as commensal.

At all events the votes are overwhelmingly, often unanimously, for the mutualism interaction. Participants routinely describe the exchange as humans providing a home for teddy bears, whilst the bears provide us with love and cuddles. There have been rare instances of suggestions of predation of bears due to the damage they have suffered from being chewed and played with and, just once, parasitism due to teddies relying on us to reproduce them.

However, the parasitism suggestion is compelling on closer inspection.

Teddy bears rely on humans for reproduction, the key biological outcome. A taxon unable to reproduce is doomed to extinction. Teddies require our resources, energy and time to reproduce. Without us they would become extinct. In return we get a hard-to-define good feeling, which in raw evolutionary terms is scant compensation for the use of our resources, although the power of this emotional driver is so potent, not least the emotional investment from the adult giver (Vargas 2009a, 2009c; Nieuwenhuys 2011). The teddy-human relationship reveals the complexities in valuing nature. Teddies have a direct, instrumental worth to their manufacturers and within the consumer economy. They also have an intrinsic value to their owners which is very strong. The natural history of teddy bears has managed to monetorise their value in a way that still eludes so much of our natural capital (eg pandas and rain forests). Indeed, such is the increasing prevalence of natural capital within UK government environment policy, it is perhaps only a matter of time before Professor Dieter Helm (of the UK Natural Capital Committee) highlights the importance of the 'teddy bear approach' to natural capital accounting.

Given this parasitism, why do audiences overwhelmingly characterise the human-teddy interaction as a beneficial mutualism? Many parasites manipulate host behaviour. Perhaps our affection for teddy bears based on the nebulous hugs and love represents just such a parasitic smoke screen.

For many parasites the most challenging stage in their life cycle is dispersal and finding a host. Most teddy bears are not bought by their owners, who are often babies when their first teddy appears. Instead teddies are gifted from family and friends; it is adult humans who choose the teddy bear (Sutton-Smith 1985; Morris *et al* 1995; Varga 2009a). In doing so adults act as the vector to transmit the bear to a new host. Getting out of the shop into a child's bed is the vulnerable stage for a teddy. Any design that does not make it is literally left on the shelf, is unlikely to be reproduced. There will be intense selection to be attractive to adult humans and cute features are most likely to invoke that response. Indeed, Morris *et al* (1995, 1699), in their study of young children's preferences for infantile features in teddy bears, point out that 'teddy bears are now better at being bought by adults, not better at being cuddled by young children'. 'Irresistible cuteness' (Morreall 1991) has human adults firmly in its grip. Intriguingly children's responses to cuteness vary markedly with age. In a test of preferences Morris, Reddy and Bunting (1995) found that up until the age of four children did not preferentially select baby-featured bears, but increasingly did so from the age of six. The selection of teddies as gift bears for babies by adults is likely to maintain the importance of juvenile features, but selection by children in outlets such as Build a Bear may shift the ratios of bear types.

The selection for juvenile characteristics and loss of adult bear morphology suggests that adult human choice has been a powerful evolutionary filter on bear design. Once a teddy has found a host the bear can lose and discard parts of its anatomy such as eyes, ears and limbs with no apparent loss to its lovability (the author's bear only has one remaining eye and one intact, attached arm. The other arm leads a peripatetic existence around the house too). Damage to hosted bears is routine and characteristic, but does not undermine the affection (Blackmore and Young 1972; Caldas-Coulthard and van Leeuwen 2009). Many adult parasites show marked atrophy once established in or on their final host. Bear-like teddies do still occur, partly an adult market choosing collectables and partly as a result of the modifying effect of popular children's books and television, eg *We're going on a Bear Hunt* (Rosen and Oxenbury 1993), which has a distinctly wilder look (complete with claws), as may be expected of a bear humans chose to hunt.

There are also occasional radiations responding to brief opportunities, most notably the 'c,c,c' Care Bears of the 1980s associated with the television series. However, without the television modification of the environment Care Bears have become scarce, perhaps because their exaggerated cuteness (heads larger than bodies, non-functional, stubby arms) look grotesque in isolation.

In summary, the overall trend for the increasing frequency of juvenile mammal characteristics in manufactured teddy bears is the result of intense natural selection at the vulnerable dispersal stage as teddies need to move from shop to juvenile human. Teddies are chosen primarily by adult relatives of the children. Doting parents select for cute, juvenile features and act as vectors transmitting the teddy parasites to new hosts. Teddy reproduction depends wholly on host resources, but humans are oblivious due to behavioural manipulation of our emotions by teddy bears.

If this sounds grim the teddy bears are not to blame. They cannot help being teddies. In the case of teddies, their soft toy cuddliness, human-like form and child's play associations, both wild and innocent, made for a powerful combination, if the environment was right. Their origins are as part of a diverse cuddly toy fauna in the early 20th century which coincided with an ecological opportunity created by changing attitudes to wildness and childhood. Their biogeographical spread encompasses all westernised cultures. Their success as they out-competed other species of cuddly toy animal was accelerated by contingent events created by Teddy Roosevelt's mythologised encounter with a bear. Since then their fortunes have waxed and waned, suffering major declines during periods of environmental stress or competition from novel toys but also radiations associated with new environments created by books and television, although these highly specialised forms may be more vulnerable to extinction as environments change. Teddy bears remain a widespread and abundant taxon and seem likely to do so, just so long as their human hosts thrive. Whilst the supposedly real wilderness of mountains and forests is a fraught and artificial cultural construct, the basic biology of natural selection occurs in our homes, shops and internet. The teddy bear is a playful, protective presence in our beds, benign in nature, perhaps a nostalgia for a time when the dangers of the wilderness were the fearsome but familiar animals. Teddy is a comfort against the grim, daily news from the contemporary wilderness of mass extinctions, emergent diseases, climate change and civil collapse.

Bibliography and References

Blackmore, D K, and Young, C M, 1972 Some observations of the diseases of *Brunus edwardii* (species nova), *The Veterinary Record* 90, 382–5

Bradshaw, J W S, and Paul E S, 2010 Could empathy for animals have been an adaptation in the evolution of *Homo sapiens*? *Animal Welfare* 19, 107–12

Caldas-Coulthard, C R, and van Leeuwen, T, 2003 Teddy bear stories, *Social Semiotics* 13 (1), 5–28

Casstree, N, 2005 *Nature*, Routledge, London.

Gould, S J, 1980 *The Panda's Thumb*, Penguin Books, Harmondsworth

Gould, S J, 1989 *Wonderful Life. The Burgess Shale and the Nature of History*, Penguin Books, London

Jenks, C, 2005 *Childhood*, Routledge, London

Jones, O, 2018 Bear necessities: toys, settings and emotional becoming, *Children's Geographies* 16 (4), 459–60.

Livingston, R W, and Pearce, N A, 2009 The teddy-bear effect: does having a baby face benefit black chief executive officers? *Psychological Science* 20 (10), 1229–36

Pierce, N E, Braby, M F, Heath, A, Lohman, D J, Mathew J, Rand D B, and Travassos M A, 2002 The ecology and evolution of ant association in the Lycaenidae (Lepidoptera) *Annual Review of Entomology* 47, 733–71

Morreall, J, 1991 Cuteness, *British Journal of Aesthetic* 31 (1), 39–47

Morris, P H, Reddy, V, and Bunting, R C, 1995 The survival of the cutest: who's responsible for the evolution of the teddy bear? *Animal Behaviour* 50, 1697–1700

Morrongiello, B A, and Hogg, K, 2004 Mothers' reactions to children misbehaving in ways that can lead to injury: implications for gender differences in children's risk taking and injuries, *Sex Roles* 50, 103–18

Murphy, B M, 2013 *The Rural Gothic in American Popular Culture. Backwoods Horror and Terror in the Wilderness,* Palgrave MacMillan, Basingstoke

Nash, R, 1967 *Wilderness and the American Mind*, Yale University Press, New Haven

Nieuwenhuys, O, 2011 Can the teddy bear speak? *Childhood* 18 (4), 411–18

Philo, C, 2018 When Teddy met Teddie, *Children's Geographies* 16 (4), 455–8

Pilgrim, D, 2012 The Golliwog Caricature, www.ferris.edu/jimcrow/golliwog/

Pope, H G jr, Olivardia, R, Gruber, A, and Borowiecki, J, 1999 Evolving ideals of male body image as seen through action toys, *International Journal of Eating Disorders* 26, 65–72

Ray, S J, 2014 Rub trees, crittercams, and GIS: the wired wilderness of Leanne Allison and Jeremy Mendes' Bear 71, *Green Letters* 18 (3), 236–53, DOI: 10.1080/14688417.2014.964282

Rosen, M, and Oxenbury, H, 1993 *We're Going on a Bear Hunt*, Walker Books, London

Sutton-Smith, B, 1986 *Toys as Culture*, Gardner Press, New York

Thomas, K, 1983 *Man and the Natural World. Changing Attitudes in England 1500–1800*, Allen Lane, London

Varga, D, 2009a Gifting the bear and a nostalgic desire for childhood innocence, *Cultural Analysis* 8, 71–96

———, 2009b Teddy's bear and the sociocultural transfiguration of savage beasts into innocent children, 1890–1920, *The Journal of American Culture* 32 (2), 98–112

———, 2009c Babes in the woods: wilderness aesthetics in children's stories and toys, 1830-1915, *Society and Animals* 17, 187–205

3

Bears within the Human Landscape: Cultural and Demographic Factors Influencing the Use of Bear Parts in Cambodia and Laos

Elizabeth O Davis and Jenny Anne Glikman

Two species of bear are endemic to East and Southeast Asia, the Asiatic black bear or 'moon' bear (*Ursus thibetanus*), and the sun bear (*Helarctos malayanus*). The moon bear primarily occurs at more northerly latitudes, while the sun bear occurs at more southerly latitudes, although there is overlap in their ranges throughout Southeast Asia (Garshelis and Steinmetz 2016; Scotson *et al* 2017). Historically, the parts of both species have been used and traded as medical and non-medical commodities in East and Southeast Asia. As commodities and thus objects of consumption, bear parts assist individuals in 'symbolic actions' (Gell 1986). As an example of one identified symbolic consumption chain, elder Vietnamese males use bear bile as a means of communicating 'respect and identity' and as a means of maintaining good health (Drury 2009a).

Knowledge of the historic bear part trade and consumption throughout East Asia is dominated by information about their use by the Chinese. Bear parts have been used in China for thousands of years (Mills and Servheen 1994), and it is estimated that the first written use of bear gallbladder was around 600 CE (Common Era), when it was prescribed for ailments such as liver disease and haemorrhoids (Dutton *et al* 2011; Mills and Servheen 1994). Other parts of the bear were prescribed medically in China as well, with the bone, blood and fat all stated to be effective in curing various diseases. Use is still common throughout China, particularly because bears are farmed[1] for their bile, and thus bile products are relatively accessible (Dutton *et al* 2011).

Bear populations in Asia were noted to be declining nearly three decades ago (Mills and Servheen 1991). Despite subsequent efforts to understand the extent to which these populations were declining, little has been found other than overwhelming evidence that, along with deforestation of bear habitat, the bear part trade is precipitating this decline (Crudge *et al* 2018a). Even though understanding the illegal trade in wildlife parts necessitates understanding of the human actors involved (Wallen and Daut 2018), sociological research has only recently begun to emerge. Additionally, this research has to date been largely focused on the Vietnamese and

---

[1] The process of bear farming developed in North Korea in the 1980s as a means of obtaining 'medicine for all'. The technique then spread to China and throughout Asia and Southeast Asia. In bear farming, a catheter is inserted into a bear's gallbladder and bile is extracted. It has been 'rebranded' as a conservation-positive measure, but numerous studies have found that for endangered animal farming this is usually not true (Damania and Bulte 2007; Kirkpatrick and Emerton 2010; Livingstone and Shepherd 2014). Usually, bile farms are comprised of Asiatic black bears; however, sun bears have been observed on some farms (Livingstone *et al* 2018).

Chinese markets. Drury (2009b, 2011) has performed extensive work into understanding Vietnamese motivations behind consumption of animal products, and has highlighted bear bile/gallbladder as a commonly used medicine. Similarly to the Chinese markets, Drury found that use of bear bile appeared to be broadly applicable across class lines in Vietnamese culture by virtue of its accessibility (Drury 2011); however, the current decline in the bile farm industry may encourage greater exclusivity in bile use in Vietnam (Crudge *et al* 2018b). Although several Chinese studies have investigated bear bile's medical efficacy (Feng *et al* 2009), to our knowledge only one study has attempted to investigate the social dimensions of bear bile use in China (Dutton *et al* 2011).

Motivations for behaviours, it is argued, are influenced by the attitudes, values and beliefs of an individual (Homer and Kahle 1988), which in turn are influenced by the cultural framework of the individual (Waylen *et al* 2010), and demographic factors (Booth and Nolen 2012). Within Southeast Asia there has been substantial research into consumer preferences and motivations for purchasing bear parts in Vietnam (Drury 2011; Vu 2010), with the implication that the cultural and demographic framework is being considered. Yet, to date, no study has been published on cultural dimensions of bear parts use in Cambodia, and only one study has been published in Laos (Davis *et al* 2016). This preliminary study uncovered spatially distinct use in its sample from northern Laos, with differences in the values, attitudes, beliefs, knowledge and behaviours held by individuals of the Laos cultural group compared to Chinese and Western tourists in Laos. Laos individuals[2] had a greater preference for wild bile, compared to the Chinese and Western individuals sampled. Chinese individuals, in particular, were more likely to cite a preference for alternatives such as synthetic or farmed bile. Additionally, Chinese tourists to Luang Prabang were more likely to hold conservation-positive attitudes and values, in comparison to the Laos individuals surveyed. As will be discussed at greater length throughout this chapter, this corroborates the qualitative research of Davis *et al* (2016), which found little evidence for what would be termed by Western conservationists as 'conservation-positive' thinking among the Laos nationals sampled.

Within this chapter we report findings of techniques grounded in anthropological theory, which were used to collect culturally-specific information that it is hoped will complement the preliminary study in Laos, and lead to a preliminary understanding of the regional dynamics of bear part use among the Khmer in Cambodia. Unless otherwise expressed, the information discussed was obtained using semi-structured interviews (SSIs), a qualitative methodological approach that allows a deep understanding of the socio-cultural context, and for elucidating fine-scale trends and patterns of belief and action (Drury *et al* 2011).

Use of Bear Parts in Cambodia

Davis (San Diego Zoo Institute for Conservation Research – Community Engagement, hereafter denoted as SDZG), in collaboration with Free the Bears (FTB)[3], conducted qualitative, semi-structured interviews in Phnom Penh and the surrounding provinces of Kampong Speu and Kandal. Following this research, FTB and members of SDZG conducted quantitative interviews in three geographic regions within Cambodia (Fig 3.1).

---

2   The term used within this chapter for the people who inhabit Laos will be 'Laos individuals', so as to best encompass the plurality of values and beliefs that are spatially distinct within the region.

3   Free the Bears is an Australian bear welfare and conservation organisation based in Cambod ia, Laos and Vietnam. It primarily performs bear rescues, but since 2014 began the current partnership with SDZG to understand the bear part trade in Southeast Asia from a human dimension perspective.

Figure 3.1: Map of the provinces where research has been conducted in Cambodia by SDZG and FTB (map created with R and the package 'tmap' (R Core Team 2017; Tennekes 2018)).

A total of 139 SSIs of Khmer-identifying individuals were completed from urban and rural individuals, male and female, and from a variety of self-stated socio-economic levels. The self-stated socio-economic levels were obtained by having each individual state their own perceived stratification of society, and their role within that stratification. Self-definitions of status are well-used in social research (Grella 1990; Kraus *et al* 2012), and as a method of socio-economic definition it is considered to be less biased than directly asking about income, a notoriously sensitive question (Galobardes and Demarest 2003).

Participants were asked about their general perceptions of bears within Cambodia, since the baseline beliefs, emotions and perceptions associated with bears was unknown. Indeed, no historic or modern knowledge exists about the 'role' of bears within Cambodian society, and thus this study attempted to provide a basic grounding in Khmer cultural feelings towards bears. Across the sample, the primary stated emotion held towards bears was that of fear, although this fear was reported as being the result of unfamiliarity with bears. Furthermore, only a third of the sample (35.3 per cent) stated that they would feel fear. The following emotions stated were 'happy/excited' (29.3 per cent), as expressed by this female participant:

> [I] would be happy because [I] really want to see them. Not afraid – nothing to be afraid of.
> – Twenty-eight-year-old Khmer female, gas station attendant

When asked what they thought would be other emotions towards bears, the answers became highly diverse, ranging from love, to fear, to 'it depends'. Significantly, this means that there appears to be no 'social belief'4 constructed about bears in the Khmer mental framework.

Bear part use by the Khmer was identified as being demographically and spatially variable, and relatively prevalent within the population. The initial SSIs performed found that most individuals did not use bear parts, and would often either not know what those parts were used for, and/or they would express their discomfort at the use of parts. Nonetheless, 13 per cent of the participants did admit to using bear parts or admitted to being interested in using them.

In both the quantitative and qualitative study, bear part use appeared to be gender-mediated. One identified novel use of bear parts is that of bear gallbladder wine for pregnant women, and women suffering from unidentified post-partum 'weakness'. This use, as well as some reservations about such use, is illustrated in the following quote from a respondent in Phnom Penh:

> My sister and aunty were given gallbladder after giving birth. People forced it on my sister. But Western [medicine] is better, don't have to take gross, disgusting things after birth. Just rest for a week and [then you are] up and walking.
> – Nineteen-year-old Khmer-Chinese female, receptionist

Among women who have used bear parts this use arguably exists within a sphere of 'folk knowledge', ie 'publicly shared conceptualisations' about, for example, effectively handling a pregnancy (Geertz 1973, quoted in Read and Behrens 1989). Although bear gallbladder may not truly be effective for treating post-partum weakness, it is believed to be so, and may continue to be used for this purpose, due to these shared notions of bear gallbladder effectiveness that is present in some Khmer communities. Moreover, across the world and certainly in Asia, women and men alike embrace folk knowledge when considering parenthood and pregnancy (Cline 2010; Hansen 2012; Qamar 2016). This type of knowledge can be non-adaptive, as the folk knowledge can be to the detriment of women (Greenhalgh 1994), and as such the effect of bear gallbladder/bile wine on pregnant and post-partum women should be explored in future studies. Moreover, synthetic, herbal and Western alternatives all exist and are readily available, and could substitute for bear bile wine.

---

4   Beliefs about social groups are termed 'social beliefs' if it can be proven that a belief is held on condition of others also holding that belief (this statement applies equally to behaviours) (Greenwood 2003).

Western social norms appear to be influential among the higher status, urban Khmer population. This was supported by the fluency with which most of these individuals spoke English, the desire many stated of seeing Cambodia become more like a Western country, and the continual emphasis on scientific medicine over Khmer traditional practices, illustrated in the following quote:

> I don't place value on traditional healing. I'm not educated to believe it works. I would consult with a professional.
>
> – Thirty-three-year-old Khmer male, NGO worker

Indeed, the terminology used by upper status individuals to describe medicine reflected a greater influence of Western social norms. In the more rural areas of Cambodia, the accepted term for Western medicine is '*barang* medicine', literally 'French medicine', though used colloquially to indicate Western medicine. However, among the more upper status individuals sampled in Phnom Penh, the term most often applied was 'scientific medicine'. Linguistically, this marks Western medicine apart from traditional Khmer medicine by implying that traditional Khmer medicine is not scientific or 'tested'.

The discovery that the predominant view is that bears are considered positively in Cambodia is important for bear conservation. Bears are seen as negative components of human landscapes in many parts of the world (Treves and Karanth 2003), with 'tragic consequences', such as the sabotage of conservation initiatives (Redpath *et al* 2017) and consistent human resistance (Fritts *et al* 2003). It is therefore encouraging that the majority of the Khmer sampled here appear to like bears and value bears being in Cambodia, despite fear being dominant among a third of the individuals sampled. However, this should be considered in the context of the qualitative sample, which was primarily urban. Individuals in other parts of Cambodia may feel more or less negatively towards bears, compared to the individuals sampled here.

Further differences in how bear parts are used were found throughout Cambodia. In field sites in the Cardamom Mountains (Fig 3.1, Pouthisat/Pursat and Kâmpong Spœ/Kampong Speu), individuals ate bear meat more frequently than individuals did in any other field site. This is likely because the Cardamom Mountains are source sites for bears, and thus although individuals may transport other bear parts such as bile, gallbladder and paws out from the area, they will consume the bear meat 'on site'. Yet, although consumption of bear meat was more frequent in the Cardamom Mountains, it did occur in other field sites, and has been found by other conservation organisations to be one of the meats consumed by high-status Khmer individuals within Phnom Penh (Flora and Fauna International, *pers comm*).

Use of animals for human purposes occurs for many reasons. In Cambodia, the drivers behind the consumption of bear products have been poorly understood, as are the products that are actually consumed and valued. Previous research has indicated that bear parts are used primarily for medical reasons in Asia, yet this use has been dominated by assumptions of use being Chinese-mediated and solely related to prestige, or solely cultural in nature. Based on the results of the data collected here, use of bear parts in Cambodia is affected by a variety of factors, including culturally and demographically specific norms, and geographic area. Moreover, what parts are used, by which groups, is flexible and varied.

FIGURE 3.2: Map of the provinces where research has been conducted in Laos by SDZG and FTB (map created with R and the package 'tmap' (R Core Team 2017; Tennekes 2018)).

Use of Bear Parts in Laos

As in Cambodia, baseline beliefs about and perceptions of bears were unknown for Laos nationals. Using semi-structured interviews (SSIs) Davis sampled 79 individuals, split by gender and of varying ages (all over 18 years old). Davis found that when considering attitudes towards bears, the Laos cultural group had a generally positive perception of bears. These positive perceptions were found previously (Davis *et al* 2016), and within studies that have explored conflict issues such as bears' crop-raiding (Scotson *et al* 2014). However, this positive social belief does not preclude use of bears for their resources, nor does a positive individual belief appear to decrease bear part use. It has been argued that in 'modern' Western societies an individual who respects/loves an animal will be less likely to harm it or use its parts, an effect conceptualised as mutualism (Manfredo *et al* 2009). However, it is argued that 'mutualism' in modern societies is distinct from the conception of mutualism held by individuals in 'hunter-gatherer' societies, who use animals yet perceive a 'relationship of mutual responsibilities' (Manfredo *et al* 2009). This 'relationship of mutual responsibilities' should not be considered as directly analogous to the 'noble ecological savage' concept, however. Rather, mutualism in a hunter-gatherer society consists of respect towards animals, with no cognitive dissonance about using animal-based resources, even if such use harms the environment. Conversely, the mutualism effect seen in 'modern' societies is argued to be the result of a growing 'egalitarian' culture, wherein individuals believe that animals and humans hold the same rights, and that animal resources should not be utilised (Manfredo *et al* 2009). This belief system is argued to be a result of post-materialism, which is a national state that Laos has not yet achieved (Lintner 2008). Moreover, this effect of mutualism has not been fully explored in non-Western societies, and has indeed been argued by some to be incompatible in different economic and cultural contexts (Kaczensky 2007). Rather, individuals in Luang Prabang may be ascribing to a more animistic framework, wherein an animal can be greatly valued, yet still be consumed. This duality is seen within China, where the tiger is both a valued (albeit complex) symbol of identity (Jalais 2018), as well as a highly sought-after object of consumption, to the extent that the tiger has become extirpated from China (Walston *et al* 2010).

The extent of the use of bear parts by participants was found to be approximately 16 per cent. The stated aspirations of use reveal how problematic this is in light of the context of the country. Laos (Fig 3.2) is a hub for illegal wildlife trading, including trade in bears and their parts (Krishnasamy *et al* 2018; Livingstone *et al* 2018). Supply of whole bears and bear parts to other countries is a pressing problem for Laos bear populations, but these results arguably show that equally worrying is demand from the in-country population. In Luang Prabang, the main use cited for bear parts was for medical purposes, although individuals did also discuss use of bear parts for handbags and clothes. Bear parts being used for medical purposes is in all probability the most likely use in Laos for economic reasons; a superficial internet search shows that bearskin shoes can cost well over $1,000[5], which is nearly five times the reported monthly salary of the average Laos individual in the capital of Vientiane. This average monthly salary may be even lower in a provincial town like Luang Prabang (Check in Price 2018).

---

5   This figure was found on the website 'shangqite.com', which appeared to sell clothing made from many endangered and threatened species. The website now appears to be down (or at least inaccessible to United Kingdom IPs). However, Shangqite products can still be purchased on eBay and other online retailers, and a Google image search will find many pictures of Shangqite's luxury leather goods.

Attitudes of the Laos cultural group do not appear to be changing away from use. Reasons for not using bear parts were mainly the expense of bear parts, as well as the perceived difficulty by some of accessing them. A common hope among most of the individuals sampled in Luang Prabang was that bear gallbladder/bile would be more accessible for people in the future. The individuals who expressed this sentiment qualified it by saying that bear bile is effective and good for health, and thus 'good for everyone to use'. Indeed, many individuals were hopeful that bear gallbladders would become increasingly more available:

> In the future, so many people will want [bear] gallbladder that it will be sold openly at the market.
> – Forty-two-year-old Lao Loum female, food seller

Additionally, addressing demand for bear parts may be challenging due to the social networks present in the area. One uncovered trend was a village practice of a hunter sharing out bear gallbladder among the community. This exchange could be a form of social capital, ie 'relationship investment' (Lin 1999). Although the villagers pay for the gallbladder, it is a relatively nominal amount compared to the effort and risk associated with poaching a bear. Therefore, it could be in the best interests of hunters to continue poaching bears. As Lin (1999) points out, generous gestures, such as the poaching of a bear for the community, at risk to oneself, can create social debt among the members who benefit. The poacher then benefits from the efforts of those in social debt to repay it. Consequently, the landscape of use in Luang Prabang should be considered as a patchwork. Within Luang Prabang town, it may be less likely that the influence of one's social groups, and by extension the social capital dynamics within these groups, will have as much of an effect as they may do in surrounding rural areas. This may be for several reasons. One is that it takes more effort for an individual in Luang Prabang town to go out into the countryside to poach a bear. Another may be because individuals in Luang Prabang town have better access to Western medicine, compared to villages that are a boat ride or difficult motorbike ride away. As bear bile is often used to treat bruising and/or broken bones, it may be considered a 'quick fix' and a more convenient alternative to making a long trip to the hospital in Luang Prabang.

Although it is a positive finding that the Laos individuals in this sample mostly feel happy about seeing bears, the impact of village social networks, along with lack of access to medicine, may hamper even well-informed and targeted conservation efforts. An additional point is that the Laos individuals interviewed appear to hold beliefs and feelings that are more similar to what is perceived to be the case in agricultural societies, ie societies where humans and domestic and wild animals live in close proximity (Armstrong Oma 2010). In these societies, it is argued, bonds exist between humans and animals, regardless of the function of the animals, and indeed in some cases precipitated by the use of animals as a resource (Armstrong Oma 2010). Thus, the perception that use of animals naturally precludes use of animals as resources does not appear to be valid in this context. It is entirely possible that in the capital of Laos, Vientiane, individuals are more likely to reflect Western-influenced attitudes and beliefs; however, this sample of Laos individuals did not appear to reflect neo-Western ideology about the environment. As has already been shown in Luang Prabang, Western-influenced demand reduction efforts probably will not resonate among the Laos cultural group individuals there (Davis *et al* 2016).

Can we Generalise about Bear Part use in Cambodia and Laos?

Some overarching trends in use can be found between Cambodia and Laos. In Laos and the province of Cambodia with the most direct contact to Laos, Stung Treng, use of bear bile seems to be as a topical ointment for reducing bruises, usually those resulting from motorcycle accidents. However, this is a very different use from the 'general health tonic' that bear bile is cited to be in urban Cambodia and in Vietnam (Drury 2009a). Additionally, the use of bear bile to treat post-partum illness appears to be specific to Cambodia, with no current evidence that this belief exists in Laos. Nonetheless, this does not mean that such use does not occur within Laos.

In both Laos and Cambodia there appears to be an emerging trend of bearskin handbags, although bearskin shoes, wallets and belts have also been cited as being purchased. This is likely a result of increasing affluence connected to the higher price tag of bearskin products. Buying a bearskin handbag communicates the individual's wealth (Husic and Cicic 2009). Desire to enhance one's prestige is a human constant that transcends cultural boundaries (Barkow 1975). This particular form of conspicuous consumption may be connected to the desire to emulate Chinese individuals, who are known to be a major market for exotic animal clothing and accessories (Sharma 2005). Although the Chinese have somewhat fraught relationships with the Southeast Asian countries (Fox and Castella 2013), there is no denying that they are a powerful cultural influence in the region (Chirot and Reid 2011). Although there is currently no published information about Chinese use of bearskin handbags, they have been recorded for sale on exclusively Chinese platforms (D Veríssimo, *pers comm*).

Perhaps the most important generalisation that can be made about use in Cambodia and Laos is that in both areas bear bile and associated bear parts used for medicine are 'non-essential'. Unlike rhino horn, individuals do not believe that use of bear parts is a matter of their life or death. Rather, bear bile and gallbladder are believed to be effective, yet expensive, alternatives to available Western medicine. Therefore, there should be less resistance by consumers towards shifting away from bear bile/gallbladder use and embracing the cheaper and more readily available Western options.

Further Research and Future Steps

As shown within this chapter, cultural context and demographic factors are important for understanding and interpreting individual actors' rationales for using bear parts. It is apparent here that consumer groups vary in motivations for, and expressions of, bear part consumption between the urban and rural divide (Singh 2008). This is by no means the only significant demographic variable affecting use of bear parts. The results presented here from Cambodia indicate that gender is clearly important in influencing admittance of use, and in influencing how bear parts are used. This demographic dichotomy is less apparent in Laos, compared to Cambodia, but it is probable that gender is significant within Laos as well. Yet, despite its ethnic diversity, Laos may be more homogenous in expressions of bear sentiment and bear part use, compared to Cambodia, although some trends of belief are apparent in Laos. For example, bear conservation organisations that work in Luang Prabang should focus on methods to reduce bear part demand that are separate from the cruelty component of bear bile extraction and snare hunting. From the results presented here and in Davis *et al* (2016), perceptions of cruelty towards bears is nearly non-existent. By extension, cruelty is an ineffective advantage mechanism in a region like Luang Prabang, Laos.

As is the case for many illegal wildlife trade (IWT) issues, the conservation problem of use of bear parts in Asia is ultimately an issue of halting human demand for the parts. It has been shown that artificially flooding the supply, ie with farmed bear bile, has only contributed to the increasing decline of bear populations throughout Southeast Asia (Crudge *et al* 2018a). Attempts at enforcement of regulations against hunting bears will constantly struggle in the face of the sheer quantity of poaching that occurs in the region (Gray *et al* 2018). Therefore, it is essential that conservationists fully understand the human communities who drive demand for bear products. In recognition of this, the first goal of the recently created Sun Bear Action Plan is to address human demand for bear products (Crudge *et al* 2018b). Understanding demand benefits greatly from the application of techniques used by anthropologists (Schultz 2011), as these techniques are often designed to understand human behaviour. Moreover, many anthropologists seek to understand the influence of cultural factors on a group's behaviour, ie 'cultural behaviour'. A full understanding of cultural factors has increasingly been shown to be important. Ultimately, the research presented here will be invaluable for informing future management decisions and conservation efforts within Cambodia and Laos.

ACKNOWLEDGMENTS

The research presented here was only possible due to the support and collaboration of in-country partner Free the Bears (FTB), a non-profit bear rescue organisation.

BIBLIOGRAPHY AND REFERENCES

Barkow, J, Akiwowo, A A, Barua, T K, Chance, M R A, Chapple, E D, Chattopadhyay, G P, Freedman, D G, Geddes, W R, Goswami, B B, Isichei, P A C, Knudson, M S, Manson, S M, Parker, C E, Price, J A, and Sarles, H B, 1975 Prestige and Culture: A Biosocial Interpretation, *Current Anthropology* 16 (4), 553–72

Booth, A L, and Nolen, P, 2012 Gender differences in risk behaviour: does nurture matter? *The Economic Journal* 122 (558), F56–F78

Check in Price, 2018 *Average and minimum salary in Vientiane, Laos* [online], available from: http://check-inprice.com/average-and-minimum-salary-in-vientiane-laos/ [16 April 2018]

Chirot, D, and Reid, A (eds), 2011 *Essential outsiders: Chinese and Jews in the modern transformation of Southeast Asia and Central Europe*, University of Washington Press, Washington DC

Cline, E M, 2010 Female spirit mediums and religious authority in contemporary southeastern China, *Modern China* 36 (5), 520–55

Crudge, B, Lees, C, Hunt, M, Steinmetz, R, Fredriksson, G, and Garshelis, D (eds), 2018a *Range-wide Conservation Action Plan for the Sun Bear, Helarctos malayanus, 2018–2028*, IUCN SSC Bear Specialist Group/Free the Bears/TRAFFIC

Crudge, B, Nguyen, T, and Cao, T T, 2018b The challenges and conservation implications of bear bile farming in Viet Nam, *Oryx*, 1–8

Damania, R, and Bulte, E, 2007 The economics of wildlife farming and endangered species conservation, *Ecological Economics* 62 (3), 461–72

Davis, E O, O'Connor, D, Crudge, B, Carignan, A, Glikman, J A, Browne-Nuñez, C, and Hunt, M, 2016 Understanding public perceptions and motivations around bear part use: A study in northern Laos of attitudes of Chinese tourists and Laos nationals, *Biological Conservation* 203 (2016), 282–9

Drury, R, 2009a Identifying and understanding consumers of wild animal products in Hanoi, Vietnam: implications for conservation management, unpublished PhD thesis, University College London

———, 2009b Reducing urban demand for wild animals in Vietnam: examining the potential of wildlife farming as a conservation tool, *Conservation Letters* 2 (6), 263–70

———, 2011 Hungry for success: urban consumer demand for wild animal products in Vietnam, *Conservation and Society* 9 (3), 247

Dutton, A, Hepburn, C, and Macdonald, D, 2011 A stated preference investigation into the Chinese demand for farmed vs. wild bear bile, *PLoS ONE* 6 (7), e21243 doi:10.1371/journal.pone.0021243

Feng, Y, Siu, K, Wang, N, Ng, K M, Tsao, S W, Nagamatsu, T, and Tong, Y, 2009 Bear bile: dilemma of traditional medicinal use and animal protection, *Journal of Ethnobiology and Ethnomedicine,* 5 (1), 2

Fox, J, and Castella, J C, 2013 Expansion of rubber (Hevea brasiliensis) in Mainland Southeast Asia: what are the prospects for smallholders? *The Journal of Peasant Studies*, 40 (1), 155–70

Fritts, S H, Stephenson, R O, Hayes, R D, and Boitani, L, 2003 Wolves and humans, in *Wolves: behavior, ecology and conservation* (eds L D Mech and L Boitani), The University of Chicago, Chicago, 289–316

Galobardes, B, and Demarest, S, 2003 Asking sensitive information: an example with income, *Sozial-und Präventivmedizin* 48 (1), 70–2

Garshelis, D, and Steinmetz, R, 2016 *Ursus thibetanus* (errata version published in 2017), The IUCN Red List of Threatened Species 2016: e.T22824A114252336. http://dx.doi.org/10.2305/IUCN.UK.2016-3.RLTS.T22824A45034242.en [12 April 2018]

Geertz, C, 1973 *The interpretation of cultures*, Basic Books, New York

Gell, A, 1986 Newcomers to the world of goods: Consumption among Muria Gonds, in *The Social Life of Things* (ed A Appadurai), Cambridge University Press, Cambridge

Gray, T N, Hughes, A C, Laurance, W F, Long, B, Lynam, A J, O'Kelly, H, Ripple, W J, Seng, T, Scotson, L, and Wilkinson, N M, 2018 The wildlife snaring crisis: an insidious and pervasive threat to biodiversity in Southeast Asia, *Biodiversity and Conservation* 27 (4), 1031–7

Greenhalgh, S, 1994 Controlling births and bodies in village China, *American Ethnologist* 21 (1), 3–30

Greenwood, J, 2003 Social Facts, Social Groups and Social Explanation, *Noûs* 37 (1), 93–112. Retrieved from http://www.jstor.org/stable/3506206

Grella, C E, 1990 Irreconcilable differences: Women defining class after divorce and downward mobility, *Gender and Society* 4 (1), 41–55

Hansen, T, 2012 Parenthood and happiness: A review of folk theories versus empirical evidence, *Social Indicators Research* 108 (1), 29–64

Homer, P M, and Kahle, L R, 1988 A structural equation test of the value-attitude-behavior hierarchy, *Journal of Personality and Social Psychology* 54 (4), 638

Husic, M, and Cicic, M, 2009 Luxury consumption factors, *Journal of Fashion Marketing and Management: An International Journal* 13 (2), 231–45

Jalais, A, 2018 Reworlding the ancient Chinese tiger in the realm of the Asian Anthropocene, *International Communication of Chinese Culture* 5 (1–2), 121–44

Kaczensky, P, 2007 Wildlife value orientations of rural Mongolians, *Human Dimensions of Wildlife* 12 (5), 317–29

Kirkpatrick, R, and Emerton, L, 2010 Killing tigers to save them: fallacies of the farming argument, *Conservation Biology* 24 (3), 655–9

Kraus, M W, Piff, P K, Mendoza-Denton, R, Rheinschmidt, M L, and Keltner, D, 2012 Social class, solipsism, and contextualism: how the rich are different from the poor, *Psychological Review* 119 (3), 546

Krishnasamy, K, Shepherd, C R, and Ching, O O, 2018 Observations of illegal wildlife trade in Boten, a Chinese border town within a Specific Economic Zone in northern Laos, *Global Ecology and Conservation*, e00390

Livingstone, E, Shepherd, C, 2014 Bear farms in Laos expand illegally and fail to conserve wild bears, *Oryx*, 1–9

Livingstone, E, Gomez, L, and Bouhuys, J, 2018 A review of bear farming and bear trade in Lao People's Democratic Republic, *Global Ecology and Conservation*, e00380

Manfredo, M J, Teel, T L, and Henry, K L, 2009 Linking society and environment: A multilevel model of shifting wildlife value orientations in the western United States, *Social Science Quarterly* 90 (2), 407–27

Mills, J, and Servheen, C, 1991 The Asian trade in bears and bear parts, WWF, Washington DC, 113

———, 1994 The Asian trade in bears and bear parts: impacts and conservation recommendations, *Bears: Their Biology and Management*, 161–7

Qamar, A H, 2016 Belief in the Evil Eye and Early Childcare in Rural Punjab, Pakistan, *Asian Ethnology* 75 (2), 397

R Core Team 2017 R: A language and environment for statistical computing. R Foundation for Statistical Computing, Vienna, Austria. URL https://www.R-project.org/

Read, D, and Behrens, C, 1989 Modeling Folk Knowledge as Expert Systems, *Anthropological Quarterly* 62 (3), 107–20

Schultz, P W, 2011 Conservation means behaviour, *Conservation Biology* 25 (6), 1080–3

Scotson, L, Vannachomchan, K, and Sharp, T, 2014 More valuable dead than deterred? Crop-raiding bears in Laos, *Wildlife Society Bulletin* 38 (4), 783–90

Scotson, L, Fredriksson, G, Augeri, D, Cheah, C, Ngoprasert, D, and Wai-Ming, W, 2017 *Helarctos malayanus*, The IUCN Red List of Threatened Species 2017: e.T9760A45033547. http://dx.doi.org/10.2305/IUCN.UK.2017-3.RLTS.T9760A45033547.en [12 April 2018]

Sharma, C, 2005 Chinese Endangered Species at the Brink of Extinction: A Critical Look at the Current Law and Policy in China, *Animal Law* 11, 215

Singh, S, 2008 Contesting moralities: the politics of wildlife trade in Laos, *Journal of Political Ecology* 15 (10), 1–20

Tennekes, M, 2018 tmap: Thematic Maps in R, *Journal of Statistical Software* 84 (6), 1–39

Vu, Quyen Thi, 2010 An analysis of attitudes and bear bile use in Vietnam, Education for Nature – Vietnam (ENV), Hanoi

Wallen, K E, and Daut, E, 2018 The challenge and opportunity of behaviour change methods and frameworks to reduce demand for illegal wildlife, *Nature Conservation* 26, 55

Walston, J, Robinson, J G, Bennett, E L, Breitenmoser, U, da Fonseca, G A, Goodrich, J, Gumal, M, Hunter, L, Johnson, A, Karanth, K U, and Leader-Williams, N, 2010 Bringing the tiger back from the brink—the six percent solution, *PLoS Biology* 8 (9), e1000485

Waylen, K A, Fischer, A, Mcgowan, P J, Thirgood, S J, and Milner-Gulland, E J, 2010 Effect of local cultural context on the success of community-based conservation interventions, *Conservation Biology* 24 (4), 1119–29

4

Bears in Gay Culture:
Histories, Discourses and Anthropomorphism

GARETH LONGSTAFF

The emergence and alignment of gay male culture and sub-culture to the discourse and image of the bear has an uneven and complex history. Gay male bears and the signification of the bear are now entrenched in the commodification of gay culture, and many of the social and sexual practices allied to bears problematically appropriate and subvert both gay and straight male identity politics. An implicit trademark of gay bear identity 'is the adoption of a conventionally masculine appearance and the accompanying rejection of the stereotyped notion that gay men cannot demonstrate masculine behaviour' (Suresha 2002). Yet, many of the social and sexual practices associated with bear culture underscore some broader conflicts across gay and straight male culture. Significant tensions which exist, such as the relationship between male social, erotic and sexual desire, the ontological and psychological position of men, patriarchy, hetero-sexism, homophobia, normativity, misogyny, and the problems of discriminatory and intersectional positions allied to factors such as race, age, class and geography, all underpin the identity of the gay bear. This chapter will examine and position some of these issues and consider how the varied histories, discourses and visual signification of the bear as a gay man and a wild animal have been anthropomorphically assimilated and employed to construct the bear as a specific symbol of gay masculinity and culture. Just as gay bears attempt to 'challenge relational aspects of masculinity, encouraging a traditionally masculine appearance while allowing for non-traditional male expressions of affection, intimacy, and nurturance' (Manley *et al* 2007, 92) they do so in ways which might be viewed as reductive and reflective of patriarchal and phallocentric dominance. In this way the gay bear functions as a crucial paradox in contemporary gay male culture; at once a way for gay men to negotiate and express their masculinity and desire, whilst also remaining a contentious symbol of how gender binaries and discriminatory sexual constructs might be reiterated and reinforced.

GAY BEARS: INDETERMINATE HISTORIES

The history and development of gay bears as well as their formation as a gay male subculture allied to the image of the bear as an animal are multifaceted. More so, it is difficult to assign a specific chronology to when gay male bears and a gay bear community first developed. In both volumes of *The Bear Book: Readings in the History and Evolution of a Gay Male Subculture* (Wright *et al* 1997) and *The Bear Book II: Further Readings in the History and Evolution of a Gay Male Subculture* (Wright *et al* 2001) there are perhaps the most detailed and extended accounts of gay bear history. Editor Les Wright proposes that there are foundational tensions between images of gay bears and attitudes which are 'vaguely defined, sometimes in self-contradicting ways, and [...] interpreted variously' (1997, 21). On the one hand the process of positioning and identifying gay bears seems to shift around the question of 'What is a bear?' and how denotatively 'it may describe physical size, refer to male secondary sex characteristics, to alleged behaviours or personality traits of bears' (ibid). On the other hand, these features may also give rise to an 'array of *connotative* associations [...] suggesting a large or husky body, heavy body hair, a lumbering gait, an epicurean appetite, an attitude of imperturbability, a contented self-acceptance of his own masculinity' (ibid). Within gay bear culture there are many empowering affirmations which circulate around how 'Bear masculinity as a social construct [is] distinct from both heterosexual and gay masculinity, encompassing values of self-acceptance, sexual freedom, and emotional intimacy among men' (Manley *et al* 2007, 106–7). In turn, and for some, this allows for the 'expression of a masculine physicality and the acceptance of maturation' so that self-identifying gay bears can 'relinquish concerns to defend their masculinity against the onslaught of both heterosexist and ageist stereotypes' (ibid, 107).

Whilst Wright cites 1986 as 'The birth of the bear "movement"', there is also a diffuse yet substantial archive of material that suggests the emergence of gay bears happened through a more arbitrary range of transitions and developments. Aspects that are associated with the development of gay bears permeate through a mixed archive of reference points from the late 1940s onward. Examples such as the bodily aesthetics of Steve Reeves in Gladiator Movies, Bob Mizier's Athletic Model Guild (AMG) and the proliferation of Beefcake magazines such as *Physique Pictorial* connect to the emergence of a post-war youth culture reliant on rebellion and disillusion. Instances where this might be articulated in celebrity culture include Marlon Brando in *The Wild One* (Laszlo Benedek, 1953) and James Dean in *Rebel Without a Cause* (Nicholas Ray, 1955). John Rechy's 1963 novel *City of Night* also documents the complexity of gay urban subcultures that rely upon the construction of self-identifying masculine men who sexually desire other men similar to themselves. Furthermore, several examples of early 'anecdotes of private circle[s] or bar circles of self-identifying bears' include the 1966 formation of a gay male 'bear' club in the Los-Angeles Satyrs MC club and the existence of a group of lovers of a '"Papa Bear" in Dallas, Texas' (Wright 1997, 25–6) around 1975. In addition, in 1976, an American network of '"chubbies" (big men) and "chasers" (men who were sexually attracted to them) emerged as a new national organization called "Girth and Mirth"' (Hennen 2005, 29) which as a precursor to the bear movement linked larger male bodies to ideological ideas of 'the wilderness, and more conventional notions of masculinity' (ibid). This also suggests a rich history aligned to 'the broader spectrum of back-to-nature masculinity movements dating back at least two centuries' (ibid, 29) in an American context, recognising that gay bear culture relies upon 'fantasies of escape [and] [...] an enthusiastic nostalgia [for] Rodeos, Wild West shows, cowboy lore, and wilderness adventure novels' (ibid).

The first media reference to gay 'bears' is thought to have appeared in the *Advocate* on 26 July 1979 in an article by George Mazzei called 'Who's Who in the Zoo: A Glossary of Gay Animals'. Whilst this is journalistically playful, there is also a precedent outlined here in terms of what gay bear culture is and was to become over the next 40 years. This in its entirety is key to how the combinations of desire, community, lifestyle and politics work to forge gay bear culture, its signification and anthropomorphic features discussed later in this chapter:

Bears are usually hunky, chunky types reminiscent of railroad engineers and former football greats. They have larger chests and bellies than average, and notably muscular legs. Some Italian-American bears are leaner and smaller; its attitude that males a Bear. *General Characteristics*: *Hair*. Their tangled beards often present no discernible place to insert a comb. *Laughter*. Bears laugh a lot and are generally good-natured. They make wonderful companions since they are prone to reach for the check [...]. *What they Eat*: beer is their favourite food. When they stay out past their hibernation time on weeknights, their lower bear nature takes over and they drink more Scotch and water than is good for them [...]. *Mating Peculiarities*: before asking you home, Bears ascertain that you will stay and cuddle all night even if nothing else happens. They may wear full leather at all times, but bears are not usually kinky. They are fascinated by nipples – others' as well as their own – and spend hours playing with them [...]. *Natural Habitat*: Bears are fascinated by motorcycle runs – possibly because it provides an excuse to keep a can of beer in their paws at all times. Although titillated by the motorcycle mystique, they prefer to let other woodland creatures ride in competitions [...] *Domestic Rating*: Bears are wonderful around the house since they don't need much exercise to keep their distinctive shape and are extremely loving, loyal and dependable [...] (Wright 1997, 42).

This is an early indication and account of bear identity as both gay and anthropomorphic which teasingly relies upon the construction of the gay bear as a gay male type allied to the bear as an animal. Moreover, it alludes to the notion of a 'pastoral fantasy encoded in bear semiotics [that] can be linked with earlier movements aimed at revitalizing an "essential" masculinity under assault from the feminizing effects of civilization by retreating to the wilderness, if only symbolically' (Hennen 2005, 27). It is also interesting to note that gay historians such as George Chauncey (1995) also claim that in early 20th century New York there were 'masculine identified man-loving men known as "wolves"' (cited in Wright 1997, 23) which indicates a much earlier archive and genealogy of gay masculinity allied to the traits of these animals.

In the mid-20th century, an elaborate web of subcultures and codes allied to leather, denim, motorcycles, work-wear, uniforms, facial and bodily hair, and the assertive display of masculinity and muscularity emerged in American popular culture. This was absorbed and assimilated by an increasingly visible gay male consumer. Whilst not explicitly linked to the identity politics of gay bears as a cohesive community, examples might include the work by Tom of Finland that erotically and explicitly references a composite or 'distinctly hybrid type' (Ramakers 2000, 138) linked to leather, uniforms, masculinity and interplays of power and sadomasochism. This is seen also in aspects of Robert Mapplethorpe's work. In photographs such as *Brian Ridley and Lyle Heeter* (1979) and *Patrice, N.Y.C* (1977) there is an emphasis on the objects and signifiers allied to gay male sadomasochistic desire and fetishist practices. For instance, and in the work which endures in his name, Mapplethorpe photographs Lyle Heeter in a way which represents features that have now been authenticated and embodied by gay bears. The heavy-set beard, his precisely worn Leatherman outfit, his pose as an S&M master, and the fixed and highly charged sexual gaze all point towards tropes that have been assimilated and adapted within gay bear culture.

These examples, and the early precedents of what a gay bear might 'be', indicate that the use of the term itself is both a way to self-identify and a means to categorise its contentiousness. Another striking example of this is Hal Fischer's *Gay Semiotics: A Photographic Study of Visual Coding among Homosexual Men* (1977) which documents the emergence of gay men in San Francisco who self-identify with aspects of what would later be termed bear culture. This photographic account places emphasis on aspects of dress and bodily appearance as key signs of gay male desire and community. Here gay men code their sexual identities and identifications through Levi jeans, Adidas trainers, checked flannel shirts, leather chaps, beards, cock rings and distinctively colour-coded handkerchiefs ('hanky's). Whilst there is no explicit reference to a 'gay bear' the accoutrements that are used by gay male individuals and 'types' such as 'street fashion leather' and 'street fashion jock' are key to the later emergence of gay bears and bear culture. Here a meticulous compound of metaphoric references and metonymic codes was absorbed and adapted from heterosexual, hetero-normative and even homophobic male culture to then be expressed as bear culture.

Alongside the sexual and erotic elements, men who would later identify as bears began to form and meet in groups to share and experience similar bodily and social desires. 'Beards meeting Beards' (London) and 'bartmanner Koln' (Bears Cologne) emerged in the early 1980s. In synchrony with this, the wider consumption and mediation of bears as representational signs of desire and identification also appeared in publications such as *Drummer Magazine* (1975–99) and the work of its editor in chief Jack Fritscher, who also founded the 'homo-masculine' magazine *Man2Man* (1979–82). Here the coding and construction of gay masculinity *as* masculine relied upon the fetishization of jockstraps, leather, cigars, hirsuteness, and a rougher, coarser and seemingly authentic steer towards the expression of gay manliness. This broader growth and ultimate commodification is also associated with publisher Richard Bulger and photographer Chris Nelson's collaborative launch of *Bear Magazine* in the USA in 1987. These early publications begin to create evidence of how 'a masculine physical image allowed members of the bear community to identify and recognize other individuals within the bear community, and strengthened their affiliation with the community' (Manley *et al* 2007, 99). These kinds of images and publications also meant that bears formulated 'a gendered strategy for repudiating effeminacy that simultaneously challenges and reproduces norms of hegemonic masculinity' (Hennen 2005, 25). This is also connected to how bear culture emerged during the late 1980s and its association with 'the AIDS pandemic and the effect of AIDS-related wasting syndrome on the erotic imagination of gay men' (ibid, 29). The bear as the embodiment of a virile, self-assured and fleshier body emerged in stark contrast to those gay male bodies that were unnecessarily stigmatised by AIDS and catastrophically 'linked with disease and death' (ibid).

In addition, these disparate examples are framed by the symbolic and ideological impact of the Stonewall Riots in 1969 that amplified the myth of a cohesive and unified gay community and movement. It also facilitated an ambiguity allied to gay bears expressing their identity via the resistant and empowering moment of 'coming out', but doing so in a way that emphasised a dominant strain of gay 'homo-masculinity' and homo-normative identity politics tethered to the emergence of gay clones in North American cities such as New York and San Francisco. In many ways this 'requirement for internal self-identification, most likely followed by a public expression of that identity, and possibly voluntary association with a group of like-minded individuals' (Wright 1997, 22) progressively augmented the gay bear community and concurrently held it open to scrutiny from other groups of sexual and gendered minorities.

To map this it may be best to use Wright's claim that '"bears" represent a link in the historical continuity of masculine-identified gay men' (ibid, 23) as concomitant to the homosexual expression of what Michel Foucault identified as 'a secret that always gave itself away' (1998, 43). More specifically, and since the 19th century, gay masculinity is a sexually categorised and identifiable 'personage, […] past, case history […] in addition to being a type of life, a life form and a morphology' (ibid). Here a crucial polarity and identificatory politics between hyper-masculine and non-masculine gay men emerges. This can be seen in the crude binary of masculine/feminine and straight/gay but more so in the discursive and cultural construction of historically derogatory identifications and categorisations such as queen, faggot, fairy and sissy. The alignment of such terms problematically attaches feminine and feminised traits to the personification of gay male effeminacy as both a subordinated and ridiculed form of gay masculinity. As a concentrated and ultimately commodifiable response it may be that gay bears have emerged as a symbolic and embodied reaction to the alignment of gay masculinity with effeminacy as an expression of gay male community, desire and visibility.

In their qualitative interviews of six self-identifying gay male bears, Manley, Levitt and Mosher (2007) build on this issue by asking 'What does it mean to you to be bear-identified?' (94). In their work they ask participants to 'define their bear identity, discuss how they became involved in the bear community, and describe whether their bear identity influenced their sense of self, masculinity, and relationships'. In the responses a range of answers suggest that 'the bear community affirmed and transformed traditional images of masculinity' (ibid, 104) in a way which renegotiated and reimagined relationships, identities and emotions. For instance, they find that whilst many gay bears embrace non-monogamy and promiscuity, they also use their gay bear identity and aspects of community to construct strong networks and bonds of 'nurturance, expression[s] of emotion, and affection with other men' (ibid, 105). In contrast, the argument that gay bears present 'self-concepts and subjective practices associated with hegemonic masculinity and negative attitudes towards effeminacy' (Guedes 2018, 120) simultaneously suggests that aspects of bear culture are vulnerable to sexual risk, mental health issues and the replication of heterosexist and homophobic tendencies such as anti-effeminacy and misogyny.

SHIFTING DISCOURSES OF GAY BEARS

In a contemporary context and in response to the commodification of gay male culture there seems to be a deceptively coherent politics of representation associated with gay male bears, despite the fact that their history is implicitly plural and uneven. As a result, the meanings and discourses that have come to be attached to them are immediately recognisable and riven with ambiguity. Foucault (1998, 101) claims 'it is in discourse that power and knowledge are joined together. And for this very reason, we must conceive discourse as a series of discontinuous segments whose tactical function is neither uniform nor stable'. The discourses of a particular sexual, social, and/or political group or individual will also produce 'different and even contradictory discourses within the same strategy' (ibid, 102). In this way, gay bears and the discourses that have come to be associated with them mark out a concurrently stable *and* unstable array of identities and identifications. Critical and cultural theorists who have worked on gay male and/or queer histories also attend to this simultaneity whereby the identities of gay men and identifications that are made with them do so in response to an intersectional and situational rhetoric of social, cultural and political conditions. Eve Kosofsky-Sedgwick recognises that the construction and representation of gay desire (and the binary tensions between the constructions of gay men in relation to their straight male counterparts) is founded on 'an understanding of their irresolvable instability' (1990, 10). This irresolution occurs between the binaries of gay/straight that are always unsteady, and also forms as an implicit feature of how gay sexual desire is articulated and signified. In this instance, sexual identity and desire, and more the ways in which gay bears espouse and appropriate straight male identities, may be underpinned always by an 'internal incoherence and mutual contradiction' (ibid, 1), in contrast to the dangers of 'discursive and institutional "common sense"' (ibid). In this way, both poles in the relationship between gay bears and straight male culture are defined by their incoherent and reciprocal paradoxes so that neither is more or less consistent or identifiable. In this way, incoherence and contradiction become the foundation to how gay bear culture is articulated and sustained. This also guides an argument that is informed by the claim that homosexuality, as a sexual definition, and gay identity in language have problematically taken on 'the distinction between relations of identification and relations of desire' (ibid, 159). Alan Sinfield observes that these modes of identification and strategies are at once 'ineluctably marginal' (1998, 40), whilst also constituting 'partially alternative subjectivities' (ibid). That is, gay bear culture and bear communities that are assembled, shared and experienced proliferate a repetitious process of 'interaction with others who are engaged with compatible preoccupations' (ibid); that is, the idealised gay *and* non-gay men who seem to inhabit a similar subject position to the gay bears' own desires and constructs of machismo, masculinity, authenticity and power.

In addition to works such as this, where gay bears are not necessarily examined analytically or empirically, there is also a strong body of work that specifically positions gay bears conceptually and critically to reposition the methodological, epistemological and ontological potentials of their meaning. Martin Levine (1992) and Shaun Cole (2000a, 2000b) assert that bears are a 1980s adaptation of the 1970s gay clone. They exist as a compound of ideological, subjective and unconscious responses to how and why discourses such as gay liberation, capitalism and AIDS are mapped together. Cole (2000a) claims that, a lot like gay clones, bears 'gloried in what they perceived [as] a "real" masculinity – hairiness, big bulky bodies, muscle developed by manual labour, rather than in the gym, often a belly' (ibid, 125). This, twinned with a reworking of clone fashion such as 'jeans, plaid shirts, work boots' (ibid), points towards the emergence of gay bear culture as a renegotiated version of gay clone culture 'reflecting (and continuing) the desire to appear to be "real" men' (ibid).

Here the sophisticated process of appropriating 'real' masculinity and the strategic ways in which it was adapted and expressed is reliant upon an imaginary version of how the 'real man' has been performatively and representationally mediated in culture. Similar to the ways in which gay male culture has appropriated the image of the bear in nature, gay clones did so with the image of heterosexual masculinity in homosocial spaces of exchange. Embodied and affective processes of '*how*' straight male dress and behaviours were appropriated were key to the emergence of the gay clone and the ways in which they transformed existent heterosexual associations 'with a new meaning of eroticism and overt sexuality' (Blachford 1981, 200). More powerfully, and as Cole (2000b) surmises, 'what the gay clone did leave was the legacy of the masculinization of homosexuality and an emphasis of overt masculine images and physiques' (ibid, 135). Still, and rather than it being a critique or reaction against clone culture, the emergence of gay bears might be more usefully positioned as a resignification and re-empowerment of former social and cultural systems of reductively hegemonic masculinity. As Hennen (2005, 32) suggests, the 'bear look was a reaction not against the clone's masculinity *per se* but rather against his hypermasculinity and the particular way that the clone displayed the body to signal that masculinity—hard, lean, muscled, toned, and smooth'.

Levine (1992, 84) aligns the gay clone to the emergence of 'urban neighbourhood[s] housing a dense concentration of gay institutions and residents' referred to as 'ghettos' (ibid, 70). More so, he goes on to suggest that 'because of its uniform look and life-style' (ibid) clone identity was promoted through 'gay media, arts and pornography' (ibid) as symbolic and indicative of 1970s post-Stonewall liberation and pre-AIDS gay life. Here, a collection of socio-cultural features connect and shape the identity of the gay clone which are also foundational to the gay bear. Hedonism aligned to specific frameworks of knowledge and understanding, motifs and codes appropriated from hyper-masculine ideals such as the cowboy, the biker and the blue collar worker were 'conveyed through both butch presentational strategies and cruising, tricking and partying [and] in particular butch attire, muscles and masculine environments' (ibid, 83). More so, the idea developed that 'social context' shaped the forms of clones' lives. That is, 'AIDS, gay liberation, male gender roles, and the ethics of self-fulfilment, constraint, and commitment' (Levine 1992, 82) correlate with some of the ways in which gay bear culture has also developed and sustained itself in relation to dressing down, natural and chubby bodies, hairiness, and the pursuit of an authentic gay masculine self.

In *Gay Pornography: Representations of Sexuality and Masculinity* (2017), John Mercer uses the earlier discourse of gay clone culture to analyse gay bear porn (128–34). Here the nodes of identification between gay clones *and* gay bears in porn are positioned as key to their emergence as sexually arousing images. A composite of the clone, the hypermasculine gay man, gay daddies, leather men, and the increase of barebacking all have the capacity to transect in the sexually explicit image of a gay bear. This image 'translates itself into the ways in which the term "bear" is used in gay porn and the types that are presented as representative of the bear aesthetic or the values of bear culture' (ibid, 129). In this way, the bear has become a kind of 'hybridised hypermasculine ideal, with a relatively flexible iconography that can be deployed across a range of contexts' (ibid). Pornography allows for the ideological and idealised fantasy of the bear to circulate and map into a vast visual supply of burly bodies, mature men, tattoos, beards and body hair, and other fetishes ranging from cigar smoking, sportswear, cock-rings and BDSM. It also places gay bears in homosocial and all-male settings such as the army barracks, the public toilet, the prison and the sex club, which in turn function as spaces where highly charged, intense and promiscuous (often group) sex occur. Mercer usefully suggests that this kind of 'repurposing, re-appropriation and bricolage' (ibid, 131) which finds its heritage in clone culture, works to position the gay bear in gay porn as 'an adjective to describe a physicality, a type or style, rather than [...] any affiliation to a [gay] subculture' (ibid) *per se*. Here, a mixture of dress, pornography, lifestyle, community and sex inhibit and underpin the visual and embodied processes of self-presentation and self-recognition cultivated in contemporary gay bear culture and its adaptation and considered use of the bear as animal.

ANTHROPOMORPHISM AND SIGNIFICATIONS OF THE GAY BEAR

The histories and discourses allied to gay bears shift over space, place and time. Yet in synchrony with these changes, a prevailing and highly recognisable visual culture associated with gay bears has emerged. One of its key features is the anthropomorphic representation of the bear and/or allusion to its traits. Here the behaviours and attributes of the bear as a wild animal are reiterated, assimilated and adapted to capture and signify the imagined and ideological politics, lifestyles and desires of the gay men who self-identify as bears. This may be most obviously seen in the visual techniques and modes of representation that have been used to promote and sustain gay bears as a socio-cultural and consumer group. More so, and in the West, there are perhaps thousands of examples which attempt to advertise, brand, market and thus encapsulate this complex rhetoric of desire, anthropomorphism, appropriation and belonging that upholds the ideological construction of the gay male bear and gay bear culture.

For instance, the UK-based Millivres Prowler Group (MPG), which produces porn features, publishes several gay magazines, and operates the Prowler adult stores in London and Brighton, uses the imprint of a bear's paw as its primary branding tool. The paw itself alludes to, but does not directly reference, gay bear culture whilst also becoming an instantly universal symbol of identification. The Prowler stores also stock and sell a huge range of bear-related items by designers such as Bobo Bear that use a mixture of comic book graphics and illustration to exploit and explore the imagined amalgamation of bear and man together. In turn, this kind of visual and coded rhetoric is often used to promote club nights and bear pride events whereby gay men and bears idealistically and anthropomorphically co-exist. In his article 'Grizzly Love: The Queer Ecology of Timothy Treadwell', Colin Carman (2012) claims that the bear enthusiast, film-maker and environmentalist Treadwell commits to 'becoming-animal' (ibid, 516) through a queer ecological bond with the grizzly bears he lives alongside. Carman suggests that 'the relationship between Treadwell and the grizzly can be easily resituated in relation to that master signifier of masculinity, the bear, so readily evoked in contemporary gay male culture' (ibid, 522). Although extreme and abstracted from the language of gay pornography, advertising and consumerism, we see with the likes of Prowler and Bobo Bear that there is an alliance between Treadwell's ecological desire to become-bear and the ways in which gay bear culture is 'invested in the erotics of bear worship' (ibid, 522) through commodities and material pleasures. Both work with the blurred boundaries and renegotiation of the 'human-animal divide, and its construction of the grizzly as consistent with many gay men's self-identification as a "bear"' (ibid, 511). Just as 'Treadwell's […] queer anthropomorphism amalgamates man and bear' (ibid, 514) so do the gay consumerist codes allied to anthropomorphic bears and their gay male counterparts in the visual imagery where wild bears are humanised and repositioned as gay men.

The XXL club night in London which caters for gay 'bears and their admirers' and uses the tagline 'one club fits all' also exploits a range of sophisticated graphic and photographic techniques to capture an appealing and visually provocative purview of gay bear life in urban space. The emblem for the club night uses the image of a brown bear walking across green grass with a perfect blue sky above. Here the visual and ideological constructions allude to a slicker and more marketable version of the wild or natural outdoors that appeals to a logocentric gay male audience. This also corresponds to aspects of what John Mercer (2017, 133) describes in bear porn as 'log-cabin fantasia' and the ways in which bears are often located or understood through a spatial and temporal 'return to nature, the rural location and the rugged epitome of masculinity represented by the lumberjack, the farm labourer or indeed the country bumpkin'(ibid). In this way, a metonymy of the gay bear captures and amplifies a 'disparate mixture of cultural and gender stereotyping, nostalgia and romanticism with which the bear is most closely associated' (ibid). Other examples of this include the gay dating/hook up app 'Scruff' and several porn companies and websites such as Butchdixon.com and RawFuckClub.com which present a strategically explicit and semantically astute series of visual and graphic references to gay bear culture as promiscuous, virile, heroic and mature. Beyond representation and mediation there are also discursive, affective and embodied practices in language and behaviour that are in some way influenced and defined by the intersections of the bear as gay man and as a wild animal. For example, a slang term such as 'Grrrr' which is widely used in gay culture as a way of indicating that a guy you have seen is sexually attractive/desirable adopts the sound that a bear may make in the wild. This anthropomorphism of gay bears is conveyed and communicated through mutable processes of identification that seem to reflect the paradoxical position of gay bear culture itself. At once familiar, yet also subject to shifts and changes in terms of its meaning and interpretation.

For the gay men who embrace and embody it, bear culture offers an affirmation of community, inclusivity, sexual expression and self-representation. For those who doubt it, gay bear culture relies upon a problematic level of appropriation that legitimates elements of hetero-sexism, patriarchy, hegemony and gender hierarchy. More specifically this can be allied clearly to the ways in which gay bears have come to construct themselves (and other gay bears) as masculine gay men. The promise of an authentic or genuine discourse of gay masculinity provides gay bears with an imagined and performative rhetoric of belonging demonstrated in the images and language of the movement. The demonstration of this in their shifting history and the association of groups such as clones to bears seems to be reliant on this search for an authentically gay *and* masculine ideology and aesthetic. Yet, and as a consequence, this kind of identity construction is also defined by an anxiety and reluctance towards the construction of the effeminate homosexual as 'the culturally accepted meaning of homosexuality, and the stereotype of homosexuality' (Cole 2000b, 125). The gradual emergence and assimilation of gay bears as a type of 'rugged masculinity' (ibid, 128) has connoted and conveyed a desire to construct and attain a 'real' masculine body, attitude and persona connected to a range of overlapping bodily and personality traits. On the one hand this might be allied to 'toughness, virility, aggression, strength [and] potency' (ibid), yet on the other there is scope for these same men to embrace cuddliness, tolerance, humour, tactility and pragmatism.

Yet problematically, gay bear identity construction has often relied upon hegemonic and overtly macho forms of heterosexual and at times heterosexist masculinity. This indicates that in gay culture the effeminacy/machismo binary has endorsed a version of gay masculinity that continues to be 'pervaded by the tyranny of gender divisions' (Marshall 1981, 154). However, and in contrast to this potentially reductive type of masculinity, the gay bear has also emerged as a form of gay masculinity that 'through appropriation opened up radical and transgressive possibilities' (Cole 2000b, 128). In this way, the gay bear has the power to create and sustain an individual sense of agency and control over its own body and its performative potentials. As Hennen (2005, 34) observes, 'when gay bears "do submission" or "do effeminacy" with their bodies, they in fact exercise a kind of embodied agency, insofar as the Bear body is perceived by heterosexual men as both "not heterosexual" and "not effeminate."' Here the possibilities of what gay can 'be' are opened up more. The anthropomorphic opportunities of men aligning their desires and bodies to the image of bears in the wild are analogous to the idea that just as 'bears emerge from hibernation with a ferocious hunger. Perhaps one day, the Bears [...] will demonstrate the same ferocious hunger for change in the gender politics governing resistant masculinities' (Hennen 2005, 42). In this way and through the combined potentials of agency and appropriation it may be that in gay bear culture the image and ideology of the anthropomorphic bear shifts the emphasis away from hyper-masculine and authenticating discourses of attaining a 'real' masculinity towards a more liminal and subversive politics of self-realisation and transgression.

BIBLIOGRAPHY AND REFERENCES

Blachford, G, 1981 Male Dominance and the Gay World, in *The Making of the Modern Homosexual* (ed K Plummer), Barnes and Noble, New Jersey, 184–210

Carmen, C, 2012 Grizzly Love: The Queer Ecology of Timothy Treadwell, *GLQ: A Journal of Lesbian and Gay Studies* 18 (4) 507–28

Chauncey, G, 1995 *Gay New York Gender, Urban Culture, and the Making of the Gay Male World 1890–1940*, Basic Books, New York

Cole, S, 2000a "Macho Man": Clones and the Development of a Masculine Stereotype, *Fashion Theory* 4 (2), 125–40

———, 2000b *Don We Now Our Gay Apparel: Gay Men's Dress in the Twentieth Century*, Berg, London

Fischer, H, 1977 *Gay Semiotics: A Photographic Study of Visual Coding Among Homosexual Men*, NFS Press, San Francisco

Foucault, M, 1998 *The History of Sexuality: 1 - The Will to Knowledge*, Penguin Books, London

Guedes, D D, 2018 Gay bear subculture: self-concepts, subjective practices and mental health, *Journal of Psychology, Diversity and Health* 7 (1), 120–33

Hennen, P, 2005 Bear Bodies, Bear Masculinity: Recuperation, Resistance or Retreat, *Gender and Society* 19 (1), 25-43

Levine, M P, 1992 The life and death of gay clones, in *Gay culture in America: Essays from the field* (ed G Herdt), Beacon Press, Boston

Manley, E, Levitt, H, and Mosher, C, 2007 Understanding the Bear movement in Gay Male Culture: Redefining Masculinity, *Journal of Homosexuality* 53 (4), 89–112

Marshall, J, 1981 Pansies, Perverts and Macho Men: Changing Conceptions of Male Homosexuality, in *The Making of the Modern Homosexual* (ed K Plummer), Barnes and Noble, New Jersey, 133–54

Mercer, J, 2017 *Gay Pornography: Representations of Sexuality and Masculinity*, I.B. Tauris, London

Ramakers, M, 2000 *Dirty Pictures: Tom of Finland, Masculinity and Homosexuality*, St Martin's Press, New York

Sedgwick, E K, 1990 *Epistemology of the Closet*, University of California Press, Berkeley and Los Angeles

Sinfield, A, 1998 *Gay and After*, Serpents Tail, London

Suresha, R, 2002 *Bears on Bears: Interviews and Discussions*, Bear Bones Books, New York and London

Wright, L, (ed) 1997 *The Bear Book: Readings in the History and Evolution of a Gay Subculture*, Routledge, London

———, (ed) 2001 *The Bear Book II: Further Readings in the History and Evolution of a Gay Subculture*, Routledge, New York

5

Bears, Wildmen, Yeti and Sasquatch

Jeff Meldrum

Humans have long held an affinity with bears, and a fascination for their superficial, but remarkable, similarity to people. This allure has even taken the form of worship, or *arctolatry*. Some have argued that the romantic notions of ancient bear cults and Paleolithic shrines are more the result of taphonomic processes and the imaginations of early discoverers (Wunn 2001). Wunn (2001, 457) concludes, 'Conceptions of cave bear worship during the early and middle Paleolithic period belong to the realm of legend.' Not all might agree, but in any case, in the more recent past, bear worship is manifest among ethnic groups across northern Eurasia, stretching from the Basques of the Pyrenees to the Ainu of Hokkaido. Intertwined with these practices is the frequent folk belief that humans descended from bears. For example, the ancient royal lines of Denmark and Sweden are declared to result from a cross between a woman and a bear (Magnus 1555). Indigenous peoples of North America also held the notion that bears and humans can interbreed. For example, the Haida of the Pacific coast of Alaska and Canada hold a tradition of a woman taken as a wife by a bear. The daughter of this pairing eventually returned to live with the Haida, and according to the legend, this primal bear-human goddess is the ancestor of all those entitled to wear the prestigious bear clan crest (Smith 1909).

Bears exhibit notable likenesses to humans in both anatomy and behaviour. Bears walk on plantigrade feet, they can stand upright, they nurse their young from paired pectoral mammae as do humans, they are omnivorous and intelligent, and they have colour vision. Medieval physicians recognized the similarity between bears and humans and, prior to knowledge of the great apes, considered the bear one of the animals most closely related to humans (Pastoureau 2011). Poet and environmental activist Gary Snyder (1990, 175) mused, 'After you take a bear's coat off, it looks just like a human.' In fact, as any hunter who has dressed a bear carcass can attest, the resemblance in musculoskeletal anatomy is so striking that some texts on forensic anthropology include specific references to bear skeletal anatomy in order to differentiate it from human remains. There was a case in rural Idaho involving the discovery of a decomposing carcass in a garbage bag that turned up in a drawn-down reservoir. Initial examination raised concern that it was perhaps the corpse of a missing person. Consultation with local anthropologists determined that it was actually a hunter's butchered bear remains (Meldrum, *pers comm*).

The Wildman

Bears have not been, however, the only anthropomorphic entities in the forests. In classical times, through the Middle Ages, the figure of the hair-covered Wildman – satyr, silvanus, woodwose and leshy – was also the denizen of the forests. Traditions likewise recount sexual encounters between these Wildmen and human females. From the 12th to the 16th centuries, the iconic Wildman (and Green Man) was a popular figure adorning heraldic crests and standing vigil over cathedral portals. With the age of enlightenment, the prominent position of the Wildman eventually faded into the mists of mythology. Just as the mystical position of the bear was displaced by the rise of science and influence of Christianity, so it seems was the role of man's presumed wild and hairy, and sometimes lascivious, forest-dwelling alter ego.

By the 18th century, accounts by Western explorers and scientists renewed fascination with notions of exotic man-like creatures in the far-off frontiers in Africa and Asia. Linnaeus (1735) dubbed these the Anthropomorpha, or man-shaped creatures. Indeed, he recognized two types of humans, contrasting *Homo sapiens* – man the wise – with *Homo troglodytes* – the cave man (also known as *Homo sylvestris* – the forest man). This was not a cave man in the cartoon Alley Oop[1] sense, popular from the 1930s through to the 1970s. Linnaeus' troglodyte was envisioned as entirely hair-covered, nocturnal, devoid of speech or material culture. In its various depictions, the troglodyte was figured alongside the then poorly understood members of the Simia (the imitators), ie the monkeys and apes. These included recognizable, but indeed anthropomorphised after a stylised fashion, depictions of a modern baboon, chimpanzee and orangutan. In a later edition of *Systema Natura*, Linnaeus abandoned Anthropomorpha for the more exclusive Primates – humans, apes and monkeys, although now excluding the sloths. But the troglodyte never gained general acceptance as a real entity. Johann Friedrich Blumenbach (1779) dubbed it Linnaeus' 'Great Mistake', attributing it to confused descriptions mixing traits of humans and the orangutan. To natural theologians of the day, these man-shaped creatures, ape or Wildman, represented missing links in creation's Great Chain of Being. Rather than reviling them like many clerics of the times, as a mockery of humanity, as disparaging caricatures of man's creation in the similitude of God, they instead perceived them as completing the perfection of God's creation by bridging the apparent gap perceived between humanity and the animal kingdom.

The Yeti

Given these two strikingly anthropomorphic creatures – the bear and the Wildman – the potential for conflation is obvious. Such blurring is all too evident in the lore surrounding a modern 'Wildman' – the abominable snowman, or *yeti*. Indeed, the etymology of the various names for the *yeti* demonstrate this tendency for amalgamation – eg the Tibetan *Miché* translates as *man-bear*. In the Himalayas there are two recognized bear species: the Himalayan or Asiatic black bear (*Ursus thibetanus laniger*) [Syn: *Selanarctos thibetanus*] and the Himalayan brown bear (*Ursus arctos isabellinus*). The existence of a yet unrecognized hominoid remains in question; therefore many offer the bear as an explanation for anomalous Wildman encounters. Indeed, the *yeti* might have languished in the realms of legend were it not for the evidence of footprints. These seemed to attest to the physicality of the creature and none took on such an iconic quality as the footprint photographed close-up by mountaineers Eric Shipton and Michael Ward in 1951 (Ward 1997). There have been numerous interpretations offered to account for its unusual appearance (Meldrum 2018). Given the crispness of the outline, in particular the toes and the snow ridges between them, it is difficult to imagine much distortion by melting or sublimation, and even

---

[1]   Alley Oop was a syndicated comic strip created by V T Hamlin. Its title character was a club-wielding caveman residing in the prehistoric kingdom of Moo, who offered a satirical look at suburban life in mid-20th century America.

more difficult to imagine inconsistent distortions manifested, but left unmentioned, along the trackway, which was observed for more than a mile. Since close-ups of only one footprint were taken, it cannot be determined whether this singular image is an accurate representation of the foot anatomy, or a depiction of artefacts unique to this particular print. Sceptics dismiss it as merely the overstep of a bear's fore and hind paws. They further generalise in their assumptions by explaining away all footprints attributed to the *yeti* as misidentified bear tracks (Taylor 2017; Messner 1998).

I personally researched and catalogued the photographic evidence of any and all footprints attributed to the *yeti*. Numerous published photos of footprints, and several unpublished or little-known photos, were identified. It became clear that the majority of 'yeti' footprints were largely unintelligible due to melting and sublimation, and therefore *indeterminate*. Indeed, it was confirmed that a significant fraction of the minority were blatantly bear tracks, and only a very few footprints pointed to a potential hominoid trackmaker. I often pondered how it was that the Sherpas so adamantly identified obvious bear tracks as *yeti*. Were they so disingenuous that they would assert whatever they suspected the Western explorer wanted to hear? Or were they so naïve as to not apprehend the distinctions between a bear paw print and a hominoid footprint? An insight shared by an Indian author shed light on this question for me. For the Sherpa, the Western boundary between the physical and the spiritual is far less distinct, if even acknowledged. For them the *yeti* is the 'Spirit of the Mountain', capable of corporeal expression in any of a variety of forms: a pilgrim, a wildman, a bear (Lall 1988). Enigmatic tracks discovered on barren glaciers at high altitude must be the spoor of the *yeti* corporeal, even if from one's perspective it is merely a bear traversing a high snowy pass between forested valleys.

That numerous examples of tracks attributed to the *yeti* are in fact made by bears is a certainty, but is it justified to generalise that *all* 'yeti' tracks are left by bears? It would seem not. Some described encounters and a very few documented footprints do point to a possible hominoid. Foremost among these rare examples are what should have displaced the Shipton-Ward footprint as the 'type specimens' of yeti footprints, ie those discovered by Edward Cronin and Jeff McNeeley in 1972, on a biological survey expedition in the Upper Barun Khola of Nepal (Cronin 1979; McNeeley *et al* 1973; McNeeley and Wachtel 1988). The tracks were pristine, laid down overnight with no opportunity for melting or sublimation in the sun. There was no issue of distortion, only a question of interpretation. The footprints extended for miles. They reportedly maintained a bipedal gait throughout – no evidence of the distinct appearance of fore paws vs hind paws, as in a quadrupedal bear trackway, even when ascending a steep incline through deep snow. Not only were multiple photographs taken of the prints, but a plaster cast was made and photographed as well. Unfortunately, the cast was seized by customs agents at the Nepalese border and is now unaccounted for. Using the combined photos of the cast and footprints, I undertook an exercise to build up a model in clay of the inferred foot responsible for that print. The result portrays what appears to be the footprint of a hominoid – not a bear (Meldrum 2018).

KNOWN SYMPATRY OF BEARS AND HOMINOIDS

While Africa has its anthropomorpha in the form of the chimpanzees (Bantu – *mockman*) and gorillas (Carthigian Hanno – tribe of hairy women), there are no sympatric bears to conflate visual or trace encounters. The only African bear is found in the Atlas Mountains of Morocco (*Ursus arctos crowtheri*). On the other hand – or foot – the islands of Borneo and Sumatra harbour the orangutan (Austronesian – *man of the woods*), as well as two subspecies of the Malayan sun bear. *Helarctos malayanus malayanus* inhabits Asian mainland and Sumatra; *H. m. euryspilus* occurs only on the island of Borneo. The specialised adaptations of the foot of the highly arboreal *quadrumanus* orangutan leaves little room for confusion with bear tracks, on those rare occasions it ventures to the ground. But southeast Asia reportedly harbours a diminutive wildman, known by various names, including the now popularised *orang pendek*. This hairy biped is said to leave small broad humanoid footprints with narrow heels, which has raised the potential for conflation with sightings and footprints of standing sun bears (Forth 2008).

THE SASQUATCH

The indigenous peoples of the Pacific northwest of North America are certainly familiar with bears. Native to North America are the American black bear (*Ursus americanus*), the grizzly or brown bear (*Ursus arctos*), and in the remote northern Arctic, the polar bear (*Ursus maritimus*). As elsewhere, bears hold a significant position in the natural and cultural landscape of these tribal peoples. They too have a distinct notion of a Wildman in their lore. In the Pacific northwest, these hominoid entities are portrayed prominently in costume, on totem poles, and as clan crests. Various tribes have their own names for them, eg '*sokqueatl*,' '*soss-q'tal*' or '*sesqac*', most appellations translating roughly as 'Wildman of the woods'. An anglicised form of these variant names was popularised by reservation schoolteacher and writer J W Burns, who attributes the term '*sasquatch*' to Charlie Victor, an old hunter from the Skwah Reserve near Chilliwack, British Columbia. (Burns 1929). Early European explorers and settlers to North America occasionally reported encounters with wildmen, perhaps influenced by traditions from the Old World. But the *sasquatch* and Bigfoot, as it came to be called in the United States after the late 1950s, was described as a giant ape, from 7–10ft tall, leaving 16in. footprints (Genzoli 1958). Could such a creature, a large relict hominoid, even sustain itself in the montane forest ecosystem of western North America?

Based on native traditional stories and contemporary eyewitness observations, *sasquatch* seem to have a catholic diet, and therefore would occupy the niche of a generalised omnivore. Bears, as well as humans, also share an omnivorous diet. Some sceptical wildlife biologists object to the premise of a *sasquatch* since a large mammalian species – namely bears – already occupies the omnivore niche. However, 'large omnivore' is a broad-brush characterisation of a dietary niche, which hardly justifies invoking the principle of competitive exclusion – ie that only one species can occupy a single niche. There would seem to be ample evidence of niche partitioning and possibly character displacement in terms of intelligence, social organisation and population density, daily activity patterns, masticatory adaptations and digestive physiology, and locomotor adaptations attributed to bears and *sasquatch* respectively. For example, bears have evolved from a carnivore ancestor that possessed a protruding snout, sporting large canines, carnassial pre-molars and molars, and a relatively short and simple digestive tract. *Sasquatch*, being a hominoid primate, would likely have evolved from a largely frugivore/folivore ancestor, with a flatter lower face, thick enamelled and enlarged premolars and molars, shorter canines, long complex digestive tract with slow passage and hindgut fermentation aiding in digestion and detoxification of plant secondary compounds. The adaptations derived in the bear and *sasquatch* respectively would constitute two distinct ways to be a large omnivore (Meldrum and Mionczynski 2007).

BIGFOOT LOOKALIKES?

Given this broadly convergent, yet distinct evolution, it would seem that if a black bear can make a living in a given habitat with diverse available resources, then very likely a *sasquatch* could as well. Indeed, there is much overlap in the distribution of substantiated reports of *sasquatch* and the known range of black bears. This was dramatically demonstrated by Lozier *et al* (2009). To draw attention to their concern over indiscriminate application of ecological niche modelling (ENM) software to predict species distributions, the authors ran a test case using *ostensibly* 'suspect' *sasquatch* data. The results showed remarkable overlap between resulting distributions of *sasquatch* and black bear. Their conclusion was, 'Thus, the two "species" do not demonstrate significant niche differentiation with respect to the selected bioclimatic variables. Although it is possible that *sasquatch* and *U. americanus* share such remarkably similar bioclimatic requirements, we nonetheless suspect that many Bigfoot sightings are, in fact, of black bears' (Lozier *et al* 2009, 1626). This is the argument, albeit qualified, employed by some ideological sceptics. Joe Nickell (2013), writing for *Skeptical Inquirer*, in a piece titled 'Bigfoot Lookalikes', offered this, together with a blatantly back-handed caveat, 'Let it be understood that I am in no way saying that all Sasquatch/Bigfoot sightings involve bears. After all, some are surely other misidentifications or hoaxes involving people in furry suits.' Nickell concludes that standing bears are the best lookalike for the upright hairy man-beasts called Bigfoot. As will be seen, any similarity is largely limited to upright posture, hairiness and colour, in spite of the contrived comparisons Nickell offers (Fig 5.1).

Although Lozier *et al* (2009) appeared to have undertaken this exercise rather tongue-in-cheek, in reality all three authors were actually quite interested in the *sasquatch* phenomenon and wanted to more closely examine these data with some ecological niche modelling (ENM) in order to see what conclusions could be reached. One of the paper's authors, Peter Aniello, who

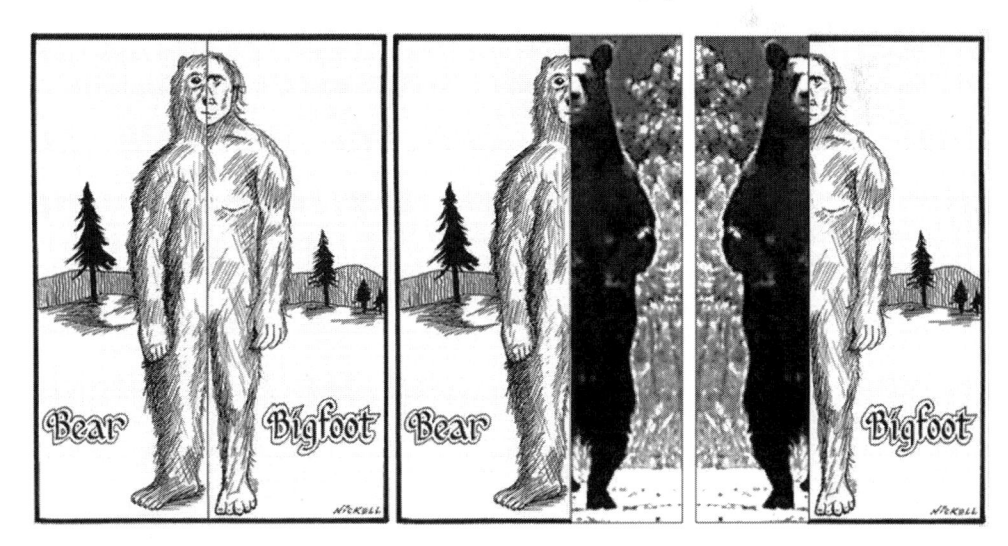

FIGURE 5.1. (LEFT) UPRIGHT BEAR OFFERED AS A BIGFOOT LOOKALIKE BY NICKELL (2013). (CENTER) COMPARISON OF NICKELL'S BEAR FIGURE ALONGSIDE AN ACTUAL UPRIGHT BLACK BEAR, HIGHLIGHTING THE INACCURACIES OF THE FIGURED BEAR ANATOMY. (RIGHT) REAL BEAR CONTRASTED WITH NICKELL'S BIGFOOT SKETCH.

has published in and serves on the editorial board of the *Relict Hominoid Inquiry*[2], said, 'The results were actually remarkably consistent, both using the full [Bigfoot] dataset and just a subset for which footprint observations were available, and with points withheld to be used as check points. In fact, the ENM came out exactly how you would expect an ENM to look for a real animal fitting the description of a Bigfoot. But to get this published in the *Journal of Biogeography*, (and, I'm sure Jeff L. [Lozier] and Bill [Hickerson] were thinking, to avoid the negative experiences you (Jeff M. [Meldrum]) have gone through in academia!), the paper had to be framed as "look how great the ENM can look even if you're using suspect data"' (Aniello, *pers comm*). This is an informative caveat, and one revealing of the inherent bias against scholarly discussions of the evidence for *sasquatch*, and the tendency to offer instead the simplistic explanation that all *sasquatch* encounters are merely bear misidentifications.

The chance of mistaking a bear sighting for a *sasquatch* is conceivable, but unlikely for a knowledgeable experienced observer under favourable conditions. In fact, quite the opposite might be more likely the case. The initial reaction of many disinterested eyewitnesses to a possible *sasquatch* sighting is to rationalise what they have seen, as simply a bear. Their inclination is to account for their experience within a familiar framework – 'It was dark and hairy and upright, so it must have been a standing bear.' However, any resemblance ends there. Bears rarely walk for more than a few steps in an upright posture before dropping again to all fours. Their bipedal gait is usually halting and awkward on relatively short hindlimbs. Their forelimbs do not swing alternately with each step, but instead are held out forward in front of the body, constrained by the sloping shoulder anatomy of a quadruped, lacking a clavicle.

Bears have characteristic physical features that distinguish them from the typical description of *sasquatch*. Notable 'field marks' aid in the reliable identification of wildlife species. Field marks for bears include: prominent ears atop their heads, long snouts, sloping shoulders due to their lack of collar bones (clavicles), and short legs. Dr John Bindernagel, a Canadian wildlife biologist who pursued an interest in the possible existence of *sasquatch*, concludes that regular misidentifications are unlikely, especially in the case of daytime sightings lasting more than one or two seconds. He notes that, unfortunately, most field guides do not provide information that would help an eyewitness identify their sighting as a *sasquatch* (Fig 5.2):

> As a result, most wildlife biologists continue to insist on misidentified bears as the most likely explanation for *sasquatch* reports despite its unbear-like appearance. The continued absence of the *sasquatch* from current mammal field guides constitutes an authoritative statement against the existence of this species in North America (Bindernagel 2004, 56).

The Evidence of Footprints

As with the *yeti*, there are footprints attributed to *sasquatch* that would seem to clearly attest to the physicality of the species: its dimensions, gait, range and behaviour. Even renowned primatologist John Napier, based on a narrow sample of alleged *sasquatch* footprints and, at that time, rather limited available empirical analyses of hominoid footprints, concluded that the footprint evidence affirmed the existence of *sasquatch*. In his conclusion he states, 'I am convinced that

---

2   The *Relict Hominoid Inquiry* (RHI) is a refereed online scholarly journal, since 2012 (www.isu.edu/rhi).

BLACK BEAR *Ursus americanus*

Height (upright) ... 5-6 ft.

Weight .... 300 lbs. (150-700)

Color .... Black, Brown
Cinnamon, White

SASQUATCH *sp. indet.*

Height (upright) ... 7-10 ft.

Weight .... 600–1,000 lbs.

Color .... Black, Brown
Blond, White

DISTINGUISHING FIELD MARKS

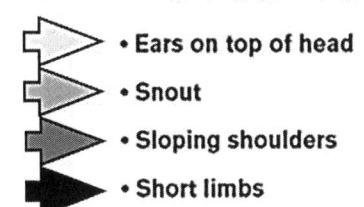

• Ears on top of head

• Snout

• Sloping shoulders

• Short limbs

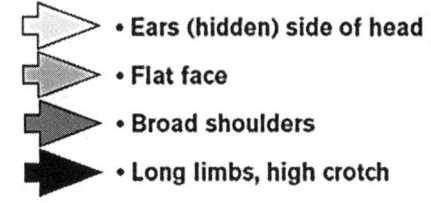

• Ears (hidden) side of head

• Flat face

• Broad shoulders

• Long limbs, high crotch

FIGURE 5.2. THE DISTINGUISHING FEATURES, OR FIELD MARKS, DIFFERENTIATING A SASQUATCH FROM A BLACK BEAR, AS WELL AS A HUMAN HIKER (MELDRUM 2013).

the Sasquatch exists, but whether it is all that it is cracked up to be is another matter altogether. There must be *something* in northwest America that needs explaining, and that something leaves man-like footprints. The evidence I have adduced in favor of the Sasquatch is not hard evidence; few physicists, biologists or chemists would accept it, but nevertheless it is evidence and cannot be ignored' (Napier 1973, 205). Unfortunately, it *has* remained ignored or off-handedly dismissed by science, despite the fact that the sample of documented footprints now numbers in the several hundreds and has been the focus of numerous published studies (eg Bindernagel 1998, Krantz 1999, Meldrum 2004, 2006, 2007).

What is the potential for mistaking known wildlife signs as alleged *sasquatch* tracks? A review of a typical field guide to animal tracks and signs once again confirms the bear as the most likely candidate for misidentification. However, only very exceptional guides offer assistance with alleged *sasquatch* footprints (Fig 5.3). While many fleet-footed animals walk and run on a reduced number of toes in a digitigrade or unguligrade fashion, such as the wolf or deer, the hind foot of the bear resembles a human's pedal appendage in its flat-footed, or plantigrade, appearance and its primitive retention of all five distinct toes that make contact with the ground. The bear's toes are arranged essentially in an uneven arc across the end of the foot, with the inner or medial toe being the smallest, and often leaving an indistinct impression. In contrast, the *sasquatch* toes are more or less aligned in an oblique toe row, with the inner or 'big' toe the largest and often the longest. Hominoids have broad flattened nails rather than the recurved claws of a bear. Seasonally, however, bear claws may be worn down from digging in the soil, to the point that they may leave little trace in a footprint, even in soft soil.

Another distinguishing feature of the bear track is the shape of the heel. The heel pad of the bear is tapered to a blunt point and is usually separated from the interdigital pad by a prominent crease. The heel tapers because the bear paw is not completely plantigrade, or flat-footed. Instead, the heel is actually elevated slightly, producing the taper of the underlying pad. In heavy mature bears the heel is pressed to the ground and the pad may be more filled out and rounded. As in most quadrupeds, a greater portion of bodyweight is differentially carried over the bear's

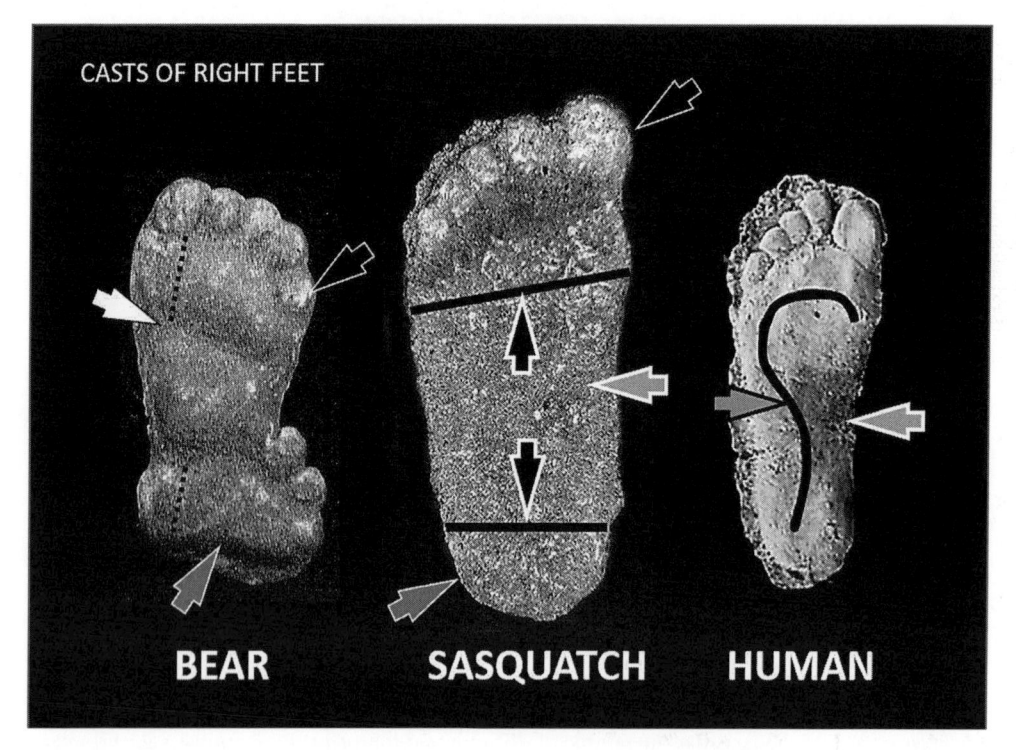

Figure 5.3. Distinguishing features differentiating the footprint attributed to sasquatch from the overlapping fore and hind paw prints of a bear (Meldrum 2013).

forelimbs so that the imprints of the forepaws are generally deeper. In contrast, the habitually bipedal *sasquatch* has a true plantigrade foot, and given its large size, has a broader rounder heel pad to cushion that point of weight-bearing beneath the calcaneus, or heel bone.

The pattern and spacing of footfalls also distinguish reputed *sasquatch* tracks from bear tracks. Generally, the four-legged or quadrupedal pattern of the bear track is evident in the series of alternating fore and hind paws. At normal walking speeds, the paws are well separated and the interval between right and left paws, or straddle, is pronounced. The bear's forepaw lacks a hinter pad and merely has a wedge-shaped interdigital pad. It is noticeably concave on its proximal border, giving it a bean-shaped outline, or cashew-shape considering its asymmetry. However, with age this concavity may tend to fill out somewhat. At swifter speeds, the hind foot imprint often oversteps, overlaps, or is directly superimposed upon the forepaw imprint. The latter two circumstances can give the impression of a single elongate footprint. This precise overlap or register of the fore and hind paws happens infrequently and inconsistently, but can give the impression of tracks left by an animal walking on only two legs, although with a very short step length.

One clue to distinguish such an overlapping track is to look at the shape of the heel. If the overlapping forepaw occupies the position of the 'heel' of the elongate footprint, the bean-shaped pad of the forepaw will exhibit a concave trailing edge instead of a rounded convex outline. If the hind paw dominates the hindmost part of the print the characteristic tapering heel of the bear hind paw will be evident. In either case, there will likely be extraneous toes visible, which are lying outside the overlapping prints, or that are not altogether obliterated by the superimposed paw.

In spite of these distinctions, occasionally bear tracks have been attributed to *sasquatch*, generally by persons unfamiliar with wildlife signs, but even occasionally by experienced hunters. Dr Lynn Rogers is of course very familiar with bear tracks as a result of his many years of experience studying bears. He has personally examined casts of alleged *sasquatch* footprints. As he hefted a large exceptionally clear cast from the west coast of Washington that was collected by an on-duty deputy sheriff, he observed, 'A lot of times bear tracks are reported as people tracks [and sometimes *sasquatch* tracks], but I cannot explain this track. I don't know how they would fake it. The big toe compared to the other toes in a human-like pattern is not like a bear at all. I just cannot explain this' (quoted in Meldrum 2006).

There is no question that footprints and upright hairy figures have been and will be occasionally misidentified, but this does not explain the numerous credible sightings by knowledgeable observers and the persistent examples of distinct well-documented footprints. It should be obvious to any experienced tracker or expert in foot morphology that all footprints attributed to *sasquatch* cannot be casually dismissed as bear footprints, nor, in particular, can or should the observations of experienced outdoorsmen and biologists be brushed aside as simply cases of misidentification, or for that matter, as hoaxes.

What is to be made of these purportedly unattributable footprints? They constitute the most pervasive, compelling body of data indicating the existence of an as-yet-unrecognized (hardly unknown) species of hominoids – *relict hominoids* – persisting in various quarters of the globe. After all, *something* is leaving these footprints. From stone to plaster to digital cameras, these enigmatic giant humanoid footprints have been recorded in Native American petroglyphs, and cast and photographed by roadbuilders, wildlife biologists, law enforcement officers and citizen scientists. For decades, a sample has accumulated revealing a remarkable record, not of merely enlarged facsimiles of human feet, nor misapprehended bear tracks, but of consistent footprints of a large bipedal hominoid evolved and adapted to rough and steep terrain (Meldrum 2004,

2007). In the absence of a type specimen of the trackmaker, a name has been attached to the footprints – an ichnotaxon (Fig 5.4, 5.5). The nomen is *Anthropoidipes ameriborealis*[3] (Meldrum 2007). Most significantly, this recognition affords the establishment of a description and diagnosis of the distinguishing characteristics of these footprints, differentiating them from bear, human and other hominoids.

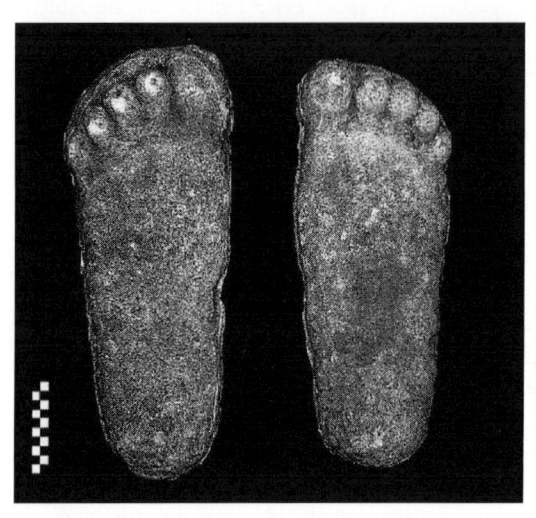

FIGURE 5.4. THE RIGHT AND LEFT FOOTPRINT CASTS TAKEN BY ROGER PATTERSON AT THE BLUFF CREEK CALIFORNIA FILM SITE ON OCTOBER 20, 1967, CONSTITUTING THE TYPE SPECIMENS OF THE ICHNOTAXON *ANTHROPOIDIPES AMERIBOREALIS* (MELDRUM 2007).

Herein I have concentrated on the footprint evidence raising the possible existence of *sasquatch* and perhaps other species of relict hominoids, such as the *yeti*. Space does not permit a comprehensive discussion of the other forms of evidence – hair, DNA, bioacoustic data, photographic and ethnographic evidence as well as eyewitness accounts. Nor are we afforded an examination and weighing of the expert evaluation and commentary accumulating in the literature, often in the face of considerable sceptical pushback. The original proposed inclusion of a chapter on *sasquatch* in this volume acknowledges the inclination by many, intentional or otherwise, to account for, rationalise and *dismiss* all prospects of relict hominoids as merely a collection of bear misidentifications, hoaxes or folklore. However, addressing this topic in this vein affords an opportunity to address and perhaps assuage this dismissive attitude.

Naturally, there are bound to be cases of misidentification, when inexperienced or less critical witnesses ascribe a particular flash of dark fur in the bush to a *sasquatch*, or assume a specific plantigrade pentadactyl footprint could be attributed to a relict hominoid. But to imply that *all* sightings and *all* footprints can be dismissed as encounters with bears (or outright hoaxes), simply because *sasquatch* is assumed, *a priori*, not to exist is hardly reasonable, and in no way *scientific* (Bindernagel 2010). In spite of repeated caveats about the unreliability of eyewitness testimony, many qualified and experienced observers have had otherwise inexplicable experiences with a consistent phenomenon that has a remarkably sensible ecogeographic and anthropologic context. These experiences are corroborated by the documentation of a footprint record that differentiates it consistently and convincingly as a bipedal hominoid, in a biomechanically sound fashion, from other forms of common wildlife (Meldrum 2004). The existence of *sasquatch* and other Wildmen, or relict hominoids, can by no rational means be considered *impossible*. Indeed, it is quite *probable* when considering the increasingly bushy nature of the hominoid family tree and recognizing that several of its branches represent lineages that have persisted alongside *Homo sapiens* until the very recent past – perhaps even to the present (Meldrum 2012a, b).

---

3   *Anthropoidipes ameriborealis* = North American ape foot.

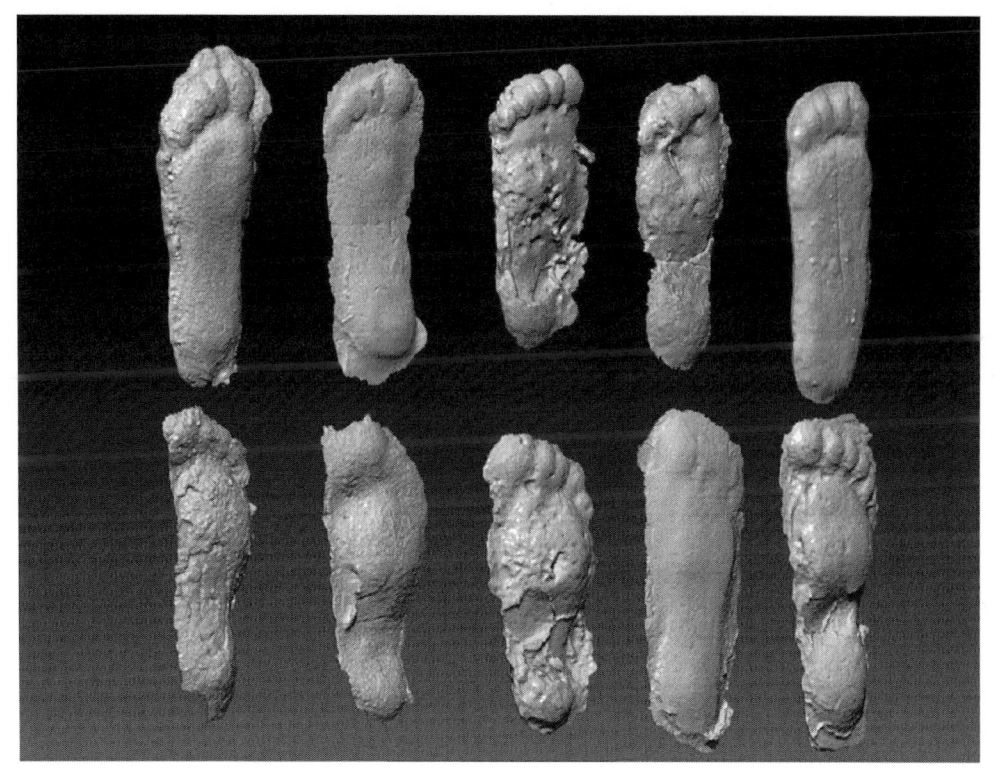

FIGURE 5.5. TEN CASTS BY BOB TITMUS AT BLUFF CREEK CALIFORNIA FILM SITE, TAKEN APPROXIMATELY 10 DAYS AFTER THE FILM WAS CAPTURED BY PATTERSON AND GIMLIN, WHICH CONSTITUTE THE REFERRED MATERIAL TO THE ICHNOTAXON *ANTHROPOIDIPES AMERIBOREALIS* (MELDRUM 2007).

BIBLIOGRAPHY AND REFERENCES

Aniello, P, 2009, Personal communication (email exchange with the author), 27 August

Bindernagel, J A, 1998 *North America's Great Ape: The Sasquatch*, Beachcomber Books, Courtenay, BC.

Bindernagel, J A, 2004 The Sasquatch: An Unwelcome and Premature Zoological Discovery? *Journal of Scientific Exploration* 18 (1), 53–64

Bindernagel, J A, 2010 *The Discovery of Sasquatch: Reconciling Culture, History, and Science in the Discovery Process*, Beachcomber Books, Courtenay, BC.

Blumenbach, J F, 1795 *On the Natural Variety of Mankind*, 3 edn, in *The Anthropological Treatises of Johann Friedrich Blumenbach* (trans. and ed. Thomas Bendyshe (1865), Longman Green, London

Burns, J W, 1929 Introducing B.C.'s Hairy Giants, *MacLean's Magazine*, April 1 issue, 9, 61, 62

Cronin, E W, Jr, 1979 *The Arun: A Natural History of the World's Deepest Valley*, Houghton Mifflin, Boston

Deans, J, 1889 The Story of the Bear and His Indian Wife. A Legend of the Haidas of Queen Charlotte's Island, B.C., *The Journal of American Folklore* 2 (7), 255–60

Forth, G, 2008 *Images of the Wildman in Southeast Asia: An Anthropological Perspective*, Routledge, New York

Genzoli, A, 1958 Huge footprints hold mystery of friendly Bluff Creek Giant, *The Humboldt Times*, 15 October 15

Krantz, G S, 1999 *Bigfoot Sasquatch Evidence*, Hancock House Publishers, Blaine, Washington

Lall, K, 1988 *Lore and Legend of the Yeti*, Book Faith India, New Delhi

Linnaeus, C, 1735 *Systema naturae sive regna tria Naturae systematice proposita per classes, ordines, genera, & species*, Lugduni Batavorum (Haak), Leiden

Lozier, J D, Aniello, P, and Hickerson, M J, 2009 Predicting the distribution of Sasquatch in western North America: anything goes with ecological niche modelling, *Journal of Biogeography* 36, 1623–7

Magnus, O, 1555 *Historia de gentibus septentrionalibus, earumque diversis statibus, conditionibus, moribus, ritibus. necnon universis pene animalibus in Septentrione degentibus, eorumque natura* Reprinted as Olaus Magnus, *A Description of the Northern Peoples, 1555: Volume I: Description of the Northern Peoples*, 1555 v. 2 (Hakluyt Society, Second Series) 28 October 1998 (trans. P G Foote)

McNeely, J A, Cronin E W, Jr, and Emery, H N, 1973 The Yeti – Not a Snowman, *Oryx* 12, 65–73

McNeely, J A, and Wachtel, P S, 1988 *Soul of the Tiger: Searching for Nature's Answers in Southeast Asia*, Doubleday, New York

Meldrum, D J, 2004 Midfoot flexibility, fossil footprints, and Sasquatch steps: New perspectives on the evolution of bipedalism, *Journal of Scientific Exploration* 18, 67–79

Meldrum, D J, 2006 *Sasquatch: Legend Meets Science*, Doherty, New York

Meldrum, D J, 2007 Ichnotaxonomy of giant hominoid trackways in North America, in Cenozoic Vertebrate Tracks and Traces (eds S G Lucas, J A Spielman, and M G Lockley), *New Mexico Museum of Natural History and Science Bulletin* 42, 225–31

Meldrum, D J, 2012a Are other hominins (hominoids) alive today? *The Relict Hominoid Inquiry* 1, 67–71

——, 2012b Adaptive radiations, bushy evolutionary trees, and relict hominoids, *The Relict Hominoid Inquiry* 1, 51–6

Meldrum, D J, 2013 *Sasquatch Field Guide*, Paradise Cay Publications, Arcata, California

Meldrum, D J, 2018 Book Review: Yeti: The Ecology of a Mystery, *The Relict Hominoid Inquiry* 7, 69–96

Meldrum, D J, and Mionczynski, J, 2007 Footprint evidence for an unrecognized hominoid in the forest habitats of the Pacific and Inter-Mountain West, *Proceedings of the Idaho Chapter of the Wildlife Society*, 33–4

Messner, R, 1998 *My Quest for the Yeti: Confronting the Himalayas' Deepest Mystery*, St Martin's Griffin, New York

Napier, J, 1973 *Bigfoot: The Yeti and Sasquatch in Myth and Reality*, Dutton, New York

Nickell, J, 2013 Bigfoot Lookalikes: Tracking Hairy Man-Beasts, *Skeptical Inquirer* 37 (5), September/ October, available from: https://www.csicop.org/si/show/bigfoot_lookalikes_tracking_hairy_man-beasts [6 November 2018]

Pastoureau, M, 2011 *The Bear: History of a Fallen King*, Belknap Press, Cambridge, Mass

Smith, K L, 1909 The Totem Poles of Alaska, *The Topeka State Journal*, 25 December

Snyder, G, 1990 *The Practice of the Wild*, North Point Press, San Francisco

Taylor, D C, 2017 *Yeti: The Ecology of a Mystery*, Oxford University Press, Oxford

Ward, M, 1997 Everest 1951: the footprints attributed to the Yeti—myth and reality, *Wilderness & Environmental Medicine* 8 (1), 29–32

Wunn, I, 2001 Cave bear worship in the Paleolithic, *Cadernos Lab. Xeolóxico de Laxe Coruña* 26, 457–63

6

Bears in Children's Literature

TRACY HAYES, HEATHER PRINCE AND IAN CONVERY

This chapter explores bear illustrations in children's literature through a transdisciplinary, boundary-crossing approach that utilises a short story to introduce key points for discussion. Commencing with an overview of bears and the various ways they have been represented in literature, we consider a wide range of disciplines including natural science, social and cultural studies, and children's geographies. We then focus specifically on children's literature, which tends to relate to pedagogies more than other disciplines (Nikolajeva 1996). Yet the aim of most literature is to show or teach us something new, or to encourage us to look at something in a different way, and the distinction between literature created for children and 'older readers' is frequently an arbitrary one. The traditional tales from which many children's stories are developed – encompassing folk tales, legends, myths, fables – come from a time before the concept of childhood existed. They have evolved from oral stories that originally contained elements of violence, child abuse/neglect, cruelty and obscenity. Over time they have become sanitised and purified, deemed more fitting for the ears of children (Nikolajeva 1996). The stories we now perceive as classic children's stories were mostly adapted from adult versions, and the methods we chose for doing this reflect how we experience and know the world, and how we want children to do so (Holton and Rogers 2004). However, books for children are not just about the words, the pictures are also important, providing them with an artistic value and stimulating the imagination (Roncken and Convery 2016).

We make the argument that bear illustrations are more than just images: they inform our perceptions and anticipation of the real animal and may determine our resultant behaviour towards it. Our focus may be anglocentric, a reflection of the lived experiences of the authors, however links may be made between the work shared here and work from other cultures, other languages, other ways of being. Bears, in their real and cultural form, are truly globalised creatures. There are eight bear species: American Black Bear, Asiatic Black Bear, Brown Bear, Giant Panda Bear, Polar Bear, Sloth Bear, Spectacled Bear and Sun Bear. They are one of the most widely distributed terrestrial mammals, with a current global distribution including North and South America, Canada, Asia, Europe and circumpolar arctic regions (Bear Trust International 2011). It is believed that bears have at one time or another lived in the wild on all continents except for Australia; however in recent times their range has been significantly reduced due to increasing pressures from human activities such as agriculture, urbanisation and the demands of an expanding human population. For example, Dixon *et al* (2007) highlight how the long-term survival of Florida black bears is threatened due to loss and fragmentation of habitat, together with the impact of unregulated hunting.

There are various ecology and conservation-based arguments for the conservation of large carnivores; this chapter draws from these, whilst taking a value-based approach that recognises the '… long-intertwined history of humans and these species and the role they played and play in the human psyche' (Redford 2005, 5). The relationship between humans and large predatory animals like bears is a complex one of blurred boundaries and ambiguities and this is evident in the varying representations of them. Animals in literature are seen as both symbols of the non-human world and symbolic of human character traits. Indeed, 'Folklorists have long viewed animal tales as vehicles to convey a culture's ideas about relationships, both among humans and between humans and animals' (Melson 2005, 15). Within these animal tales, there are many different images, dependent on the nature of the book, and whether it is based on fiction/non-fiction, fantasy or fact. Their inclusion may have the aim to entrance, bewitch and entertain, or to educate and inform. Conservation stories (see for example, Gross *et al* 2018) are used in various ways, for example to encourage people to visit places and to help them connect with the animals and the landscape. The task of these stories is to illuminate, enhance and bring meaning to experiences. Conservation stories have a foundation in empirical science, yet embrace narrative, emotive methods to convey information in a manner that resonates with listeners and readers. These are more than *just stories*, they are peer-reviewed for robustness, with a strong evidence-base and, as argued by Leslie *et al* (2013, 1126), aim to help '… bring conservation science to life'.

Within books for children, there is a recognised genre of eco-edutainment books, which have the aim of providing advice on '… how to save the world from environmental catastrophe […] such books articulate and spread "eco-knowledge", encouraging children to become environmentally aware world citizens' (Larsson 2012, 200). This genre includes picture books (see for example, Op de Beeck 2005). The animal illustrations in these books tend to be realistic and contribute to the environmental message of the book. Although, interestingly as highlighted by Op de Beeck (ibid), many of the books that convey an environmental message are actually printed and distributed in a non-sustainable manner. In contrast to this genre, animals in popular stories designed to entertain the reader often show little resemblance to the real creature, for example Winnie the Pooh (written by A A Milne and illustrated by E H Shepard), Paddington Bear (written by Michael Bond and illustrated by Peggy Fortnum) and the various incarnations of Care Bears (American Greetings Corporation n.d., see also Jeffries, this volume). A notable exception to this is the illustrations in the original version of Kipling's *The Jungle Book* (1894). These were drawn by Kipling's father, John Lockwood Kipling, who was a '… talented artist, sculptor, writer, designer and teacher' (Pan Macmillan 2017, non-paginated), and are more realistic of both animals and humans. Over the years, the illustrations have radically altered and when we consider more recent versions, often based on the Disney film (*The Jungle Book*, 1967), Baloo the Bear is very different to the original: he is an altogether softer, less scary version than the original story book version drawn by Kipling's father, who would have observed bears in the wild.

With literature designed to be read to or by children, often conflated within the concept of 'children's literature', the intended audience is broader than just children; it includes the adults responsible for sourcing and reading the books – parents, carers, teachers and librarians. The decision as to which books to read is often based on adults' nostalgia for the '… good old stories of their childhood' (Nikolajeva 1996, 54). Other adult roles include the writer, illustrator, the narrator/creator: these are texts created by adults for children. As Melson (2005, 18) highlights, within these adult creations '… these symbolic images are also a window into a culture's ideas about children and animals and how they are related'. Indeed, children's literature is one of the few socio-cultural creations in which the creator and the reader (adults) are from a different community to the recipients (children); as identified by Nikolajeva (1996) this necessitates two systems of codes, one addressed to the child, the other, often unconsciously, addressed to the adult beside or behind the child. Between them they create an interrupted reality (ibid, 55).

The subtext of animal images is 'replete with "boundary issues" about human-animal distinctiveness, with ethical implications for animal welfare, animal rights, and ecological consciousness' (Melson 2005, 18). In their examination of how biodiversity was represented in children's books, Sousa *et al* (2017) found that in 164 books aimed at children aged six to eight years, living beings were found in 98 per cent and habitats in 80 per cent of the books. However, the representations were '…strongly biased towards anthropomorphization [*sic*] of nonhuman animals who inhabited limited common habitats. This may contribute to the idea that all biodiversity lives in forests and humanized [*sic*] habitats…'. Furthermore, their work highlights that indirect experiences such as reading books and looking at pictures play a key role in the development of children's attitudes towards, perceptions of, and emotions about biodiversity. When we extend this to the representation of bears, it becomes increasingly important to consider the level of anthropomorphism. Is the bear shown to be soft, cuddly, cute and furry – a friend to the child – that can potentially encourage a 'playful, embodied engagement in the world' (Holton and Rogers 2004, 163)? Or is it more accurately portrayed as a fierce, scary predator, an animal deserving of respectful avoidance? We will now share a short story that we will use to raise key points for consideration in the remainder of the chapter. The ellipses at the end of four sentences within this story, plus the final question, suggest points at which to pause and focus the discussion.

Come on Bear

'*Come on Bear, I've made you some porridge. Come and get it before it goes cold.*' She places the bowl on the ground and steps away to hide behind a tree. And waits. And waits. And waits. No sign of bears. Reluctantly, she picks up her bag and heads home, vowing to return tomorrow with a different flavour porridge. Perhaps bears prefer honey flavoured oats? Pooh Bear loves honey, Paddington likes marmalade. But when it comes to porridge, the only concern seems to be if it is too hot, too cold or just right …

She's loved bears from a very young age. Her cot was filled with soft toys, gifted on her birth. These were added to over the years, resulting in a motley collection adorning her now grown-up bedroom. Most are bears, accompanied by one little rabbit, a large green frog and a spotted dog. She prefers the furry bears, they're cuddlier. Each bear is named. The first one was called 'Bubba', her earliest attempt at saying bear. The next was Ted-ted, then Teddy and Freddy the twins, followed by Samuel, Poley (the polar bear), Orange-Ted and John. The newest one is simply called Bear, and when you squeeze his tummy, he growls. He was a gift from her Uncle Ian who had been to see real bears in the wild. This one was scarier than the others, with sharp claws, a long nose and small, squinty eyes. She hid him at the end of the bed when the lights went out. He was a daytime, playtime bear. Bubba, with his big blue eyes and fluffy ears, was her sleepy-time pal …

There are bear pictures on the walls of her bedroom, and shelves lined with books. Winnie-the-Pooh, Paddington, Rupert, Yogi and Boo-Boo, their names etched on the spines of the books. She loved the stories by Jill Murphy, Jane Hissey and the story-collections by lots of different authors. Her absolute favourite was a beautifully illustrated book by Jackie Morris (2014) titled 'Something about a Bear'. She liked this because it tells you where to find bears and how to care for them. She'd drawn pictures of each bear and stuck them to the map on the back of her door.

Each night she'd pick a bear and dream of visiting the place where it lived, whispering to herself, *'watch out, bear, I'm coming to get you'* …

'*I'm going on a bear hunt. I'm going to find a real bear. I've waited long enough,*' she announced to her parents. Old enough to travel alone, she got on a plane to Canada and started to walk. She'd read the books. She'd bought the trail map showing the best places to find bears. She'd spoken to other tourists staying in the hostel. She now knows where the bears live. She's going to find one and take a photo of herself with the bear. It will become her bear, which as everyone knows, is the best bear of all. But bears are not easy to find. They don't like people. People shout, throw things and spray them with foul-smelling scents. The Big Brown Bear smells the girl before he sees her. He smells the porridge too. It smells of 'human'. Despite his hunger, he keeps his distance. By the fourth day, he's tempted closer. He's getting used to the smell of this human, who doesn't seem scary, and he's getting hungrier. The world is getting colder. He wants to sleep, but his stomach needs filling. The seventh day dawns, the porridge smells particularly inviting. Hmmm, maple syrup and pecans. Too good to resist. He creeps up to the bowl, reaches out a paw, hungrily brings the porridge up to his mouth. FLASH! Startled he rears up on his hind legs, lashing out with his paws. He hears a scream and a bang. Then it all goes dark …

The girl got a photo of her bear eating porridge. The hunter got his trophy and triumphantly shared his story of saving the girl from the Big Fierce Animal. After all, what choice did he have? You can't let bears attack humans, can you?

Too hot, too cold or just right …

As you may recognise, this is a reference to the well-known, traditional story of *Goldilocks and the Three Bears*, a story that Southgate (2013) claims was first told by Eleanor Mure in 1831 to entertain her nephew. It was subsequently published in written form in 1837 by author and poet Robert Southey (Carpenter and Prichard 1984), with many subsequent retellings, mostly featuring bears who wear clothes, live in houses full of furniture and eat human food (see for example, as retold by Baxter and illustrated by Ailie Busby 2011). This form of illustration is also apparent in many other books for children, for example the *Teddy Bears' Picnic* (most versions) or *The Bedtime Bear* (words by Whybrow and illustrations by Axel Scheffler 2016). When we think about the food eaten by bears in most children's books, it is very different to the diet of real bears. Bears are omnivorous animals; in the wild they will feed on a wide range of foods, depending on the species of bear and its preferred habitat. This includes vegetation, berries, nuts, insects, deer fawns, elk and moose calves, fish, fruits, nests of bees, invertebrates, small vertebrates and carrion. A brown bear's diet may be approximately 85–95 per cent vegetation such as grasses, sedges, bulbs and roots, whilst polar bears, the most carnivorous of all bears, live almost entirely on a diet of seals and other marine mammals (Bear Trust International 2011).

Does it matter if the story book diet of porridge, sandwiches, honey and cakes is not an accurate depiction of a bear's diet? Perhaps not in the story book of a very young child, who then grows into an awareness of the different needs of a real bear. However, for many people, especially those in more urbanised areas, bears and humans no longer coexist. In the UK there are no real wild bears; they were hunted and persecuted, leading ultimately to their eradication. Here they now exist only in zoos, museums and in our books and films. When humans and wild bears come into close contact there can be a real cause for concern, particularly when it comes to food. There are many reports of bears getting too close to humans in search of food, stories of people leaving food for bears to tempt them closer, of bears scavenging through rubbish dumps, becoming pests through habituation, and calls for humans to be bear aware (see for example, Healey 2016). Climate change is altering the habitats available for bears to live as wild bears, forcing more confrontations with humans, and making it of greater importance to develop a better understanding of how to coexist with bears, based on research into first-hand experiences of nature.

In one relevant study, Burgess and Mayer-Smith (2011) investigated children's perceptions and experiences of nature during a residential outdoor environmental education programme and analysed how this contributed to an understanding of how nature experiences may arouse 'a love of life and all living things' (ibid, 27). Although their study did not relate this to the representation of nature in children's literature, it did highlight the importance of first-hand experiences in nature. For example, they observed:

> …increases in child ren's aesthetic, humanistic, moralistic, symbolic, naturalistic, and scientific-ecological valuing of nature […] involvement in the environmental education program appeared to help children not only understand the natural world but also reduce their concerns and negative feelings about wild animals, heights, and the dark (ibid, 38).

After their experiences, one of the children commented, 'You don't want a bear to get along with humans or eat our food because if it got too friendly then you'd have to put it to sleep.' Another remarked, '… my favorite [*sic*] memory is probably seeing the cougar marks on the tree and the bear marks, that was like scary awesome!' They were reported as having developed a greater respect for predators in the wilderness, and the need to allow them space.

Bubba, with his big blue eyes and fluffy ears, was her sleepy-time pal …

Most people recognise that there is a need to address the negative impacts that human activities have on the natural world, and within this, for many researchers (authors included) there is a specific focus on how we can involve young people in this process. Hayes' doctoral study (Hayes 2017) responded to these concerns by exploring young people's relationship with nature, considering how this is nurtured through the projects offered to them. The young people (11–25) were from diverse backgrounds, with a wide range of individual needs. The key themes that emerged highlighted the role of the practitioner/facilitator; peer, family and school pressures to 'grow-up' and be responsible; the importance of playfulness, kindness, comfort and belonging. One of the key findings was that young people (and practitioners) responded most enthusiastically when the facilitator of outdoor learning experiences was engaging and lively. These findings were captured in storied form (like that used in this chapter), which have proved useful for generating discussions. A less traditional, unexpected outcome from this research was a range of teddy bears called Adventure Bears that are designed to be played with outside. They are neither fluffy nor furry, nor even particularly 'bear-like'. They are made from material that can be easily washed and dried, and do not have claws or teeth or anything scary. Unlike the real thing they can be played with and cuddled in bed. They have this in common with most bear illustrations in children's literature, which demonstrate a range of features, particularly facial features, depending on the nature of the story.

Enculturation, the gradual acquisition of the characteristics and norms of a culture, begins with toys, then picture books, nursery rhymes, fairy tales, fiction and non-fiction books. Dobrin and Kidd (2004) explore the interplay of children's environmental experiences with the texts aimed at them, which include cultural, multimedia and literary forms. They are concerned that, whilst children may have exposure to cultural products that represent the natural world, this needs to go alongside close contact with nature, with opportunities for exploration and embodied learning. Books alone are not enough. In children's literature, sometimes the animals are illustrated in character form as toys (the bear is noticeably a teddy bear), other times they are more representative of an animal. With contemporary fiction, the story may result from the prior existence of a film or a toy, rather than vice versa (Kuznets 1994). We can think of toys as three-dimensional illustrations, images brought to life, embodied in fabric form, sometimes fluffy, sometimes not. We experience nature, culture and family as an interwoven entity and the connections and attachments we make can be very strong and meaningful. These include the connections we make with nature (non-humans), and those we make with each other. Soft toys, fairy tales and nursery rhymes provide children with an introduction to some of the creatures with whom we live, helping them to feel a sense of familiarity and desire to learn more. As children grow, they may move on to develop a relationship with a pet animal. However, as the stories show, predatory animals do not make good pets. We can potentially habituate them, but not tame/domesticate them, and it remains an uneasy relationship. We may easily substitute a dog for a wolf; however, a substitute bear can really only be a toy.

Watch out, bear, I'm coming to get you …

We're going on a bear hunt; this represents a call to adventure heard in many playgrounds, early-years settings and nature centres across the Western world. For many it echoes the words from the story of the same title by Michael Rosen (1993, illustrated by Helen Oxenbury) and enables the facilitator of these experiences to adopt a playful approach, drawing from children's stories and games (Hayes 2016). In Rosen's story, the family head out to look for a bear and when they find it, they get scared and run back home to hide. This story gets closer to the reality of encountering a real live bear and shows how our expectations and perceptions may be different from this. As Kuznets (1994, 8) highlights, the illustrations are integral to this process; not only do they shape our 'aesthetic vision', they influence our expectations. We understand that the images we see are not real, yet they imperceptibly influence our perceptions of real animals (Bekoff 2014). What we see is a human interpretation, based on socio-cultural stereotypes.

This process of enculturation continues as we grow, develop and experience more of the world. There are so many books, toys, games, films for all ages, along with a desire for the real, for wildness, for contact with nature, for adventure. Nature-based tourism is a subset of ecotourism, and within this bear-watching is recognised as big business (see Chapter 10 in this volume). It is criticised as often more 'about purchasing *experiences* rather than *things*, with particular emphasis on photographic tourism' (Lemelin 2006 cited in Nevin *et al* 2012, 271). This can bring humans and bears into conflict. If we believe that an animal will naturally want to harm, kill or eat us, then getting in first becomes justifiable, a case of self-defence (Bekoff 2014), and the mere idea of co-existence becomes untenable and foolhardy.

He hears a scream and a bang. Then it all goes dark ...

There is well-documented hazard to wildlife of people trying to get too close, trying to get photos/selfies, of wildlife becoming habituated to humans, perceived as a greater risk, leading to animals being further hunted, persecuted and endangered as a result. For example, there is a video of a woman feeding breakfast to a bear which went viral on social media (Rumble 2018) and attracted an envious response from others keen to do the same. Actions like this can contribute to a devastating loss of wildlife, particularly predators, due to ignorance, misinformation and lack of understanding. Careless, selfish actions can be destructive. What will we do when all the 'big scary animals' are not just rare, they are gone? One organisation trying to address this is the US National Park Service (2018), which in its online advice to visitors reminds us:

> Watching wildlife safely is the responsibility of all park visitors. When you visit national parks, you are entering animals' habitat and should behave like a polite guest. In fact, the safety and health of wildlife depends on the thoughtful choices park visitors make. Wildlife face some serious risks when humans get close enough to interact with them...

Relating this hazard to children's literature, we have to remember that like the girl in the story, the hunter may have grown up reading stories about bears. In his books the focus may have been more about hunting, adventure and practical skills. In his case, he has been enculturated to see bears as a threat and as something to be hunted. Returning once more to the girl in our story, who is so desperate for a picture of her bear that she tempts it with food, we are reminded of another story that was shared on social media of a woman whose determination to feed bears in her garden ultimately resulted in 'food conditioning problem bears' who were unfortunately shot and killed. We are cautioned to remember '... that many wildlife departments have policies that are unfair to the animals they deal with – and will punish an animal even if, as in this case, humans are the ones at fault' (Schelling 2015). This honest advice is not reflected in most bear illustrations in children's literature. Bekoff (2004, 113) warns us that '... there are hidden costs and collateral damage when animals are misrepresented, disparaged and objectified'. Berkowitz (2011) reminds us of the importance of oral storytelling which challenges children to use their own imaginations to bring the spoken word to life, and not to rely on the images created by an illustrator. This also serves to highlight the importance of first-hand experience of nature to counter these issues, and to meaningfully develop an understanding of the natural world.

What choice did he have, you can't let bears attack humans, can you?

If we adopt an anthropocentric view of the world, nature is seen as expendable, with the needs of humans coming first. In contrast, for many people the threat of climate change, anthropocentric damage to the planet and loss of diversity are of pressing concern, and they (authors included) do not see nature as expendable. We are challenged to find an effective way to co-exist with animals, particularly predators. As so eloquently argued by Bekoff (2014) this may involve a process of rewilding – our hearts and our landscapes – to effectively address some of the tensions and conflicts involved. In his exposition of 'Why Big Fierce Animals Are Rare', Colinvaux elucidates the interconnectedness of all living things, sharing the spaces and resources available on this planet, existing '...together in some form of accommodation, living and letting live, always suited to the ways of life they must follow, often present in teemingly diverse array' (1980, 2). However, humans as a species are not very good at this (as evidenced by a large body of literature, including the global Living Planet Report (WWF 2016) and the UK-focused State of Nature Report (Hayhow *et al* 2016)) and we tend to forget that we too are animals. Our ways of life dominate, and our needs and desires result in devastating loss of wildlife. Some of the first species to go extinct are the top carnivores, including big cats, wolves and bears. They are our prime competitors for resources and the animals we perceive as most likely to kill us. And yet they are also the main characters in our childhood stories. The Red Riding Hood story does not work in the absence of wolves. Goldilocks and the One Bear does not have the same appeal as when there are three. Unless action is taken to conserve and, where necessary, rewild our world (and our lives) these wonderful creatures will become little more than artefacts, photos and stories of fantastical creatures that once roamed the land, until all that remains is their illustrated form, enlivening the text in children's literature. Perhaps it is time for some honest stories for children of all ages to share? Alongside the tales of teddy bears that entrance, entertain and delight, let us add some stories that encourage respect for bears (and other predators) and illustrate the need for them to be given the space to be bears, in all their wondrous and fearsome glory.

BIBLIOGRAPHY AND REFERENCES

American Greetings Corporation, no date *Care Bears*, available from: http://www.americangreetingsentertainment.com/brands/care_bears [25 February 2018]

Baxter, N, and Busby, A, 2011 *Goldilocks and the Three Bears*, Penguin, London

Bear Trust International, 2011 *Bear Species of the World*, available from: https://beartrust.org/wp-content/uploads/2012/08/Bear-Species-of-the-World_Bear-Trust-2011.pdf [25 February 2018]

Bekoff, M, 2014 *Rewilding our hearts: Building pathways of compassion and coexistence*, New World Library, California

Berkowitz, D, 2011 Oral storytelling: Building community through dialogue, engagement, and problem solving, *YC Young Children* 66, (2), 36

Bond, M, and Fortnum, P, 1958 (1997) *A Bear Called Paddington*, reprint, Picture Lions, HammersmithBurgess, D J, and Mayer-Smith, J, 2011 Listening to children: Perceptions of nature, *Journal of Natural History Education and Experience* 5, 27–43

Carpenter, H, and Prichard, M, 1984 (2005) *The Oxford Companion to Children's Literature*, reprint, Oxford University Press, Oxford

Colinvaux, P, 1980 *Why Big Fierce Animals Are Rare,* Penguin, London

Dixon, J D, Oli, M K, Wooten, M C, Eason, T H, McCown, J W, and Cunningham, M W, 2007 Genetic consequences of habitat fragmentation and loss: the case of the Florida black bear (*Ursus americanus floridanus*), *Conservation Genetics* 8, (2), 455–64

Dobrin, S I, and Kidd, K B (eds), 2004 *WildTHINGS: Children's Culture and Ecocriticism,* Wayne State University Press, Detroit, Michigan

Gross, L, Hettinger, A, Moore, J W, and Neeley, L, 2018 Conservation stories from the front lines, *PLoS Biol* 16, (2)

Hayes, T A, 2017 Making sense of nature: A creative exploration of young people's relationship with the natural environment, unpublished PhD thesis, Lancaster University/University of Cumbria, UK

———, 2016 A playful approach to outdoor learning: Boggarts, Bears and Bunny Rabbits!, in *Play, Recreation, Health and Well Being* (eds J Horton and B Evans), vol 9 of *Geographies of Children and Young People* (ed T Skelton), Springer, Singapore

———, 2013 Seeing the world through their eyes. Learning from a 5 ½ year old, a rabbit and a boat ride with aunty, *Horizons* 63, 36–9

Hayhow, D B, Burns, F, Eaton, M A, Fulaij, A T, August, A, Babey L, Bacon, L, 2016 State of Nature 2016, The State of Nature partnershipHealey, J B, 2016 *When Bears Attack: Close Encounters of the Terrifying Kind*, Skyhorse Publishing, New York

Holton, T L, and Rogers, T B, 2004 'The World around Them': The Changing Depiction of Nature in *Owl Magazine*, in *WildTHINGS: Children's Culture and Ecocriticism* (eds S I Dobrin and K B Kidd), Wayne State University Press, Detroit, Michigan

Kipling, R, and Kipling, J L, 1894 (2016) *The Jungle Book*, reprint Pan Macmillan, LondonKuznets, L R, 1994 *When toys come alive: Narratives of animation, metamorphosis, and development*, Yale University Press, New Haven

Larsson, B, 2012 The cosmopolitanization of childhood: eco-knowledge in children's eco-edutainment books, *Young* 20 (2), 199–218

Leslie, H M, Goldman, E, Mcleod, K L, Sievanen, L, Balasubramanian, H, Cudney-Bueno, R, Feuerstein, A, Knowlton, N, Lee, K, Pollnac, R, and Samhouri, J F, 2013 How Good Science and Stories Can Go Hand-In-Hand, *Conservation Biology* 27 (5), 1126–9

Melson, G F, 2005 *Why the Wild Things Are: Animals in the Lives of Children*, Harvard University Press, Cambridge, MA

Milne, A A, and Shepard, E H 1926 (1994) *The complete tales of Winnie-the-Pooh*, reprint, Penguin, London

Morris, J, 2014 *Something About a Bear*, Frances Lincoln Children's Books, London

Nevin, O T, Swain, P, and Convery, I, 2012 Nature Tourism: Do Bears Create a Sense of Place?, in *Making Sense of Place: Multidisciplinary Perspectives* (eds I Convery, G Corsane and P Davis), The Boydell Press, Woodbridge

Nikolajeva, M, 1996 *Children's Literature Comes of Age: Toward a New Aesthetic*, Garland Publishing Inc, London

Op de Beeck, N, 2005 Speaking for the trees: Environmental ethics in the rhetoric and production of picture books, *Children's Literature Association Quarterly* 30, (3), 265–87

Pan Macmillan, 2017 *Illustrating Rudyard Kipling's The Jungle Book*, available from: https://www.panmacmillan.com/blogs/classics/john-lockwood-kipling-the-jungle-book [9 March 2018]

Redford, K H, 2005 Introduction: How to Value Large Carnivorous Animals, in *Large Carnivores and the Conservation of Biodiversity* (eds J C Ray, K H Redford, R S Steneck and J Berger), Island Press, Washington, DC

Roncken, P, and Convery I, 2016 Representations of nature in children's literature, in *Shifting Interpretations of Natural Heritage* (eds I Convery and P Davis), The Boydell Press, Woodbridge

Rosen, M, and Oxenbury, H, 1993 *We're Going on a Bear Hunt*, Walker Books, London

Rumble, 2018 *Woman and bear casually enjoy breakfast together*, available from: https://rumble.com/v32d9r-lady-feeds-her-bear.html [25 February 2018]

Schelling, A, 2015 *Woman Feeds Bears – And Ends Up Killing Them*, available from: https://www.thedodo.com/bears-killed-woman-fed-1306465728.html [25 February 2018]

Sousa, E, Quintino, V, Teixeira, J, and Rodrigues, A M, 2017 *A Portrait of Biodiversity in Children's Trade Books*, Brill, Leiden, Netherlands

The Jungle Book 1967 Directed by Wolfgang Reitherman [animated film], Walt Disney Pictures, Burbank, California

Whybrow, I, and Scheffler, A, 2016 *The Bedtime Bear (Tom and Bear)*, Macmillan Children's Books, London

WWF, 2018 *Living Planet Report – 2018: Aiming Higher* (eds M Grooten and R E A Almond), WWF, Gland, Switzerland

7

Knowing Individual Bears

OWEN T. NEVIN, IAN CONVERY AND JOHN KITCHIN

Knowing individuals is important. It is hard to think of a more open-ended truism with which to start a chapter on knowing individual bears, but for behavioural ecologists, it is not only important, it is essential. As Barrie Gilbert notes in the foreword to this volume, the consequences of 'not knowing' individual bears and/or 'their place' can be serious. Whether that knowledge of individuals is applied in the academic pursuit of ethology (the study of behaviour in wild animals), as a naturalist guide within the ecotourism industry or to improve husbandry in an agricultural setting, including bear farming for bile across China and southeast Asia (see Chapter 8, this volume), it draws on a deep history and heritage. In this chapter, we outline the history and trajectory of bear identification and in doing so reflect on antecedents of human/other animal relations that span millennia.

Our behavioural research with brown bears in Glendale Cove on Knight Inlet in British Columbia began in 1996 and has continued over a period of more than 20 years in partnership with Knight Inlet Lodge (KIL), a commercial bear viewing lodge based in the cove. While not unique, this long-term commitment to research by a commercial partner offers a model by which generational scale studies can be conducted beyond the boundaries of parks and protected areas, which, after all, is where most wildlife resides. As Western (2015) notes, globally most biodiversity lives outside of protected areas, though it is undoubtedly richer within protected areas (Gray *et al* 2016). This has profound implications for how we interact with wildlife, and in particular how people relate to charismatic megafauna.

Ethological studies at KIL have included investigation of the impact of viewing activities on the foraging energetics of bears (Nevin 2003; Nevin and Gilbert 2005b, 2005c); temporal-spatial refuging (Nevin 2003; Nevin and Gilbert 2005b, 2005c); breeding behaviour (Nevin and Gilbert 2005a); and the selection and use of mark trees in olfactory communication (Clapham 2012; Clapham *et al* 2012, 2013, 2014). In parallel, GPS telemetry and genetic sampling have addressed spatial movement, habitat use, connectivity, dispersal and relatedness, while social science research has explored the relationship between people and bears, and their cultural meanings (Nevin *et al* 2012, 2014). Much of the detailed behavioural study on the site is facilitated by the maintenance of a register of individually identifiable bears of known age-sex class. Photo-identification techniques allowed individual bears to be distinguished (Fig 7.1); coat colouration and scar patterns were recorded with sketches and descriptions, supplemented by a catalogue of reference photographs. Each bear was given a unique numeric code with sex determined by urination pattern, direct observation of genitals or the presence of cubs (Nevin 2003; Nevin and Gilbert 2005b). Coat colouration in particular can change greatly throughout the season and so regular, ongoing observation of the bears is required to ensure gradual change is documented; likewise, body mass can change by large amounts as hibernation approaches, changing the overall shape of the bear.

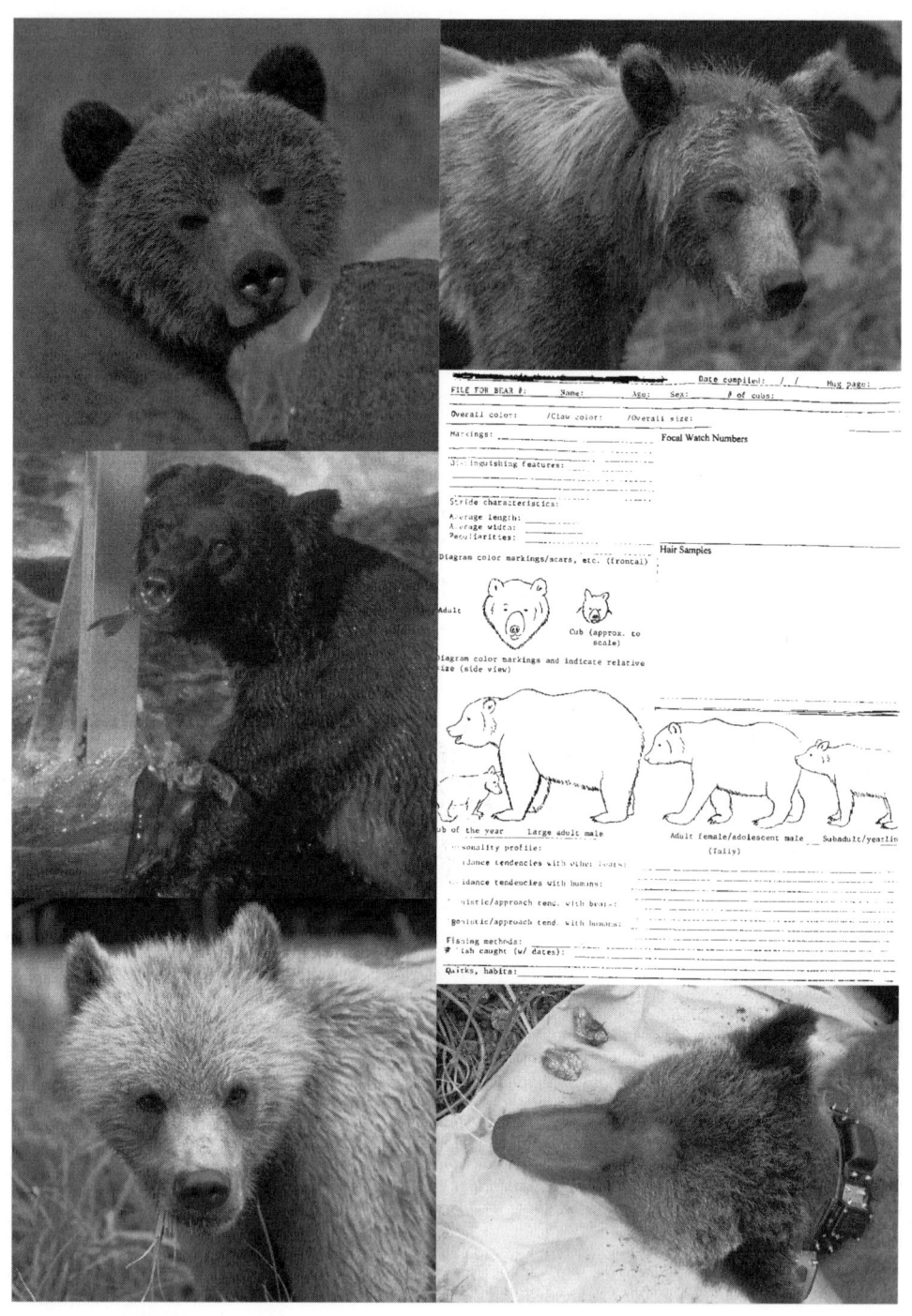

FIGURE 7.1. INDIVIDUALLY IDENTIFIED BEAR FACES AND AN EXAMPLE OF A BEAR IDENTIFICATION DATA SHEET (NEVIN 2003).

Features like scars and claw colour are more stable over time and are key to confidently identifying individuals; this requires close observation through high power optics. While not a unique identifying characteristic, the behavioural characteristics of an individual bear can greatly assist in the process of identification. This approach has been effectively applied with bears for several decades (eg Stonorov and Stokes 1972). While the importance of the individual in the study of behavioural ecology can be traced back to the very foundations of the discipline (Tinbergen 1962), the roots go much deeper than that.

THE HUMAN-ANIMAL RELATIONSHIP

As humans, we have a long and complex set of relationships with the other species with whom we share the planet. Over the last 200,000 years or so human society has embarked on a remarkable socio-evolutionary journey; from hunter-gatherers, to settled agricultural communities and more recently to industrial urban environments. This journey has seen our species move further into a 'human' world and away from what may be defined as a natural world (DeMello 2012; Nöth 1998; Bulbeck 2005; Zedrosser et al 2011). This is significant for a number of reasons, not least because the natural world offers a canvas for human cultural expression (DeMello 2012; Nöth 1998; Bulbeck 2005; Trigger 2008). More fundamentally, however, we are inextricably linked and dependent upon the natural world for a wide range of resources (DeMello 2012; Oma 2010; Ingold 2006), though given our technological advances, sedentary pastimes and online existence (Soga and Gaston 2016), we appear to have lost sight of this dependency. As Sorman (2014) memorably writes in the novel *La peau de l'ours,* from a bear perspective human life is 'absurd, poor, violent and incredibly dry'.

We eat animals, cloth ourselves in their hides, keep them as pets, write about them, study them, worship them, fear them, love them. We watch films about animals and take holidays that centre on viewing them. Our relationship with the natural world is fluid and ever changing, complicated and contradictory (Jones 2000; Oma 2010; DeMello 2012; Bulbeck 2005; Blewitt 2010). Much significance lies in how we define both animals and nature; they are often viewed as a thing, a commodity and an unconscious actor in the generalised human biosphere (Jones 2000). It could be argued that the current interest in natural capital and monetised approaches to nature moves us further in this direction, arguably 'a neoliberal road to ruin' as George Monbiot famously put it in *The Guardian* (Monbiot 2014).

This longer-term perspective concerning human-nature relations is important because humans are responsible for the current biodiversity crisis. The Global Planet Index (Living Planet Report 2018) shows a decline of 60 per cent in population abundance for 4005 species between 1970 and 2014; the UN's Sustainable Development Goals include 'urgent and significant action to reduce the degradation of natural habitats, halt the loss of biodiversity and by 2020 to protect and prevent the extinction of threatened species' (Goal 15.5), and there is evidence of a 'biological annihilation', and an ongoing 'sixth mass extinction event', that threatens biodiversity and the ecosystem services it provides (Cellebos et al 2017). Although often thought of as a discipline focused on the protection of biodiversity, contemporary models of conservation also recognise the role of humans in conservation practice; for some commentators, conservation is as much about human survival as it is about protection of other species (Blewitt 2010; Lovelock 2006; Smith and Wishnie 2000; Lescureux et al 2011). As we (Convery and Nevin) often say to our students, managing animals is reasonably easy; the tricky part is working with people. Put another way, humans are as reliant on ecosystem goods and services for survival as any other species on the planet, which effectively makes conservation an essential survival strategy. Understanding human behaviour and attitudes towards nature is therefore as important to conservation biology as gathering information on species and ecosystems; for conservation to be successful it must connect deeply with everyday lives, histories and experiences, reflecting the values of those affected most by changes in land use and the presence of protected species (Bagchi and Mishra 2006; Smith and Wishnie 2000; Wilkie *et al* 2010; Zedrosser *et al* 2011; Xu *et al* 2007; Jim and Xu 2002; Blewitt 2010; Lovelock 2006; Lescureux *et al* 2011; Peterson *et al* 2010; Bulbeck 2005).

The Brown Bear

The brown bear (*Ursus arctos*)is the world's most widely distributed bear species, found on all major land masses across the Northern Hemisphere; although considered a 'Species of Least Concern' by the IUCN Red List (McLellan *et al* 2017), some smaller populations have become genetically isolated and are considered threatened, while some are now extirpated (McLellan *et al* 2017; Ordiz *et al* 2011; MacDonald and Barrett 1993; Zedrosser *et al* 2011). Geographic distribution earmarks the brown bear as the world's most successful wide-ranging large carnivore (Zedrosser *et al* 2011); the brown bear owes its success to its adaptability and omnivorous lifestyle (McLellan *et al* 2017; MacDonald and Barrett 1993; Stayaert *et al* 2011). Found in coastal areas, in mountain habitat at elevations of over 5,000 metres and in arid desert, the brown bear feeds on regionally abundant food, from salmon in North American coastal habitat to moth larvae in interior mountainous habitat (McLellan *et* al 2017). The result of varied regional adaptation to resources is a variety of morphological differences between populations; for example, bears that feed on salmon grow much larger than those with lower protein content in their diets, such as those living in interior mountain habitats in North America (Hilderbrand *et al* 1999; Nevin and Gilbert 2005b, 2005c).

In Europe, modern humans and brown bears have co-existed for at least 30,000 years (Ordiz *et al* 2011). In the introduction to this volume, we highlighted how our early human-bear interactions formed an important part of our understanding of the world, a feature also noted by Black (1998). During their evolutionary journey, bears and people have shared space and resources; in some areas local ecological knowledge regarding safe to eat and medicinal plants was discovered after watching bears (Beider 2005). It is significant that bears, like humans, are omnivores, and we have shared resources in many areas across the globe (Black 1998; Hallowell 1926; Russel and Enns 2002; Clark and Slocombe 2009). Stories of bear-human encounters through the ages have created the myth of an animal able to bridge the boundaries between human and animal (Clark and Slocombe 2009; Schwartz *et al* 2003; Black 1998; Hallowell 1926; Sorman 2014).

As Serra (2013, 76) notes, there is a deep significance of the bear in European history and mythology. Citing Michel Pastoureau (2007), Serra describes a deeply-rooted relationship between humans and bears, a history that interlaces power relations and religious domination:

> The bear is the only animal that can be represented standing upright, it can stand, sit, sleep on its side or on its stomach, run, swim, dive, roll, climb, jump and even dance...raises its head to contemplate the sky and the stars.

The bear used to occupy a place between the human and the divine:

It was the king of the natural kingdom, emerging from the pagan North, until the early Middle Ages when the Catholic Church supplanted it with the lion. Pagan festivities relating to the bear slowly metamorphosed into Saints Days whose legends include a bear (Valentine, Eligium, Vincenzianum, Blaise) or saints with the Latin root *ursus* in their names (Saint Ursus, Ursicenus, Ursula)…the Catholic Candelora, the presentation of Jesus in the temple and the feast of light, replaced the antique feast that celebrated the end of the hibernation months for the bears (Serra 2013; Pastoureau 2007).

HUMANS AND BEARS: A CULTURAL RELATIONSHIP

It is clear that bears occupy an important role in many cultures around the world (Schwartz *et al* 2003; Black 1998; Beider 2005; Pastoureau 2007). As discussed above, attributes of 'person-hood' stem from the bear's physical appearance and occasional bipedal posture (Schwartz *et al* 2003; Black 1998). Bears are easy to anthropomorphise due to their physical characteristics (DeMello 2012; Hallowell 1926). Indeed, various bear-related myths, rituals and beliefs reflect what we know of ourselves; in many respects our relationship with nature is mediated through cultural interpretations of bear species (Black 1998). While global cultural beliefs and values vary enormously (Clark and Slocombe 2009; Peterson *et al* 2010; Black 1998; Jones 2000), there is a remarkable degree of cultural similarity in our attitude toward bears (Black 1998; Beider 2005; Pastoureau 2007). Stories, myths and beliefs about bears provide compelling evidence of a broadly homogenous cultural worldview (Black 1998).

The ability to stand and move in a bipedal posture, coupled with other traits deemed similar to humans, such as eye location, has given rise to a variety of stories. These feature half-human creatures, they suggest that hibernation is a way for the animals to cross the boundary between our world and the underworld, between the physical realm and the spiritual; stories of copulation between women and bears gave rise to mythologies of shared ancestry, explained the strength of an individual or blood line (Black 1998; Beider 2005; Pastoureau 2007; Hallowell 1926). Hallowell (1926) relates that for many North American cultures, a direct reference to bears is taboo as they are often thought to understand human speech. 'King of the Forest' or 'King of the Mountain' is a common name given to bears across Europe and North America, 'grandfather' or 'old man', 'uncle', 'cousin' and 'brother' are also regularly recorded (Hallowell 1926; Black 1998; Lescureux *et al* 2011). These references of kinship are seen to help to reduce conflict with an animal that can be dangerous and quick-tempered if not treated with respect, even after death (Clark and Slocombe 2009; Lescureux *et al* 2011; Black 1998; Hallowell 1926; Beider 2005; Pastoureau 2007).

There has always been some degree of anthropomorphism in our understanding of bears, generating cultural and emotional connections that do not, at first appearances, sit well with modern, largely Western scientific traditions (Clark and Slocombe 2009). This has implications for bear-related community conservation, where the local cultural context is of central impor-tance. Cultural perspectives of bears tend to be emotional and value-laden (Wheeler 2013); however, there is a strong tie between these anthropomorphic, respectful and ritual interactions which acknowledges, and in many ways relies on, the recognition of bears as individuals.

This individual recognition and respect appears to be lost as a cultural norm in Europe as bears and other wild animals are hunted to extirpation in many areas of the continent. They were no longer 'brother or cousin'; the forest too had become something very different in the minds of humans and we see the emergence of the wild-wood narrative as a place for ungodly people and animals (Schwartz *et al* 2003). By the time Europeans were colonising the 'New World of North America' in the 1600s, attitudes toward wild animals and the spaces they occupied had created a very new understanding of nature (Schwartz *et al* 2003). Wolves and bears (sometimes known rogue individuals) were viewed as dangerous, and were systematically removed from human spaces (such as farms) by hunters. Driven from our lives into stories and myths, safely away from children and the future of European culture; stories of attacks, regardless of their rarity; fear – these often now dominate contemporary perceptions of bears (Moen *et al* 2012; Schwartz *et al* 2003).

Over the years, settlement, agriculture, industry, religion, politics and the arts have redefined the bear and created a new world for them to occupy, real or imagined (Watts 2000; Jones 2000). The distance between 'us and them' expanded. Over time bears were pushed to the margins (Pastoureau 2007; Beider 2005), and when Europeans colonised the New World, their ideas about bears went with them, this time with guns. The untamed nature of America was 'cleansed', along with the genocide of native peoples; and any species viewed as dangerous, unproductive or ungodly were controlled, pushed to the periphery of our lives (Schwartz *et al* 2003).

In this separation, individual human experience of nature generally, and wild places and carnivores in particular, becomes remote and second-hand. Kahn and Friedman (1995) coined the phrase 'Environmental Generational Amnesia' and this general concept could be well applied to the loss of personal, individual interactions of earlier generations with individual bears and their knowledge of them and how to live with them to the point where the bear became a generic other to be feared. The realm of the bear became wilderness, the forest.

Humans And Bears: A Modern Relationship

Human development and expansion over the last 200 years or so has had a major impact on brown bear populations globally. Increased persecution, habitat loss and fragmentation has led to population declines and extirpations (Lescureux *et al* 2011; Lescureux and Linnell 2010, Zedrosser *et al* 2011; Ordiz *et al* 2011). However, the 20th century has seen a shift in attitudes (Kaczensky *et al* 2011; Zedrosser *et al* 2011), and conservation projects on all three continents where brown bears are found have seen a recovery for many local bear populations (Zedrosser *et al* 2011; Lescureux *et al* 2011). However, much of this support comes from people who live in towns and cities away from the rural areas where bears live and there remain local concerns (both real and imagined) about living in close proximity to bears (Lescureux *et al* 2011). Tourism has driven much of this shift in attitude, and it has helped to persuade local communities that bears are of value (Nevin *et al* 2012). Globally, remote 'backcountry' areas are attracting more visitors than ever before and nature tourism is the fastest growing sector in the $3.5 trillion global annual tourism market (Mehmetoglu 2006). The changing social and economic value of these 'wilderness' ecosystems has the potential to influence land planning, resource extraction and conservation decision-making (Swain 2006).

Ecotourism provides an avenue for the rediscovery of the individual bear and can have positive benefits not only for bears but also the ecosystems they inhabit and the local economy (Morzillo *et al* 2010; Nevin *et al* 2012, 2014). For many bear populations future survival will depend on understanding how local people perceive them and choose to respond to their presence (Lescureux *et al* 2011). Negative associations with large carnivores have the potential to increase conflict between people and bears, with real-life possibility of negative consequences for both (Kaczensky *et al* 2011; Loginov 2012; Lescureux *et al* 2011). There is still a great deal of controversy over the hunting of bears; a report published at the start of 2014 found that bear tourism in British Columbia generated more income for the province than bear hunting (CREST 2014).

The presence of tourists, their expectations and perceptions can affect the conservation value of the landscape through their consumption of specific species. The act of viewing bears in their natural setting, interacting with wildlife in close proximity, is a highly important aspect of the tourist experience (Lemelin 2006). Much of what motivates the nature tourist is captured in the concept of sense of place in that the setting of the bear encounter often adds greatly to the perceived value of the experience (Nevin *et al* 2012, 2014). As Biel (2006) indicates, their meaning and significance far outweigh their simple presence. Understanding the impact of this growing industry on the environment, and the motivations and perceptions of the tourist, offers a way of potentially influencing future conservation strategies (Nevin 2010). In British Columbia (Canada), established ecotourism activities centred on bear viewing have been proven to have positive impacts for the animals being viewed (Nevin 2003; Nevin and Gilbert 2005b, 2005c). At the same time our increased presence in these landscapes is bound to increase interactions with these animals; we need to approach this new paradigm with care and understanding to prevent further negative interactions (Nellemann *et al* 2007; Zedrosser *et al* 2011); recognising and knowing individual differences between bears can facilitate this greatly.

Studies that explore the behavioural responses of bears to people suggest the 'less aggressive' brown bears of Europe have become more accustomed to the presence of people over a longer period of time; the survivors being the bears that have adapted an anti-predator response to people (Ordiz *et al* 2011; Moen *et al* 2012). These European bears are today studied in multi-use landscapes where human activity dissects the habitat available to bears (May *et al* 2008; Bischof *et al* 2009). Proximity to human settlement and activity is seen to impact on the behaviour of bears; activity may disturb and displace the animals (Bischof *et al* 2009; Nevin 2009; Nevin 2008; Nellemann *et al* 2007). Brown bears in North America and Russia are thought to react more aggressively to people (Moen *et al* 2012), largely because the population has had less time to develop an anti-predator response to humans as hunting has taken place over a much shorter period of time (Ordiz *et al* 2011; Schwartz *et al* 2003). However, First Nations Canadians did, and do, hunt bears, especially those individuals known to have attacked humans (Clark and Slocombe 2009; Schwartz *et al* 2003).

Bears tend to avoid people, unless surprised due to wind direction or physical environmental barriers (Schwartz *et al* 2003; Moen *et al* 2012). In many areas bears will avoid human presence in a landscape, taking cover during times of high human activity (May *et al* 2008; Olson *et al* 1997). Activities such as hunting, although targeted to males, can affect the survival of other age-sex classes of bears by displacing them from resources and limiting the time spent feeding (Ordiz *et al* 2011; May *et al* 2008; Bischof *et al* 2009). At the same time in BC tourist activity is seen to have positive benefits for the population (Nevin 2003; Nevin and Gilbert 2005b, 2005c). Bears adjust their feeding times to avoid people or take refuge from potentially infanticidal males by feeding during the bear viewing times (Nevin 2003; Nevin and Gilbert 2005b, 2005c). In a relatively short period of time, motive and attitude change towards the Knight Inlet population of bears has seen both an improvement in the bear-human relationship and an increase in the population (Nevin and Gilbert 2005b, 2005c; Hamilton *et al* 2004; Lloyd 1979). Particular, regularly sighted bears develop a loyal following among both naturalist guides and ecotourists. Learning from this relationship could be a valuable conservation aid in a wider context.

Human geo-social movements have driven an understanding of animals that is based on a hunter-hunted relationship; learning about these encounters as we do from stories that can persist through generations (Clark and Slocombe 2009) limits our view of bears in today's world to that of an aggressive animal (Rogers and Mansfield 2011). Understanding of hunted species is generic; the individual behavioural responses by a hunted animal cannot be repeated; the animal dies, therefore understanding potential interaction with individuals over time becomes limited (Knight 2005). Stories emanating from these encounters do persist (Clark and Slocombe 2009). From a North American aboriginal perspective, refraining from hunting certain individuals in a local population of bears was seen as beneficial; long-term knowledge of dominant males offered security against the influx of new males that may behave unpredictably (Clark and Slocombe 2009). Not viewing animals as individuals makes it easier for us to exploit them but limits our ability to form the geographically appropriate relationships that will improve human-animal interactions (Jones 2000). Taking into consideration the potential for increased interactions in the future in a growing variety of landscapes, we should seek to improve the perceptions and relationships with bears before we perpetuate further negativity (Nellemann et al 2006; Rogers and Mansfield 2011).

Human-animal interactions in the modern world take place in such varied social, regional and value-laden contexts that they prompt a case by case revaluation of the relationship as a one size fits all approach is inappropriate (Jones 2000). We may choose to view human manipulation and interaction with the environment as ubiquitously negative or inevitable and beneficial when one considers the limited number of truly pristine environments where people have never ventured: however, human environmental manipulation is widespread and has shaped many of the landscapes that we consider wild (Farina et al 2005; Nevin et al 2012). Bears are known to interact with humans and human modified environments in a number of well-documented ways. Bears avoid busy roads, except for some females and cubs who are potentially drawn to roadsides by male absence (Graham et al 2010). In Glendale Cove (KIL), as in other tourist areas, female bears are drawn to areas of high human presence as this enables access to food away from males (Nevin and Gilbert 2005b, 2005c; Olson et al 1997). Other studies have focused on the use of landscapes by bears, how far from roads they sleep, how they may avoid food-rich areas in the hunting season (Ordiz et al 2011).

Individual behaviour is the result of interactions over time where animals and humans learn appropriate response to the other party (Oma 2010). As social animals, brown bears have extended maternal care periods associated with learning; bears have well-developed cognitive abilities and are able to learn and interpret their environment in a variety of complex and as yet unexplored ways (Huber 2010; Deecke 2012).

Living and working with the same set of animals on a daily basis results in mutual familiarity (Knight 2005). Social animals in a domestic setting transfer the trust associated with conspecifics to humans; humans also transfer the same trust to the animals (Oma 2010). This is also possible with wild animals; the legacies of Fossey, Goodall and Galdikas speak of this relationship eloquently. The (in some quarters) controversial work of Lynn Rogers (see Rogers in this volume) with black bears in Minnesota challenges our view that animals such as bears can be safely habituated to proximal human interaction. Lynn's work depends on habituation, 'the waning of response to neutral stimuli' (Rogers and Mansfield 2011). His work, a systematic review of bear behaviour over decades, leads him to the conclusion that bears view the humans as neither threat nor competitor; his work relies on correct interpretation of bear behaviour and appropriate response. Inappropriate response to bear threat or stress, which can be outwardly as subtle as a yawn, is seen to be a major cause for bear attacks (Rogers and Mansfield 2011; Rogers 2011). The idea that humans and animals are at conflict in any area undoubtedly suggests intent on the part of both human and animal, much of this rhetoric unhelpfully framed by the terminology used (Peterson *et al* 2010). It is perhaps more appropriate to view bear behaviour as a response to human stimulus and respond accordingly to avoid negative encounters (Rogers and Mansfield 2011; Nellemann *et al* 2006; Clark and Slocombe 2009).

IMAGES AND OUR UNDERSTANDING OF BEARS

This brings us back to knowing individual bears and the importance of representation and images, which have long played a role in our understanding of and communication about the natural world, from cave paintings to natural history programmes; contemporary image collection also forms an important part of data collection. It would seem that forming connections with animals is important to humans; physical, mental, visual or emotional connections matter (DeMello 2012; Bulbeck 2005). Exploring, understanding and representing nature has been a human obsession for thousands of years (Hayes 2008). Since the invention of cameras, we have focused on animal subjects (Pollo *et al* 2009), in part fuelling a multi-billion-dollar film-making industry. These films often exaggerate the separateness and distance between the human world and the natural world; driven by an aesthetic value of 'wildness', any evidence of human presence is removed (Bulbeck 2005; Blewitt 2010). Of course, this is almost entirely a fiction; human-animal interactions have for millennia been an inevitable part of human life (Robinson 2006; Bulbeck 2005; Blewitt 2010). Increasingly however, wildlife film is where animals are given life and meaning (Porter 2006; Davies 2000). The aesthetic value of wildlife remains significant even if we never physically experience it (Porter 2006).

As mentioned earlier, much of our behavioural work with bears is dependent on the ability to identify and track individuals through time and space based on catalogues of images (see, for example, Clapham *et al* Chapter 13 in this volume). This is, however, incredibly time and resource intensive. Through years spent watching bears and learning to recognise individuals, we have gained the skills and understanding to identify individual bears from their faces alone, subconsciously picking up on subtle differences between bears, just as we do with human faces, although likely with less accuracy. Primatologists frequently use faces to recognise individuals, but it is much rarer in non-primates or species with no discernible marking patterns on their faces. The obvious question for the 'iPhone X' generation of researchers is if we can confirm human identification from facial recognition software, can this process be extended to bears?

The use of remote cameras has been growing as a methodological approach in wildlife biology (reviewed by Elmeligi *et al* 2018); they are less intrusive, less costly and require fewer man-hours to effectively generate an abundance of data than direct observational techniques (Karanth and Nichols 1998). While efficient, this does not expose the researcher to the repeated interactions which allow the development of reliable individual identification for animals which, like bears, lack readily identifiable patterns in the form of spots and stripes. How then to gain the efficiency while retaining the individual insight?

MacLeod *et al* (2001) called for a concerted effort to automate species identification through computationally intensive approaches and in fact drew attention to a number of successful applications of these techniques in differentiating similar species (eg the Natural History Museum, London's use of DAIST (Digital Automated Identification System) to identify 15 species of parasitic wasp from digital images of their wings). More recently, deep learning and neural network approaches have been applied to the identification of more diverse groups of species (Norouzzadeh *et al* 2018).

Current work in this field involves Melanie Clapham (see Chapter 13) as a team member. The BearID project (http://bearresearch.org/) aims to progress the field of conservation technology by developing face recognition software that can identify individual brown bears from images of their faces. Applying this technology to camera trap imagery would provide bear researchers with a new technique to monitor wild populations of brown bears and ask a wider variety of applied research questions, with implications for other threatened wildlife; providing answers that could aid conservation efforts worldwide.

Bibliography and References

Bagchi, S, and Mishra, C, 2006 Living with large carnivores: predation on livestock by the snow leopard, *Unica unica. Journal of Zoology* 268, 217–24

Beider, R E, 2005 *Bear,* Reaktion Books, London

Biel, A W, 2006 *Do Not Feed the Bears*, University Press of Kansas

Bischof, R, Swenson, J E, Yoccoz, N G, Mysterud, A, and Gimenez, O, 2009 The magnitude and selectivity of natural and multiple anthropogenic mortality causes in hunted brown bears, *Journal of Animal Ecology* 78, 656–65

Black, L, 1998 Bear in Human Imagination and in Ritual, *Ursus* 10, 343–7

Blewitt, J, 2010 *Media, Ecology and Conservation*, Green Books, Devon, UK

Bulbeck, C, 2005 *Facing the Wild: Ecotourism, Conservation & Animal Encounters*, Earthscan, London

Clapham, M, 2012 An assessment of the chemical signalling strategies employed by brown bears (Ursus arctos) to communicate with conspecifics, PhD thesis, Lancaster University, UK

Clapham, M, Nevin, O T, Ramsey, A D, and Rosell, F, 2014 Scent marking investment and motor patterns are affected by the age and sex of wild brown bears, *Animal Behaviour* 94, 107–16

—— 2013 The function of strategic tree selectivity in the chemical signalling of brown bears, *Animal Behaviour* 85, 1351–7

——, 2012 A hypothetico-deductive approach to assessing the social function of chemical signaling in non-territorial solitary carnivore, *Plos One* 7(4): e35404. doi:10.1371/journal.pone.0035404

Clark, D, and Slocombe, S, 2009 Respect for Grizzly Bears: An Aboriginal Approach for Co-existence and Resilience, *Ecology and Society* 14, 42

CREST, 2014 *Economic Impact of Bear Viewing and Bear Hunting in the Great Bear Rainforest of British Columbia*, Center for Responsible Travel, available from: http://www.responsibletravel.org/projects/documents/Economic_Impact_of_Bear_Viewing_and_Bear_Hunting_in_GBR_of_BC.pdf

Davies, G, 2000 Visual animals in electronic zoos. The changing geographies of animal capture and display, in *Animal spaces, beastly places* (eds C Philo and C Wilbert), Routledge, London

Deecke, V B, 2012 Tool-use in the brown bear *Ursus arctos, Animal Cognition* 15, 725–30

DeMello, M, 2012 *Animals and Society*, Columbia University Press, New York

Elmeligi, S, Convery, I, Deecke, V, and Nevin, O T, 2018 Virtual collecting: Camera-trapping and the assembly of population data in twenty-first century biology, in *Naturalists in the Field: Collecting, recording and preserving the natural world from the fifteenth to the twenty-first century* (ed A MacGregor), Brill, Leiden, Netherlands, 863-90

Farina, A, Santolini, R, Pagliaro, G, Scozzafava, S, and Schipani, I, 2005 Eco-semiotics: A new field of competence for ecology to overcome the frontier between environmental complexity and human culture in the Mediterranean, *Israel Journal of Plant Sciences* 53, 167–75

Graham, K, Boulanger, J, Duval, J, and Stenhouse, G, 2010 Spatial Temporal use of roads by grizzly bears in west-central Alberta, *Ursus* 21, 43–56

Gray, C L, Hill, S L, Newbold, T, Hudson, L N, Borger, L, Contu, S, Hoskins, A J, Ferrier, S, Purvis, A, and Scharlemann, J P, 2016 Local biodiversity is higher inside than outside terrestrial protected areas worldwide, *Nature Communications* 7, 12306 doi: 10.1038/ncomms12306

Hallowell, I, 1926 Bear Ceremonialism in the Northern Hemisphere, *American Anthropologist* 28, 1–175

Hamilton, A N, Heard, D C, and Austin, M A, 2004 *British Columbia Grizzly Bear Ursus arctos population estimate 2004*, BC Ministry of Water, Land and Air Protection, Victoria, BC, 1–7

Hayes, M A, 2008 Into the Field: Naturalistic education and the future of Conservation, *Conservation Biology* 23, 1075–9

Hilderbrand, G V, Schwartz, C C, Robbins, C T, Jacoby, M E, Hanley, T A, Arthur, S M, and Servheen, C, 1999 Importance of meat to population productivity and conservation of North American brown bears, *Canadian Journal of Zoology* 77, 132–8

Huber, D, 2010 Rehabilitation and reintroduction of captive-reared bears: feasibility and methodology for European brown bears *Ursus arctos*, *International Zoo Yearbook* 44, 47–54

Ingold, T, 2006 Rethinking the Animate, Re-animating Thought, *Ethnos* 71 (1), 9–20

Jim, C Y, and Xu, S S, 2002 Stifled stakeholders and subdued participation: Interpreting local responses toward Shimentai Nature Reserve in South China, *Environmental Management* 30, 327–41

Jones, O, 2000 Unethical geographies of human-nonhuman relations. Encounter. Collectives and spaces, in *Animal spaces, beastly places* (eds C Philo and C Wilbert), Routledge, London

Kaczensky, P, Jerina, K, Jonozovic, M, Krofel, M, Skrbinsek, Rauer, G, Kos, I, and Gutleb, B, 2011 Illegal killing may hamper brown bear recovery in the Eastern Alps, *Ursus* 221, 37–46

Kahn, P H, and Friedman, B, 1995 Environmental views and values of children in an inner-city black community, *Child Development* 66 (5), 1403–17

Karanth, K U, and Nichols, J D, 1998 Estimation of Tiger Densities in India Using Photographic Captures and Recaptures, *Ecology* 79 (8), 2852–62

Knight, J, 2005 Introduction, in *Animals in Person: Cultural Perspectives on Human-Animal Intimacy* (ed J Knight), Berg, Oxford and New York, 1–13

Lemelin, R H, 2006 The Gawk, The Glance, and The Gaze: Ocular Consumption and Polar Bear Tourism in Churchill, Manitoba, Canada, *Current Issues in Tourism* 9, 516–34

Lescureux, N, and Linnell, J D C, 2010 Knowledge and Perceptions of Macedonian Hunters and Herders: the Influence of Species Specific Ecology of Bears, Wolves and Lynx, *Human Ecology* 38, 389–99

Lescureux, N, Linnell, J D C, Mustafa, S, Melovski, D, Stojanov, A, Ivanov, G, and Avukatov, V, 2011 The King of the Forest: Local Knowledge About European Brown Bear *Ursus arctos* and Implications for Their Conservation in Contemporary Western Macedonia, *Conservation and Society* 93, 189–201

Lloyd, K, 1979 *Aspects of the Ecology of black and grizzly bears in coastal British Columbia* [online], MSc thesis, University of British Columbia, Canada

Loginov, O, 2012 Status and Conservation of Two Brown Bear Subspecies in Kazakhstan, *International Bear News* 21, 24–5

Lovelock, J, 2006 *The Revenge of Gaia*, Penguin Books, London

MacDonald, B, and Barrett, P, 1993 *Collins Field Guide. Mammals of Britain and Europe*, HarperCollins, London

MacLeod, R, Herzog, S K, Maccormick, A, Ewing, S R, Bryce, R, and Evans, K L, 2011 Rapid monitoring of species abundance for biodiversity conservation: Consistency and reliability of the MacKinnon lists technique, *Biological Conservation* 144, 1374–81

May, R, Dijk, J, Wabakken, P, Swenson, J, Linnell, J, Zimmerman, B, Odden, J, Pederson, H, Reidar, A, and Landa, A, 2008 Habitat differentiation within the large-carnivore community of Norway's multiple-use landscapes, *Journal of Applied Ecology* 45, 1382–91

McLellan, B N, Proctor, M F, Huber, D, and Michel, S, 2017 *Ursus arctos* (amended version of 2017 assessment), The IUCN Red List of Threatened Species 2017: e.T41688A121229971, http://dx.doi.org/10.2305/IUCN.UK.2017-3.RLTS.T41688A121229971.en

Mehmetoglu, M, 2006 Typologising nature-based tourists by activity – Theoretical and practical implications, *Tourism Management* 28, 651–60

Moen, G K, Stoen, O, Sahlen, V, and Swenson, J E, 2012 Behaviour of Solitary Adult Scandinavian Brown Bears *Ursus arctos* when Approached by Humans on Foot, *Plos One* 7, 2

Monbiot, G, 2014 Put a price on nature? We must stop this neoliberal road to ruin, *The Guardian*, available from: https://www.theguardian.com/environment/georgemonbiot/2014/jul/24/price-nature-neoliberal-capital-road-ruin [3 July 2019]

Morzillo, T A, Mertig, A G, Hollister, J W, Garner, N, and Liu, J, 2010 Socioeconomic factors affecting local support for black bear recovery strategies, *Environmental Management* 45, 1299–1311

Nellemann, C O G, Stoen, J, Kindberg, J E, Swenson, I, Vistnes, G, Ericsson, J, Katajisto, Kaltenborn, B P, Martin, J, and Ordiz, A, 2007 Terrain use by an expanding brown bear population in relation to age, recreational resorts and human settlements, *Biological Conservation* 138, 157–65

Nevin, O T, 2003 Towards a Theory of Carnivore Density: the influence of prey abundance and risk-sensitive behavioural change on individual access to high energy food salmon: impacts on the density and viability of bear populations, unpublished PhD thesis, Utah State University, Logan, Utah, USA

——, 2008 Tempro-spatial influence of forest road re-commissioning on movement patterns and travel corridors in brown bears (*Ursus arctos*) in second growth temperate rainforest ecosystems in coastal British Columbia, unpublished report, University of Cumbria, UK

——, 2009 An assessment and review of potential impacts of timber extraction from harvest blocs around Pete Lake in the Knight East Landscape Unit in the population of brown bears *Ursus arctos* in the Glendale Tome Browne drainage, unpublished report, University of Cumbria, UK

——, 2010 Importing carnivore encounters: conservation and ecotourism in a new carbon economy, paper presented at the *24th International Congress for Conservation Biology, 3–7 July 2010, Edmonton, Alberta*.

Nevin, O T, and Gilbert, B K, 2005a Observations of autumn courtship and breeding in Brown Bears, *Ursus arctos*, from coastal British Columbia, *Canadian Field-Naturalist* 119 (3), 449–50

——, 2005b Perceived risk, displacement, and refuging in brown bears: positive impacts of ecotourism? *Biological Conservation* 121, 611–22

——, 2005c Measuring the cost of risk avoidance in brown bears: further evidence of positive impacts of ecotourism, *Biological Conservation* 123, 453–60

Nevin, O T, Swain, P, and Convery, I, 2012 Carnivore tourism: do motivated tourists change the social, economic and conservation value of the wild places they visit?, in *Making Sense of Place* (eds I Convery, P Davis and G Corsane), Boydell & Brewer, Woodbridge

———, 2014 Bears, placemaking, and authenticity in British Columbia, *Natural Areas Journal* 34 (2), 216–21

Norouzzadeh, M S, Nguyen, A, Kosmala, M, Swanson, A, Palmer, M S, Packer, C, and Clune, J, 2018 Automatically identifying, counting, and describing wild animals in camera-trap images with deep learning, *Proceedings of the National Academy of Sciences* 115 (25) E5716-E5725; https://doi.org/10.1073/pnas.1719367115

Nöth, W, 1998 Ecosemiotics, *Sign Systems Studies* 26, 332–43

Olson, T L, Gilbert, B K, and Squibb, R C, 1997 The effects of increasing human activity on brown bear use of an Alaskan river, *Biological Conservation* 82, 95–9

Oma, K A, 2010 Between trust and domination: social contracts between humans and animals, *World Archaeology* 422, 175–87

Ordiz, A, Stoen, O, Delibes, M, and Swenson, J E, 2011 Predators or prey? Spatio-temporal discrimination of human-derived risk by brown bears, *Behavioural Ecology* 166, 59–67

Pastoureau, M, 2007 *The Bear: History of a Fallen King*, Belknap Press of Harvard University Press, Cambridge, Massachusetts, USA

Peterson, M N, Birckhead, J L, Leong, K, Peterson, M J, and Peterson, T R, 2010 Rearticulating the myth of human-wildlife conflict, *Conservation Letters* 3, 74–82

Pollo, S, Graziano, M, Giacoma, C, 2009 The ethics of natural history documentaries, *Animal Behaviour* 77, 1357–60

Porter, P, 2006 Engaging the Animal in the Moving Image, *Society and Animals* 14 (4) 399–416

Robinson, J G, 2006 Conservation Biology and Real-World Conservation, *Conservation Biology* 20 (3) 658–69

Rogers, L, and Mansfield, S, 2011 Misconceptions about black bears: response to Geist, *Human-Wildlife Interactions* 5, 173–6

Rogers, L, 2011 Does diversionary feeding create nuisance bears and jeopardize public safety? *Human-Wildlife Interactions* 5, 287–95

Russel, C, and Enss, M, 2002 *Grizzly Heart*, Random House, Toronto, Canada

Schwartz, C, Swenson, J, and Miller, S, 2003 Large carnivores, moose, and humans: A changing paradigm of predator management in the 21st Century, *Alces* 39, 41–63

Serra, I, 2013 On Men and Bears: A Forgotten Migration in Nineteenth-Century Italy, *History Workshop Journal* 76 (1), 57–84

Smith, E A, and Wishnie, M, 2000 Conservation and Subsistence in Small-Scale Societies, *Annual Reviews Anthropology* 29, 493–524

Soga, M, and Gaston, K J, 2016 Extinction of experience: the loss of human-nature interactions, *Front Ecol Environ* 14, 94–101

Sorman, J, 2014 *La peau de l'ours*, Gallimard, Paris

Steyaert, S M J G, Støen O G, Elfström, M, Karlsson, J, Lammeren, R V, Bokdam, J, Zedrosser, A, Brunberg, S, and Swenson, J E, 2011 Resource selection by sympatric free-ranging dairy cattle and brown bears *Ursus arctos*, *Wildlife Biology* 17, 389–403

Stonorov, D, and Stokes, A W, 1972 Social behavior of the Alaskan brown bear, *International Conference on Bear Research and Management* 2, 232–42

Swain, P, 2006 *The value of watchable wildlife: measuring the impacts of bear viewing in British Columbia*, unpublished MSc thesis, University of Central Lancashire, UK

Tinbergen, N, 1963 On aims and methods of ethology, *Zeitschrift für Tierpsychologie* 20, 410–33

Trigger, D S, 2008 Indigeneity, ferality, and what 'belongs' in the Australian bush: Aboriginal responses to 'introduced' animals and plants in a settler-descendant society, *Journal of the Anthropological Institute* 14, 628–46

Watts, M J, 2000 Afterword, Enclosure, in *Animal spaces, beastly places* (eds C Philo and C Wilbert), Routledge, London

Wheeler, W, 2013 Postscript on Biosemiotics: Reading Beyond Words – And Ecocriticism, *New Formations*, 137–54

Wilkie, D S, Redford, K H, and McShane, T O, 2010 Taking of Rights for Natural Resource Conservation: A Discussion About Compensation, *Journal of Sustainable Forestry* 29, 135–51

Xu, A, Jiang, Z, Li, C, Da, S, Cui, Q, Yu, S, and Wu, G, 2007 Status and conservation of the snow leopard *Panthera uncia* in the Gouli Region, Kunlun Mountains, China, *Oryx* 42, 460–3

Zedrosser, A, Steyaert, S M J G, Gossow, H, and Swenson, J E, 2011 Brown Bear Conservation and the Ghost of Persecution Past, *Biological Conservation* 1449, 2163–70

Bears in the Public Gaze

Bears Behind Bars:
Captive Bears Throughout History

KOEN CUYTEN AND IAN CONVERY

Bears and humans have co-existed for thousands of years. All eight species of bear have occupied a particular niche in human culture and development, from prehistoric times through to the World Wildlife Fund (WWF) adoption of the panda bear as the organisation's logo. The most 'exotic species' of bear (such as sloth bear and the polar bear) have sparked the interest of animal collectors since at least 2500 BCE. Ever since that time, bears have featured in private animal collections, and with the rise of the modern (public) zoo in the 18th century, exhibited for human entertainment in zoological gardens, museums, circuses, street theatre, cafes, film and TV. They have danced, walked the tightrope, dressed up as children, and played the part of human friend (eg *Grizzly Adams*) and adversary (eg *The Revenant*), all in the name of entertaining humans. They have also played a role in traditional medicines, particularly in the East where for hundreds of years bear bile has been used for a range of curative properties.

As a result, captive bears are found all over the world, even in the most remote places. Unfortunately, many captive bears are still housed in small barren 'crush cages', deprived of even the most basic needs and care such as water, proper food and shelter. Globally, various species of bear are privately owned (often illegally); they are kept in backyards, next to petrol stations or roadside restaurants, or on public display at a beach or café to attract customers. Most of these bears will have health problems and display chronic behavioural problems associated with captivity. These bears are usually wild-caught as cubs, a practice that is a significant threat to the wild population in many regions. Other bears feature in circuses, typically performing by balancing on a rope during the show then spending the rest of the day confined in small circus trailers. We are perhaps most familiar with bears from visits to a zoo, where the quality of the enclosure varies from a cage barely larger than the bear[1] to large naturalistic enclosures that resemble the bears' wild habitat.

Today, the best zoos in Europe promote *ex-situ* captive bears as 'ambassadors', with a focus on education, conservation and scientific research to benefit the species and their *in-situ* habitat in the wild. Initiatives such as the European Endangered Species Programs (EEP), the European Studbooks (ESB) and the Regional Collection Plans (RCP) managed by EAZA (the European Association of Zoos and Aquaria) aim at conserving healthy populations of animals in captivity while safeguarding the genetic health of the animals under their care. There are also bear sanctuaries in Europe (and to a lesser extent in Asia and North America) that care for the many bears rescued from exploitation and poor levels of maintenance. Such sanctuaries, like the Bear

---

[1] We have witnessed this ourselves in (nameless) zoos throughout Eastern Europe and Central Asia.

Forest in the Netherlands, provide the best of veterinary care, husbandry and enrichment to give formerly mistreated animals a bear-worthy life.

In this chapter, we consider two main areas of bear captivity: bears as entertainment, focusing on dancing bears, and bears in medicine, focusing on bile farming. We will then discuss the role of bear sanctuaries in providing care and respite for rescued bears.

As reported elsewhere in this volume, bears have captivated our imagination for thousands of years. They were one of the first 'zoo animals' as they are relatively easy to keep; for example, there are records of Syrian brown bears (*Ursus arctos syriacus*) being brought into Egypt by pharaoh Sahure for his enjoyment during the 5th dynasty (2500 BC) (Kisling 2001). In 1500 BC, Queen Hatshepsut (Egypt's first and only female pharaoh) had a facility that could be considered the earliest zoo. Among the animals she imported from the Punt (an African country in what is now Ethiopia and Somalia or the Horn of Africa) were rhinos, giraffes, leopards, monkeys and more familiar species like cattle and hounds. Under King Ptolemy II (285–246 BC) the greatest animal collection in the ancient world came into being at Alexandria. Supposedly, he had a polar bear (*Ursus maritimus*) in his collection, but it may well have been a light colour variation of the Syrian brown bear (Brown 1993).

After Roman conquest, the menagerie in Alexandria served as a staging post in the supply of wild African mammals to Rome. As with lions, Roman rulers considered the bear as a symbol of strength and power and they used bears in warrior contests, chariot races and circus-like performances. Bears and lions were commonly used because they could still be found in southeastern Europe at the time. Bears were forced to fight bloody battles 'to the death' with dogs, unarmed prisoners, gladiators or other wild animals like giraffes. These battles were held in vast arenas such as Circus Maximus in Rome, which held 150,000 spectators at a time. Roman Emperor Caligula (AD 37–41) used 400 bears during a single 'game' and Emperor Gordian (AD 238) used no less than 1000 bears in a single event (Epplett 2001).

Bears have been used in street entertainment throughout Asia and Europe for many centuries. During the Middle Ages (476 to 1453), for example, bears were trained to 'dance' and were led around on chains for public amusement. Another form of popular entertainment was bearbaiting, which occurred in England (mainly in London) from the time of the Norman Conquest (1066) into the 19th century. Bears were kept in bear gardens or bear pits for this purpose. Bear gardens were round and open structures, often with three levels of seating (galleries) surrounding a 17 m diameter inner ring. Some gardens contained several rings, where a variety of performances took place, including gorillas riding on horseback and bears or bulls fighting mastiff dogs or each other (Brown 1993). It was a cruel form of entertainment, with bets taken on how many dogs would be killed before the bear or bull died. Similar to the Roman circus, the London bear gardens offered brutal and gory entertainment, and were notoriously raucous and disorderly events (Brown 1993). However, bearbaiting was not just for the 'common people'; English royalty also enjoyed such events and there are records of 13 bears being used for one event for the entertainment of Queen Elizabeth I. Like other members of the 'elite', the Queen was by all accounts an aficionado of these animal baiting games (Brown 1993).

There is a long and interesting history charting the temporal, spatial and ethical journey from bearbaiting to zoos, in the theatre (Fig 8.1) and circuses (Fig 8.2); there is, however, insufficient space in this chapter to pay any more than cursory attention to the various staging points along the way. Bear pits date back to the Middle Ages; strong fortifications and large moats around towns lost their strategic importance, so they began to be used as animal enclosures.

FIGURE 8.1. A CIRCUS POSTER OF PERFORMING BEARS DURING THE VICTORIAN AGE – COURTESY OF HERITAGE AUCTIONS, HA.COM.

FIGURE 8.2. POLAR BEARS IN THE HAGENBECK CIRCUS – UNKNOWN SOURCE.

Bears were often kept in these moats, and the 'bear pit' was dug several metres into the ground and fortified with a strong stone wall, in the middle of which would be a climbing tree and a small pool of water (Kisling 2001). Arguably the best known of all the bear pits was the one at Bern, Switzerland. Bern has kept and exhibited bears for more than 500 years, from medieval times until the death of a 28-year-old brown bear called Pedro in 2009 (at which point the bear pit closed, Fig 8.3). Even in early modern zoos, bears were housed in bear pits, such as at the Jardin des Plantes in Paris (opened 1794) and the London Zoological Gardens (opened 1828). Even some zoos founded in the 1930s and 1940s built bear pits because they were inexpensive and still considered a suitable way to keep bears (Kisling 2001).

The 19th century saw a substantial increase in the number of zoological gardens opened to the public to display exotic animals for public education and entertainment (Kisling 2001). Since the mid-20th century zoos have

BEAR PIT

FIGURE 8.3. THE BERN BEAR PIT 'VIEWS OF THE ZOOLOGICAL GARDENS', 1831. COURTESY OF ZSL.

become increasingly focused on biodiversity conservation and have become more complex operations dealing with animal husbandry, education, field conservation and research. Many zoos nowadays have bears in their collections and, through proper education programmes, use them as ambassadors for bears in the wild. By creating interactive exhibits, interpretive tours and educational programmes that bring people face-to-face with living animals, zoos and aquariums profoundly influence their visitors in significant ways (Davis 1996).

Another popular form of entertainment where animals were widely (and still are) used is the circus. The modern circus originated in England during the mid- to late 1700s (Brown 1993). Although bears have been used extensively for entertainment purposes for thousands of years, they were 'late arriving' in the modern circus. Bears were intensively trained only to perform tricks from the end of the 19th century onwards (Brown 1993). Nearly all bear species have been or are still used today in circuses. The most commonly used bears are the Eurasian brown bear (*Ursus arctos arctos*) and the polar bear. In Asia, the Asiatic black bears (*Ursus tibethanus*) are more commonly used in circus performances. Southeast Asia has circuses where even the smallest of all bears, the sun bear (*Helarctos malayanus*), is used to perform tricks. Even giant pandas (*Ailuropoda melanoleuca*) and sloth bears (*Melursus ursinus*) have featured in circus acts. Since the early 21st century, the use of bears in circuses has diminished as more and more countries ban the use of (wild) non-domesticated animals in traveling circuses. However, Palmer (2016) states that as part of a PETA[2] investigation into circuses in Suzhou, China, bear cubs were found chained by their necks and tethered to a wall, forcing them to remain upright to train them to walk on their hind legs. There are similar PETA reports of mistreatment linked to circuses in Vietnam. Clearly, there is still work to be done.

Dancing Bears

Another notable (and long-lived) aspect of bear entertainment is bear dancing. During the 18th and 19th centuries, it was common to find groups of wandering minstrels and storytellers in Europe, who would often have dancing bears amongst their troupe (often wearing period costumes). Serra (2003) relates the seasonal travels of *orsanti* (bear-trainers), from the Italian Apennine region to the rest of Europe in the mid-19th century. These migrants roamed Italy and Europe, reaching as far as Turkey, Russia and Scandinavia, with their carts and their animals: 'a strange company of men, boys, bears, and monkeys.' Their ranks included the famous bear-trainer, Guglielmo Puelli, who apparently travelled to Finland and Russia, where he purchased a 'giant bear', and reached Sweden in 1880. Puelli slept with the bear to protect himself from the northern frost and the bear defended him if brawls broke out. 'He is a better friend than a human being' (Serra 2003, 60). The French novelist Victor Hugo writes of the world of the travelling entertainers in *L'homme qui rit* (1869). Until the end of the 19th century, this form of travelling entertainment was also common practice in the United States, where bears featured in well-known Vaudeville acts. Bears became common street entertainment during the late 19th and the early 20th centuries in the United States, throughout Europe and into Asia (eg Turkey). Even in more recent times (the end of the 20th century, early 21st century), dancing bears were trained by Romany peoples from Eastern Europe and Asia (Fig 8.4), and by the nomadic Kalandar people from India (who tend to use sloth bears).

Indeed, according to D'Cruze *et al* (2011), the Kalandar community of South Asia has performed with dancing sloth bears since the late Vedic era (1000–700 BCE). As the kingdoms in India disappeared, the 'dancing' bear trade transitioned to become entertainment for villagers and tourists who paid to watch bears. Poached from the wild as cubs, they were trained using cruel and brutal methods to force them to 'dance' on the streets. They suffered ruthless physical and psychological abuse and from severe and chronic medical problems. With no anaesthesia,

---

2   People for the Ethical Treatment of Animals

FIGURE 8.4. A DANCING BEAR IN SERBIA – COURTESY OF BEARS IN MIND.

Figure 8.5. A Kalandar with dancing bear in India – courtesy of Wildlife SOS.

a red-hot poker rod would be driven through the muzzle of the bear cub (at the age of around six months) and the canines would be forcibly removed. A thick coarse rope would then be threaded through the wound and tugged to induce 'dancing' performances (Fig 8.5). Unfortunately, despite widespread media attention in India and relevant legislation (eg the Prevention of Cruelty to Animals Act, 1950, and the Wildlife Protection Act, 1972), D'Cruze *et al* (2011) report that the practice is still prevalent in rural, remote or inaccessible areas across India, though there has been significant achievement in reducing the number of bears involved. There is also a 'knock-on effect' from the reduction in Kalandar bear use; Radhakrishna (2007, 4224) reports on a Kalandar switch to monkeys (Rhesus macaques) and that, alongside the constant danger from working with bears, the public and media pressure was an additional reason for this. He records that the 'bear saving campaign had reached a crescendo and they feared they could be physically attacked by indignant tourists or common people if they continued'.

From 1995 onwards, an organisation called Wildlife SOS in India began to rescue dancing bears from the streets of India. By December 2018, there were 628 rescued sloth bears across four rescue facilities in Agra, Bannerghatta, Bhopal and West Bengal, bringing to an end this centuries-old tradition that inflicted terrible cruelty on thousands of endangered bears (Schaul 2012; Khanna 2018). Wildlife SOS developed relationships with various state agencies in order to enforce the Wildlife Protection Act of India (1972). Sloth bears are protected under Schedule I of this Act and listed as 'vulnerable' by the IUCN. Under Indian law, the possession of sloth bears and use of them for performance is now illegal and punishable with a jail sentence of three to seven years. With the cooperation of the Uttar Pradesh Forest Department, Wildlife SOS established the Agra Bear Rescue Facility, which is now globally the largest rescue centre for rescued sloth bears, housing over 270 rescued bears on about 160 acres allotted to the project by the Uttar Pradesh Government (Schaul 2012). In December 2009, Raju, the last known dancing bear to be rescued from the Kalandar community, was relocated at the Wildlife SOS Sloth Bear Rescue Centre in the Bannerghatta Biological Park. In December 2018, Raju celebrated his ninth year of freedom from captivity (Khanna 2018). However, as Kartick Satyanarayan, CEO of Wildlife SOS, notes, in order 'to protect the sloth bear population, the focus was not only on rescuing the bears but also to help alleviate the Kalandar community by providing them with an alternative livelihood' (Khanna 2018). Wildlife SOS embarked on an intensive process of engaging with the Kalandar community and living with them in over 60 villages. As Sinclair (2016, 2) notes, if the team had approached the Kalandar people that were dancing bears in a judgmental way (eg 'this is wrong', 'you are bad', 'we know better'), it is doubtful that the same level of cooperation and outcome could have been achieved. Once trust was established, the Kalandars agreed to voluntarily hand over their 'illegal' bears and in turn accept from Wildlife SOS skill training and seed funds to develop alternative livelihoods. The skill training provided by Wildlife SOS to the Kalandars involved carpet-weaving, driving, welding, grinding and packaging spices, sewing, jewellery-making, gem cutting and polishing, running tea shops and vending vegetables and goods (Schaul 2012; Kemmerer 2015).

Wildlife SOS, supported by the Ministry of Environment and Forests, the government of India and state forest departments, now has a successful model in place for the rescue and rehabilitation of wildlife. By acting respectfully and non-judgmentally and investing in long-term engagement and collaboration, the Wildlife SOS teams were able to work with the government to end the practice of dancing bears in India (Sinclair 2016). There is further good news in that enrichment activities can have a long-term effect in rehabilitating stereotypic behaviours in rescued bears (Veeraselvam *et al* 2013).

MEDICINE BEARS

Bears are associated with medicine in a number of different contexts. With reference to North American tribes, Hallowell (1926) reports that in most of the Pueblos (communities of Native Americans in the southwestern United States) the bear is the doctor 'par excellence'. He states that the Zuni (a Pueblo tribe associated with the Zuni River) view bears as 'foremost among the medicine animals of the curing society' and bear paws or claws appear in the paraphernalia of shamans or society doctors. In much of Pueblo culture, bears are represented on altars, as stone fetishes, and their images painted on masks. In Europe, the omnivorous diet of the bear gave it in many cultures the attribute of medicine animal, knowing all the plants and foods (Koloslova *et al* 2017). Clark and Slocombe (2009) report that amongst the Southern Tutchone (First Nations people of southern Yukon Territory) 'bear medicine' is used to prevent bears and people from bothering each other. This medicine consists of special Southern Tutchone words to enable safe passage when a bear is encountered on the trail. The Cheyenne (indigenous people of the Great Plains) believe the bear can cure itself if wounded and has greater healing powers than humans (Hallowell 1926). Captive bears (and their body parts) are perhaps most widely linked with traditional Chinese medicine (TCM), an association that we explore further in the following section.

Bear bile has been an important base ingredient in TCM for millennia. The first known record of the use of bear bile for its medicinal properties comes from a Tang Dynasty document that dates to AD 659 (Li 2004). The inclusion of bear bile in *The Compendium of Chinese Materia Medica* (*Bencao Gangmu*), written by the Ming Dynasty doctor Li Shizhen (1518–93), solidified its position in Chinese medicine (Li 2004). Wang and Carey (2014) state that bear bile is considered the 'king' of animal biles, both in ancient times and also in contemporary TCM, and top-grade bear bile has been valued 'more than gold' for its preventative as well as therapeutic qualities (including for liver disease, haemorrhoids, kidney problems, eye problems and even cancer).

Traditionally, bear bile was collected from an entire gallbladder taken from a bear killed in the wild (Li 2004). However, this method of bile extraction failed to provide a steady bile supply to practitioners of TCM, with inevitable supply/demand outcomes; bear bile medicines became both very expensive and increasingly desirable as a luxury commodity. In the late 1970s, however, North Korea succeeded in developing a 'technology' for obtaining bile from live bears. Consequently, bear farming was established (Li 2004) and spread throughout China and Vietnam. Over time, increasing pressure from international conservation and animal welfare groups on the major bile producing countries, South Korea, China and Vietnam, has had some success discouraging this practice (Livingstone and Shepherd 2014), though it remains legal in China (but better regulated) and is still practised to varying degrees of legality elsewhere in southeast Asia.

Moreover, whilst the government of Vietnam made it illegal to extract bear bile in 2006, there is evidence that this simply led to illegal production (Crudge *et al* 2018). Farms began appearing in Lao PDR and Myanmar, where weaker legislation, lax law enforcement, low public awareness of conservation and animal welfare concerns, and limited international scrutiny has allowed the industry to grow unchallenged (Livingstone and Shepherd 2014). In Lao PDR, the number of captive bears increased from 40 in 2008 to 122 in 2012, some of which were being housed at illegally operating breeding facilities. There was also a high mortality rate, with wild bears poached as replacements (Sukanan and Anthony 2019).

According to Li (2004), Chinese officials saw bear farming as a lucrative business and an enterprise that 'served the people's health needs'. With government support there was a mushrooming of bear farms across China and by the mid-1990s China had more than 600 bear farms keeping in excess of 10,000 bears (most of them Asiatic black bears) for daily bile extraction. 'For many years, Chinese officials and farm owners had chosen not to see the vast suffering of animals on these farms' (Li 2004). What they cared about was a steady flow of the 'liquid gold' generated by the confined and poorly kept bears (Fig 8.6). While latex and metal catheters are still used, the only method of bile extraction actually allowed under current regulations in China is to surgically

Figure 8.6. A bear on a farm in China – courtesy of Animals Asia.

create a fistula from the gallbladder to the abdomen. In 2006, the Chinese State Council Information Office said that it was enforcing a 'Technical Code of Practice for Raising Black Bears', which requires 'hygienic, painless practice for gall extraction and makes strict regulations on the techniques and conditions for nursing, exercise and propagation'. However, according to Loeffler *et al* (2009), the Technical Code was not being enforced and many bears were still spending their entire lives in small extraction cages without free access to food or water. As Jill Robinson of Animals Asia (cited by Hance 2015) notes:

> Bears are constantly thirsty and hungry, get little or no veterinary care and essentially are tortured their whole lives. Today ... thousands of moon bears lie in constant pain and anguish in cages that are no bigger than coffins. A number of crude and brutal methods are used to extract their bile – rusting catheters, barbaric full-metal jackets with neck spikes, medicinal pumps and open, infected holes drilled into their bellies. Some bears are put into cages as cubs and never released ... most farmed bears are starved, dehydrated and suffer from multiple diseases and malignant tumours that ultimately kill them.

Bile is drained once or twice a day by inserting a metal tube through the membrane that has grown over the wound. Apart from the mental trauma of being confined in an extremely small space, the bears also suffer a litany of health problems including cancer, infections and blindness (Li, 2004). All the more remarkable that Fang Shuting, the then head of the Chinese Association of Traditional Chinese Medicine, should state that 'the process of extracting bear bile is like turning on a tap: natural, easy and without pain. After they're done, the bears can even play happily outside. I don't think there's anything out of the ordinary! It might even be a very comfortable process!' (Hance 2015).

Hance (2015) states that conditions in Chinese bile farms are alarming, with bears often kept in crush cages (deliberately too small for animals to stand or move much). Conditions are often so unsanitary, and bears so sick, that public health concerns have been raised about consuming farmed bile. If the bears live long enough they can be bile milked for decades. However, they usually stop producing bile after ten or so years, at which point they are killed and their body parts sold.

The Chinese government claimed that bile farming would meet local demand for bile whilst also helping to conserve the country's wild populations of Asiatic black bears (Li 2004). However, wild bears continue to be killed for bile and poached as an illegal source of new stock for farms. Indeed, there is evidence that farming in China has resulted in the perception that bears and bear products are a readily available and acceptable commodity (Loeffler et al 2009). Dutton et al (2011) state that the introduction of farmed bear bile has had little impact on demand for wild bear bile or has in some circumstances increased it. Elsewhere in southeast Asia, Livingstone and Shepherd (2014, 1) state that in Lao PDR there is evidence that bears are still being wild-caught domestically or illegally imported internationally (in violation of national and international law). Moreover, farmed bile has not diminished the demand for wild bile, as the market value has increased dramatically in recent times. They conclude that bear farming in Lao PDR may be increasing the incentive to poach wild bears.

Whilst there is evidence that bear bile does have medicinal qualities (Feng et al 2009), for example ursodeoxycholic acid (UDCA) found in bile helps to dissolve gallstones as well as containing anti-inflammatory and antimicrobial properties (Guarino et al 2013), alternative products are increasingly available. Viable alternatives to bear bile, including synthetic bear bile and others originating from non-threatened animals and plants, have been introduced in recent years (Sha Li et al 2016; Sukanan and Anthony 2019). Despite this, bear bile continues to be in demand, and it is now also used to treat colds, hangovers (and also for getting drunk when mixed with rice wine) and more, though there is no scientific evidence supporting its effectiveness for these ailments. It is also sometimes used as an ingredient in household products like toothpaste, acne treatment, tea and shampoo as a way to expand the market for bear bile beyond traditional medicine (Animals Asia 2015).

In 2017, Vietnam's government promised to close down all its bear farms by 2022, linked to a promise by the country's traditional medicine community to stop prescribing bear bile products by 2020. The number of bears used has dropped from 4500 at its peak to around 800–900 bears in 2018. However, a recent study by Crudge et al (2018) demonstrated that demand for wild bear bile was not satisfied by the widespread availability of farmed bear bile, with consumers willing to pay more for wild-sourced products (with some reports suggesting that wild bear bile is worth up to 12 times more than farmed bear bile). Vietnamese bile producers attribute the falling demand for farmed bear bile to government intervention, shifting consumer trends and concerns over the potency of farmed bile (Roth 2018). The existence of bear bile farms presents considerable challenges to law enforcement in Vietnam (and indeed elsewhere in southeast Asia). For example, when the government outlawed bile extraction in 2005, it required that all captive bears be registered and microchipped. Keeping unregistered bears was made illegal. However, Vietnamese authorities lack the resources and capacity to monitor bear farms using microchip scanners. Overall, Crudge *et al* (2018) conclude that bear bile farming in Vietnam relies on restocking from wild populations, and farmers openly admit to extracting and selling bear bile, in clear violation of national legislation.

There has been some progress in South Korea, where the government completed a sterilisation programme on captive bears in 2017 as part of an effort to phase out farming. China, however, remains the centre of the industry and of the demand for bile products (where it is still legal). Studies are ongoing about the impact of bear farming on wild bear populations. A recent study has been set up by the China State Forestry Agency, the IUCN-SSC Bear Specialist Group and Oxford University with financial support from the Dutch NGO Bears in Mind.

BEAR SANCTUARIES

Whilst significant progress has been made in terms of reducing dancing bears, there is still much work to be done in relation to bile farming. Sadly, it is likely that one way or another, bears will continue to be held in captivity for the foreseeable future, and we will continue to require facilities that provide the best of veterinary care, husbandry and enrichment to give formerly mistreated animals a bear-worthy life.

Captive bear welfare can be greatly affected, positively or negatively, by several important aspects: enclosure size and composition (eg barren concrete enclosure versus forested enclosure with a pond to swim in), feeding and enrichment, group composition and age, health and veterinary care. As Veeraselvam *et al* (2013) indicate, enriched environments can have a positive impact on rescue bear wellbeing, and bears should be housed in an environment that closely resembles their wild habitat. Bears should be stimulated to show their natural bear behaviour, which has a positive effect on their overall wellbeing (Veeraselvam 2013; Grandia *et al* 2001).

The government of Lao PDR has also made a commitment to shut down bear bile farms in the country (Sukanan and Anthony 2019). Free the Bears Fund Inc. (FTB), an international conservationist group, seeks to help eradicate all bear bile farming in Lao PDR by 2020 and has stepped up efforts to establish sanctuaries to house bears rescued from farms. One organisation in particular, Animals Asia, has been at the forefront of the opposition to the bear bile industry for over 20 years. It has set up two large sanctuaries, in China and Vietnam, where it has been able to rescue and rehabilitate more than 600 bears, all rescued from bear bile facilities. There is hope, as Jill Robinson (cited in Hance 2015) notes: '[Rescued bears] ultimately prove to be fun-loving, trusting and forgiving of the species that caused them indescribable pain.'

The mission of Bears in Mind is to protects bears in the wild and help captive bears in need. This Dutch-based NGO has been working on conservation and bear welfare issues since 1993. Its best-known project is the Bear Forest, a bear sanctuary in Rhenen, in the Netherlands. The Bear Forest is a two-hectare semi-natural forested area on the edge of Ouwehand Zoo where rescued dancing bears, circus bears and bears used in the film industry are given the opportunity to enjoy the rest of their days in an enriched environment free from persecution. These bears effectively become ambassadors for wild bears and for those bears still kept under dire circumstances elsewhere. Thirty bears have been brought to the sanctuary over the past 25 years, with ten bears currently still living there (2019).

Most of the current residents of the Bear Forest have come from Eastern Europe, with several of the bears coming from Georgia. Three bears were rescued from a zoo closure just south of the Georgian capital Tbilisi. Unfortunately, their fate would likely be euthanasia if no solution was quickly found, and in April 2007 these three bears were airlifted to the Netherlands. Following a 30-day quarantine period, they were released in the Bear Forest. For the very first time they were able to experience the sensation of natural soil and grass beneath their paws. These three bears have become ambassadors for the many captive bears held under poor conditions elsewhere in Georgia; often in restaurants, monasteries and petrol stations. Local NGO NACRES, together with Bears in Mind, developed a Captive Bear Action Plan in 2007, which was shared with the Ministry of Environmental and Nature Resource Protection of Georgia (MoE). Later updates indicated that the number of bears in captivity in Georgia was increasing, and in 2016 the MoE was again lobbied about the (illegal) captive bear problem, and it was also presented with a plan to establish a bear sanctuary. Discussion is currently (2018–19) ongoing between the Georgian government, NACRES and Bears in Mind to finally work towards a solution for the many mistreated and often illegally kept brown bears in Georgia.

BIBLIOGRAPHY AND REFERENCES

Animals Asia, 2015 *Five bear bile uses it's hard to believe are real* [online], available from: https://www.animalsasia.org/uk/media/news/news-archive/five-bear-bile-uses-it%E2%80%99s-hard-to-believe-are-real.html [26 March 2019]

Brown, G, 1993 *The Great Bear Almanac*, The Lion Press, Sandy, Bedfordshire, UK

Clark, D A, and Slocombe, D S, 2009 Respect for Grizzly Bears: an Aboriginal Approach for Co-existence and Resilience, *Ecology and Society* 14 (1), 42–60

Crudge, B, Nguyen, T, and Cao, T T, 2018 The challenges and conservation implications of bear bile farming in Viet Nam, *Oryx,* 1–8, doi:10.1017/S0030605317001752

Davis, P, 1996 *Museums and the Natural Environment*, Cassell/Leicester University Press, London and New York (Chapter 10, Zoological Gardens and Aquaria, 208–28)

D'Cruze, N, Sarma, U K, Mookerjee, A, Singh, B, Louis, J, Mahapatra, R P, Jaiswal, V P, Roy, T K, Kumari, I, and Menon, V, 2011 Dancing bears in India: a sloth bear status report, *Ursus* 22, 99–105

Dutton, A J, Hepburn C, Macdonald, D W, 2011 A Stated Preference Investigation into the Chinese Demand for Farmed vs. Wild Bear Bile, *PLoS ONE* 6 (7), e21243, doi:10.1371/journal.pone.0021243

Epplett, W C, 2001 *Animal Spectacula of the Roman Empire,* The University of British Columbia, Vancouver, Canada

Feng, Y, Siu, K, Wang, N, Ng, K-M, Tsao, S-W, Nagamatsu, T, and Tong, Y, 2009 Bear bile: dilemma of traditional medicinal use and animal protection, *Journal of Ethnobiology and Ethnomedicine* 5, 2

Guarino, M P L, Cocca, S, Altomare, A, Emerenziani, S, and Cicala, M, 2013 Ursodeoxycholic acid therapy in gallbladder disease, a story not yet completed, *World Journal of Gastroenterology* 19 (31), 5029–34

Hallowell, A, 1926 Bear ceremonialism in the Northern Hemisphere, *American Anthropologist* 28, 1–175

Hance, J, 2015 Is the end of 'house of horror' bear bile factories in sight?, *The Guardian,* available from: https://www.theguardian.com/environment/radical-conservation/2015/apr/09/bear-bile-china-synthetic-alternative [25 March 2019]

Hugo, V, 1869 *L'homme qui rit,* Éditions Pocket, ParisKemmerer, L, 2015 Chapter 11: Dirty Dancing – Caring for Sloth Bears in India, in *Bear Necessities: Rescue, Rehabilitation, Sanctuary, and Advocacy* (ed L Kemmerer), Brill, UK, 116–27

Khanna, B, 2018 India's last dancing bear celebrates 9 years of freedom, *Deccan Herald*, 18 December 18, available from: https://www.deccanherald.com/city/raju-india-s-last-dancing-bear-708711.html [26 March 2019]

Kisling, V N, 2001 *Zoo and aquarium history: Ancient animal collections to zoological gardens,* CRC Press, Taylor and Francis Group, London

Kolosova, V, Svanberg, I, Kalle, R *et al,* 2017 The bear in Eurasian plant names: motivations and models, *Journal of Ethnobiology and Ethnomedicine* 13, 14, https://doi.org/10.1186/s13002-016-0132-9

Li, P J, 2014 China's bear farming and long-term solutions, *Journal of Applied Animal Welfare Science* 7, 71–81

Li, Sha, Hor, Yue Tan, Wang, Ning, Hong, Ming, Li, Lei, Cheung, Fan and Feng, Yibin, 2016 *Substitutes for Bear Bile for the Treatment of Liver Diseases: Research Progress and Future Perspective,* School of Chinese Medicine, Li Ka Shing Faculty of Medicine, The University of Hong Kong, Pokfulam, Hong Kong

Livingstone, E and Shepherd, C R, 2016 Bear farms in Lao PDR expand illegally and fail to conserve wild bears, *Oryx* 50, 176–84

Loeffler, I K, Robinson, J, and Cochrane, G, 2009 Compromised health and welfare of bears farmed for bile in China, *Animal Welfare* 18: 225–35

NACRES, 2017 *Captive Bears in Georgia, Bejan Lortkipanidze,* unpublished (internal) report available from the Bears in Mind office, Rhenen, the Netherlands

Palmer, A, 2016 *How Bears Are Trained for the Circus* [online], available from: https://www.peta.org/blog/bears-trained-circus/ [26 March 2019]

Radhakrishna, M, 2007 Civil Society's Uncivil Acts: Dancing Bear and Starving Kalandar, *Economic and Political Weekly* 42 (42), 4222–6

Roth, A, 2018 As Bear Bile Farms Close, Captive Animals at Risk, *National Geographic* [online], available from: https://www.nationalgeographic.com/animals/2018/07/bile-bears-killed-vietnam/ [26 March 2019

Schaul, J, 2012 Wildlife SOS India Nearly Extinguishes a 400-Year-Old Practice of Dancing Bears, *National Geographic,* October [online], available from: https://blog.nationalgeographic.org/2012/10/11/wildlife-sos-india-nearly-extinguishes-a-400-year-old-practice-of-dancing-bears/ [26 March 2019]

Serra, I, 2013 On Men and Bears: A Forgotten Migration in Nineteenth-Century Italy, *History Workshop Journal,* 76 (1), 57–84

Sinclair, M, 2016 *Internationalization of animal welfare standards. Encyclopaedia of food and agricultural ethics,* Springer, New York City, USA

Van Dijk, J, 1998 *Project Proposal Bulgaria, dancing bear problem,* unpublished (internal) information available from the Bears in Mind office, Rhenen, the Netherlands

Veeraselvam, M, Sridhar, R, Jayathangaraj, M G, and Perumal, P, 2013 Behavioural study of captive sloth bears using environmental enrichment, *International Journal of Zoology* https://doi.org/10.1155/2013/526905

Wang, D Q, and Carey, M C, 2014 Therapeutic uses of animal biles in traditional Chinese medicine: an ethnopharmacological, biophysical chemical and medicinal review, *World Journal of Gastroenterology* 20 (29), 9952–75

9

The Bear in the Museum

Peter Davis

One of my earliest childhood memories was of a school visit to Towneley Hall Museum and Art Gallery in my home town of Burnley. Before the visit, rumours had been spreading amongst my classmates of the terror that would be felt when we came face-to-face with 'the bear'. However, I rather liked him, and it is good to know that this Himalayan black bear is still there, standing at the top of the stairs, grasping a tree branch and threatening any visitor daring to enter his domain. In his original condition when arriving at Towneley he would have been less worrisome, having been sent around 1908 from Kashmir as a rug by a native of Burnley, William Theodore Taylor. The bear, mounted in his current menacing position in 1920, first appeared in the Towneley Hall exhibition catalogue in 1928. According to curator Mike Townend (4 April 2018, *pers comm*), 'He has been the highlight, as well as the terrifying part, of many a child's visit and continues to be so.' Websites now refer to him as 'Towneley's famous bear' and he acquired the name 'Bill' some 15 years ago for reasons unknown.

My next memorable bear encounter was at Sheffield Museum, where as a junior curator one of my tasks was to carve new wooden claws for the polar bear that stood on open display in the entrance hall; for some reason visitors felt fake bear claws were ideal mementoes of their visit to Weston Park. Despite its poor condition – and threatening gaze – the Sheffield public loved this bear and there was an outcry from local people when it was removed from display in the 1980s. Although a replacement polar bear was found and is also valued by visitors, Sheffield folk still remember the original specimen – now exhibited at Eureka in Halifax.

These two examples demonstrate that visitors to museums – especially local repeat visitors – clearly form an affinity with bears in museums. These mounted bears fascinate us, carrying the significance of their species and the environments they once inhabited. It is interesting that – rather like bears in zoos – they frequently receive familial names, a feature that Swinney (2011) terms 'rampant anthropomorphism'. By being attributed with names they go beyond being a scientific exhibit, they become more than *Selenarctos thibetanus* or *Ursus maritimus*, these animals acquire new meanings whilst retaining elements shown in life. As Marvin (2006, 164) – referring to polar bear taxidermy exhibits – notes, 'What we have are the last traces of the animal and they still have power.' However, Ryan (1998, 117) suggests mounted animals demonstrate authenticity and docility; in other words that despite their intrinsic power we can approach them safely. That feature, held only by bears in museums, explains why they are so significant.

Live Bears In Museums

In the past the distinctions between zoological gardens, museums and botanical gardens were blurred, and some museums accommodated live bears to attract visitors. The gardens of the Yorkshire Museum in York were created in 1830 for the Yorkshire Philosophical Society (YPS) by the landscape architect Sir John Murray Naysmith (1803–76). In 1825, the society appointed the geologist John Phillips (1800–74), the nephew of pioneering geological cartographer William Smith (1769–1839), as the first Keeper of the museum. This position effectively launched his career, and in helping to found the British Association for the Advancement of Science, he organised its inaugural meeting hosted by the YPS in York in 1831. An outstanding figure in geology, Phillips was elected Fellow of the Royal Society in 1834; he held academic posts at Kings College London, Dublin and Oxford. In York, where he remained as Honorary Curator until 1844, Phillips – in addition to his curatorial duties – took responsibility for Naysmith's botanical garden. In 1830, following a proposal by a group of society members, a small menagerie was installed in the garden, the exhibits including a golden eagle, several monkeys and a bear. In 1831, the bear escaped from its cage and chased Phillips and William Vernon Harcourt (1789–1871), first President of the YPS, into an outbuilding. Following this misdemeanour, it was offered to the Zoological Society of London, which agreed to take the bear. Transport, however, was an issue, but the zoo's resourceful Secretary offered an interesting suggestion:

Zool. Soc. London, Dec. 26th 1831

Sirs,

We shall feel much pleased in taking your bear on the terms proposed in your letter of 21st.

The best mode I can conceive of forwarding him to us is by one of the York coaches, you booking him on as an outside Passenger, and promising the Guard a recompense on his delivering him safe in London. Be so good as to send us a line to inform us of the Coach by which the animal is to travel and the place and probable time of his arrival in town. You will also oblige me by stating to whom we shall pay the price of the animal.

I hope I shall have the opportunity of showing you our Garden and your old friend as a happy occupier of them.

(quoted in Pyrah 1988, 47)

Hence the bear travelled as a pillion passenger from York to London, accompanied by Henry Baines, an employee of the YPS. Sarah King (May 2018, *pers comm*) notes that Baines 'worked for the YPS for another 20 years or so afterwards, so he must have got over it'. The responses of the bear's fellow passengers are not known. I suggest this is perhaps one of the more unusual stories of a bear in the museum context.

The blurred boundaries between zoos, museums and botanical gardens illustrated by this example have largely disappeared, and live bears are now the prerogative of zoological gardens. However, captive bears can be seen outside the confines of zoos, for example in Bern in Switzerland (the bear being the city's heraldic emblem) where they have been exhibited since 1513. A new and spacious bear park was created in 2009 on the banks of the River Aare, replacing the old bear pit. Interestingly, the latter is now scheduled as a cultural monument of national significance, another heritage legacy from human engagement with these animals.

CELEBRITY BEARS

The bears on show at Towneley and Sheffield Museums demonstrate that many bear specimens on display or held in museums' research collections have been regarded as 'celebrities', acquiring personalities in their own right or by association. As Alberti (2011, 1), referring to mounted animals generally, recalls, 'Their fame in life and their iconic status in death defy taxonomy.' Creating 'animal biographies' – tracing the history of specimens before and after death – enables us to chart the shifting cultural and scientific meanings of these animals, and to contemplate how people have reacted emotionally to them. Biographies of animals often demonstrate a journey from nature to culture, from life in the wild to an 'afterlife' in human society. For the majority of people, encounters with bears are most likely to occur not in the wild but within the confines of a zoo or a museum – the ways in which bears are exhibited there impact on our understanding and emotional responses, albeit influenced by the knowledge and attitudes that the viewer brings to the encounter. Many bears in museums have fascinating biographies and afterlives, including the following.

Christopher Robin Milne, A A Milne's son, appears as Christopher Robin in the *Winnie-the-Pooh* tales. His bear was named after Winnie, a black bear that Christopher enjoyed visiting in London Zoo. Winnie had been a celebrity at London Zoo in the 1920s, a star attraction for visitors and known for her friendliness; she died in 1934. However, her skull was re-discovered and identified during research on the skeletal collections of the Hunterian Museum of the Royal College of Surgeons in London; hence, the skull of the bear that inspired the *Winnie-the-Pooh* books is now on public display there. Winnie was a celebrity and today her skull retains that status.

The panda *Ailuropoda melanoleuca* is the icon of the World Wide Fund for Nature (WWF) because of its rarity and endangered status. It was believed once to be a member of the raccoon family but DNA analyses have revealed it is indeed a true bear (O'Brien *et al* 1985). Several pandas have achieved cult status – and almost all specimens in zoos have been given familial names – but arguably still the best known in the UK is Chi-Chi. Caught in May 1955 in Baoxing, Sichuan, she travelled twice via Beijing to Moscow, and then to Berlin, Frankfurt and Copenhagen Zoos before she arrived at London Zoo on 5 September 1958, where she lived until her death in 1972. Nicholls (2011) has described the life and afterlife of Chi-Chi in detail, including the account of the international team involved in the post-mortem and the debates about the taxonomic status of the species. Following the post-mortem, what remained of Chi-Chi was given to the Natural History Museum, London, where she was prepared as a mounted specimen by senior taxidermist Roy Hale and placed in a habitat diorama where today she still attracts the attention of visitors. However, she is much more than an exhibit, having – in life and death – aided our understanding of the species and altered public perceptions of this endangered animal. The endearing image of pandas – and how this is captured in the WWF logo – has had a marked effect on our environmental consciousness. Created by naturalist and artist Peter Scott, we can be almost certain the original logo was modelled on Chi-Chi. As Nicholls (2011, 183) notes, 'It is her image that has inspired millions to reflect on humankind's position among other species and our profound impact upon them.'

A rather gentle-looking polar bear displayed in Leicester Museum was adopted as an emblem by the Leicester confectioner that produced the 'Glacier Mint', a sweet developed by Eric Fox, one of the original founders of the company. From 1922, the mints have been sold with the 'Peppy the polar bear' icon, typically depicted as though standing on all fours on one of the clear, ice-like mints. Collected in Greenland, the mounted bear was originally purchased by Fox in the 1920s from the taxidermy studio of Rowland Ward. Fox displayed the bear in the original factory and, to gain more publicity, it was taken to carnivals and even to football matches. Falling out of favour in the 1960s and forgotten, Peppy was re-discovered in the factory in 2003 and subsequently acquired by Leicester Museum, being restored over a period of six years. This

FIGURE 9.1. KNUT ON DISPLAY IN THE NATURAL HISTORY MUSEUM, BERLIN. PHOTOGRAPH BY CAROLA RADKE, AND REPRODUCED COURTESY OF THE MUSEUM FÜR NATURKUNDE, BERLIN.

bear has since regained its celebrity status on public display and in the media, and Leicester Museum continues to search for other bears known to have been used by the Fox company for advertising purposes.

Unlike Peppy, not all polar bears gain positive publicity. In 2011, the death of Knut, one of the world's most famous polar bears, reopened the ethical debate on humankind's relationship with, and attitudes to, wild animals, and especially the place of polar bears in captivity. Knut was born in Berlin Zoo in December 2006; rejected by his mother, he was hand-reared. His abandonment, appealing looks and close relationship with his keeper turned him into a media star and an environmental advocate, acting as a mascot for the German government's campaign against climate change. Knut died aged four in 2011, and a bronze statue of him was placed on display in the zoo in 2012. The decision by the Berlin Natural History Museum to prepare Knut for display raised controversy when a manikin to take his fur was revealed in 2013. Evidently this bear, in life, had aroused the sympathy of the zoo's visitors and the media in general, so the idea of a 'stuffed' Knut appalled many. However, the museum dismissed criticism of the decision to display Knut, making the case that it gave an opportunity for visitors to the city to continue to see him. In 2013, Knut became Berlin's climate ambassador at the Naturalis Biodiversity Centre in Leyden, the Netherlands, where he delighted more than 150,000 visitors. In Berlin, Knut has been part of the exhibition 'Masterpieces of Taxidermy' since July 2014 and retains his appeal (Fig 9.1). Evidently, the decision taken by the museum has been vindicated.

BEARS WITH ATTITUDE

Bill, the Towneley Hall bear (Fig 9.2) stands upright behind glass, claws digging into an upright tree branch. His mouth is wide open, demonstrating perfect teeth, a warning not to approach too close. He may not be the largest of bears – on average, this species, the Asian black bear, measures from 56 to 65in. nose to tail and weighs from 200 to 265lb – but he still spells danger. More threatening is the brown bear kept in the Gun Room at Manderston Hall near Duns in the Scottish Borders. According to the FENSCORE database (fenscore.natsca.org) it is 'Reputed to be the tallest mounted bear in Britain'; this specimen (Fig 9.3) also has a threatening upright stance and dwarfs its owner, Lord Palmer. This bear was shot in Russia by his relative, Sir James Miller (1863–1906). Miller also brought home a live brown bear to Manderston and it too has been mounted in this upright position. At the Valley Center History Museum in California there is a taxidermy mount of a grizzly bear shot in the area that was said to weigh more than 2200lb; on display it stands nearly 8ft tall, an enormous specimen.[1] In Sheffield, the polar bear now on display features as the frontispiece in *Nanoq: flat out and bluesome* (Snaebjörnsdóttir and Wilson 2006) – again in an upright stance – although seemingly searching for seals and not showing any threat behaviour. 'Snowball', a polar bear on display in Springfield Science Museum, Massachusetts, featured at Forest Park Zoo until her death in 1979. According to the museum's website

[1]   This bear, originally on display at the San Diego Natural History Museum (founded 1874) and subsequently acquired by Valley Center in 2002, delivers a salutary message about the impacts of hunting and the decline of large carnivores in the state. The grizzly bear was designated the official state animal in 1953 and still adorns the state flag and seal; however, the last known record of a California grizzly was the animal shot and killed in Fresno County in 1922. A wild grizzly bear was spotted several times in Sequoia National Park in 1923 but then never seen again. It is ironic that California's official animal was declared extinct in the state by 1924, the only evidence of its past existence being museum specimens.

FIGURE 9.2. 'BILL' THE TOWNELEY HALL BEAR. PHOTOGRAPH BY JON THOMPSON, REPRODUCED WITH PERMISSION OF TOWNELEY HALL MUSEUM, BURNLEY.

FIGURE 9.3. REPUTED TO BE THE TALLEST MOUNTED BEAR IN BRITAIN, THIS BROWN BEAR CAN BE SEEN AT MANDERSTON HOUSE, DUNS, SCOTLAND. REPRODUCED COURTESY OF THE LORD PALMER AND THE MANDERSTON ESTATE.

the bear's standing pose, mounted by taxidermist Glen Ives, 'is a natural position polar bears assume when they are on ice floes searching for seals'. This positive attitude to displaying this large carnivore is commendable; sadly, it is in contrast to other preparations, notably the Dover Museum polar bear, donated by a relative of the explorer and doctor, Reginald Koettlitz, who had brought it back from the Arctic in 1897. Fitted with a lamp holder in its paw, it stood in the Dover surgery of the Koettlitz family from 1890 to 1960; the lamp holder has been removed, but this bear continues to act as a reminder of humankind's arrogance and lack of respect for nature. In Warwick the brown bear on display – again in an upright stance – inherited from the Warwick Natural History and Archaeological Society in 1932 is celebrated because its pose reflects the 'Bear and Ragged Staff' of the county symbol; in heraldry the bear represents courage.

The upright stance of many bears in museums is a legacy of their own history as trophy specimens. A quarter of the taxidermy polar bears pictured in *Nanoq* strike the same pose and five specimens reveal their teeth and claws; of the bears on all fours, nine also adopt a threatening gaze – in total 43 per cent suggest 'danger' to visitors. Bears are impressive animals due to their size, but are only dangerous to irresponsible or unlucky humans, so we have to question why so many have been prepared in this fashion. Marvin (2011, 203) considers the relationship between animals and hunters, and suggests the afterlives of trophy animals can be interpreted 'not as a celebration of how the animal lived; rather … as a celebration of the process of how the hunter was able to bring about its death'. In effect, the taxidermy animal is linked to the autobiography of the hunter or collector rather than the biography of the animal itself. When animals such as bears are transferred from the private homes of hunters to the public domain in a museum, they retain part of that autobiography. These bears in museums – many acquired from private individuals – are still tainted by the kudos acquired by the hunters who faced them, killed them and had them prepared in a fashion that suggests their own courage. Marvin (2011, 216) argues that in the move from private collection to the museum a specimen 'ceases to be a personal trophy … rather it becomes an impersonal representative of the species'. However, as we have seen, bears in museums counter this 'impersonal representative' argument; they have a knack of acquiring new identities and new personas, their appeal to the visiting public leading to the adoption of familial names and a sense of public ownership.

The postures and attitudes adopted by 'trophy bears' are in marked contrast to bears placed within a re-creation of their natural habitat in carefully constructed dioramas. These efforts to reveal their true nature can be seen in many of the world's large museums; painted backdrops provide landscapes that give a vivid impression of place, modelled vegetation and rocks create an illusion of reality and the bears themselves are mounted in varied postures – digging, scratching, fishing and doing what bears do in the wild. An excellent example of such a diorama exists in the natural history museum in Milan, Italy (Fig 9.4). Such attempts to re-create a habitat, a time and an event – effectively trying to return bears back to the wild – rely on the knowledge of the ecologists who have studied bears in their environment, but also the skill of the artist and the taxidermist in creating this illusion.

MUSEUM BEARS AND CONSERVATION MESSAGES

Large scale dioramas – such as that above – were created first in American museums and continue to provide an enduring and accurate picture of the natural world as it was in the early 20th century. The technique of placing animals within a 'natural' setting was readily adopted in Euro-

Figure 9.4. A diorama of brown bears at the McNeil River Reserve in Alaska, displayed at the Natural History Museum, Milan. Photograph by Giorgio Bardelli and Reproduced Courtesy of Museo Di Storia Naturale Di Milano/Giorgio Bardelli.

pean countries, notably in Sweden, where the Biological Museum in Uppsala was specifically designed for a series of habitat dioramas, and in Stockholm, where the concept of the large scale open diorama was pioneered by Gustaff Kolthoff as early as 1880 (Wonders 1990). Other European museums, such as the natural history museum in Bern, Switzerland, created outstanding examples that take the art to its limit. The museologist A E Parr observed a distinct difference between the 'reality' of European dioramas and a 'lighter spirit of sentimental realism' which characterised the North American versions. 'He believed that when nature is interpreted so as to inspire the viewers' imagination, it possesses a special value that is destroyed by absolute verisimilitude. In North America, where a sentimental identification with the wilderness landscape and a tendency towards nature worship has strong historical traditions, it is not surprising that a romantic attitude toward nature prevails in the habitat dioramas' (Wonders 1990). This link between wilderness, sentiment, the conservation movement and the development of the diorama is an important one; museums are seen to be reacting positively to new concerns closely allied to the educational aims of museums and responding to growing environmental concerns. Even as early as 1915, O C Farrington recognised that (in North America) there had been a revitalisation of natural history museums, the growing recognition of the value of 'nature study', and the 'realisation of how rapidly many of the forms of nature are disappearing' (Farrington 1915). In dioramas, museum visitors had the opportunity to meet a polar bear in an Arctic landscape or witness brown bears capturing salmon. It was the spiritual and emotional response to the diorama that made it such a dramatic tool in display. As Coleman (1939) observed, 'Habitat groups and the beginning of ecological study reflected the desire of the layman and scientist alike to accept nature whole. Appreciation of nature now became the theme. Conservation was taking the place of use as the ultimate motive.'

Surviving dioramas are now, in many cases, a glimpse of the past, as species and habitats have indeed been lost. In one sense this makes dioramas an important historical source (and still an inspiration and perhaps even a warning), but in another sense they are a fabrication. Should the foreground of a Rocky Mountain diorama contain human footprints, discarded packaging or rusting Coke cans? Curators are taking more innovative steps to put across messages about the threats to biodiversity when interpreting dioramas. Bern Museum has re-written all the labels associated with its dioramas to draw attention to the plight of threatened habitats and the declining range of the species exhibited. Chicago's Field Museum dioramas are now 'set ... amid the latest in interactive, multimedia technology to convey the exhibit's central message – the interconnectedness of life ... the exhibit examines the impact of development and human activity, particularly human overpopulation that threatens the natural world' (Anon 1993). Bears displayed in museums have real potential to deliver such conservation messages.

To change our attitudes to bears, aid public understanding and promote conservation of bear habitats, museums need to adopt new interpretive techniques and capitalise on new technologies and social media. The range of options that new technologies bring to inform the public of issues related to bear ecology and behaviour, and the importance of bears as top predators and their significance in supporting biodiversity, has never been greater. However, other techniques, especially the use of art and art installations, have become one of the methods utilised by museums to explore conservation issues, particularly climate change. For example, the artwork *Hermaphrodite Polar Bear* by Gary Hume, exhibited at the Walker Art Gallery in Liverpool, at first sight has a comic edge, but its real message is to expose the tragic fate of polar bears, increasingly influenced by chemicals drifting to the Arctic through wind and ocean currents. These accumulate in the tissues of polar bears, causing severe hormonal disruptions in adults, resulting in foetal deformities and an inability to reproduce. Another good example is the polar bear carved by ice sculptor Mark Coreth from a ten-ton block of ice, displayed in Piccadilly Gardens in Manchester on 31 March 2011. Over the next few days the ice bear melted, reflecting the impact of global warming on the Arctic ice and the implications for polar bears and other marine life. The sculpture celebrated the launch of the Manchester Museum's Living Worlds gallery that also emphasises the connections between all living things, asking hard-hitting questions about the choices humankind can take with respect to nature and the environment.

THE BEAR BONES

The skull of the 'Banwell Bear' – excavated from Banwell Cave by William Beard in the 1820s – is on display in the Foundation Stones gallery in the Museum of Somerset, Taunton, and is part of the collection of Somerset Archaeological and Natural History Society. Ice age animal remains are found frequently in the caves of the Mendip Hills, animal carcasses having been washed into the caves by storm water; their bones inform us of the fauna that existed during that period of Somerset's history. This cave bear (*Ursus speleaus*) was alive during the Pleistocene period, some 80,000 years ago; it would have stood some 2.5m tall and been a formidable predator.

This specimen is just one example of the rich collections of bear material that are held in museums in the UK – both fossil material and that of recent bear species. Fossil material is especially well represented; cave bear and brown bear, alongside hyaena, bison, reindeer, wolf and fox, are found in many museums such as the National Museum of Wales, which holds specimens from Coygan Cave (Carmarthen) and Paviland Cave (Gower, Glamorgan). Fossils from well-known caves such as Kent's Cavern (near Torquay) and Cresswell Crags (near Worksop) have been widely scattered in UK museums. Sheffield Museum, for example, has extensive fossil bear material from Cresswell Crags and limestone areas of the Peak District (Windy Knoll and Hartle Dale), including teeth, claws and limb bones of cave bear and brown bear. The limestone caves of the Yorkshire Dales have provided even small local museums with fossil bear material – the Craven Museum in Skipton boasts 'the finest collection of bear pelvic bones in the country' while the Upper Wharfedale Folk Museum in Grassington also displays brown bear skeletal material from the same source, the cave system of Elbolton Pot.

More recent specimens – especially skeletal material – are also extensive in regional museums in the UK. Analysis of data from a very small sample of museums – Bristol, Leeds, Glasgow's Hunterian Museum, Sheffield, Sunderland and the Great North Museum: Hancock, Newcastle – indicates the wide range of specimens available for research, education and display. Even in such a restricted number of collections (six) it is perhaps surprising that altogether some 118 bear specimens have been catalogued and it is likely that other material not yet digitised exists. Mounted animals include sun bear (*Ursus malayanus*) (two specimens), brown bear (*Ursus arctos*) (five), polar bear (*Ursus maritimus*) (four), American black bear (*Ursus americanus*) (two), Himalayan black bear (*Ursus thibetanus*) (two) and one unidentified animal. Complete articulated skeletons are rare, but the Hunterian Museum in Glasgow has complete skeletons of brown bear and sun bear (*Helarctos malayanus*). However, skulls of bears are especially well represented, with polar bear (19 specimens) being most common; others include sloth bear (*Melursus ursinus*) (11), Asian (Himalayan) black bear (four), brown bear (five), American black bear (three), sun bear (two), panda (*Ailuropoda melanoleuca*) (one) and unidentified specimens (25). The remaining items include trophy heads, teeth, vertebrae, limb bones and partial skeletons of these bears, many of which remain unidentified. The Hunterian is unusual in also holding wet-preserved bear material. Together these specimens are a remarkable resource, as even in this limited group of provincial museums the range of bear material is remarkable and all of the world's eight species are represented.

Bears – or parts of bears – travel on a rite of passage when they enter the museum through the process of accessioning. They are numbered, documented, photographed and digitised, and through these processes assume a new role or 'afterlife'. They have become cultural objects and can fulfil a variety of roles in education and research, while retaining much of the power and fascination the bear had in life. The curator of these specimens now has a significant and demanding role – and a moral obligation – to interpret these bears in a dignified fashion, providing a narrative that recognises their magnificence as top predators. Multiple narratives are possible, including bear distribution, taxonomy, ecology, behaviour, conservation and bear-human interactions – the choice of narrative lies with curators and educators – so how do they wish to portray bears? As Swinney (2011, 230) writes, 'It is through the stories that we tell about these animals that they spring into afterlife.'

ACKNOWLEDGMENTS

I am grateful to Alistair McLean (Sheffield Museums), Isla Gladstone (Bristol Museum), Bryan Morgan (Craven Museum), Maggie Reilly (Hunterian Museum, Glasgow), Rebecca Machin (Leeds Museum) and Stephen Kelly (Tyne and Wear Museums) for information about bear specimens in their collections. Sarah King (The Yorkshire Museum) directed me to information on John Phillips' encounter with the bear and Mike Townend provided background to the Towneley Hall bear. Lord Palmer and his secretary, Ann Turnbull, kindly provided information and images of the bears at Manderston House, Duns.

BIBLIOGRAPHY AND REFERENCES

Alberti, S J M M (ed) 2011 *The Afterlives of Animals*, University of Virginia Press, Charlottesville and London

Anon, 1993 Messages from the wilderness, *Museum News* 72 (1), 19

Coleman, L V, 1939 *The Museum in America: A critical study*, 3 vols, American Association of Museums, Washington DC

Farrington, O C, 1915 The Rise of Natural History Museums, *Science*, 13 August 1915, 206

Marvin, G, 2006 Perpetuating Polar Bears: the Cultural Life of Dead Animals, in *Nanoq: flat out and bluesome. A Cultural Life of Polar Bears* (eds Snaebjörnsdóttir and Wilson), Black Dog Publishing, London, 157–65

———, 2011 Enlivened through Memory: Hunters and Hunting Trophies, in *The Afterlives of Animals*, (ed S J M M Alberti), University of Virginia Press, Charlottesville and London, 202–18

Nicholls, H, 2011 The Afterlife of Chi-Chi, in *The Afterlives of Animals* (ed S J M M Alberti), University of Virginia Press, Charlottesville and London, 169–85

O'Brien, S J, Nash, W G, Wildt, D E, Bush, M E, and Benveniste, R E, 1985 A molecular solution to the riddle of the giant panda's phylogeny, *Nature* 317, 140–4

Pyrah, B J, 1988 *The history of the Yorkshire Museum and its geological collections*, William Sessions, York

Ryan, J, 1998 *Picturing Empire: Photography and the Visualisation of the British Empire*, Reaktion Books, London

Snaebjörnsdóttir, B, and Wilson, M, 2006 *Nanoq: flat out and bluesome. A Cultural Life of Polar Bears*, Black Dog Publishing, London

Swinney, G N, 2011 An Afterword on Afterlife, in *The Afterlives of Animals* (ed S J M M Alberti), University of Virginia Press, Charlottesville and London

Wonders, K, 1990 The illusory art of background painting in habitat dioramas, *Curator* 33 (2), 90–118

10

Museum Polar Bears and Climate Change*

Henry McGhie

Polar bears have been around for a long time although, as species go, not too long. A fossil jawbone from Svalbard, with DNA well-preserved in the frigid climate, was used to show that the species diverged from the brown bear just 150,000 years ago. Chemical analysis of the fossil, which was 110–130,000 years old, showed that the bear had a marine, carnivorous diet, as in today's polar bears (Lindqvist 2010). During the great ice ages polar bears occurred far to the south of their present range: there is a magnificent mounted skeleton of a polar bear in Stavanger Museum of Archaeology, discovered beneath the floor of a house in southwest Norway in 1976 (Blystad *et al* 1983). The skeleton dates from the late Pleistocene, 12,400 years ago, when polar bears were not quite so polar as they are now (north polar, arctic or ice bear may be more appropriate names anyway); it was found in a well-preserved state, with seal bones in its stomach. Today, polar bears live around much of the Arctic, in 19 subpopulations (although there is apparently a lot of exchange of animals between areas) (eg Obbard *et al* 2010).

Development of an Icon

Polar bears have been closely associated with the Arctic throughout modern history and make a number of appearances in Western art (see Donald 2010). They feature in many images relating to Britain's conquest of the Arctic and in search of the Northwest Passage. Notable among these is Richard Westall's (c. 1806) rather ludicrous image[1] of a young Horatio Nelson beating off a polar bear with the butt end of his musket, recalling an incident in Svalbard: the bear looks more terrified than terrifying. Edwin Landseer's *Man Proposes, God Disposes*[2] (exhibited in 1864) shows two furtive polar bears – one reviewer at the time likened them to 'monster ferrets' – atop the remains of a wrecked ship, or possibly some kind of shelter or grave. One gnaws on a human rib while the other tears at a piece of red cloth atop a cairn. Landseer uses the polar bear within his Arctic sublime, a nature red in tooth and claw that challenged British imperialist confidence, and drew on his rather bleak take on a Darwinian struggle for existence (Donald 2007, 94–100). Perhaps he also sought to assuage the forlorn Franklin expedition's members against charges of cannibalism that were widely reported and sensationally denied (see Høvik 2013, 118). Briton

---

* This chapter is dedicated to the memory and inspiration of the late Stephen Kellert.

[1] The Westall image can be seen at: https://www.google.com/search?q=nelson+and+the+bear&source=lnms&tbm=isch&sa=X&ved=0ahUKEwjs867fsM3iAhXxyYUKHRqGD6sQ_AUIESgC&biw=1536&bih=747#imgrc=Mw2rQfys3366nM

[2] Landseer's *Man Proposes, God Disposes* is available from Wikimedia commons, https://en.wikipedia.org/wiki/Man_Proposes,_God_Disposes#/media/File:Manproposesgoddisposes.jpg

Riviere's *Beyond Man's Footsteps* (1894) presents a different image, of a lone polar bear surveying its icy home, with more than passing similarity to *Monarch of the Glen* (or the opening credits of Disney's *Lion King*). The English artist John Macallan Swan, known especially for imaginative images of animals, painted many sensitive pictures incorporating polar bears, going about their lives freely and without human influence, based on close observation of animals at Regent's Park Zoo, London. *We Were the First that Ever Saw* (c. 1900) shows an apparent mother and two young bears swimming freely among icebergs, similar to another painting, *Adrift* (c. 1905, see Fig 10.1). Another painting, *The Abandoned Boat* (undated), has much in common with Landseer's painting described above: a group of five polar bears climb from icy water into an abandoned boat, although these appear to be more curious than ravening.

FIGURE 10.1. *ADRIFT* BY JOHN MACALLAN SWAN, © ABERDEEN CITY COUNCIL (ART GALLERY & MUSEUMS COLLECTIONS).

The popular image of the polar bear was transformed through the 20th century in Canada, the US and the UK. Originally often portrayed as a powerful, vicious and dangerous creature, the image of the powerful polar bear was continued in the 20th century in Disney's *White Wilderness* and, later still, the BBC's *Frozen Planet* (2011), replete with scenes of nature red in tooth and claw, as polar bears and other large predators attack their prey, often shown in slow motion for dramatic effect, or set to a classical music soundtrack somehow playing in the Arctic wilderness. Through the 1950s–80s, high levels of sport hunting of polar bears became a growing concern, with an estimated 5–10,000 bears being killed annually (Stirling 1988, 188; Archibald 2015, 272).

At the same time, an environmental ethic became increasingly prevalent in Western society, as did a general acceptance of the key role that large predators play in maintaining healthy ecosystems. Trophy hunting ended with the conservation reassessment of 'Threatened' status for polar bears in 2008. These shifts in perception were accompanied by, or enabled by, a change in the dominant imagery of polar bears, notably in magazines such as *National Geographic*. The popular image of the polar bear became that of a vulnerable, sensitive, threatened animal in need of human care. Typically, close-up photo opportunities presented by darted polar bears were used to full advantage. The visual language of helicopters, men with rifles and subdued animals surrounded by people (again usually men) was common to sport hunting and to biological investigations of the bears, reinforcing the polar bear's image as subdued by people, and either weak, threatened or overcome.

POLAR BEARS AND CLIMATE CHANGE

The Arctic has emerged as one of the regions most intensely impacted by climate change, with temperature increases far in excess of the global average increase. Sea ice is reduced with rising temperatures; Arctic sea ice declined at a linear rate of 14 per cent per decade from 1979 through 2011 (Stroeve *et al* 2012) and continues to decline (eg NOAA 2017). Polar bears are strongly identified with Arctic climate change, with a well-understood narrative linking their lives to their habitat: annual sea ice. No ice, no bears. Changes in sea ice are known to alter polar bear abundance, behaviour, distribution, productivity, fasting behaviour and body condition (see Derocher *et al* 2013, Wiig *et al* 2015 for references; Atwood *et al* 2016; Ware *et al* 2017), so continued climate warming will increase future uncertainty and pose severe risks to the welfare of polar bear subpopulations (Wiig *et al* 2015).

The link between polar bears, Arctic sea ice and climate change is so strong that the official International Union for the Conservation of Nature Red List Assessment was based solely on projected declines of sea ice: 'all polar bears depend on sea ice for fundamental aspects of their life history, and loss of sea ice is the primary long-term threat to the species.' The polar bear was assessed as 'Vulnerable' to extinction, based on an assessment of the loss of sea-ice habitat alone. Polar bears were predicted to be very likely (71 per cent probability) to face a reduction of 30 per cent in global population size within three generations (30–50 years) from 2015, but a small (7%) likelihood of a larger population decline (of more than 50 per cent). The assessors acknowledged that other factors could also impact numbers, for example declines of prey, hunting or other human-bear conflict (see Wiig *et al* 2015).

DEVELOPMENT OF A [CLIMATE] ICON

Awareness of the threat posed to polar bears by climate change rose steadily, so the polar bear became the 'poster child' of climate change and 'the most political of all animals': 'the nightly news regularly depicts a lonely polar bear isolated on a small iceberg floating out to sea, implicitly on a course to extinction' (Owen and Swaisgood 2008, 123; see also Dunaway 2009; Born 2018). As the impacts of climate change are increasingly felt around the world, the narrative of the future of polar bears becomes a potential early warning system of the future ahead for other regions, wildlife, human communities and human society. The latter part of the 20th century thus saw a major perception shift of threats to polar bears over a relatively short time, from a species primarily threatened by over-hunting to one impacted by a more abstract, insidious and intractable environmental problem. Dorothea Born has explored the development of the polar bear as a climate change icon, through the pages of *National Geographic*. She identifies a three-stage trajectory: firstly, polar bears were anthropomorphised; then polar bears were visually connected to the endangered Arctic. Lastly, they emerged as ambassadors of a threatened ecosystem and icons of climate change. She notes that images of polar bears raise personal concern and awareness, and a localised account of climate change, but they do not make its causes – or possible solutions – visible, nor relevant to many viewers (Born 2018, 1).

Imagery of polar bears and the Arctic are part of a longer trajectory: Denis Cosgrove notes how the prevalent imagery of polar bears on ice floes presents both environment and fauna to be read 'as passive victims of anthropogenic processes underway in far distant locations' (Cosgrove 2008, 1878). He also suggests that the relative [psychological] distance – distanciation – of people and nature has increased in environmental imagery, with the polar bear and climate change as a prime example (Cosgrove 2008, 1878). Cosgrove argued for a more critical approach to use of imagery in environmental communications, to help shape and promote alternative attitudes to nature (Cosgrove 2008, 1879).

Jon Mooallem (2013) has questioned the effectiveness of the polar bear as an icon for climate change, recalling a visit to the California Academy of Sciences. An exhibit about polar bears and disappearing glaciers was being replaced by an exhibit about more local climate change impacts – worsening droughts, forest fires and climate change. 'Never mind the polar bears. Concentrate on how bad it's going to be for you', the museum's director told Mooallem (Mooallem 2013, 20).

The strength of the connection of the polar bear with the narrative of climate change can be seen from the fact that climate change deniers have sought to influence public opinion on anthropogenic climate change by attacking research on polar bears and on sea ice extent. This is based on a kind of magical thinking that, by seeding doubt on the science of polar bears' relationship with sea ice, the multitude of other climate change evidence must somehow be open to question. This is the same tactic as was used by creationists and intelligent design proponents, who sought to debunk the scientific narrative around the evolution of the peppered moth in relation to industrialisation. One prominent voice 'against' scientific consensus on polar bears, who typically uses the non-peer-reviewed blogosphere as a platform, has been linked to right-wing think tanks (receiving payments from them); her anti-science views circulate widely among right-wing blogs (see Harvey *et al* 2018).

Putting an Icon to Work

While the scientific and popular narrative of the connection between polar bears and climate change became increasingly clear, there was a growing awareness that the prevalent narrative was too fatalistic. Manzo (2010), and O'Neill and Nicholson-Cole (2009), discuss 'fear appeals', a typically alarmist form of communication prevalent in mass media that speaks of emergencies, catastrophes and hyperbole. Polar bears were, and are, heavily implicated in these fear appeals, as icons of climate change. This is highly problematic, as O'Neill and Nicholson-Cole found that 'fear-inducing communication approaches were found to enhance a sense of fatalism and thus act to encourage disengagement with climate change rather than positive engagement' (O'Neill and Nicholson-Cole 2009, 370). In other words, while a narrative may be being communicated, it is actually inhibiting people's sense of their own, or others', ability to do anything about climate change, or polar bear conservation. Conservation biologists, too, have recognised the importance of framing their work on polar bears within a framework of possibilities. Steve Amstrup, a leading American polar bear biologist, had the realisation one sleepless night that the dire prognosis for polar bears that he and co-workers had issued 'had been perceived by the general public as a prediction of unavoidable doom for the species'. Frustrated at media versions of scientific reports he and his colleagues had produced, he wrote to his collaborators that 'I am also sure that if the general public thinks nothing can be done, THEN NOTHING WILL BE DONE!' Instead, Amstrup realised that he and colleagues should present 'the prognosis for polar bears in a way that emphasizes that there is hope if we do the right things' (quoted in Swaisgood and Sheppard 2010, 627).

In a study in Norwich (UK), O'Neill and Hulme (2009) found that icons, including an image of a polar bear, raised participants' perception of the level of threat posed by climate change. The polar bear was the best understood icon of climate change and the icon that participants were most drawn to (O'Neill and Hulme 2009, 407). However, polar bears were also considered to be the least relevant icon to participants, their local community, people in the UK and people in the world, falling far behind other images in this respect. Overall, there was the rather ambivalent finding that polar bears are engaging icons for climate change, but they did not make climate change more relevant to people. So, polar bear images may raise concern or catch people's attention, but they do not necessarily facilitate action or constructive emotional responses.

Contrary to some of the above findings, Janet Swim and Brittany Bloodhart (2015) explored the efficacy of both emotional and more scientific, objective appeals in motivating people (in the US) to donate money to polar bear conservation. They found that empathy and hope were most important in appeals to environmentally minded people, and a combination of empathy, hope, worry, personal guilt and boredom motivated non-environmentally minded people to donate. Perhaps this can be explained by the close connection between the raising of participants' awareness of the issues with the opportunity for participants to act on their thoughts and feelings: a kind of 'buy with one click'. Connecting challenge (information on polar bears' conservation status and the need for action by people) with support (making it easy for participants to act on their responses) presents a realistic model for participants to connect their thinking, feeling and doing around polar bears, creating an environment for, and raising a sense of, empowerment (see also Lorenzoni *et al* 2007; McGhie *et al* 2018).

Linking polar bears and climate change on the one hand, and personal action on the other, has been repeatedly found to be distancing (see above), but this presents some opportunities. Polar bears' fate, like climate change in general, is perceived to be distant – psychologically distant – in terms of a number of dimensions: temporal, social, geographical and in terms of uncertainty. Psychological distance has been linked with the way that people represent concepts mentally and with personal action; perhaps counter-intuitively, increased psychological distance has been found to facilitate choices that are more abstract and linked with people's core values, although psychological closeness has been linked to increased concern (Spence *et al* 2012). The projected decline of polar bears over decades, and of wider environmental change, is challenging as it is concerned with timescales longer than everyday concerns (Stehr and von Storch 1995; Lorenzoni *et al* 2000). The three generations of polar bears involved in the species' conservation status assessment equates with the 50-year period that has been suggested as the upper time limit of people's ability to conceptualise the future (see O'Neill and Nicholson-Cole 2009, 361). Polar bears, identified as appealing in their own right in some studies, could be deployed to help people explore the psychologically distant aspects of climate change, and to connect the future of the bears with the future of human communities and society over the similar time frame.

Polar Bears, Climate Change Engagement and Museums

Museums present particular opportunities for people to explore and connect polar bears, climate change and human society. However, they have been slow to adopt (or rediscover) a more active, future-focused frame (eg Davis 1996; Janes 2015; McGhie *et al* 2018; McGhie 2018a, b). While a doom-and-gloom niche is highly prevalent in mass media and in conservation biology, a more solutions-focused hope niche is scarcely occupied (see Swaisgood and Sheppard 2010), providing a great opportunity for museums.

In museums, 'engagement' is often thought of as a time-bound activity that takes place in museums and is separated from the impact of the engagement. In an alternative model, climate change engagement may be defined as 'an ongoing personal state of connection' – as opposed to participation in a time-bound process of engagement – with the issue of climate change woven into people's everyday lives (Lorenzoni *et al* 2007, 446; Whitmarsh *et al* 2011). A state of engagement incorporates a broad range of aspects that constitute what we think, feel and do about climate change – cognitive, affective and behavioural aspects. Simply knowing more about climate change does not necessarily promote action and, as information has an impact on affective and behavioural aspects, may inadvertently disempower action (as seen above). Engaging constructively with all three aspects presents a plausible route towards constructive engagement with the topic in people's daily lives, connecting people's thoughts, values and concerns with choices and actions (Lorenzoni *et al* 2007; McGhie *et al* 2018), to promote a deeper personal connection with nature (see Arbuthnott *et al* 2014; Bruni *et al* 2018). O'Neill and Nicholson-Cole (2009), whose work has been discussed above, found that imagery could have positive effects on people's attitudes and motivational state concerning climate change action. Images that made participants feel most able to do something about climate change tended to show activities linked to energy and energy-saving devices in people's homes (thermostats, low-energy light bulbs, solar panels, wind turbines) and transport choices (cycling and trams), connecting with people's day-to-day activities and lifestyle choices. Similar results have been found in the UK, US and Australia (O'Neill *et al* 2013), and in Germany, Switzerland and Austria (Metag *et al* 2016). Museums could use 'their' polar bears to connect the local with the global, and to explore, critique and debate the gap that exists between personal lifestyles, political will and action, and more distant concepts and places, including polar bears in the Arctic. Museums are ideal locations to adopt such an approach: it has been previously found that people are more receptive to information in museums, and more likely to reflect on options for personal action (Arbuthnott *et al* 2014).

The late Stephen Kellert, of Yale University, established a typology of nine basic human attitudes to nature based on surveys and questionnaires (Kellert 1978). This work has been used extensively to explore attitudes between different [human] age groups, genders and cultures (see Kellert 1996). Importantly, it reveals that a very small minority of people consider animals from a primarily scientific viewpoint. This should be noted by all museums, which often place nature within a scientific frame. Kellert's work can be a powerful tool for developing activities relating to the environment where people are in mixed groups or come from different backgrounds and interest groups, typical of a museum setting (see table 10.1). Kellert's framework can be used to great effect to explore attitudes to polar bears, and to promote an understanding of different

Table 10.1: Kellert's attitudes to nature, applied to polar bears

Attitude	Primary interest	In relation to polar bears
Naturalistic	Primary interest and affection for wildlife and the outdoors.	Polar bear in wild nature. Human experience of wild nature.
Ecologistic	Primary concern for the environment as a system, for interrelationships between wildlife species and natural habitats.	Polar bear as part of an ecosystem, within a foodweb. Interactions and interdependencies between polar bears and other species. Life history in relation to seasonal changes. Participation of people within ecosystems and foodwebs, and relationships between human actions and polar bears.
Humanistic	Primary interest and strong affection for individual animals, principally pets. Regarding wildlife, focus on large attractive animals with strong anthropomorphic associations.	Polar bear as a large, attractive animal. Empathy with polar bear. Anthropomorphic views of polar bears, or all polar bears, as an individual 'character'.
Moralistic	Primary concern for the right and wrong treatment of animals, with strong opposition to exploitation of and cruelty toward animals.	Ethical responsibility towards polar bears.
Scientistic	Primary interest in the physical attributes and biological functioning of animals.	Understanding the lives of polar bears, in relation to their physiology, biology, life history.
Aesthetic	Primary interest in the artistic and symbolic characteristics of animals.	Artistic and poetic approaches to polar bears, and their habitat. Polar bears in visual and literary culture. Polar bears as stand-ins for human thoughts and concepts.
Utilitarian	Primary concern for the practical and material value of animals.	The practical use of polar bears, their impact on economy, their impacts on other resources useful to humans.
Dominionistic	Primary satisfactions derived from mastery and control over animals typically in sporting situations.	Hunting, exploration, other 'quests' and conquests involving polar bears.
Negativistic	Primary orientation an avoidance of animals due either to indifference, dislike or fear.	Fear of polar bears.

relationships with the animals. Museums could use 'their' polar bears to explore climate change, polar bears, people's personal lifestyles and geopolitics within this framework. This would present a more nuanced opportunity for people to explore concerns, possibilities and actions, both individually and collectively. Museums could use their resources to critique, disrupt and challenge preconceptions about 'the future' and the place of polar bears in that future, drawing on scientific research and creative experiences linked with personal action (see also McGhie, Mander and Underhill 2018).

Kellert's work formed a conceptual basis for the transformation of a formerly 'traditional' natural history gallery at Manchester Museum (part of the University of Manchester, UK). The new gallery, Living Worlds, opened in 2011, and explores the relationships between people and nature, a deliberately ambiguous statement that refers to people individually and collectively (McGhie 2012; McGhie 2018a). A polar bear, in the museum since the early 20th century, now occupies a prominent place at the head of the gallery in a case called 'Connect', 'escaping' from a diorama-like setting to approach rainforest animals and British predatory animals. This aims to both disrupt the 'environment in a bubble' of traditional dioramas and to emphasise the connectedness between different environments, and indeed the connection between people's individual and collective choices and their impacts. The same bear 'escaped' from this permanent setting to take part in a temporary exhibition on climate change in 2016 (see Fig 10.2); its place on the gallery was taken by an empty chair inside the case. The exhibition 'Climate Control' encouraged people to explore the past and the future. The polar bear was placed within a narrative connecting fossil plants and coal, industrialisation and the effects of climate change around the world. The polar bear was placed on open display with a chair in front of it, mirroring the chair placed in the empty case on the Living Worlds gallery. Visitors were encouraged to sit in the chair, to see the polar bear 'face to face'. The words 'powerful', 'free', 'wild', and the question 'are we so different?' were projected on the wall behind the polar bear, to disrupt the fatalistic narrative outlined earlier. Visitors were encouraged to respond in various ways: placing black stickers to represent individual carbon footprints; contributing ideas for a more sustainable future; and voting on their views about climate change in terms of who will be affected by it, and who cares about it, to promote a sense of agency and collective action. As with the 'donate now' project described earlier, asking people to respond to the exhibition with their immediate emotional reactions and thoughts aimed to foster greater empowerment and more awareness of the thoughts, values and actions of others who visit the museum (see McGhie, Mander and Underhill 2018).

DISCUSSION

In a complex, environmentally compromised world, with widespread confusion and disinformation on polar bears, climate change and a wide range of other enviro-social problems, a stronger role for museums is more needed than ever (Janes 2015; McGhie 2018b). Museums can create a platform for people to explore and express ideas around citizenship and the world they want, and to explore the impacts of that world both nearby and farther afield. This has a strong connection with the plight of polar bears. Rather than repeating doom-laden messages, museums can use polar bears in their exhibitions to make the connection between visitors' lives (their worlds) and the world of the polar bear. Framing the connection between a possible shared future, and alternative futures where there are no polar bears, presents a plausible role for museums. Highlighting both the vulnerability of people, and polar bears, and the resilience and adaptability, both of people and polar bears, can be an important part of this alternative framing. Helping people, and polar bears, to face the challenge of climate change will be increasingly important. The discussion of climate change, and of museums, is often devoid of a vision of the future. What kinds of futures are possible, and what would it take to create them? What kind of world is acceptable to each of us? What part will we, and polar bears, play in that world? The psychological distance between people and polar bears represents a wide, creative space to explore connections and consequences, with highly abstract options and possibilities, rather than simply addressing immediate concerns.

FIGURE 10.2. A TAXIDERMIED POLAR BEAR PLAYS A PART IN THE *CLIMATE CONTROL* EXHIBITION AT MANCHESTER MUSEUM, 2016 (GARETH GARDNER/MANCHESTER MUSEUM, UNIVERSITY OF MANCHESTER).

While environmental communicators may advise against the use of charismatic megafauna such as polar bears in climate change or other environmental communications (eg Futerra 2010), museums present the unusual place in society where polar bears are part of the expectation. Visitors expect to encounter them. We can use that encounter to provide deep, rich and meaningful experiences that imagine and begin to create futures, both for people and for polar bears. Rather than foregrounding local, personalised risks of climate change, we can connect our futures – individually and collectively – with those of the polar bears, to promote a world that is liveable for both.

Bibliography and References

Arbuthnott, K D, Sutter, G C, and Heidt, C T, 2014 Natural history museums, parks, and connection with nature, *Museum Management and Curatorship* 29 (2), 102–21

Archibald, K, 2015 From fierce to adorable: representations of polar bears in the popular imagination, *American Review of Canadian Studies* 45 (3), 266–82

Atwood, T C, Peacock, E, McKinney, M A, Lillie, K, Wilson, R, Douglas, D C, Miller S, and Terletzky, P, 2016 Rapid environmental change drives increased land use by an Arctic marine predator, *PLoS One* DOI:10.1371/journal.pone.0155932

Blystad, P, Thomsen, H, Simonsen, A and Lie, R W, 1983 Find of a nearly complete Late Weichselian polar bear skeleton, *Ursus maritimus* Phipps, at Finnøy, southwestern Norway: a preliminary report, *Norsk Geologisk Tidskrift* 63, 193–7

Born, D, 2018 Bearing witness? Polar Bears as icons for climate change communication, in *National Geographic. Environmental Communication* DOI: 10.1080/17524032.2018.1435557

Cosgrove, D, 2008 Images and imagination in 20th-century environmentalism: from the Sierras to the Poles, *Environment and Planning A* 40, 1862–80

Davis, P, 1996 *Museums and the Natural Environment*, Leicester University Press, Leicester

Derocher, A E, Aars, J, Amstrup, S C, Cutting, A, Lunn, N J, Molnár, P K, Obbard, M E, Stirling, I, Thiemann, G W, Vongraven, D, Wiig, Ø, and York, G, 2013 Rapid ecosystem change and Polar Bear conservation, *Conservation Letters* DOI: doi.org/10.1111/conl.12009

Donald, D, 2007 *Picturing Animals in Britain 1750–1850*, Yale University Press, London

Donald, D, 2010 The Arctic fantasies of Edwin Landseer and Briton Riviere: Polar Bears, wilderness and notions of the sublime, *Tate Papers* 13 (Spring 2010), available from: http://www.tate.org.uk/research/publications/tate-papers/13/arctic-fantasies-of-edwin-landseer-and-briton-riviere-polar-bears-wilderness-and-notions-of-the-sublime [20 June 2018]

Dunaway, F, 2009 Seeing global warming: contemporary art and the fate of the planet, *Environmental History* 14 (1), 9–31

Futerra, 2010 *Branding Biodiversity* [online], available from: http://www.futerra.co.uk/downloads/Branding_Biodiversity.pdf [22 June 2018]

Harvey, J A, van den Berg, D, Ellers, J, Kampen, R, Crowther, T W, Roessingh, P, Verheggen, B, Nuuten, R J M, Post, E, Lewandowsky, S, Stirling, J, Balgopal, M, Amstrup, S C, and Mann, M E, 2018 Internet blogs, Polar Bears, and climate-change denial by proxy, *Bioscience* 68 (4), 281–7, doi:10.1093/biosci/bix133

Høvik, I, 2013 *Heroism and Imperialism in the Arctic: Edwin Landseer's Man Proposes – God Disposes*. Nordlit 2008. ISSN 0809-1668

Janes, R R, 2015 *Museums Without Borders: selected writings of Robert R. Janes*, Routledge, London

Kellert, S R, 1978 *Policy implications of a national study of American attitudes and behavioral relations to animals*. US Fish and Wildlife Service, US Government Printing Office, Washington, D.C.

——, 1996 *The Value of Life: Biological Diversity and Human Society*, Island Press, Washington DC

Lindqvist, C, 2010 Complete mitochondrial genome of a Pleistocene jawbone unveils the origin of the polar bear, *Proceedings of the National Academy of Sciences* 107 (110), 5053–7

Lorenzoni, I S, Jordan, A, O'Riordan, T, Turner, R K, and Hulme M, 2000 A co-evolutionary approach to climate change impact assessment. Part II. A scenario-based case study in East Anglia (UK), *Global Environmental Change* 10, 145–55

Lorenzoni, I, Nicholson-Cole, S, and Whitmarsh, L, 2007 Barriers perceived to engaging with climate change among the UK public and their policy implications, *Global Environmental Change* 17 (3), 445–59

Manzo, K, 2010 Beyond Polar Bears? Re-envisioning climate change, *Meteorological Applications* 17, 196–208

McGhie, H A, 2012 Living Worlds at the Manchester Museum, in *A Handbook for Academic Museums: Exhibitions and Education* (eds S S Jandl and M S Gold), MuseumsEtc, London, 222–53

——, 2018a Promoting people's connection with nature through natural history displays in museums, in *Natural History Dioramas – Traditional Exhibits for Current Educational Themes* (eds A Scheersoi and S D Tunnicliffe), Springer, Berlin, 149–61

——, 2018b Climate Change: a different narrative, in *Addressing the Challenges in Communicating Climate Change Across Various Audiences* (eds W Leal Filho, B Lackner and H A McGhie), Springer International, Cham (Switzerland), 13–29

McGhie, H A, Mander, S J, and Underhill, R, 2018 Engaging people with climate change through museums, in *Handbook of Climate Change Communication 3. Case Studies in Climate Change Communication* (eds W Leal Filho, E Manolas, A Azul, U Azeiteiro, and H A McGhie), Springer International, Cham (Switzerland), 329–48

Metag, J, Schäffer, M S, Füchslin, T, Barsuhn, T, and Kleinen-von Königslöw, K, 2016 Perceptions of climate change imagery: evoked salience and self-efficacy in Germany, Switzerland and Austria, *Science Communication* 38 (2), 197–227

Mooallem, J, 2013 *Wild Ones: a sometimes dismaying, weirdly reassuring story about looking at people looking at animals in America,* Penguin, New York

NOAA, 2017 Arctic Report Card [online], available from: https://www.arctic.noaa.gov/Report-Card/Report-Card-2017 [26 June 2018]

Obbard, M E, Thiemann, G W, Peacock, E, and DeBruyn, T D, 2010 *Polar bears: Proc. the 15th Working Meeting of the IUCN/SSC Polar Bear Specialist Group, Copenhagen, Denmark, 29 June–3 July 2009*, IUCN, Gland (Switzerland) and Cambridge (UK)

O'Neill, S, and Hulme, M, 2009 An iconic approach for representing climate change, *Global Environmental Change* 19, 402–10

O'Neill, S, and Nicholson-Cole, S, 2009 "Fear won't do it": promoting positive engagement with climate change through visual and iconic representations, *Science Communication* 30 (3), 355–79

O'Neill, S, Boykoff, M, Niemeyer, S, and Day, S A, 2013 On the use of imagery for climate change engagement, *Global Environmental Change* 23 (2), 413–21

Owen, M A, and Swaisgood, R R, 2008 On thin ice: Climate change and the future of polar bears, *Biodiversity* 9 (3–4), 143–8

Spence, A, Poortinga, W, and Pidgeon, N, 2012 The psychological distance of climate change, *Risk analysis* 32 (6), 957–72

Stehr, N, and von Storch, H, 1995 The social construct of climate and climate change, *Inter-Research CR* 5 (2), 99–105

Stirling, I, 1988 *Polar Bears*, Anne Arbor: University of Michigan Press

Stroeve, J C, Kattsov, V, Barrett, A, Serreze, M, Pavlova, T, Holland, M, and Meier, W N, 2012 Trends in Arctic sea ice extent from CMIP5, CMIP3 and observations, *Geophysical Research Letters* 39: L16502

Swaisgood, R R, and Sheppard, J K, 2010 The culture of conservation biologists: show me the hope! *BioScience* 60 (8), 626–30

Swim, J K, and Bloodhart, B, 2015 Portraying the perils to polar bears: The role of empathic and objective perspective-taking toward animals in climate change communication, *Environmental Communication* 9 (4), 446–68

Ware, J V, Rode, K D, Bromaghin, J F, Douglas, D C, Wilson, R R, Regehr, E V, Amstrup, S C, Durner, G M, Pagano, A M, Olson, J, Robbins, C T, and Jansen, H T, 2017 Habitat degradation affects the summer activity of Polar Bears, *Oecologia* 184, 87–99

Wiig, Ø, Amstrup, S, Atwood, T, Laidre, K, Lunn, N, Obbard, M, Regehr, E, and Thiemann, G, 2015 *Ursus maritimus*, The IUCN Red List of Threatened Species 2015: e.T22823A14871490, available from: http://dx.doi.org/10.2305/IUCN.UK.2015-4.RLTS.T22823A14871490.en [10 June 2018]

11

On the Oblique Imperative: What Revealing Conceals and Concealing may Reveal

Mark Wilson and Bryndís Snaebjörnsdóttir

Matrix: the cultural, social, or political environment in which something develops (Oxford Dictionary)

Look at my skin – look at my skin shine… (Dylan 1963)

It was an urgency to come here, […] My fear was that we would lose the opportunity of seeing these magnificent animals –

polar bear tourist in Kaktovik, Alaska (Goode 2016)

Since the 1980s the ecotourism sector has grown and grown. It is the fastest growing sector in tourism – growing at an annual rate of between 10%–15%. Tourism is one of the few sectors of the world economy that continues to grow despite the ups and downs in the world economy (World Tourism Forum, 2012)

In this chapter, we, as collaborative artists, follow the links between spectacle, image and eco-tourism and, in this context, challenge the viability of expectations upon which ecotourism is fuelled. Implicitly, we offer a critique on its ethical sustainability, particularly where its regulation is, at best, patchily implemented. The specific frame for our inquiry here is the research undertaken for an art project *Matrix*, commissioned by the Anchorage Museum in Alaska where, from 2015–20, we are 'Polar Lab Artists in Residence'. In this research, and the artworks arising, we have been examining interspecific, human and bear ecologies in the Arctic region.

THEATRE OF OPERATION

Somewhere out there, caught if you will like a seed, mid-flight and quivering on an obscure thread of the worldwide web, there exists a brief, 41-second clip of black and white video footage depicting an aerial search and the discovery of a freshly-dug polar bear den out on the North Slope – effectively, at the highest latitude of the USA.

We were shown this clip by US Fish and Wildlife agent Craig Perham when we met with him in Anchorage in 2015. In many ways, it is like many other clips from an archive of similar aerial surveillance missions in which an oil industry's attention, using thermal imaging Forward Looking Infra-Red (or FLIR) technology, turns away from the work of excavation, mineral extrac-

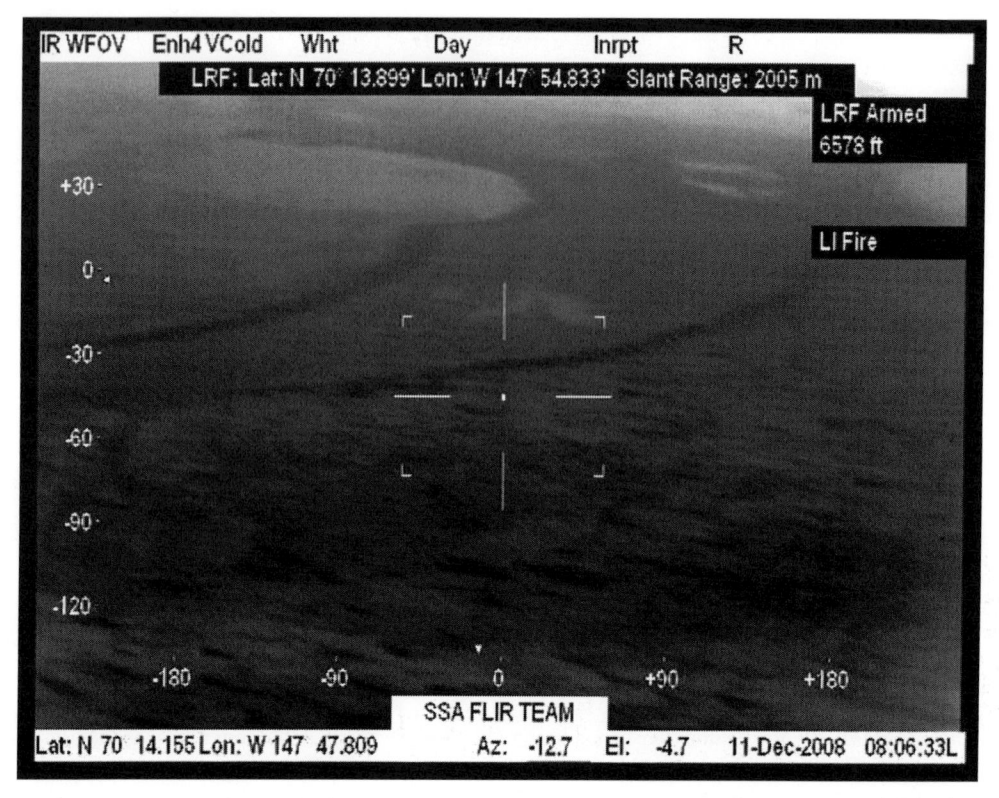

FIGURE 11.1. AERIAL FLIR STILL DURING A POLAR BEAR DEN DETECTION SURVEY, TAKEN OVER NORTH SLOPE BOROUGH COAST, FODDY ISLAND, ALASKA. PHOTO COURTESY OF U.S. FISH AND WILDLIFE, ALASKA (2008).

tion and pipeline monitoring, instead focusing on environmental stewardship and the purposes of conservation. The principle is simple – up on this Arctic coast in late autumn and early winter, biologists join together to fly with oil industry pilots in search of occupied polar bear dens. On finding these denning sites, the ice roads, built each fall to service the transport of crude oil to shipping points further down the coast, must be routed or sometimes re-routed, to a distance of a minimum one-mile radius from those locations.

The particular clip we refer to differs from others in that, during the recording, effectively at the moment the denning site is spotted, the crew are surprised (and somewhat jubilant) to detect movement and then to see the female, at the entrance to the den she's digging, seeming to sniff around in order to identify the cause of the commotion. She turns her head to stare back towards the aeroplane from which the camera is pointed.

In this moment, the subject is not the bear, but significantly, something else – something that exists between the bear and the banked snow – between the sky and the ground, between the photographically negative displacement and disorientation which is a characteristic of the technological visualisation and which makes a moonscape of the arctic plateau – and this momentary, interspecific recognition. By flying at elevations of 2000ft and beyond, this engagement is technically not supposed to happen. The idea is to detect and so protect – not to disturb and thereby put in jeopardy the processes of ursine reproduction.

There are other remarkable and notable things about the film, particularly in what it says about the way we look and see and understand our 'selves' and our human behaviour. The technology and its application in the field, which together constitute this event, is of course in many ways a modern marvel, a conservational coup and, in itself, an embodiment of ideological paradox...

FLIR was developed '... together with oil industries and the American Petroleum Institute (API) to meet their requirements for detecting and minimizing gas leaks. The use of infrared cameras has already become a standard practice in many oil and gas companies. It's a proactive way to identify sources of Volatile Organic Compound (VOC) emissions and repair leaking components before it's too late ...' (FLIR 2016). In the interests of commercial efficiency and safety, FLIR clearly offers a powerful industrial apparatus, but in the hands of the conservationist project, the device reveals something different.

In all such footage from the US Fish and Wildlife Service (USFWS) archives, the camera scans the sweeping arctic land – as it reveals, so it obfuscates. In it there are no haunting sounds of the loon, no flashing glimpses of the jaeger (skua), nor any distracting arcs of white as snowy owls dissect the tundra's horizon – in fact there seems to be little space at all, as the image on screen is reduced to blurred, pixelated divisions of black, white and grey. What we see of this coastal terrain is more a map than any recognisable articulation of hills or sea. And yet beyond this there is some dark undertone of familiarity. While the margins of the screen are populated with the tumbling numbers of live data, at the centre, the view is fixed with sights – the scoping cross-hairs which signify precise aim. In this, we are reminded that there are more ways than one, or indeed two, to apply a technology. As we watch, the dark associations of video reportage tracking 'surgical' extirpations of unwanted human agents within remote territories are inescapable. With discomfort, we carry this implicitly menacing scrutiny to the present subject. And despite how our intellect may attempt to reassure us otherwise, when we scan the land in this way, even in the service of wildlife protection, we are made to feel uneasy, because in the application of this knowledge and these tools – in this context – we seem to make a quarry from the object of our care.

REGISTERS OF PERCEPTION

What, if anything, should we construe from this? Perceptually, by looking, we render the object of our gaze doubly vulnerable. The technology turns us back on ourselves and despite our known intentions we are twice the aggressor. Our technology makes it so.

At the centre of the frame a movement is detected. The polar bear wriggles tinily and awkwardly out from her den, almost as if the land itself is giving birth.

We would argue that in this moment, in focusing our attention and triggering our emotional engagement, the power of the miniature is infinitely more moving than any high-definition recording of a snow leopard in the Himalayas or of a raptor in full stoop on its prey. How so? One of the phenomena captured in this digital moment, through this very 'distance' and 'approximation', is the very space of power.

> The poor image is a copy in motion. Its quality is bad, its resolution substandard. As it accelerates, it deteriorates. It is a ghost of an image, a preview, a thumbnail, an errant idea, an itinerant image distributed for free, squeezed through slow digital connections, compressed, reproduced, ripped, remixed, as well as copied and pasted into other channels of distribution (Steyerl 2009).

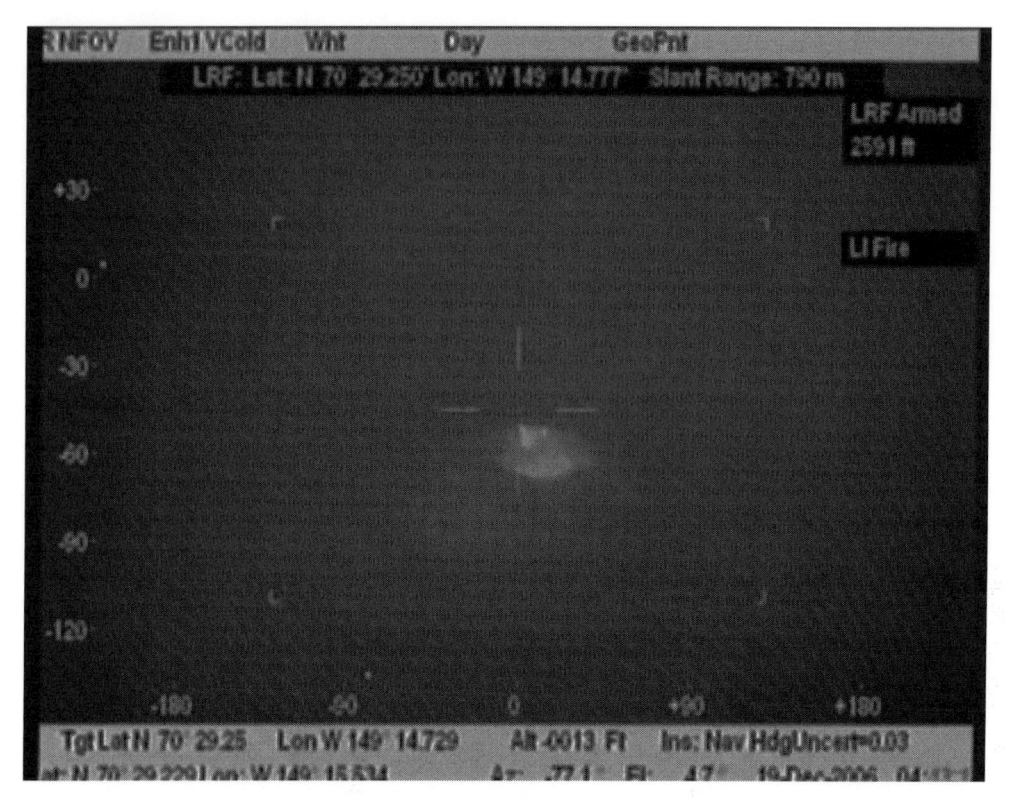

Figure 11.2. Aerial FLIR still of a polar bear excavating a den during a polar bear den detection survey, taken over North Slope Borough coast. Photo courtesy of U.S. Fish and Wildlife, Alaska (2006).

The poor image is fleeting, transient, suggesting urgency and candour. Because this recording is political – the poorness of its quality reminds us of the significance not only of the subject but simultaneously of its relation to the observer – it tilts us away from the fetishisation of an animal's image as discrete 'exoticised subject of the other' and towards our own intersections in time and space, along with all (or some) of the environmental implications of that entanglement. It resonates with a specificity of meaning that nevertheless ripples out through all the tentative uncertainty concerning our individual environmental position and responsibilities. Rather than catharsis and escape, this moving image offers us an insoluble and troublesome particle of grit. If we are to believe that photography or film has valuable work to do, then this should stand as an example of how such environmental photographic work might effectively function. The poor image-definition gives birth to/constructs/brings into being a unique moment which privileges no one thing, but records, as a set of intersecting events, the movement of the plane and camera, the technological screen and tumbling data, the rough and rolling land, the hotspot of the den, the movement of the bear and the candid surprise of the crew.

The fact that the footage maintains distance from the subject seems key to our appreciation of this intersectional view. The further alienation conveyed by the highly technological appearance and apparatus by which this scene is conveyed may ultimately be regarded as a signifier of respect

– the world of the polar bear in this context and in its enmeshing with more than one human world is spatially enfolded and ontologically parallel rather than being, for instance, symbiotic. Distance therefore allows an understanding of context and points us towards complexity. As we watch, we make the following observations:

We are aware of the probing, scrutinising purpose of the mission.

The scrutiny itself is aesthetically alienating in respect of and in contrast to the supposed, imagined and now imaged 'warmth' of the bear.

We acknowledge the significance of infrared detection, by which the 'white' is the coldest hotspot imaginable.

We see the clear inquisitiveness of the bear.

Even in this diminutive manifestation, the bear seems not to be fearful but, rather, justifiably curious and, in turn, probing in its scrutiny of the plane.

Craig Perham asks us (without really asking, or needing to ask) not to use this particular footage in whatever work arises from our research, because it is not representative of what they do. He need not be concerned.

The Oblique View

In any artwork, there are considerations of 'taste' and appropriateness that must be weighed alongside all others. In respect of any project we undertake, we are at pains to point out that it is not useful for us to be a mouthpiece for the views of any particular party. Conversely, to beautify or sensationalise, to make exotic or to scandalise, is to miss the point and to misspend the potential of otherwise hard-earned engagement – for us, as artists, the spectacle is rarely a destination – and vice versa. There are some images which have the capacity to steal attention, so profoundly and to the occlusion of all else, that their inclusion could only be a distraction, saying everything and nothing at all in a moment, engaging, hijacking or diverting attention.

An artist's role, very often, is to understand what it is that we see and calculate accordingly how we might present not the image, but the means by which that understanding is conveyed. In such cases, the way an artist presents information, or an understanding – the way chosen to withhold the spectacle rather than letting it be seen – is paramount. In fact, whatever individual thing is seen is rarely the work. The oblique view, suggesting what is beyond view, is the privilege of the artist whose view is always greater and more complex than that presented. Art exists to extend the thinking and the sense of involvement of individuals who perceive it. It is enjoyed and resented on those very same grounds. Enjoyed because it extends – resented because it appears deliberately, even wantonly, to obscure or refuse easily to relinquish. Simplicity is eschewed on the grounds that it is an illusion – complexity embraced because it acknowledges what it is that we do not yet know and that what we think we know, we may not know tomorrow. That is because our knowledge, like the world itself, is subject to change, to altered circumstance and incomprehensible ecological effect. In art, knowledge is not an answer – it is an instrument by which we're able to see things differently.

That this meagre clip provides a platform from which to write is one thing, but to consider presenting this as a visual treat has no correlation with the art we do or the motivation that underpins it. The truth is, as we craned over Craig's shoulder to look at this for the first time, there was no doubt of its capacity to move – but still, such movement would be to distract from the nuanced detail which was driving our own interest and research in this project.

Spectacle is not the same as image. Spectacle both prefigures image (in context) and is a product of image (decontextualised). In this respect, it's fascinating to look more closely at the relationship between a private experience and the distillation or reduction of that experience into an image (or series of images), the intersection of subject and phenomenon where the signifier of spectacle (which cannot ever be known through the experience of image) is sparked. What is to become of that spark? What might it more productively ignite and how might we otherwise reconcile ourselves to the loss we feel as it withdraws from us or indeed as we withdraw (as we must) from it? How can the gravity and radiance of its constellations, in our absence, do anything but fade or collapse into the flimsiest of memories?

In an image 'arms race', when the world is in competition to impress by image, nothing has value – because all images fade through familiarity or otherwise obscure and eclipse their subject. No image is detached and independent. All images are haunted emptily by those things the image cannot record and re-present. All images are a surface which, no matter what their individual power to seduce might be, ultimately offer only a hollow promise upon which it is impossible to deliver. This is the conundrum that drives the industry providing unique or 'exotic' experiences. The image that the ecotourist sends back is the trophy or certificate of a secret, private experience; an experience that importantly, for its value to be maintained, must remain largely inaccessible to others. Yet ironically, the same 'image' is the bait that draws those others to invest in that experience for themselves … we see this fragile paradigm breaking, or on the point of inducing breakdown, everywhere we look – from the dubious (and serially fatal) assisted ascents of Everest, to the environmental pressure cooker that is, for example, contemporary Icelandic tourism.

As our technology improves, it is often the case that we forget that its development, whilst serving an apparent and inevitable focus of need, becomes subject to that need and so determines, constrains and delimits the scope of the technology itself (Flusser 2000). The need here is twofold – to get closer and to extract more detail of the subject, more or less, in isolation. In other words, the hunger for objectification, quite naturally, is an isolating process, the goal of which is to pick out, to separate and to render as distinct, a unified entity. An example would be that, whilst not in any way an attempt to deny in principle the camouflaging capacity of an animal in respect of its immediate environment, the photographic endeavour might privilege distinction between that cover and the subject, thereby overcoming the guise. This is also an irksome manifestation of the modernist legacy, which attempts to unpick and objectify complex systems, re-presenting them as serial, discrete events and players.

What is it we believe we are recording and what, of value, do we miss therefore in the primacy of image and, in that, the fix on and fetishisation of focus and high-definition?

We've established that we are diverted in this endeavour from the intersectional matrix – and that by accepting an image component within a complex matrix as being hard to single out, the circumstances of its coming into being are afforded more weight and consideration … but there is more. For years, along with many artists, we have argued against the assumptions that are the basis of representation. Such assumptions are never more evident than in the lavish television documentaries typified by National Geographic or the BBC productions presented by David Attenborough. In the same way that these projects telescope time and provide an entirely unrealistic diet of continuously unfolding events and spectacle, so too, as technological capabilities increase, year by year, the resolution of the image becomes ever more sharp; so high in definition that its relation to our own experience of the world is exponentially and incrementally made ever more distant, ever more alien and unrealistic. The incremental nature of those steps has meant that viewers have simply not noticed – in short, we are all hypnotised. And again, there are consequences. We have become restless, impatient, dissatisfied – and we have developed a closely-related appetite for the exotic spectacle. Couple this with a growing awareness of environmental decline and the ethical license that a new type of tourism allows, namely the promise that by visiting a remote site you may contribute to its preservation, and you have the ingredients for a contradictory and unsustainable contract. The growth of the industry and its promise, when protracted logically, is ultimately self-cancelling.

Looking, Data and Representation

We should say a few words here on the context for *Matrix #1* (2016), the first work we made in Alaska. The matrix of the title is the environment of multiple human and interspecific interests as they intersect in specific locations on the North Slope Borough in the most northern part of Alaska. These interests, amongst others, include those of the Inupiaq communities, the oil industry, polar bears (in their denning activities and behaviours), conservation and tourism.

In all the research for the project, originally in Svalbard (2010) and later in Alaska, in Barrow and Kaktovik, we consciously rejected the idea of going into or even near polar bear dens. We made this decision on the grounds that others, with whom we were and continue to be in dialogue, already do so as part of their professional remit – it is our frank belief in any case that human proximity itself is often an endangering or compromising factor in respect of these and other species-subjects of our scrutiny. The counting of species populations, the mapping of their habitats, the monitoring of their behaviours and interactions is of course fascinating, but these studies are, or arise from, human projects designed ultimately to serve the desires and perceived needs of humans. In that respect, for us, each such project provides us with a new zone of scrutiny – and an associated set of questions. What does it say about humans, or a particular set of humans, to be studying or indeed observing for entertainment, or individual gratification, the fact of the bear, its presence and behaviours, in what we understand to be its natural habitat?

In 2014, CBC news published an article declaring: 'There is more money in looking at bears than there is in shooting them – 12 times more to be exact, according to a new study.' While this may be regarded as a move forward in our approach towards non-humans (put simply, to observe rather than kill), what is the net gain and net loss of such a business (and business it most certainly is) for humans, for the bears, for the environment we all share – and by what calculus may this be measured? Why indeed, at this point, can it be assumed that 'ecotourism' or any kind of regular, commercial, human interaction in environmentally fragile areas is important enough to outweigh the undeniable interference and potential disturbance such escalation of the business will inevitably cause?

On the subject of bears and ecotourism, in addition to commentators from a wide range of specialist perspectives – biology, zoology, ecology etc. – cultural producers, like ourselves, carry the work of these and others to a wider audience in order, in this case, to study the currency and wider effects of bear awareness upon human collective consciousness. As an effect of bringing our findings out of the field from which they derive, our observations inevitably stray from the status of data *per se*. By exposing material to the imaginings of those who are neither the professionals nor amateurs in the field, data may be said to be subject to 'contamination'. Cultural mediation is an inevitability – as a consequence of the processes of media dissemination. A further consequence of the mediating effect, however, is for these amalgams and hybrids (of what is gathered in the field and what a public brings to the subject themselves) to coalesce as compounds into new (transformed and newly identifiable) entities. As artists, however, it has often been an intention through our work to question the basis and constraints of data collection and indeed, so too, the objectives of its more serious publishing and disseminating platforms. On multiple occasions in the field, working alongside scientists (eg our exhibitions Snæbjörnsdóttir/Wilson 2015, 2017), it has been evident that scientists too are very often interested in observing and absorbing the bigger context from which data is drawn – but scientific practice is expensive and its funding is invariably politically, economically or religiously motivated. This leads in turn to particular distorting emphases in the extraction and processing of data. In our work, we have drawn attention to the many kinds of misleading and delimiting representations of species and individuals, and to the propensities and capacities which as a result are denied, stripped back and excluded by ever-narrowing research criteria, and asked, to what extent is data collection reducing our capacity to engage, to understand, to recognise the bigger, ecological picture? (NB – the metaphorical 'bigger picture' is not to be mistaken for a 'picture').

In what is shaping up to be a critique of particular kinds of scrutiny and engagement, should we then be demanding a new kind of technology, one that allows us to see, weigh and fathom relationships rather than their individualised components? Does such a technology exist already? And is it too much to propose that art, and what art has and continues to become, may be such a technology, in that it allows the weighing together of disparate materials drawn from multiple fields, methods and their co-constitutive relationships – without ever pretending to provide the last word on their extent or limits or to suggest that what is presented is anything more than an instrument (amongst many possible instruments) by which to read, a set of relations – in specific time.

In ecological thought, the drive to go-see for oneself is understandable, but inevitably there is a price, the consideration of which must, in time, outweigh the translation of desire into action. The validity of experience is not and was never contingent upon the production of a verifying image. But while the binge-like and competitive trading of images escalates, in this context it is so much more than a diversion; it is the virus that drives the demand and threatens to unravel an ever increasingly unattainable prize.

The image is a placeholder, a memento mori, a souvenir – but also, merely a token. The image as we know, after time and for the subject, comes to eclipse the original experience itself. But in its function as token, it carries new caché. As a shared document, although depleted, carrying nothing of the agency it might at least for a time have held for the image-maker, it is a surrogate of close association, temporally, once – between a person and place or event or a site. It is also the contextualising instrument, an aide-mémoire for a story.

Transcending the Singular View

So how do these ideas play out in the consideration of the material we gathered in the research, development and presentation stages of *Matrix*? They underpin, absolutely, the depleting capacity of representation – itself a subject to which we have devoted much time to, both in writing and also as embedded critique within our work.

Vilém Flusser (2000), in writing on photography, was at pains to explain how in our cultural production, paradoxically, we become the instruments of the technology we devise in order to serve our desired production. He describes the black box (housing the increasingly complex inner workings of the camera) as a phenomenon over which we have less and less control, standing between what it is we put before it (the visually recordable world) and what ultimately it allows us to produce, as image.

In a nutshell, it is in respect of such occluding capacities, not only of what we commonly understand as 'technologies', but accordingly, of any cultural form and production, that we (as artists) have been diligent over years in configuring the essence of any work as constituted in a matrix – the relationship between multiple elements, without ever relying (or being seen to rely) upon individual pieces. The 'being seen to' is important, because in a Brechtian (self-revealing) sense, even if the content is difficult to grasp in its entirety, or the ideas (justifiably, necessarily even) are challengingly complex, the process of its generation and presentation is transparent. Still evident is the acknowledgment in itself that we (artists and audience) are working this through 'together' – that there is no one answer to be found and the artwork is simply one tool, amongst many possible tools, by which to think through whatever ideas are on the table. No technology is reliable as a means by which to understand the world – any understanding it may be possible for us to achieve will always, we presume, be essentially a human understanding – because the human condition itself is the complex of registers by which we sense and acknowledge our serial and continual intersection. We are instruments of that condition and the conditioning of the culture/s into which we are born or raised – including their technologies and art. Not surprising then, as we grope for truths or understanding, that we should constantly remind ourselves to depend on no representations at all – as provided by data, scan, image, film, book, sound, audit etc. – but to triangulate consciously and constantly between all available referents, contexts, variables and other 'trace' elements. Inevitably this invites us to consider the factor of 'variability' in perception and to embrace subjectivity in our individual readings and conclusions as being indicators, moment by moment, of unassailable truth – momentary though they must inevitably be. Why? Because if we are to triangulate (and indeed the figure of 'three' summoned by triangulation is simply a convenience suggesting possibly infinite multiplicities of view) then one of the chief factors to be considered is that of temporal shift. In an ecology of view, the rolling out of time and its effects on circumstance is surely amongst the most influential and corrosive on any sense of stasis or fixity.

Fröydi Laszlo, in her essay *Place and World* (2015), in which she discusses the project and exhibition *Trout Fishing in America and Other stories* (Snæbjörnsdóttir and Wilson 2014), made reference to this essential componency as a factor of the work:

> For the viewer, this means that even the information he or she receives through the different components in an installation must combine and coalesce into a kind of crystalline or kaleidoscopic reflection. To achieve this effect, no piece may be too certain of its own truth. This means that even a self-critique of the media used to carry meaning must be strategically embedded. (Laszlo, 137–8)

In this sense, it must be evident how in the context of installation and certainly in the way that we use it, the space of exhibition itself, as instrument, is turned inside out to reveal, rather than seamlessly occlude, a set of mechanisms which interrelate. These mechanisms point from a material present to a constitutive past – research, that is, the delving inquiry into subject involving multiple parties and sites, is hauled in, evidenced and privileged strategically, in the same way as any presented fabrication or text.

Interspecific Intersection

Barrow and the North Slope Borough is a place where human interests of many kinds intersect. With the National Petroleum Reserve Alaska to the west and the Arctic National Wildlife Refuge to the east, Deadhorse and Prudhoe Bay between them, without obvious correspondence, such interests intermingle and coalesce with those of other species within a crucible of environmental contention. In *Matrix*, our interest was in this apparently human context for polar bear dens on the North Slope. As an icon, the polar bear exists (unrealistically) in a kind of splendid isolation – it roams our imagination – every bit as much as it roams the arctic landscape – as a powerful independent.

For years, as artists we have been fascinated by the individuality and ergonomics of polar bear maternity dens – their allure as places of beginning and of continuity and how, as such, they embody both a biological specificity of purpose and (to us) a cultural register, touchingly significant of environmental fragility.

Having over the last six years researched multiple unique iterations of denning, first in 'wilderness' areas in Svalbard and Greenland, by and large far from human presence, we find that in the Alaskan Arctic, the National Geographic narrative of pristine isolation and environmental perfection is misplaced – out there, polar bears share the terrain with a complex human matrix comprising the Inupiaq people, the oil industry, the tourist industry and a legion of environmental scientists. As a consequence, bears will often den in close proximity to human sites – by their own volition – and like the bears in Churchill, Manitoba, make use of the 'cover' and rewards that such proximity brings. The opportunism of bears, characteristic of predators in general, makes them stakeholders in a nexus of interspecific interests.

Just south of Point Barrow, within a few hundred yards of the most northerly projection of US soil, there exists a final scattering of makeshift hunting cabins, seasonal human dwellings in various states of disrepair, to which townsfolk too migrate in the summer. Around each cabin lie scattered respectively, chairs, lumber, packing and fishing equipment, children's swings, engine parts and so on. These always temporarily occupied and unoccupied constructions and dwelling assemblages suggested to us something analogous with the polar bear dens, central to our research.

They are not dens. They are not the places sculpted for the purpose of sheltering new life – but there seemed to us a correspondence nonetheless. Paradoxically, where one can be seen as the register of a seasonal new start, where the world itself is renewed each year in the guise of power and vulnerability, for us the other was inescapably a sign of resistance or a 'petering out' – an abandoned frontier at the edge of empire. The straggle of huts, equally disparate and individual in appearance, spoke hauntingly of the end of America, its entropic condition in the face of a north beneath which it sprawls – a place upon which its imperial ambitions seem destined now to be coldly extended, but which long after it is too late, it will not have understood.

In December 2017, President Trump of the United States announced that drilling would begin within the Arctic National Wildlife Refuge (ANWR):

> The GOP-led Congress voted [...] to lift a ban that had been in place since 1980 on oil and gas drilling in the refuge, a 19.6-million-acre section of north-eastern Alaska that is considered one of the most pristine areas in the country. The ban was removed as part of the Republican tax-reform package approved in December 2017 (*US Today* 2018)

Figure 11.3. Hunting cabins at Point Barrow. Photo courtesy of Snæbjörnsdóttir/Wilson (2015).

In September 2018, together with artist Allison Akootchook Warden, we travelled to her home village of Kaktovik, an isolated, arctic coastal settlement on Barter Island in the North Slope Borough, 60 miles from the Canadian border. Kaktovik, with a population of around 300 people, is the only village within the 19.6 million-acre ANWR.

During our visit, we attended public meetings and met with and interviewed many people from the community, including local officials, the US Fish and Wildlife Service and a researcher working on the impact of tourism in the area.

Inupiaq people have an ancient relationship with the polar bear, its habits and behaviours, and despite now sharing the wider region with incomers from over 30 nations, they maintain to this day their hunting traditions involving the animal as a source of food and clothing. In Kaktovík, however, this relationship has taken something of a turn in recent decades. Since the mid-1990s increasingly, polar bears are stranded during the autumn season on the beaches around the village and remain so until the ice re-forms in November. After a time, the whaling captains began customarily to leave the carcasses of the bowhead whales on a spit of land running parallel to the village seafront. Now, each year, up to 100 bears at a time gather there to feast off the bones.

As a consequence, tourists have been turning up during the whaling season in unprecedented droves. Jennifer Reed from the ANWR discussed the phenomenon when interviewed in September 2018:

> Before 2011, you know, visitor numbers for polar bear viewing in Kaktovik were, gosh, less than 50 annually. Today we're talking about hundreds and hundreds of visitors, many from around the world, each year.

In 2017, more than 2000 people visited Kaktovik specifically to see polar bears, an extraordinary hike in tourism for such a remote town. But not everyone is on board with the attraction. In the same article, Bruce Inglangasak, a licensed guide in Kaktovik, is quoted as saying 90 per cent of the town was against commercial tourism:

> The community was scared about, you know, activists that were going to try to get us to shut down the whaling – subsistence whaling … The tourists haven't stopped whaling, but there are still people in Kaktovik who feel like visitors gawk at their subsistence activities. It's an invasion of privacy.

With the prospect of drilling in the region, the town, already well-experienced in the vicissitudes of federal planning, not least from the ANWR assignation (1960) and its disruption of Inupiaq caribou hunting traditions, is now preparing (for good or bad) for an oil boom:

> And right now, there's plane load after plane load of tourists eager to see Alaska's most iconic endangered species. (Pemberton 2018)

The dreadful irony is that a perceived urgency drives these increasing numbers. In an article in the *New York Times* in 2016 Erica Goode quotes tourists to Kaktovik as saying:

> It was an urgency to come here […] My fear was that we would lose the opportunity of seeing these magnificent animals. (Goode 2016)

The situation in Kaktovik is even more complex than we had anticipated whilst planning our visit. Most significantly, there is no consensus amongst the people there, regarding any of the issues of contention – the ANWR, the oil and gas industries (from which each resident directly benefits financially each year)[1] or the desirability of polar bear tourism. When we interviewed Annie Sittichinli Tikluk of the Village Corporation, she told us the majority of the community see the tourists flying in from Fairbanks and Anchorage, sometimes for less than a day, to photograph the bears and then leave without any interaction with people, or benefit to the economy of the village. A further source of resentment is that they take up valuable seats on the very limited and hugely expensive plane service and this has meant, on a number of occasions, that members of the community have been prevented from accessing critical medical attention in relation to emergencies and chronic conditions alike. The people who benefit most are the two boat tour operators of the town.

We were told that, largely because of this discomfort and annoyance, a few days before our visit, the whaling captains had moved the whale remains from the usual site to a place on native land, an area not accessible to tourists at all. Although some bears remained within sight of the village, the majority migrated to this more isolated beach. As a consequence, even while we were

---

[1] Alaskan residents also receive annual dividend payments from the state's Permanent Fund, based on a five-year average of the fund's performance. The state established the Permanent Fund in 1976, as construction of the Alaska Pipeline concluded. Twenty-five per cent of revenue from mineral leases on state-owned lands and from federal mineral revenue-sharing payments go into the Permanent Fund for investment. In 2014, each Alaskan resident received $1,884 as a result of this pay-out, up from $900 in 2013 (https://www.doi.gov/sites/doi.gov/files/uploads/06102016_useiti_county_case_study_updates-north_slope.pdf, accessed 8 January 2019).

there, it was reported to us that there was considerable resentment from the incoming tourists who had invested substantial monies, some for the trip of a lifetime, to see and photograph bears.

In addition to their enforced containment through the late formation of fall ice, polar bear denning habits are also increasingly compromised by the effects of global warming and consequent sea level rise, meaning that coastal bluffs against which banks of snow have ordinarily built up are eroded and erased. Increasingly, the bears are digging their dens in earth banks.

Matrix

In the project that began for us with a speculative research visit to Svalbard in 2010 and continues (at the time of writing) on the North Slope Borough, we proposed that the ultimate challenge to representation, and yet the symbol that consequently may yet prove to be most durable, is a void – albeit a void constituted by specific contextual conditions. Into that void we would invite an audience to bring a perceptual mix of fragmentary knowledge and imaginative projection.

Matrix focuses on an evocation of the polar bear by making specific reference to the environment that is its point of individuated entry into the world – the maternity den.

The word 'matrix' signifies a substance, situation or environment in which something has its origin, takes form or is enclosed. The importance of the term in this context is as a displaced agent of potential – a locus for projection and contemplation.

The den of a polar bear is a white space in a white field. Its presence is announced discreetly as a darkening in the snow. Even experts in the field find a polar bear den remarkably hard to spot. It is a secret portal.

The prospect of entering or staring into a space, legitimised or given agency by the qualities of the absence it embodies, is powerful and compelling. By doing so, it is possible to sense and register our precarious human constructions of the world and, in this instance, our cultural conceptualisation of its possible, or inevitable, demise.

Central to *Matrix* is the idea of shelter or refuge as being a natural extension, expression and embodiment of the ontology of all living things. The polar bear den has no exterior shape. Its interiority is quintessential. It is a space, an emptiness into which new life is introduced. It declares, in very loaded terms, an absence. Before too long, vacated dens are liable to melt or collapse and so the absence implies the recent departure of the maternal family. But, in the project, the den – this space – is made to embody ideas of precarity and rejuvenation – even hope.

Through our discussions with scientists from the US Geographical Survey and US Fish and Wildlife Service, access was given to a series of recent field recordings – including diagrams and dimensions – of dens in the US Arctic. Once back in the UK, as a means of making material what is effectively a void without specific external margins, we worked with the National Glass Centre in Sunderland to construct a series of scale models (1:10) in glass, based on these carefully mapped and measured dens. The actual dens vary in their size and complexity – some comprise an entrance tunnel and a single birth chamber; some have multiple rooms and points of entry and exit, including those smaller exits made in the later stages by cubs. Accordingly, our scaled maquettes range from 250cm to 1m in length.

So, for the exhibition *Up Here* (May to October 2016), we exhibited *Matrix #1* on the top floor gallery of Anchorage Museum. The installation comprised three video and glass-maquette assemblages, a set of large framed photographs depicting individual summer shelters on the spit of land leading to Point Barrow and a video entitled *The Mariner's Oubliette*.

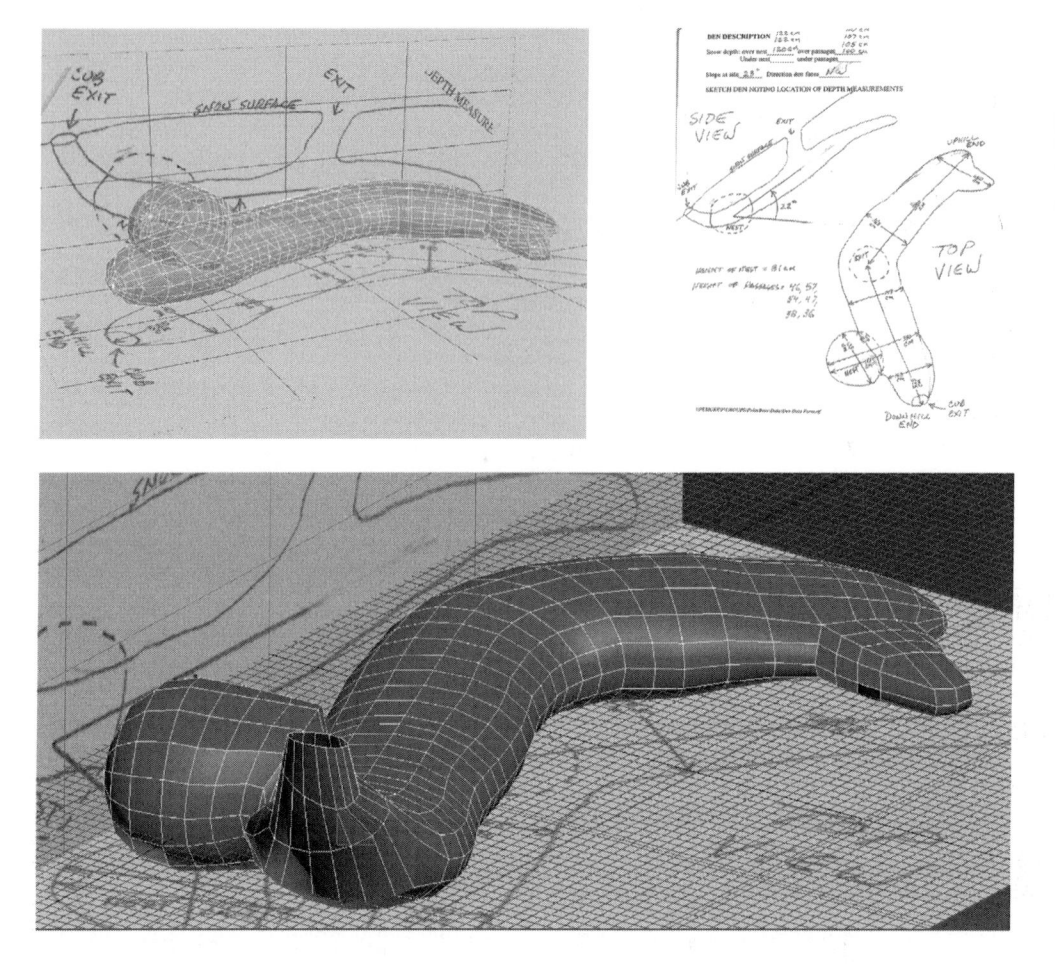

FIGURE 11.4. SNÆBJÖRNSDÓTTIR/WILSON (2016). PREPARATORY 3D VISUALISATIONS BASED ON FIELD DRAWINGS OF A POLAR BEAR DEN ON THE NORTH SLOPE BOROUGH. ORGINAL DRAWING PROVIDED BY US GEOLOGICAL SURVEY, ALASKA (COURTESY GEORGE DURNER PhD).

Within a closed vitrine, each of the glass den maquettes was placed on an elevated translucent glass floor, onto which a projector, concealed inside the vitrine base, back-projected sequences of the FLIR surveillance. The flickering light from the video refracted green and aquamarine through the underside of the glass, illuminating and animating the dens. Along with the other elements of the installation – in making visible the footage of the search through a physical mani-festation *in glass* of these hidden spaces, together with the constricted crackle of voices on board the plane, directing the sweep of the camera – we wished to bring to the viewer something of the complexity of interspecific relations in the fragile ecologies of the North and, in turn, their fateful connectedness to the resources upon which humans have globally come to depend.

In the light of our own research certainly, and in many ways more generally, ecotourism can be seen to be both an oxymoronic construction and problematic phenomenon. It seems to be an

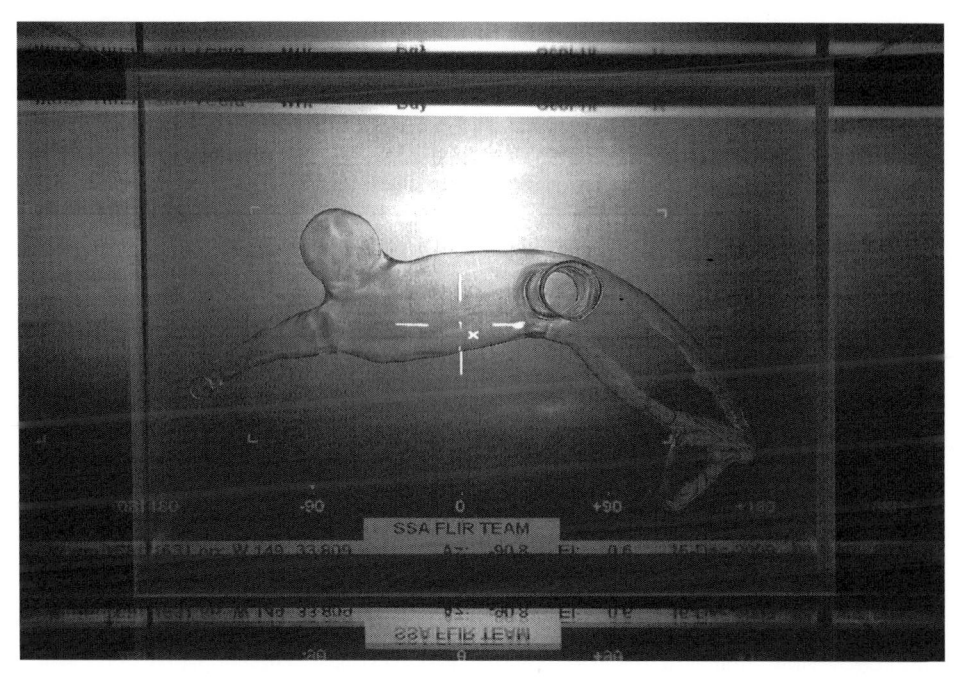

Figure 11.5. Snæbjörnsdóttir/Wilson (2016) *Matrix #1*. Glass maquette, scale 1:10 (made with the support of the National Glass Centre, Sunderland, UK).

additional, dubious and troublingly complicating factor in an already seething nexus of human/ interspecific interests and environmental frailty.

Quite what we do with this, in our ongoing work for *Matrix*, remains to be seen. The time is still a long way off when populations will be troubled by what artists say or do *per se*. Even in the circles of art, art that critiques the world and its institutions is often treated with suspicion – sometimes not particularly respected, or even understood. Artists working in this way are unashamed mongrels, dealing in the business of imponderables and hypothesis, whose mischievous enterprise mixes and melds knowledge from multiple fields and tests the strictures of those disciplines. Paradoxically, whilst the principles of interdisciplinarity are widely held to be desirable, artists as non-specialists, whose practices so easily embrace it, are not necessarily thought to be its most trusted or dependable stewards or leaders, perhaps because in respect of disciplinary structures and methodologies, subconsciously it is felt they have the least to lose. They tread in the territories of specialist others and, through dialogue and fieldwork, seek to make porous, procedures and research methods which might otherwise seem fixed and beyond question. Sometimes, locally, when we get it right, our interaction is welcomed and regarded even as useful, if only as an instrument by which issues, methods and beliefs might be considered differently.

Perhaps then, footfall is the difference by which we might justifiably weigh the relative merits of art-interventions and research in environmentally fragile areas on the one hand and the current global burgeoning of ecotourism on the other. Artists work as individuals or in small groups – their work is rarely, if ever, made for financial profit or backed to the point of influence by corporate interests. Their concern is with enquiry or critique, to make and share observations arising from their temporary entanglements in relation to specific intersections and interstices – to question publicly how else things might be. But, in the hands of business and entrepreneurial endeavour, the exponential footfall of ecotourism, engendered by an imperative to profit, will always risk compromising the delicate and 'exotic' ecologies which drive well-meaning customers to part with their cash.

As I say, how we deal with this added complication, in our project, is not clear. But, as a clearly evident extension of the interspecific biome of Kaktovik, the North Slope Borough, the Arctic National Wildlife Refuge, their denizens and their interests – in that already crowded room – it is too large an elephant to ignore.

BIBLIOGRAPHY AND REFERENCES

Canadian Broadcasting Corporation, 2014 *Bear Watching Profits*, available from https://www.cbc.ca/news/canada/british-columbia/bear-watching-more-profitable-than-bear-hunting-says-study-1.2488311 [7 August 2016]

Dylan, B, 1963 *Last Thoughts on Woody Guthrie* 12 April 1963 performance at New York City Town Hall, available from: http://genius.com/Bob-dylan-last-thoughts-on-woody-guthrie-annotated [2019]

Goode, E, 2016 'Polar Bears' Path to Decline Runs through Alaskan Village', *The New York Times* [online], available from: https://www.nytimes.com/2016/12/18/science/polar-bears-global-warming.html [9 January 2019]

FLIR, FLIR, available from http://flir.tw/ogi/display/?id=49559 [January 2019]

Flusser, V, 2000 *Towards a Philosophy of Photography* (1st English translation), Reaktion, London

Laszlo, F, 2015 'Place and World', in *Trout Fishing in America and Other Stories* (eds M Wilson and B Snæbjörnsdóttir), 133–46

Pemberton, J, 2018 *Alaska Public Media – Alaska's Energy Desk – Juneau – September 5th 2018* [online], available from: https://www.alaskapublic.org/2018/09/05/in-kaktovik-sea-ice-loss-means-a-boom-in-polar-bear-tourism/ [9 December 2018]

Steyerl, H, 2009 In Defense of the Poor Image [online], available from:

https://www.e-flux.com/journal/10/61362/in-defense-of-the-poor-image/ [2018]

US Today, 2018 Oil and gas drilling in Alaska [online], available from: https://eu.usatoday.com/story/news/politics/2018/04/19/trump-administration-takes-initial-step-steps-toward-oil-and-gas-drilling-alaskas-arctic-national-wi/533176002/ [9 December 2018]

World Tourism Forum, 2012 Pros and Cons of Eco-tourism [online], 7 April , available from: https://worldtourismforum.org/global/pros-and-cons-of-eco-tourism/ [October 2017]

EXHIBITIONS

Snæbjörnsdóttir/Wilson *Matrix #1* for International Polar Lab Group exhibition *The View From Up Here,* curated by Julie Decker, Anchorage Museum Alaska (May to September 2016)

—— *Shooting the Messenger* for International Group exhibition *Aiviq & Nanuk,* curated by Julie Decker, Anchorage Museum Alaska (October 2018 to May 2019)

—— *Trout Fishing in America and Other Stories* (2014), exhibition curated by Heather Lineberry and Ron Broglio, Arizona State Museum (October 2014 to January 2015)

—— *Beyond Plant Blindness* (2017), installation in three locations in Botaniska the Botanical Garden in Gothenburg, Sweden (April to September 2017)

12

Visitations: The Social and Cultural History of Polar Bear Narratives in Iceland and the North Atlantic

Kristinn Schram and Jón Jónsson

While bears hold a significant place in world views, material and narrative cultures around the world, the polar bear has a particular significance in the folklore of the Arctic and sub-Arctic. It should come as no surprise that this powerful and majestic animal has been respected, feared and even worshipped since the Stone Age, 50,000 years ago.

In the worldview of northern peoples, polar bears have been considered among gods and in some cases the ancestors of men. The Arctic region even draws its name from the Greek root *arktikos*, or *near the bear*, referring to the constellation Ursa Major, which, with Ursa Minor, appear in Ancient Greek mythology as the mythological mistress and lovechild of Zeus. Bear constellations are also known in the myths of indigenous groups in North America and Greenland and the Inuit concept of human-animal transformation, often involving a bear or a seal, can also be connected to the bear's role in shamanism (Thompson 1966, 167). In the British Isles, an example may be found in the bear-goddess Artio, derived from the Gaulish word for 'bear' and the Proto-Celtic *arto,* a word connected to the legendary King Arthur (Zimmer 2009). Irish family names, such as McMahon, meaning son of the bear-cub, and Mahoney, grandson of the bear-cub, also express bear-human interconnectedness among the Gaels (Jubainville 1889, 1905). Between these Inuit, Gallic and Scandinavian cultures, centrally located in the North Atlantic, lies an enlightening component in the cultural history of the bear. In this chapter we will explore what the role of the polar bear could be in the social and cultural history of Icelanders by referring to Icelandic narratives of these human-animal relations throughout the North Atlantic. These narratives demonstrate how, in a virtually bear-free country, folklore and narrative carries its inhabitants where their limited experience cannot.

Medieval Sources for Polar Bear Arrivals in Iceland

While Iceland is not a natural habitat of bears, its inhabitants' limited knowledge and experience with them mostly springs from their cultural origins in Scandinavia and the British Isles, as well as from Norse settlements in Greenland. Yet, through the centuries the polar bear, an icon of the Arctic, has on occasion come ashore in Iceland. Numerous narratives have been told and recorded of the Icelanders' interaction, or conflict, with the white bear (In Icelandic: hvítabjörn / plural: hvítabirnir), often simply referred to as bear (Icelandic: bjarndýr [literally, bear-animal]), or more recently ice-bear (Icelandic: ísbjörn). The polar bear's habitat of shores and ice lies around the Arctic Ocean, but they are often found on drift ice further south and can swim long distances in short periods of time. Their search for food can carry them far and their way of life follows that of the seal, which is its major food source. Those polar bears that have come ashore in Iceland have mostly arrived on drift ice or have swum a distance to shore. They are most likely to have come from East Greenland although it cannot be ruled out that some have come from Svalbard (Skírnisson 2009, 40).

In all, roughly 600 polar bears are said to have arrived in Iceland since its settlement (Icelandic Institute of Natural History website). Accounts of these arrivals can be found in sources of varying reliability so this number must be taken with caution. The number of accounts also constantly increases, not just by new arrivals, but by new discoveries of polar bear arrivals accounted for in early modern manuscripts and more recent newspapers and journals. Their digitisation and searchable databases have made these sources accessible, adding to the number of records. No systematic attempts were made before the 19th century to account for all polar bear visits to Iceland, so it appears to be a matter of chance if they appear in narratives. This number may therefore be too low, although many of the narratives do have a fictitious air. The numerations of the last two centuries are more reliable, showing for example that 70 polar bears arrived in Iceland in the 20th century (Halldórsson 2005). This includes the 27 bears that came ashore in the years 1917–18, which had high levels of sea ice beyond the island's shores (Skírnisson 2009, 39). From the year 2000, five bears have come ashore and all have been killed. Some of the bears in older accounts share this fate, while others disappeared out onto the ice or swam to sea. Biologist Ævar Petersen, an expert on polar bear arrivals in Iceland, has recently suggested that Iceland should be considered as the furthest reaches of the polar bear natural habitat (Petersen 2015, 72). Their comings and goings would then be a natural part of their wanderings. This is counter to other theories such as declining ice, a desperate search for food or even that these wandering bears have somehow become outcasts in the social systems of bears (Skírnisson 2009, 43–4). Petersen points out that recent research shows that the swimming capabilities of polar bears, travelling long distances without the support of land or ice, supports his suggestion of a larger range. He also mentions the many narratives of bears departing from Iceland's shores, unharmed (Petersen 2015, 72).

Narratives of the encounters between humans and bears have been known and told since the time of human settlement in Iceland, now widely acknowledged as the late 9th century. *The Book of Settlements* (Icelandic: *Landnámabók*), which contains a narrative overview of Iceland's settlers, is believed to have been written two centuries after the fact. It tells of old Ingimundur, who on his travels in north Iceland found a she-bear and her two cubs, and named the location Cublake or Húnavatn. It goes on to say that Ingimundur travelled to Norway and gave the animals to King Harold Fairhair. The *Landnámabók* (217) states that 'The men of Norway had never before seen a white bear', and the gift was rewarded with a ship, piled with wood.

Another account in the same source tells of Arngeir, who settled the Melrakkaslétta plains of northeast Iceland. He had gone off with his son Þorgils to look for sheep, but did not return. Another of his sons, Oddur, found both of them killed by a polar bear. In revenge for his father, Oddur killed the bear and ate it. After this event Oddur was described as wild and hard to deal with (*Landnámabók* [286]; see also Árnason 1956, IV 120–1). This, most likely the oldest, narrative of a bear killing a man in Iceland suggests the belief that eating bear meat induces certain characteristics and powers.

Hinting at human-animal transformation this case of contagious magic could be connected to a broader folk motif of warriors acquiring the fierce power of bears and other animals. The sagas of the Icelanders, and the younger legendary sagas, give many examples of this. Recorded in Iceland in a period ranging from the 12th to 14th centuries they hark back to oral traditions and historical times before and after the settlement of the country. A common form of animal-like warrior in these narratives is the berserk (berserkur) who becomes fearless and frenzied in battle and in some cases transforms (or transports) into the body of an animal (see e.g. Guðmundsdóttir 2007, 281). The etymology of the term, "bear-shirt" or "bear coat," in itself suggests that the warriors wore the pelts of bears and gained from them their strength and bravery. The sagas as a whole show a strong tradition of connecting warriors to powerful animals – a belief arguably supported by archaeological evidence of animal costumes used in the ritual activity of pre-Christian Scandinavia (see Gunnell 1995, 37).

Descriptions of berserks suggest a broad anthropomorphic and zoomorphic scope. Snorri Sturluson's *Heimskringla*, an account of the histories of Norwegian kings up to the 12th century, describes the berserks as warriors of the pagan god Óðinn that "went without mail and were mad as dogs or wolves, bit their shields, were strong as bears or bulls. They killed the men, but neither fire nor iron affected them. That is called going berserk (fóru brynjulausir ok váru galnir sem hundar eða vargar, bitu í skjǫldu sína, váru sterkir sem birnir eða griðungar. Þeir drápu mannfolkit, en hvártki eldr né járn orti á þá. Þat er kallaðr berserksgangr)" (Sturluson 1941, 17). A later example are the dozen berserks that appear in the legendary saga of Hrólfur kraki, among whom the most famous, and perhaps most hyperreal, is Böðvar Bjarki or Warlike Little-Bear. Bjarki is the son of Bera (she-bear) and Björn (bear) who was cursed to transform into a bear during the daytime (Hrólfs saga kraka 1960, 57). Böðvar Bjarki becomes a great warrior in the court of Hrólfur. In what turns out to be Hrólfur's last stand, Böðvar Bjarki appears to be sleeping but is actually in the field of battle defending his king in the form of a bear. Only when Böðvar Bjarki is awakened from his trance-like state does the bear leave battle – sealing their fate (Hrólfs saga kraka, ch. 25 and 50). While this account is somewhat reminiscent of shamanistic ritual it could just as well be a wandering motif derived from neighboring shamanistic societies such as the Sámi (see Tolley 2007, 6). These events in *Hrólfs saga* are meant to take place in Denmark centuries before Iceland's settlement (estimated in the late 9th century) and present rather extreme cases of the berserk. The wealth of material nonetheless would suggest a widespread knowledge of the animal warrior tradition among Nordic peoples and early Icelanders long before they recorded in written form. At some point, as in Oddur's case, these narratives enveloped the polar bear. Even Böðvar Bjarki himself, in one of his incarnations in the poetic *Bjarkarímur*, appears to be transformed, mid battle, into a *hvítabjörn* or white-bear, the common Icelandic term for the polar bear (Hrólfs saga kraka og Bjarkarímur 1904, 161).

Representations of polar bears in medieval literature and folk narrative vary significantly. In medieval literature, which is intrinsically connected with oral tradition, polar bears are used by human characters as precious commodities. They are presented to kings in the hope of reciprocity, advice and safe passage in their land. The bears do not seem to pose any danger to their handlers when they are transported across vast distances. One of the best-known polar bear accounts in medieval literature is *The Tale of Auðun of the West Fjords* (Icelandic: *Auðunar þáttr vestfirska*). A þáttr, literally a 'strand', is in fact essentially a short story, often serving as a kind of interlude in a longer saga, allowing only for the briefest action and character development. Auðun, an impoverished character from the Westfjords in Iceland, invests all he has on a living polar bear in the Norse settlement of Greenland. But rather than returning to Iceland, the ambitious Auðun is intent on presenting the bear as a gift to King Svein in Denmark. He somehow transports the living bear to Norway and must negotiate his way through the Norwegian court, without giving the bear to King Harald, Svein's sworn enemy. Managing this, as well as a quick pilgrimage to Rome to boot, Auðun returns to Iceland a man of means having gained the favour of both kings and provided them with a rare opportunity to negotiate.

In his extensive book on this story, Miller (2008) offers a nuanced reading of it, pulling together issues like luck, wealth and gift-giving and their importance in Norse culture and the human condition. But it is the particular animal and its cultural context that is, to his mind, most significant. Miller stresses that the unit of value is a white bear, an extravagant treasure but also, like Moby Dick, a blank cipher to be invested with meaning by those who encounter it.

Norwegian folklorist Knut Liestøl suggests this story, and many others like it, are likely rooted in oral traditions that eventually found their way into the migratory legends of Scandinavia (designated ML 6015/AT 1161, respectively) and particularly in western Norway (Liestøl 1933). These legends refer to an invasion by supernatural beings into the farmstead home that is only thwarted by a lone visiting 'man with no name' and his accompanying polar bear (sometimes a dog in the Icelandic variation). Interestingly, the evil beings, often in the form of trolls, mistake the bear for a white cat, and are later threatened by the farmer, who claims that 'she's had three kittens, and they're all bigger and more irritable than she is herself' (Gunnell 2004). Folklorist Terry Gunnell offers a close examination of these migratory legends and demonstrates how legends, both in Scandinavia and Iceland, come into being and migrate between countries, regularly mutating and adapting themselves (often with difficulty) to the prevailing circumstances and dominant beliefs. It is also worth noting that the mistaken identity of the bear, as a white cat, can be seen as a testament to the polar bear's rarity and exotic character in Scandinavia. This also provides the narrative function of stealth and surprise when the otherwise docile bear attacks the unsuspecting intruders.

More or Less than Human: Folk Beliefs and Legends

In Icelandic folk tales and legends from the last few centuries the polar bear is neither docile nor easily dealt with. Yet, many of them express a folk belief that attributes polar bears with various human characteristics, intelligence and, in some cases, even greater wisdom than that of humans. The most intelligent among them are said to have the acumen of 12 men (Jónsson 1979, III 192–3; Sigfússon 1982, 205–6). Some legends tell of the polar bear king who bears a horn on his head, much like the unicorn, but with a golden ring on its end. Furthermore, the animal speaks and understands human speech, a quality that features in many other bear narratives (Árnason 1956, IV 3; Sigfússon 1982, 205–6). Some legends tell of a special type of polar bear, the red-cheek (Icelandic: rauðkinnungur), which are recognised by the red colouration on the sides of their heads. They are said to be fiercer than other bears (Árnason 1954, I 608).

Commonly, folk tales and legends personify bears; they can be empathetic and are likely to reward generously any good deed that is done to their benefit. Ill deeds, on the other hand, are met with fierce revenge. These are characteristics shared with many supernatural beings in Icelandic legends but especially the elves, or hidden people, that command respect and often repay favours manifold. The bears reward human assistance with a share of their catch, two large grey seals in one example, or 13 large seals in another (Þorkelsson 1956, 299–300, 331; Jónsson 2009, 91–2). Iceland's northernmost island, Grímsey, is the background for many a polar bear narrative. One tells of a water shortage on the island remedied only when a bear arrives and strikes its paw on the rocks, from which water begins to spring. The islanders build a well on the spot and name it Bear-well (Icelandic: Bjarnarbrunnur) (Árnason 1956, IV, 28). A less appealing, but very human, trait shared by the polar bears of folk narrative is the propensity to take offence. On Grímsey, for example, it is said that bears were particularly sensitive to a particular insult: that their tail was unattractive from the rear (Icelandic: 'aftanljótur dindill') (Árnason 1956, IV, 4).

The idea that bears are actually humans under a spell appears early in Icelandic sources. Jón Guðmundsson, nicknamed 'the learned', was a self-taught polymath from the Strandir district of northwest Iceland. One of his best-known works is a natural history of Iceland from around 1600. In this manuscript Jón presents the folk belief that in some cases a polar bear's hibernation is actually an attempt to release themselves from their bear's guise. While this takes only 30 days and 30 nights, the problem is that a human is needed at the period's end to burn the guise while the bear is in its human form. Therefore, more often than not, the bear must wear his skin once again, and becomes even more difficult to deal with in his anger and greed (Hermannsson 1924, 13–14; Hreinsson 2016, 586). This motif can also be found in 19th century folk tales such as one that claims that bears give birth to human children that only become bear cubs after the she-bear strikes her paw over them. One narrative tells of a man who stole a new-born girl from a she-bear. The girl thrived well but sought more and more to be out at sea. One day she had wandered on to the ice and came across a she-bear that lifted her paw and changed the girl into a cub (Árnason 1954, I, 606).

Bears are also said to be so wise that they recognise both their potential killer and namesake among humans (Sigfússon 1982, 205–6). The belief that bears do not eat their namesakes is prominent in folk narrative. Those that bear names such as Björn, Bjarni, Bessi or Bessa are therefore safe from bear attacks and bears are safe from them, as killing one namesake among animals also brings ill fortune (Árnason 1956, IV; Sigfússon 1982, 205–6).

A related tradition of narratives tells of bears sparing pregnant women. One narrative tells of two women on the run from an assailing bear. One of them was pregnant and lagging behind the other one. But the bear ran past her, killing the other woman, before returning to the pregnant woman and laying its head in her lap. The woman interpreted this act as a request to name her unborn son Björn (Davíðsson 1978, II, 291). This and other narratives like it show a clear connection between naming folklore and pregnancy and the clemency it provides (Sigfússon 1982, 205–6; Bjarnason 1954, II, 18; Þórisdóttir 2018, 15).

It is clear that bears of these narratives have a certain code of ethics that must be honoured in their interaction with humans. As is also common in Greenlandic folklore, mutual respect must be shown at all times. In Icelandic legends, a hunted animal should be allowed its dignity in its final moments. Attacking a dying animal is considered an act of villainy and brings misfortune on the attacker (Árnason 1954, 608–9). The biologist Þórir Haraldsson's reading of polar bears in Icelandic folk tales is that they show how people related to nature and respected the various forces that reside within it, both visible and invisible. In other words, the nature of man and animal is the same, whether it is expressed through nobility or cruelty. He concludes that the tales have a moral significance and, like many other folk tales, are meant to teach that integrity leads to happiness (Haraldsson 2002, 491–2). The speech, royal status and gratitude of animals is of course not limited to Icelandic polar bear narratives. They are international legend motifs and are applied to various animal species. But perhaps because of their physicality, way of life and perseverance, polar bears take on a more human character than most other animals.

A Cruel and Dangerous Beast

Anthropomorphic qualities are not the only aspects of significance in Icelandic polar bear legends. Other examples stress the cruelty of the bear and the danger that their presence poses. Within these legends the Icelandic population, dispersed across the country's coastline, experiences the sudden arrival of the polar bear as an invasion. The bear as a menacing outsider is believed to be vicious and life-threatening, disrupting daily life and posing a risk to both humans and livestock. It is worth noting that no other wild animals pose a threat to humans in Iceland. This invasion of an external agent is therefore one of the key aspects of polar bear legends. In many, the bear invades the farmhouse itself in search of food. In some ways the bear is more like a supernatural being than an actual animal.

The unwelcome guest, a cruel beast who comes from the sea, belongs to a different world than the Icelanders. Stories of their invasion are in many ways comparable to those of precarious nature-spirits roaming on the dusky edges of the human abode, occasionally overrunning the farmstead in the twilight of the winter solstice or Yule (Gunnell 2002, 191–7). It is in this liminal period of time that the elves, or hidden people (Icelandic: huldufólk), find new habitat, and sometimes throw parties in the people's homes while they attend Christmas mass. This is also the period of time when Grýla, the mother of trolls and mischievous Yule-lads, roves the countryside looking for human children to feed the litter awaiting her return to the cave. The Yule-lads themselves also venture into the homes of men. Having been somewhat sanitised in contemporary narrative forms, these beings appear in older legends, rhymes and ballads as evil, roguish rascals that may prove quite dangerous. Nearly all of these Yule-tide beings are said to come from the hills and mountains, the uninhabitable highland interior, but with some interesting exceptions. A few legends from east Iceland tell of their arrival from the sea – much like the bears. It is also from the sea that Iceland's greatest human danger presents itself, that of the pirates who terrorised the coasts of Iceland, mainly in the 17th century, pillaging and abducting hundreds of people who were sold into slavery in far-off places such as the Barbary Coast. These narratives of external invasion commonly express a fear of the unknown and augment the threat, danger and cruelty drawn from history and shared imaginaries.

As mentioned above, this particular tradition of Icelandic narratives emphasises the cruel nature of the polar bear. As a character, its chief motive is to attack, kill and eat the farm's residents, men, women and children. These narratives are likely to have shaped contemporary views toward polar bear sightings. In light of this, it is interesting to examine if any historical sources or anecdotal evidence might be found of polar bears actually killing humans. Indeed, narratives of polar bears that may be found in folk tale collections and other sources are to a large extent folklore rather than history. One distinguishing feature of these narratives is the general anonymity of the bears' victims. Considering the intense Icelandic preoccupation with genealogy, this is somewhat suspicious. For comparison, the first alleged arrival of the plague in Iceland was traced back to a named and fully identifiable individual in 1402. Nevertheless, one cannot rule out the possibility that some accounts of polar bear attack, and their specified locations, are based on actual events.

In the oldest annals there are two accounts of bears killing a group of people. The year 1321 annals tell of a polar bear coming ashore in Heljarvík Bay in the Strandir region of northwest Iceland and killing eight people. Another account, from 1518, claims a polar bear came ashore on the Skagi peninsula, also killing eight people, who are described as 'poor women and children' (Þórisdóttir 2018, 26, 30).

Folk tale collections provide us with additional narratives that mention particular farms ruined by polar bear attacks where every resident had been killed (Þórisdóttir 2018, 42–3, 79, 81–3, 90). Many stories share the added drama of the man of the house being away as the bear attacks his homestead. On his return he is met with a ghastly sight, such as the pile of his wife and children's bones in the farmhouse or his wife's finger or arm close by. In some cases, he encounters the bear carrying the woman's breast in his mouth, spurring the farmer's pursuit and eventual revenge (Árnason 1956, IV, 3–6; Davíðsson 1978, II, 293–4; Jónsson 1979, III, 188–90). Two additional legends from Grímsey contain a curious form of child sacrifice. Evidently, it was believed that once a bear had settled in its den trouble would ensue and the animal would grow evil and cruel, having 'layed down on its paw' (Icelandic: 'lagst á hramminn'). An Icelander had therefore to attempt to draw the bear out from its den by dangling his child in front of it. Disaster followed when the bear managed to kill the child and was itself killed in revenge (Davíðsson 1979, II, 292; Sigfússon 1982, 207).

Of the numerous groups of people supposedly killed by polar bears, only six individuals are mentioned by name. Among them are two characters from 9th century settlers, Arngeir og Þorgils (mentioned earlier) and a character drawn from legends of the Westfjords: Dýra-Steinþór (Beast-Steinthor), well known for killing up to 19 or 20 bears (not to mention chopping off the hand of an ogress). His last polar bear was also his bane after charging downhill towards the bear with his halberd (a form of Viking age pole weapon; Icelandic: atgeir) acting as a lance. The power of the charge was such that the end of the halberd crushed Steinþór's chest, so both man and bear were killed (Bjarnason 1954, II, 13–19; Davíðsson 1979, III, 17). The narrative expresses the folklore motif that each hunter can only hunt a certain number of animals, usually 20, before he is himself killed in vengeance (Sigfússon 1982, 211–12). Other tales of 'heroes', such as Dýra-Steinþór, and their numerous conflicts with bears can also be found; one of them was Bjarndýra-Hálfdán, who was also killed by his last polar bear (Árnason 1956, IV, 4).

A well-known migratory legend, that has been attached to various mountain tracks across Iceland, tells of the cunningness of polar bears encountering travellers armed with either halberds or, alternatively, alpenstocks, a mountaineer's staff (Icelandic: broddstafur). While many variations may be found they essentially describe the bear sniffing the weapon and then allowing the rambler to continue on his way unharmed. On his way down the mountain pass the armed traveller meets another wanderer and lends him the weapon for protection. When the bear then sees a second traveller carrying the same weapon he chases after the initial, and now defenceless, one, who the bear then kills and eats (Jónsson 1979, III, 191–2; Árnason 1954, I, 607–8; Árnason 1956, IV, 4; Þorkelsson 1956, 369–70; Sigfússon 1982, 203–4; Friðlaugsson 1935, 392). In one curious variation, the victim is named Bessi (a derivative of the name Björn or bear); this variation thus runs counter to the naming-folklore that should have been his salvation, because the bear generally does not kill his namesake.

One more polar bear victim mentioned by name is Hjálmar Jóhannsson, who was killed in the remote Hornstrandir region of northwest Iceland. Oral narratives, told by his descendants, claim he had died from his wounds some time after attempting to fight the animal with a shark lance, a weapon commonly used in shark hunting (Jörundsdóttir 2018). According to church records, Hjálmar was born 8 May 8 1806 and died 20 December 1838. The cause of death is not stated but does briefly mention that he 'died with haste' (ÞÍ, 127; Íslendingabók).

On 30 April 30 1859, a local news item appears in *Norðri*, the local paper of the northern town of Akureyri: 'Rumour has it, that 6 bears arrived in Strandir and killed two men, before it was slain' (*Norðri* 1859, 43). This is the most recent account of a polar bear actually killing people in Iceland and is yet unsubstantiated by any other source. Rumour, indeed.

The Killing Fields

In 19th century folk tales it was believed ill fortune would follow the killing of an animal that stayed clear of humans. Such narratives of polar bears can be found on Grímsey Island and the Melrakkaslétta plains of northeast Iceland (Davíðsson 1978, II, 291; Þórisdóttir 2018, 108–9). It is nevertheless likely, at least since the early modern age, that bears would be killed if sighted, since the catch was considered a great boon. Its pelt was a precious treasure that could be sold at a high price and was coveted by both churches and kings (Teitsson 1975, 35–44). A common phrase, even in modern Icelandic, 'bjarnylur', or 'a bear's warmth', springs from folk belief recorded in both medieval literature and a mid-19th century folk tale collection. The bears are believed to be 'of a warm nature' that could be transferred to anyone that is born on a polar bear's pelt. According to this belief this individual could count on being immune from the cold, which is certainly a desirable trait in the North Atlantic climate (Hávarðarsaga Ísfirðings; Árnason 1954, I, 605.) The meat from the bears was eaten throughout the centuries and examples can even be found in the late 20th century (Petersen 2015, 69). In the last decades Icelanders have shied away from eating polar bear meat because of the risk of *Trichinella* infection, which is also one of the reasons stated for shooting polar bears on arrival to Iceland (Skírnisson 2013, 143-149). The most recent bears to arrive in Iceland have been taxidermied and are much sought after by museums, where they attract attention as objects of display.

Through the ages the killing of polar bears appears as a heroic act in the Icelandic folk narratives, stressing conflict between man and beast. It is only in the last years that questions have been raised about the necessity of shooting polar bears on arrival. Whether they appear in 19th century folk tales or contemporary news items, they often feature renowned bear-slayers, unexpected heroes, inadequate weapons and close calls. Among the unexpected heroes are members of the household forced to take on the polar bear in the absence of a more likely 'hero', who is away. Using whatever household appliances are available and taking advantage of the confines of their small turf houses, they usually prevail. A woman on the Melrakkaslétta plains, for example, hides behind the stairs that lead to where her children are concealed. As the bear tries to stretch its paws toward the children, she kills it with a pair of scissors (Davíðsson 1978, II, 292–3). Another woman similarly lures a bear toward her children before killing it with a knife (Árnason 1956, IV, 5–6). In the Westfjords, a blind man, the legend goes, manages to kill a polar bear with a knife as it attempts to squeeze in through a window (Bjarnason 1959, III, 36–8). In another story, children are hiding in the loft as the bear attempts to break through the loft hatch. Having poked up his head the bear licks its lips at the sight of the children. The oldest boy then quickly grabs a knife and cuts out its tongue and thus kills it (Árnason 1956, IV, 6). Children who kill polar bears in Icelandic folk tales are without exception boys.

Attempts to trick the bear or cleverly defend oneself are also quite illuminating. A woman living alone in Hvanndalur valley was once visited by a group of polar bears. Before they managed to break into her house, she managed to heat tar in a pot, over the fire. While forcing its way in, one of the bears poked in its rear end and the lady then poured the hot tar over it, which ignited its hair. The group stampeded out onto the ice, ridding her of the bears – at least momentarily (Sigfússon 1982, 210–11). The folk tales of Grímsey Island explain that its houses are built in long and winding passageways in order to discourage bears from such meanderings (Davíðsson 1978, II, 292).

In the Strandir district, a common spot for bear visits, the locals still tell jokes of how best to escape an attacking bear. One of them recommends choosing a companion who is somewhat slower to run. Another piece of advice, which appears quite comical, involves turning one's clothing, including gloves, inside out. If the bear gives chase one should begin by throwing a glove over one's shoulder. The bear, as the story goes, cannot tolerate inverted clothing and will sit down to turn it back to normal before continuing after its prey (Þórisdóttir 2018, 195). On inspection this hilarious advice appears, apparently without irony, in the travel books of two foreign travellers who visited Iceland, Niels Horrebow in the mid-18th century and Ebeneser Henderson from 1814–15 (Jónasson 1961, 190).

Another interesting motif can be found in a few legends where the master of the house releases a viscious bull, a bloated stallion or an exquisite saddlehorse that fights the bear. The conflict usually ends with the death of both animals (Jónsson 1979, III, 192–3; Sigfússon 1982, 209–10, 227–8). Among the more recent features in narratives of the polar bear slayer are inadequate weapons, such as a broken or ramshackle gun (Thorarensen 1971, I, 223–4). Also an important feature is how close the characters come to disaster (Jónsson 1979, III, 185–8).

'Close calls' are also a fixture of contemporary media narratives on bear arrivals in the 20th and 21st centuries. These modern narratives of bear-sighting and slaying stay relatively clear of the anthropomorphic features of traditional narratives. They focus rather on the threat of the bear and the pursuit that begins as soon as it is spotted. The tight squeezes and inadequate weaponry of the narratives also reflect how unprepared people were to meet dangerous animals. The sighting of polar bears was news in itself and no less a source of anxiety. The local paper *Austri* started the new century, 11 January 1901, by reporting the following:

> We hereby report that a bear was spotted in Steingrímsfjörður [of the Strandir region], close to the farms Skeljavík and Kálfanes; it lingered in the heath above them but sometimes ascended down to sea. It has disappeared now and is nowhere to be found. This is considered strange, indeed (*Austri* 1901, 3).[1]

It is perhaps not pure coincidence that on the same page one finds an advert for guns and ammunition, imported from Norway. A former district officer in the Strandir region, Guðjón Guðmundsson of Eyri (1890–1972), puts emphasis on how defenceless the less affluent farmers were in the past and had good reason to fear encroaching ice flows. After one such ice-winter (Icelandic: hafísvetur) in 1968, Guðjón, a polar bear slayer himself, nonetheless states, of his contemporaries, that only cowards fear the ice. He is quoted as saying that 'young people today may sometimes fear the polar bear but such fear is unnecessary in modern times, when everybody has such good guns' (Jónsson 1968, 107). Despite the late 20th century proliferation of rifles and shotguns in rural communities, the white-knuckle narratives of close calls are still a feature of news reports and often appear in literature, film and television.[2] Official and unof-

---

1 'Þess skal hér getið, að vart varð við bjarndýr í Steingrímsfirði, í sumar er leið, frá bæjunum Skeljavík og Kálfanesi; hélt það sig í heiðinni þar fyrir ofan, en kom stundum niður að sjó. Nú er það horfið fyrir nokkru og hefir hvergi komið fram. Þykir það nokkuð kynlegt' [authors' translation].
2 See for example the so-called *Nonni* books of Jón Sveinsson (1913), later adapted into a television series titled *Nonni und Manni* (1988); see also *Ikingut* (2010), a film featuring an Inuit child wandering across sea ice from Greenland to Iceland, initially mistaken for a cub.

ficial reports and sightings are also quickly distributed on social media, a potential measuring stick of social anxiety.

At the turn of the 21st century, the polar bear in Iceland has acquired connotations that district officer Guðjón of Eyri could not have dreamed up. Icelanders are active participants in global consumer culture and no strangers to the Coca-Colonisation of polar bears. The Coke-drinking polar teddies, tag-lined 'Always Cool, Always Coke', represent a sharp swing back towards anthropomorphic representation, only with a stark infantilising feature (Ellis 2009, 263; *Wagnleitner* 1994*)*. But neither is it lost on Icelanders that polar bears have taken on geopolitical and ecological significance. They feature heavily in the imagery of scientific cooperation in the Arctic. Scientific diplomacy helped maintain the high north as a region of low tension throughout the Cold War and continues to be regarded as essential to achieving Arctic sustainability in the future (Berkman 2019). As a symbol of the fragility of the Arctic, the polar bears' status as threatened or vulnerable is demonstrated by their visitations to Iceland.

The most recent polar bear arrivals in Iceland in 2008 (the first in 20 years), 2010, 2011 and 2016 garnered both international and domestic attention (Engelhard 2017). While protected under Icelandic law, the polar bear may be shot by permission of the authorities if there is believed to be a security or contamination threat. In the wake of their killing some discussion has taken place in the media and among policy-makers. Despite some public calls for rescue and even 'repatriation', a working group commissioned by the environmental ministry supported the response with the exception that a costly rescue plan be put in place subject to low-risk scenario. As yet, no such plan is in place (Guðmundsson *et al* 2008).

Nevertheless, polar bears are presented to tourists in Iceland as an accessible and familiar animal, easily bought and taken home as a souvenir. As one of the most prominent 'Arctic objects' on display in Icelandic tourism destinations and stopovers, polar bear souvenirs can be seen as fundamental parts of the 'mental map' and visual archive of the North. Exotic images of 'the North' have played a considerable part in the self-representation of Iceland in the last decades (Loftsdóttir 2018). This form of 'borealism' speaks to how Icelanders negotiate and adapt to emerging regional developments through an Arctic or 'West Nordic' identification (Schram 2011). While Iceland's Arctic status can be called into question, such narratives in many ways reflect state policy and the dynamics of globalised market forces and geopolitics. Yet one can find counter-narratives to direct at these somewhat dubious representations of Iceland and its relationship with polar bears. A case in point is a curious venture, called Fooled by Iceland, a thinly veiled spoof of a massive tourism campaign called Inspired by Iceland. The anonymous campaign, which began as a student project in the Icelandic University of Art, consisted of a series of posters distributed around Reykjavík, deactivating tourist traps and correcting falsehoods. One of the posters depicts a drawing of a polar bear and states: 'Polar bears do not live in Iceland. Sometimes they travel from Greenland on an iceberg. When they do, we kill them' (Fooled by Iceland).

This popularity of the polar bear in Icelandic representation that includes consumer products, tourism and art can be connected to its growing role in the discourse of climate change and fragile environments under threat. The polar bear's image connotes the conditions of regional groups in the Arctic, not always to these groups' liking, but to some extent addressing the challenges shared around the globe. It therefore has quite extensive significance to Arctic discourses and climate change, with unlimited potential for associations on both local and global scales as one of the primary non-human actors in the climate change discourse (Bjørst 2011, 256). In the Icelandic context, these narratives, and counter-narratives debunking common myths and deconstructing associated images of authentic Arctic Iceland, position Iceland directly within Arctic discourses. But, like Audun of the Westfjords, they project quite culturally specific values on the blank slate of the exotic polar bear.

The folklore of the bear in Iceland, and particularly the polar bear, is only to a limited extent a reflection of human-bear interaction. Rather, the bears exist in a buffer zone between the collective realm of imagination and a material reality where human-polar bear encounters are, however, distinctly possible. Within this buffer zone Icelanders may examine the blurry lines between human and animal, between the civilised and the wild, between security and danger. Through various Icelandic narratives of its *visitations* and *invasions*, in sources ranging from medieval literature and legends to new media, the polar bear is presented with many faces and in varying degrees of anthropomorphism or human-animal transformation. It can be benign and malicious, appeased or hunted, respected and feared as an outsider. It is a source of symbolic or magical strength, status, identity, warmth, food, exoticism, heroism, calamity and lingering danger. While none of the accounts of Icelanders being killed by polar bears can be taken at face value, the visitations of polar bears are perceived as a destructive force in Iceland. Despite some arguments placing Iceland within the furthest reaches of the polar bear's natural habitat, its arrival is perceived as 'unnatural'; an invasion or, more recently, a contamination risk.

In our times, the Anthropocene, the polar bear is symbolic of a climate damaged through human intervention. The polar bear has particular meanings in the folklore of northern peoples and not least on the edges of their habitat. As a symbol of conservation, climate change and Arctic cooperation, the polar bear connotes the Arctic as an image that is claimed by both Arctic and sub-Arctic countries, including the North Atlantic islands of Iceland and Greenland as well as the Nordic kingdoms that have ruled over them. Yet, narratives within 'Arctic tourism' seem to incorporate the polar bear in the country's fauna and place Iceland firmly within the Arctic despite the country's somewhat ambiguous geopolitical status. The polar bear's fleeting presence on Iceland's shores and cultural imagination therefore does not only call into question the boundaries of the human and the animal, but also the Icelanders' place in a precarious world. These projections of human aspiration and trepidation perhaps do not leave the polar bear, in itself, with much agency or room for representation. As narrated in the social and cultural history of Iceland, in the greater North Atlantic context, the *bjarndýr* remains a cypher.

BIBLIOGRAPHY AND REFERENCES

Árnason, J, 1954–61 *Íslenzkar þjóðsögur og ævintýri* I–VI. (eds Árni Böðvarsson and Bjarni Vilhjálmsson), Þjóðsaga, Reykjavík

Auðunar þáttr vestfirska, 1943 *Íslensk fornrit* 6, 359–68

Austri, 11 January 1901, 3

Bjarnason, A F, 1909, 1954, 1956 *Vestfirskar þjóðsögur* I–III, Ísafoldarprentsmiðja, Reykjavík

Bjørst, L R, 2011 *Arktiske diskurser og klimaforandringer i Grønland. Fire (post) humanistiske klimastudier*, PhD dissertation, University of Copenhagen, Copenhagen

Davíðsson, Ó, 1978–80 *Íslenzkar þjóðsögur* I–IV, 3, Þjóðsaga, Reykjavík

Ellis, R, 2009 *On Thin Ice: The Changing World of the Polar Bear*, Vintage Books, New York

Engelhard, M, 2016 *Ice Bear: The Cultural History of an Arctic Icon,* University of Washington Press, Washington

Friðlaugsson, J, 1935 Hvítbjarnaveiðar í Þingeyjarsýslu, *Eimreiðin* 41 (4), 388–403

Guðmundsdóttir, A. 2007 The Werewolf in Medieval Icelandic Literature, The Journal of English and Germanic Philology, 106(3), 277-303

Guðjónsdóttir, S B, 2014 *Björn, bersi, bangsi. Birtingarmyndir hvítabjarna í íslenskum þjóðsögum og miðaldabókmenntum,* BA-essay, University of Iceland, Reykjavík

Guðmundsson, H J, Guðmundsson, G A, Jónsson, Ó, and Stefánsson, S V, 2008 *Viðbrögð við landgöngu hvítabjarna á Íslandi,* Umhverfisráðuneytið, Reykjavík

Gunnell, T, 1995 *The Origins of Drama in Scandinavia*, D.S. Brewer, Cambridge

——, 2002 Komi þeir sem koma vilja … Sagnir um innrás óvætta á jólum til forna á íslenska sveitabæi, *Úr manna minnum: Greinar um íslenskar þjóðsögur* (eds B Hafstað and H Bessason), Heimskringla, Reykjavík

——, 2004 The Coming of the Christmas Visitors: Folk Legends Concerning the Attacks on Icelandic Farmhouses Made by Spirits at Christmas, *Northern Studies* 38, 51–75

Haraldsson, Þ, 2002 Hvítabirnir í þjóðsögum, *Úr manna minnum: Greinar um íslenskar þjóðsögur* (eds B Hafstað and H Bessason), Heimskringla, Reykjavík

Hávarðar saga Ísfirðings, 1943 *Íslensk fornrit* VI, 289–358

Hermannsson, H, 1924 Jón Guðmundsson and his Natural History of Iceland, *Islandica: An annual relating to Iceland and the Fiske Icelandic Collection in Cornell University Library* XV, Cornell University Library, Ithaca, New York

Hrólfs saga kraka. 1960 (Slay, D ed.) Den Arnamagnæanske Kommission, Copenhagen

Hrólfs Saga Kraka og Bjarkarímur. 1904 (Jónsson, F. ed.) S.I., Møllers Bogtrykkeri, Copenhagen

Hreinsson, V, 2016 *Jón lærði og náttúrur náttúrunnar,* Lesstofan, Reykjavík

Jónasson, J, 1961 *Íslenzkir þjóðhættir,* 3 edn (ed E Ó Sveinsson), Ísafoldarprentsmiðja, Reykjavík

Jónsson, G, 2009 *Skaftfellskar þjóðsögur og sagnir* II, Skrudda, Reykjavík

Jónsson, Þ M, 1978–79 *Gríma hin nýja. Safn þjóðlegra fræða íslenzkra* I–V, Þjóðsaga, Reykjavík

Jónsson, K, Sigurbjarnarson, G, and Víkingur, S, 1968 *Hafís við Ísland,* Kvöldvökuútgáfan, Akureyri

Jubainville, H d'Arbois, 1889 Gentilices en ius, *Revue Celtique* 10, 164–9

——, 1905 Les dieux celtiques a forme d'animaux, *Revue Celtique* 26, 196–9

Landnámabók, 2, Íslenzk fornrit. 1968, vol 1, Hið íslenska fornritafélag, Reykjavík

Liestøl, K, 1933 Kjetta pa Dovre, *Maal og Minne* 24, 24–8

Loftsdóttir, K, 2018 *Crisis and Coloniality at Europe's Margins: Creating Exotic Iceland,* Routledge, London

Miller, W I, 2008 *Audun and the Polar Bear: Luck, Law, and Largesse in a Medieval Tale of Risky Business,* Brill, Leiden

Norðri, 30 April 1859, 43

Petersen, Æ, 2015 *Hvítabirnir á Vestfjörðum fyrr og nú. Hornstrandir og Jökulfirðir* V (ed Hallgrímur Sveinsson), Vestfirska forlagið, Þingeyri, 58–77

Schram, K, 2011 Banking on Borealism: Eating, Smelling, and Performing the North, *Iceland and Images of the North* (Imaginaire du Nord Series), Presses de l'Université Québec, Québec

Sigfússon, S, 1982 *Íslenskar þjóðsögur og sagnir* IV (ed Ó Halldórsson), Þjóðsaga, Reykjavík

Silis, I, 1981 *Nanok,* Vindrose, Copenhagen

Skírnisson, K, 2009 Aldur og ævi hvítabjarna, *Náttúrufræðingurinn* 77 (1–2), 39–45

——, 2013 Um líffræði tríkína og fjarveru þeirra á Íslandi, *Náttúrufræðingurinn* 83 (3–4), 143–9

Slay, D, 1960 Hrólfs saga kraka. 1960 (Slay, D ed.) Den Arnamagnæanske Kommission, Copenhagen, Editiones Arnamagnæanæ, Series B. Sveinson, J, 1913

Sturluson, S, 1941. Heimskringla I., Íslensk fornrit, vol. 26, Hið íslenzka fornritafélag, Reykjavík

Teitsson, B, 1975 Bjarnfeldir í máldögum, *Afmælisrit Björns Sigfússonar* (eds B Teitsson, B Þorsteinsson and S Tómasson), Sögufélag, Reykjavík, 23–46

Thompson, S, 1966 *Tales of the North American Indians,* Indiana University Press, Bloomington, 167

Thorarensen, J, 1971 *Rauðskinna hin nýrri. Þjóðsögur, sagnaþættir, þjóðhættir og annálar* I–III, Þjóðsaga, Reykjavík

Tolley C. 2007 Hrólfs saga kraka and Sámi bear rites, Saga Book, 31

Wagnleitner, R, 1994 Introduction, *Coca-Colonization and the Cold War: The Cultural Mission of the United States in Austria After the Second World War*, The University of North Carolina Press, Chapel Hill, NC

Þórisdóttir, R R, 2018 *Hvítabirnir á Íslandi*, Bókaútgáfan Hólar, Reykjavík

Þorkelsson, J, and Pétursson, H, 1956 *Þjóðsögur og munnmæli* I, 2 edn, Bókfellsútgáfan hf, Reykjavík

Zimmer, S, 2009 The Name of Arthur: A New Etymology, *Journal of Celtic Linguistics* 13 (1), University of Wales Press, 131–6

ÞÍ Þjóðskjalasafn Íslands: Staður í Aðalvík. Prestþjónustubók 1816–52 [unprinted]

Websites/ online sources

Berkman, P A, *Science Diplomacy Action: An Incidental Serial for Rigorous Meeting Syntheses* 2019 [online], available from: https://www.uarctic.org/media/1599347/science-diplomacy-action_synthesis-no-3_arctic-science-agreement-dialogue-panel_supporting-implemention-of-the-arctic-science-agremenet-_31jan19.pdf [18 March 2019]

Fooled by Iceland [online], available from: http://fooledbyiceland.tumblr.com18.3.2019 [18 March 2019]

Halldórsson, J M, *Hvað hafa margir ísbirnir komið til Íslands? Vísindavefurinn* 22 December 2005 [online], available from: http://visindavefur.is/svar.php?id=5506 [18 March 2019]

Íslendingabók [online], available from: https://www.islendingabok.is [18 March 2019]

Icelandic Institute of Natural History website [online], available from: http://en.ni.is/zoology/mammals/polar-bears/index.html [18 March 2019]

LSJ: The Online Liddell-Scott-Jones Greek-English Lexicon [online], available from: http://stephanus.tlg.uci.edu/lsj/#eid=15561 [18 March 2019]

Pers comm

Jörundsdóttir, S H, 2018 Personal communication (interview by the author) 14 October

Film and television

Nonni und Manni 1988; *Ikingut* 2010

Bear Biology, Management and Conservation

13

Chemical Signalling in Brown Bears

Melanie Clapham, Owen T. Nevin and Ian Convery

Olfactory communication has been defined as: 'The process whereby a chemical signal is generated by a presumptive sender and transmitted (generally through the air) to a presumptive receiver who by means of adequate receptors can identify, integrate and respond (either behaviourally or physiologically) to the signal' (Eisenberg and Kleiman 1972, 1).

Brown bears (*Ursus arctos*) have been reported in literature to mark and rub on trees (Tschanz *et al* 1970; Green and Mattson 2003; Puchkovskiy 2009). This has been linked to olfactory communication among brown bears, though until recently no clear function had been attributed. In this chapter we present an overview of research conducted to explore the biological significance of chemical signalling in brown bears (from Clapham 2012; Clapham *et al* 2012, 2013, 2014). This was conducted by assessing scent marking site selection, understanding who are the signallers and receivers, and studying the postures and stereotypithy of marking behaviour. To establish why these behaviours have evolved, the significance of observed signalling behaviours can be evaluated in terms of their potential fitness benefits. Assessing the function of scent marking in brown bears provides an opportunity to establish its influence on the social behaviour of the species, thus demonstrating the importance of behavioural studies conducted *in situ*. Collectively, knowledge of this form of social behaviour provides a unique insight into the social complexity of this species.

BEARS AND TREE MARKING

Brown bears claw, bite, urinate and rub various parts of the body against trees, each being suggested as a method of chemical communication (Tschanz *et al* 1970; Lloyd 1979; Green and Mattson 2003; Puchkovskiy 2009). Brown bears are reported to use a diverse range of tree species for their marking activities; these are often referred to as 'bear trees' or 'rub trees' (Tschanz *et al* 1970; Puchkovskiy 2009). The use of 'traditionally rubbed trees' by brown bears is highlighted by Green and Mattson (2003). These are trees that are repeatedly used for marking by bears over successive years, and their non-random selection is said to indicate their importance within intraspecific communication (Tschanz *et al* 1970; Green and Mattson 2003; Clapham 2012; Clapham *et al* 2013), rather than an individual response to external stimuli as suggested by Meyer-Holzapfel (1968, in Burst and Pelton 1983). The continual use of previously marked trees was also found in black bears (*U. americanus*) (Burst and Pelton 1983), and in giant pandas (*Ailuropoda melanoleuca*), termed 'scent stations' by Swaisgood *et al* (2004). Schaller *et al* (1985) categorised the term 'scent post' as trees with visible scent deposits by giant pandas, not just clawed trees. It appears that multiple species of bears use traditional marking sites, but how do bears select which trees to use? Are there certain tree characteristics that are important to bears?

Prior to our work on tree species selection in brown bears, we considered evidence collected from three distinct geographic areas: Russia, the continental USA and Greece. These studies, while restricted in number, provided a strong theoretical underpinning for our work on marking site selection.

Puchkovskiy (2009) assessed the selectivity of such trees across different forested landscapes in Russia. He found a strong element of selectivity according to tree species, with selection favouring coniferous over broadleaf species (Puchkovskiy 2009). Among coniferous trees, rarer species in forest stands, fir (*Abies* spp.) and pine (*Pinus sibirica*) – termed 'cedar' in Puchkovskiy 2009 – were actively selected at a higher rate than the dominant species (spruce: *Picea* spp.). Brown bears invested more effort in selecting these rarer species of tree for marking than any other species available to them. A possible motivation behind this selection could be that fir and pine trees provide a supplement to the olfactory signal.

Wiley (1983) suggested that to have evolved, chemical modes of signalling must have provided a fitness benefit to signalling individuals which outweighed the costs endured. It is well documented that mammals, particularly large species, select conspicuous objects on which to deposit chemical odours (Macdonald 1980, 1985; Wiley 1983). Brown bears also appear to select conspicuous objects by selecting the rarer tree species for scent marking. The low rates of occurrence of both fir and pine within forest stands in Russia may have rendered their presence conspicuous.

In contrast, Green and Mattson (2003) found no evidence of tree species selectivity for scent marking by brown bears in the Greater Yellowstone Ecosystem. They indicated that the dominant species within the study area 'had a strong effect on marking', but did not link this to which species were marked predominantly (Green and Mattson 2003). However, they did find a difference between the diameter of marked versus unmarked trees, but did not refer to this as a scent marking strategy. Instead they suggested that the properties of a tree enhance rubbing as a pleasure stimulus, rather than to aid in chemical signalling. Though not suspected by the authors, it is possible that in this location bears were selective on the size rather than the species of tree for marking; perhaps size could also render a tree conspicuous.

Karamanlidis *et al* (2007) reported that brown bears in Greece mark wooden power poles processed with a preservative coating, usually creosote. Power poles are placed 50–100m apart, with vegetation in the direct vicinity cleared (Karamanlidis *et al* 2007). Corridors form between these locations, creating a network of travel routes (Karamanlidis *et al* 2007). The selection of power poles for scent marking may initially seem unconventional; however, once again the unusual/conspicuous object within the local environment is selected. Creosote may act as an additional attractant to supplement the olfactory signal or as a novel odour for 'scent rubbing' (Gosling and McKay 1990).

Study Site

Glendale Cove is situated along Knight Inlet, on the south-central coast of British Columbia, Canada. During spring/summer brown bears are attracted to the tidal marshes to feed on sedges (*Carex* spp.). This coincides with the breeding season (beginning in late May and continuing until mid/late July) when adult males, lone adult females and courting pairs can be seen in this area. At this time of year, females with dependent young are often viewed towards the far north of the estuary, feeding along the inter-tidal zone (Nevin 2003; Nevin and Gilbert 2005a). Approximately 40–50 brown bears use the Glendale spawning channel as a primary energy resource during hyperphagia, due to the abundant return of pink salmon (*Oncorhynchus gorbuscha*) (Nevin 2003; Nevin and Gilbert 2005b; Clapham *et al* 2012). Data were collected between 1 June and 31 July in 2009 and between 1 June and 5 October in 2010 and 2011.

Identifying Brown Bear Marking Trees

Traditional marking trees can be distinguished from trees that have merely been scratched or rubbed on a single occasion by following certain criteria (Clapham *et al* 2013). Traditionally used trees usually have:

- remnants of hair attached to the bark or resin
- altered bark texture which may appear smoothed
- visible claw and bite marks, often contributing to a large wound on the tree.

It is also possible to identify recent use by the presence of freshly exposed resin, lacerated bark which has not yet fallen to the ground, lighter exposed wood and loosely attached hair which would be displaced by wind or rain.

For our research (Clapham 2012; Clapham *et al* 2013), in order to identify if bears were behaving selectively when choosing marking sites, we documented both marking and non-marking trees. We recorded the tree species along with diameter at breast height (dbh) and the angle of the tree. We also documented features of the marks including: height of the tallest visible mark from the base of the tree, descriptions of the marks, and any evidence of over-marking through different aged marks. Once a marking tree has been recorded, 5m radius sample plots were then conducted to identify the local tree composition, noting the species, dbh and angle of each tree. Line transects were conducted systematically throughout the surrounding forest to assess the availability of tree species on a landscape scale. In addition, transects were conducted following wildlife trails to assess the composition of trees on trails compared to the wider landscape.

Description Of Marking Trees

A total of 50 traditional marking trees were located and of these almost 50 per cent (23) were amabilis fir (*A. amabilis*). The remaining trees were: Sitka spruce (*Picea sitchensis*) (11), western hemlock (*Tsuga heterophylla*) (eight), western red cedar (*Thuja plicata*) (seven) and red alder (*Alnus rubra*) (one). These trees were significantly larger (dbh) than unmarked trees and the maximum height of marks was 2.02m ± 0.22.

Dead trees, which had been marked while alive, were occasionally still marked, although it is more difficult to identify this visually due to the lack of fresh sap (Fig 13.1a). The longevity of marks varies greatly; for example, marks caused by a wet bear rubbing a tree can be visible for less than two hours (Fig 13.1b) while biting or clawing marks remain fresh throughout the current year (Fig 13.1c).

The species of tree upon which marks are made also has a great influence on the appearance of those marks. While Amabilis fir and Sitka spruce trees often had large scars due to bark being removed by biting or clawing (Fig 13.1d and e), western red cedar and western hemlock were not found to scar in this way but rather displayed variation in bark texture between marked and unmarked areas (Fig 13.1f and g). Areas which had been rubbed also exhibited a shiny appearance. Marking trees typically had no lower branches, although this is the general growth form within the stands where these trees were found.

Fig 13.1 Photographs of trees marked by bear rubbing. a) Dead amabilis fir; such trees are still marked by bears, but lack characteristic signs such as sap and fresh wounds. b) Red alder marking tree recently rubbed by a bear with a wet pelage. This type of sign will dry within a few hours. c) Fresh and scarred claw marks on an amabilis fir marking tree. The lacerated bark to the right of the photograph displays fresh claw marks. d) Large scar on an amabilis fir caused by the removal of bark through clawing and biting by bears over many years. e) Small scar on a Sitka spruce. The lack of moss growing below the scar indicates that the tree is still frequently used. f) Western red cedar displaying evidence of rubbing by bears through the shiny appearance and change in texture of the bark. g) Western red cedar displaying evidence of rubbing by bears through the shiny appearance and change in texture of the bark. h) Red alder displaying evidence of rubbing by bears. Note the darker appearance of the bark in comparison with the trees in the background. This tree did not satisfy all the criteria to be classed as a traditional marking tree. (Clapham 2012).

Fig 13.2 Photograph of a stomp trail leading to a brown bear marking tree. This trail was visible for the entire fall season of 2011.

Red alder was the only broadleaf hardwood species to be identified as a traditional marking tree. Marks on red alder appear visually similar to marks on western red cedar and western hemlock. Rubbing by bears darkened the already smooth bark of the one red alder marked frequently (Fig 13.1h). A series of depressions (footprints) leading to the mark tree was evident at some locations (Fig 13.2). These are created by bears grinding and stomping their feet in succession as they approach the marking tree. When this stomping behaviour was observed directly, lasting visible marks were not always left, depending on the substrate. Therefore, while not all trees had easily observable stomp trails these may have been present in a form not detectable to the human observer, eg scent.

LOCATION AND SELECTION OF MARKING TREES

We found that marking trees were primarily located on forest edges bordering either the Glendale estuary or riverbanks along the valley. These trees were clustered near productive food resources where levels of bear activity were higher. Searches across the landscape found some marking activity; however, these trees were much more widely spaced than those surrounding the estuary.

The species of tree selected for marking differed significantly from a random selection among those available on both a local scale and a landscape scale; this was similar to the findings of Puchkovskiy (2009) in Russia. Amabilis fir, Sitka spruce and western red cedar were all selected for marking more frequently than would be expected based on their abundance in the landscape. On a local scale, ie within a 5m radius, Amabilis fir and western red cedar were selected significantly more than expected.

Detailed analysis of these data (Clapham 2012; Clapham et al 2013) reveals that the initial criteria of a marking tree is primarily that of location, and then of tree selectivity by species and size. It has been suggested that, due to increased intraspecific competition, scent marks should be concentrated in areas where the defence of a resource is needed to facilitate the function of chemical signals in influencing the behaviour of receivers (Dawkins and Krebs 1978; Lloyd 1979; Gosling 1981, 1990; Smith et al 1989). In the Glendale drainage, marking trees were located on trails leading to the estuary/river, with patterns of use dictated by temporal food availability. Marks appear to be placed in areas frequented by females, to which males are attracted. Once these areas are established, marking trees are selected based on context. In forests, trees are not conspicuous unless they differ from their surroundings. Selection depends on the species and size of the tree, with other properties likely playing a secondary role. The strategy of placing scent marks along well-used travel routes and on conspicuous trees that differ from their surroundings increases the likelihood of the scent mark being encountered and demonstrates the mitigation of time and energy expenditure in relation to potential fitness costs by the signaller.

THE SOCIAL FUNCTION OF CHEMICAL SIGNALLING IN BROWN BEARS

To examine marking behaviour in more detail, cameras were placed at 21 traditionally marked trees which showed signs of recent activity (Clapham 2012; Clapham et al 2012, 2014). Cameras were positioned to capture both marking behaviour at the tree and the behaviour on approach and departure.

Data were collected across 1,265 trap nights during the breeding season and 1,024 trap nights during the non-breeding season, with a trap night defined as a 24-hour monitoring period by a single camera. Scent marking and investigatory behaviour were documented outside of the breeding season to assess for potential seasonal differences. Camera traps were located surrounding the estuary in the spring and repositioned facing marking trees in areas of high activity during the pink salmon run from August onwards (Nevin and Gilbert 2005c). The age-sex class of the individual(s) captured by the cameras was recorded and their behaviour classified using an ethogram, or set of behavioural definitions, developed specifically for this project (Table 13.1). Courting pairs were classified as individuals and, where images of an individual were separated by less than five minutes on a single camera, they were not considered independent events. Twenty-five individual bears were identified during the breeding season. In the non-breeding season 52 individuals were identified; 11 of these were seen in both seasons.

Table 13.1 Behavioural ethogram of investigatory and marking behaviour exhibited by brown bears in the Glendale drainage (Clapham 2012; Clapham *et al* 2013)

Course	Behaviour	Description
Approach/Leave	Walk	Approach or depart the tree by walking at a normal pace, rear legs bending: a regular walking gait
	Stomp	Approach or depart the tree at a slower pace with
		rear legs extended as brought forward
		grinding of the pad, especially rear, into the ground in succession
		pacing back and forth in front of the tree; whereby stepping in the same depressions made in the ground each time
Investigation	Investigate	Direct contact of nose with tree (quadrupedal)
		Head angled towards tree with
		neck stretched
		nose lifted/twisted
		Changing course of direction to approach tree
		Hesitating and visibly angling body/head towards tree
		Smelling ground in direct vicinity of tree
	Investigate bipedal	Investigating the tree standing on rear legs only
Scent marking*	Sit**	Sitting at the base of the tree with or without direct contact of the back to the tree, on haunches
	Back	Direct contact of the back on tree standing on rear legs only (bipedal)
	Flank	Direct contact of the flanks, rump, and/or shoulders on tree (quadrupedal)
	Head	Direct contact of the head and/or neck on tree, ventral or flank towards the tree (quadrupedal or bipedal)
	Claw	Raking the tree with claws once or repeatedly (quadrupedal or bipedal)
	Bite	Biting the tree, but not consuming the wood (quadrupedal or bipedal)
	Chest	Direct contact of the chest with the tree (bipedal)
	Stomp	Stomping in between other scent marking behaviours

* As urination cannot be reliably detected in captured images, the presence or absence of urination within the behavioural sequence was not included in analysis.

** As anal sacs containing secretions have been reported in brown bears (Rosell *et al* 2011), sitting at the base of trees may function in deploying secretions.

MARKING EVENTS

Camera traps captured a total of 1,050 independent events across the study period with different age-sex classes frequenting sampling locations in proportion to their occurrence in the general population observed at that time. The presence of bears on these trails was, therefore, shown to be representative of the observed population.

The frequency of marking by individuals was significantly different between age-sex classes during the non-breeding season. Comparison of frequencies of events at a population level revealed variation in marking and investigatory behaviour as a product of age-sex class and season. Across both seasons, adult males marked trees more than expected when using trails containing marking trees. Females with young, however, marked and investigated in proportion to their use of trails across both seasons and adult females marked less than expected across both seasons. No females with young less than one year of age were captured on cameras during the breeding season. Subadults marked less than expected during the breeding season and as expected during the non-breeding season.

Using these data, we assessed the social function of chemical signalling in brown bears, based on the behaviour of different age-sex classes at marking trees, comparing between breeding and non-breeding season (Clapham 2012; Clapham *et al* 2012, 2014). We concluded that scent marking functions primarily to communicate dominance between adult male brown bears. Other age-sex classes may eavesdrop upon these signals; for example, Jojola *et al* (2012) found that captive subadult brown bears investigate the anal gland secretion (AGS) of adult males more intensively than that of females. Marking trees did not appear to be used by adult females to advertise oestrus; instead we hypothesised that substrate marks alone may be sufficient to attract mates and further research is needed on this type of scent marking. Females with young cubs changed their behaviour outside of the breeding season, which was thought to function in the engagement of young with marking trees at a time of year when they are less vulnerable to infanticide.

STEREOTYPITHY IN MARKING BEHAVIOUR

Despite many anecdotal accounts, Tschanz *et al* (1970) were the first to provide a detailed description of marking postures used by brown bears. Recorded in captivity, they state that bears rubbed all parts of their body and head against trees, pit walls, stall gates and on the ground whilst bipedal, quadrupedal, sitting or lying down (see Tschanz *et al* 1970 for a detailed account of individual marking postures). Urination took place simultaneously with rubbing in males during all postures, but only during bipedal back rubbing in females (Tschanz *et al* 1970). They describe a wide range of rubbing postures, but found that bipedal back rubbing was the most prevalent and was recorded in all males studied (Tschanz *et al* 1970). This posture is described as:

> In the upright position, the neck and shoulder is used, in that touching the back and the head is accomplished by bending the knees and rubbing the length of the tree, or rubbing the middle by swinging from side to side in pendulum form. Both methods have been seen to be used in combination (translated from Tschanz *et al* 1970, 52).

Males used a wider variety of rubbing postures than females; females most often rubbed as per the above description, while additionally pulling available branches to the head and throat

(Tschanz *et al* 1970). However, as males investigated scents left on the ground, at shoulder height and bipedal, the mode of rubbing is said to be irrelevant to the effect of the scent upon other individuals (Tschanz *et al* 1970). Alternatively, multiple marking postures may create a more complex chemical signal (Johnston 2005), in that scent is deposited from multiple locations on the body; mosaic chemical signals are thought to aid in individual recognition (Johnston 2005) and scent-matching (Gosling 1982).

Male giant pandas display a wider variety of marking postures than females; urine deposited via a handstand position is only displayed by males (Kleiman *et al* 1979; Schaller *et al* 1985; Swaisgood *et al* 2000; Liu *et al* 2006). When studied in a captive setting, more energy is invested in investigating elevated scents (urine and anogenital gland secretion) than those placed at lower levels (White *et al* 2002). White *et al* (2002) reported that subadult males displayed avoidance behaviour when adult male urine was placed to replicate the handstand posture. It may be, therefore, that handstand marks function to signal competitive ability and possibly aggressive intent between adult males (White *et al* 2002).

A wide range of postures and patterns are employed by members of the order Carnivora to mark their scent onto objects, and therein signal to conspecifics. While there is much anecdotal evidence on the marking behaviour of brown bears, until relatively recently (Clapham 2012; Clapham *et al* 2014) no published empirical data examined marking patterns displayed by wild populations. Our work has defined behaviours related to the approach, investigation and/or marking of a tree by bears. Analysis of each event where a bear, of known age-sex class, had investigated or marked on a tree using these behavioural categories revealed strong stereotypithy in marking behaviour (Figs 13.3 and 13.4 display two examples of classified behavioural

Fig 13.3 Camera trap photographs of an adult female investigation sequence, displaying: a) approach to the tree (unknown), b) quadrupedal investigation, c) bipedal investigation, and d) depart (walk). (Clapham 2012).

FIG 13.4 CAMERA TRAP PHOTOGRAPHS OF AN ADULT MALE BROWN BEAR SCENT MARKING SEQUENCE, DISPLAYING A)
APPROACH-WALK, B) QUADRUPEDAL INVESTIGATION, C) FLANK RUB, D) BACK RUB, E) SIT, F) BACK RUB, G) STOMP, H) BACK
RUB, I) STOMP, J) FLANK, K) BACK RUB, L) DEPART (WALK).

sequences, with descriptions from the ethogram where the repeatable, or stereotyped, nature of
these sequences can be seen). This was particularly apparent for adult male bears and less so for
subadult bears and cubs.

CONSTRUCTING SCENT MARKING HYPOTHESES FOR URSIDS

Chemical signalling is thought to provide a fitness benefit to signallers as a method of manip-
ulating receivers to the signaller's reproductive advantage (Dawkins and Krebs 1978). However,
receivers are also under selection to respond appropriately to signals in relation to their own
reproductive success, and adjust their behaviour if the signal is beneficial (Johnstone 1997).
Indeed, signals must be appropriate to the sensory and cognitive capabilities of the intended
receiver to elicit a response (Guilford and Dawkins 1991; Johnstone 1997). Fitness costs could be
reduced if animals behave strategically, and use the physiochemical characteristics of their environment to their advantage (Müller-Schwarze 2006). Brown bears select trees for scent marking,
which has advantages over auditory or visual signals in that scents persist in the absence of the
signaller (Doty 1986), but this would be true of marking onto any object. We argued that their
selectivity of trees on which to mark and the location of these trees displays an economical system
of signalling whereby signallers limit the energetic costs of producing scent marks by placing
marks strategically to intercept potential receivers (Clapham 2012; Clapham et al 2013). Studying
the efficacy of marking strategies has provided evidence concerning the function of scent marking
in brown bears. The fitness benefits individuals gain at marking trees may be highlighted by the
amount of time and energy bears invest in signalling and/or receiving scents. This led to the

documentation of stereotyped patterns of tree marking behaviour, with variations indicated by age-sex class.

In Clapham (2012) it was suggested that the behavioural strategies used by brown bears when tree marking are comparable to those of species with known methods of scent deposition, where chemical signalling has been identified. Kleiman (1966) stated that a scent mark can be distinguished by identifying specific behavioural and biological changes in an individual, not attributed to the deposition of excreta. During our research (Clapham 2012; Clapham *et al* 2012, 2013, 2014) specific behavioural patterns have been observed in brown bears which cannot be purely attributed to the deposition of excreta or the relief of an irritant. Observations of selected marking postures indicated that brown bears primarily use trees to rub the flanks, dorsal surface (back), head and chest (Clapham 2012; Clapham *et al* 2012, 2014). The utilisation of a tree to rub the back is feasible as it is an unreachable area. However, the flanks, head and chest are accessible for the bear to make contact with using their claws alone. Given the thickness of the pelage of bears, it seems unlikely that a tree would provide a greater alleviation than contact with the claws. In addition, marking trees usually lack lower limbs (Green and Mattson 2003; Clapham 2012), are not selected based on lean, and therefore apparently do not provide any additional benefit over claw-use.

If rubbing behaviour was not communicative, there would be no requirement for individuals to use the same trees. These rubbing locations could be on trails as bears passed through the forest, though there would appear to be little requirement for them to be clustered near food resources. Instead, rubbing locations could be situated throughout the landscape, with trees used at random and little investigation of trees by other bears. Conversely, brown bears mark in high traffic areas, select conspicuous trees based on their species and size, use the same trees as conspecifics, vary the frequency of use of marking trees depending on their age and sex class, vary their frequency of use between breeding or non-breeding season, and display stereotyped postures and patterns when tree marking. All of these support the hypothesis that tree marking has a functional role in chemical signalling in brown bears.

The use of scent marking for chemical signalling among mammalian populations is well studied. Through hypothesis-driven research, the mechanisms, strategies, social functions and potential fitness benefits of scent marking behaviour have been determined for many species. However, despite their ecology hypothetically favouring chemical methods of communication, the Ursidae have received little attention. As sexual selection and the physical environment dictates chemical modes of signalling for many species of large mammal, an increased knowledge of scent marking behaviour in bears will permit greater understanding of their ecological needs and selective pressures. This chapter has highlighted the knowledge gained from our research on chemical signalling behaviour in brown bears. Using purely observational studies, the location of marking trees, frequency of scent marking by different age-sex classes, time and energy invested in marking and receiving scents and specific behaviours exhibited at marking trees all indicate that chemical signalling is taking place when brown bears mark trees. In our studies, adult males appeared to invest the most time and energy in marking behaviour, which could indicate they gain net fitness benefits from chemical signalling. The behaviour of other age-sex classes at marking trees, particularly subadults and females with young, seems to be dictated by the behaviour of adult males in the area at that time, causing seasonal variation. We hypothesised that marking trees function to signal competitive ability between individuals, with dominant individuals signalling their high competitive ability and receivers detecting these cues and modifying their behaviour accordingly. Within this hypothesis, marking trees may also function in individual recognition of conspecifics, and could facilitate scent matching. This research was the first to publish data on the social function of scent marking in brown bears and the first to relate scent marking strategies and related marking behaviours to cost/benefit reasoning. It should be considered a preliminary study, from which hypotheses can be developed, and are now being developed, by other research groups in addition to ours.

BIBLIOGRAPHY AND REFERENCES

Benner, J M, and Bowyer, R T, 1988 Selection of trees for rubs by while-tailed deer in Maine, *Journal of Mammalogy* 69, 624–7

Burst, T L, and Pelton, M R, 1983 Black bear marks trees in the Smokey Mountains, *International Conference for Bear Research and Management* 5, 45–53

Clapham, M, 2012 *An assessment of the chemical signalling strategies employed by brown bears (Ursus arctos) to communicate with conspecifics*, PhD, Lancaster University, UK.

Clapham, M, Nevin, O T, Ramsey, A D, and Rosell, F, 2014 Scent marking investment and motor patterns are affected by the age and sex of wild brown bears, *Animal Behaviour* 94, 107–16

——, 2013 The function of strategic tree selectivity in the chemical signalling of brown bears, *Animal Behaviour* 85, 1351–7

———, 2012 A hypothetico-deductive approach to assessing the social function of chemical signalling in a non-territorial solitary carnivore, *PLoS ONE* 7, e35404

Dawkins, R, and Krebs, J R, 1978 Animal signals: information or manipulation? in *Behavioural Ecology: An Evolutionary Approach* (eds J R Krebs and N B Davies), Blackwell Scientific Publications, Oxford, 282–309

Doty, R L, 1986 Odor-guided behavior in mammals, *Experientia* 42, 257–71

Eisenberg, J F, and Kleiman, D G, 1972 Olfactory Communication in Mammals, *Annual Review of Ecology and Systematics* 3, 1–32

Gosling, L M, 1981 Demarkation in a gerenuk territory: an economic approach, *Zeitschrift für Tierpsychologie* 56, 305–22

———, 1982 A reassessment of the function of scent marking in territories, *Zeitschrift für Tierpsychologie* 60, 89–118

———, 1990 Scent marking by resource holders: alternative mechanisms for advertising the costs of competition, in *Chemical Signals in Vertebrates* (eds D W Macdonald, D Müller-Schwarze and S E Natynczuk), Oxford University Press, Oxford

Gosling, L M, and McKay, H V, 1990 Scent-rubbing and status signalling by male mammals, *Chemoecology* 1, 92–5

Green, G I, and Mattson, D J, 2003 Tree rubbing by Yellowstone grizzly bears Ursus arctos, *Wildlife Biology* 9, 1–9

Guilford, T, and Dawkins, M S, 1991 Receiver psychology and the evolution of animal signals, *Animal Behaviour* 42, 1–14

Johnston, R E, 2005 Communication by mosaic signals: Individual recognition and underlying neural mechanisms, in *Chemical Signals in Vertebrates* 10 (eds R T Mason, M P LeMaster and D Müller-Schwarze), Springer, USA

Johnstone, R A, 1997 The evolution of animal signals, in *Behavioural Ecology: An Evolutionary Approach*, 4 edn (eds J R Krebs and N B Davies), Blackwell, Oxford

Jojola, S M, Rosell, F, Warrington, I, Swenson, J E, and Zedrosser, A, 2012 Subadult brown bears (Ursus arctos) discriminate between unfamiliar adult male and female anal gland secretion, *Mammalian Biology* 77 (5), 363–8

Karamanlidis, A A, Youlatos, D, Sgardelis, S, and Scouras, Z, 2007 Using sign at power poles to document presence of bears in Greece, *Ursus* 18, 54–61

Kleiman, D G, 1966 Scent marking in the Canidae, *Symposium of the Zoological Society of London* 18, 167–77

Kleiman, D G, Karesh, W B, and Chu, P R, 1979 Behavioural changes associated with oestrus in the giant panda, *International Zoo Yearbook* 19, 217–24

Liu, D, Yuan, H, Tian, H, Wei, R, Zhang, G, Sun, L, Wang, L, and Sun, R, 2006 Do anogenital gland secretions of giant panda code for their sexual ability? *Chinese Science Bulletin* 51, 1986–95

Lloyd, H A, 1979 Aspects of the Ecology of Black and Grizzly Bears in Coastal British Columbia, unpublished MSc thesis, University of British Columbia, Vancouver

Müller-Schwarze, D, 2006 *Chemical Ecology of Vertebrates*, Cambridge University Press, New York

Murie, A, 1981 The grizzlies of Mount McKinley, *U.S. Department of Interior, National Park Service, Science Monograph Series* 14, 251

Nevin, O T, 2003 The Influence of Prey Abundance and Risk-Sensitive Behavioral Change on Individual Access to High-Energy Food (Salmon): Impacts on the Density and Viability of Bear Populations, unpublished PhD thesis, Utah State University, Utah

Nevin, O T, and Gilbert, B K, 2005a Observations of autumn courtship and breeding in brown bears, Ursus arctos, from coastal British Columbia, *Canadian Field Naturalist* 119, 449–50

——, 2005b Measuring the cost of risk avoidance in brown bears: Further evidence of positive impacts of ecotourism, *Biological Conservation* 123, 453–60

——, 2005c Perceived risk, displacement and refuging in brown bears: positive impacts of ecotourism? *Biological Conservation* 121, 611–22

Pocock, R T, 1921 The external characters and classification of the Procyonidæ, *Proceedings of the Zoological Society of London* 91, 389–422

Puchkovskiy, S, 2009 Selectivity of tree species as activity target of brown bear in taiga, *Contemporary Problems of Ecology* 2, 260–8

Rosell, F, Jojola, S M, Ingdal, K, Lassen, B A, Swenson, J E, Arnemo, J M, and Zedrosser, A, 2011 Brown bears possess anal sacs and secretions may code for sex, *Journal of Zoology* 283, 143–52

Schaller, G B, Jinchu, H, Wenshi, P, and Jing, Z, 1985 *The Giant Pandas of Wolong*, University of Chicago Press, Chicago

Smith, J L D, McDougal, C, and Miquelle, D, 1989 Scent marking in free-ranging tigers, Panthera tigris, *Animal Behaviour* 37, 1–10

Stefanov, I S, 2012 Macromorphometric study on the paranal sinuses in a brown bear Ursus arctos, *Bulgarian Journal of Veterinary Medicine* 15, 57–61

Swaisgood, R R, Lindburg, D G, White, A M, Hemin, Z, and Xiaoping, Z, 2004 Chemical communication in giant pandas, in *Giant Pandas: Biology and Conservation* (eds D G Lindburg and K Baragona), 257–91, University of California Press, California

Swaisgood, R R, Lindburg, D G, Zhou, X, and Owen, M A, 2000 The effects of sex, reproductive condition and context on discrimination of conspecific odours by giant pandas, *Animal Behaviour* 60, 227–37

Tschanz, B, Meyer-Holzapfel, M, and Bachmann, S, 1970 Das Informationssystem bei Braunbären, *Zeitschrift für Tierpsychologie* 27, 47–72

White, A M, Swaisgood, R R, and Zhang, H, 2002 The highs and lows of chemical communication in giant pandas (Ailuropoda melanoleuca): effect of scent deposition height on signal discrimination, *Behavioral Ecology and Sociobiology* 51, 519–29

Wiley, R H, 1983 The evolution of communication: information and manipulation, in *Animal Behaviour*, 2 edn (eds T R Halliday and P J B Slater), Blackwell Scientific Publications, London

Yuan, H, Liu, D, Sun, L, Wei, R, Zhang, G, and Sun, R, 2004 Anogenital gland secretions code for sex and age in the giant panda, Ailuropoda melanoleuca, *Canadian Journal of Zoology* 82, 1596–1604

Zhang, J, Liu, D, Sun, L, Wei, R, Zhang, G, Wu, H, Zhang, H, and Zhao, C, 2008 Potential chemosignals in the anogenital gland secretion of giant pandas, Ailuropoda melanoleuca, associated with sex and individual identity, *Journal of Chemical Ecology* 34, 398–407

14

Reducing Uncertainty in Bear Management

Sarah Elmeligi, Owen T. Nevin and Ian Convery

Once globally abundant ranging across Asia, Europe and North America, grizzly bears (*Ursus arctos*) have been classified as threatened, endangered or vulnerable in most parts of their range (Weilgus 2002). In Canada, the grizzly bear is classified as 'Special Concern' by the Committee on the Status of Endangered Wildlife in Canada (COSEWIC 2018); in the contiguous United States, they are listed as 'Endangered' under the Endangered Species Act (US Fish and Wildlife Service 2018). From the 1940s to 1960s, habitat loss resulting from expanding human settlements and agriculture (Shelton 2001) combined with increasing negative interactions between people and bears led to the killing of grizzly bears and dramatic decreases in population sizes (McCracken 1957). Habitat loss from industrial land use practices and conflict with people continues to impact grizzly bear populations in Canada (Benn and Herrero 2002; Nielsen *et al* 2006).

Human use and development, such as roads, communities, industrial development and recreational use, impact grizzly bear habitat both inside and outside of protected areas in western Canada (Nielsen *et al* 2006; Sorensen *et al* 2015). Grizzly bears in western Canada exist in a multi-use landscape with home ranges often overlapping federal and provincial management agency jurisdictions (eg federal and provincial protected areas, other public lands, and private land; Bourbonnais *et al* 2013). Each of these jurisdictions has different management responses to grizzly bear behaviour and habitat use detailed in their respective management plans. Primary human use in each of these jurisdictions is also variable (eg recreation, private land use, and industrial or commercial use). As a result, how people react to grizzly bears and their expectations regarding bear management change across the landscape. Grizzly bears with home ranges overlapping multiple jurisdictions must navigate a complex variety of human uses and potential management responses.

There are many challenges regarding researching grizzly bear habitat use and activity in areas of human use. Their large home ranges can render data collection challenging across varying spatial scales. The diversity of habitats they can occupy across various densities and intensities of human use can make inferences at the population level difficult to defend. They are also complex animals that can make decisions based on complex stimuli and learn over time, which can render robust statistical analyses at the population scale difficult or inappropriate based on the dataset. Grizzly bears inherently exhibit a high level of individual variation, which makes it difficult to create population-based management protocols or recommendations. All these factors create a relatively high level of uncertainty in grizzly bear management.

Uncertainty is defined by missing or inadequate information on the probabilities of various management outcomes (Bormann and Kiester 2004); failure to acknowledge and treat the sources of uncertainty can lead to poor management decisions (Regan *et al* 2005). This is particularly important in conservation biology as managers and scientists attempt to better understand ecosystem complexities to implement effective management actions (Drechsler 2004). Challenges arise, however, as many ecological processes are so complex and non-linear that accurate predictions can be impossible (Bormann and Kiester 2004). Attempting to increase understanding can often lead to a reductionist approach to management, where complex factors are not wholly considered in management recommendations (Ludwig *et al* 1993; Ascher 2001). To further complicate the situation, poor linkages between science and environmental policy and management can exist and sometimes be attributed to scientific uncertainty and a lack of consensus among scientists (Moore *et al* 2009). These problems can lead to management decisions that are not created with sufficient information and result in unexpected or undesired outcomes.

While wildlife responses to human use can be difficult to measure and produce uncertain results, gauging the type and severity of human use impacts is nonetheless essential for management plans to be successful. To truly achieve sustainability, it is critical to understand how human use and development affects ecological integrity in various temporal and spatial scales (Petersen 2000).

Alleviating Uncertainty by Moving Towards Coexistence

One of the easiest ways to address uncertainty in grizzly bear management may be to focus management efforts on human use, rather than on the grizzly bears themselves. This can be accomplished by considering human-bear coexistence across the landscape. The concept of coexisting with grizzly bears can be perceived as impossible by some, as challenging by others, and totally possible by others. There is debate amongst bear biologists regarding what coexistence truly means and how it is achieved in daily life. Coexistence with bears may be defined as bears and people being able and willing to share similar habitats at similar times without conflict. People define coexistence differently based on their own preconceived notions of what is possible, where they live, and what kind of grizzly bear population they are being asked to coexist with. Coexistence may also be scale-dependent. For example, people and bears may both occupy the same protected area, valley bottom, specific trail or mountain meadow. Therefore, the scale at which a management agency defines coexistence will impact management tactics across the landscape (eg human development nodes and preservation zones), valley bottom (eg seasonal area closures), or specific trail (eg human travel restrictions, trail routing).

The opposite of coexistence is human-bear conflict. These are situations where people and bears in similar habitats at similar times lead to a negative interaction. These include times when people feel fearful, bears damage property, or bears attack aggressively. Managing to reduce human-bear conflict is complicated by the high level of individual variation exhibited between bears in response to human use (Elmeligi and Shultis 2015; Chi and Gilbert 1999; Nevin and Gilbert 2005a, b; Elmeligi 2017). Grizzly bear habitat use in response to people is complex, as is the human response to grizzly bears.

With their large home ranges, grizzly bears move across jurisdictional boundaries regularly. This can be problematic when they go from an area with a high level of protection (eg a national park) to an area with little protection (eg private land, industrial landscape). Human-bear conflict can result in areas where management approaches may not be tolerant of human-bear coexistence. This risk increases if an individual bear assumes that the human response to a particular behaviour (eg foraging on natural food sources in close proximity to people) will be static across human-created jurisdictional boundaries. This is rarely the case, however. In these areas, biological sciences alone cannot provide a complete understanding of, or solutions to, conflict; half of the challenge in addressing human-wildlife conflict is in understanding and working with the human dimension (Madden 2004). It is too simplistic to utilise linear relationships to score habitat quality and trail user expectations of where and what kinds of management should occur. The reality is that there is no clear 'winner' in these situations (Shanley *et al* 2013). People will need to make some sacrifices, just as bears will need to adjust their habitat use.

Taking a conservative and adaptive management approach is one way to cope with this high level of complexity and uncertainty. This may involve diversifying policies and practices, especially when uncertainty is high (Bormann and Kiester 2004). Another way to reduce uncertainty is to include social studies that define human motivation and responses as integral parts of management or the ecosystem being studied (Ludwig *et al* 1993). Grizzly bears are individual, people are individual, and human use can take infinite forms and levels of intensity. It is this diversity that makes coexistence possible, but it is the threatened and endangered status of grizzly bear populations that makes it necessary.

Current Management Approaches

Managing bears

Managing vulnerable and sensitive species, like grizzly bears, while facilitating a safe and positive human experience in bear-country is the essence of the dynamic management challenge in many areas in western Canada. Several management agencies have objectives surrounding the maintenance of grizzly bear habitat and provision of safe human access to bear habitat. According to the Canada National Parks Act (2013), the 'maintenance and restoration of ecological integrity ... is the first priority of the Minister when considering all aspects of the management of parks' (Section 8 (2), p 5). The Government of Alberta *Grizzly Bear Response Guide* (Government of Alberta 2016) considers an effective management strategy as one that balances the protection of life and property as a priority, as well as meeting objectives for grizzly bear management. The Government of British Columbia uses a procedure manual to prevent and respond to conflict between people and bears (Government of BC 2016), which also prioritises human safety and recognizes that many variables can influence the response of officers to conflict situations with large carnivores.

Typical responses to managing human-bear conflict focus on managing the bear and/or its habitat. Exactly how this is done varies between managing agencies across human-created jurisdictional boundaries. For example, food conditioned or habituated grizzly bears in Alberta can be relocated for their first 'offence', although preventative action, such as monitoring bears and managing human use, is stated as the initial response. In British Columbia, however, a bear exhibiting similar behaviour is monitored; relocation only becomes a management response when a bear has begun displaying aggressive behaviour (eg bluff charges) towards people. In national parks, Parks Canada has a policy to not relocate bears at all. While each of these approaches addresses uncertainty in bear management by managing individual bear behaviour, there is no certainty from the bear's perspective of management response to its behaviour. This highlights how uncertainty actually goes both ways – managers deal with uncertainty in terms of research applying to the population level, and bears deal with uncertainty in terms of management response across jurisdictional boundaries.

Changes in management response have higher risk implications for subadult grizzly bears who are most likely to disperse across the national park boundaries in Alberta and British Columbia. This age/sex class has the highest levels of human-caused mortality in British Columbia (McLellan 2015) and Alberta, but McLellan and Hovey (2001) found no clear relationship between the survival of young bears and their tendency to disperse. This may be more directly related to where they disperse from and to. In the case of Banff and Jasper National Park, grizzly bears are dispersing from a highly protected landscape without motorised recreation or industrial activity to an unprotected landscape with a higher road density and higher intensity of human activity (eg motorised recreation and industrial activity). Bears dispersing into areas with human settlement have higher rates of mortality (McLellan and Hovey 2001). If a subadult has been raised by a female who selected habitat nearer to human use areas, it follows this bear may seek similar habitats when it disperses. Subadults that spent more time moving around roads on Alberta private lands had a higher chance of being killed (Kite *et al* 2016). This issue is compounded if a subadult bear has learned, through years of living in a national park, that people do not represent a substantive threat. The mortality risk to these individuals increases when they leave the boundaries of the protected areas, but their survival has implications for the provincial recovery of the species.

This dynamic showcases the need for interagency, multi-stakeholder cooperation in grizzly bear management. The Interagency Grizzly Bear Committee (IGBC) in the United States is a multi-stakeholder group coordinating grizzly bear population recovery policy, planning, management and research that formed in 1983 to recover grizzly bears in the lower 48 states. The IGBC consists of representatives from the US Forest Service, the National Park Service, the US Fish and Wildlife Service, the Bureau of Land Management, the US Geological Survey, state wildlife agencies and some Native American tribes with grizzly bear habitat (IGBC 2016). By working collaboratively between agencies and, in many cases, with landowners, the Yellowstone grizzly bear population has exceeded recovery goals (IGBC 2016). No such formal collaborative exists in Canada.

Within Alberta, interagency cooperation should consist of all relevant land managing agencies, including Parks Canada and Alberta Environment and Parks, as well as private landowners, industrial stakeholders and First Nations governments. Only by working and planning together can mortality across jurisdictional boundaries be reduced for those bears living at the interface between federal and provincial land. The interdisciplinary problem-solving workshops described in Rutherford *et al* (2009) instigated this type of collaboration in the national parks and were successful in improving communication within the local community; these efforts should be expanded to include multiple locations outside of protected areas (Rutherford *et al* 2009).

Managing people

All managing agencies recognize the importance of managing people who use grizzly bear habitat. The Parks Canada Charter (2002) defines a comprehensive mandate for park management and includes elements of 'fostering public understanding, appreciation and enjoyment' (p 1). This mandate complements one of the principal components of the provincial Alberta Grizzly Bear Recovery Plan, which is to reduce human-bear conflict and encourage coexistence between the public and grizzly bears (Government of Alberta 2008). Understanding public attitudes and support for grizzly bear management in protected areas is, therefore, an important component of meeting management objectives at both the federal and provincial level.

How people react to a grizzly bear encounter is not always addressed in the management of human-bear encounters, but it can play an essential role in the outcome of the encounter. For example, a person who reacts aggressively may prompt a grizzly bear to do the same. Research found that dogs off leash was the second most common way human behaviours contributed to carnivore attacks (Penteriani *et al* 2015). Working with people to adjust their behaviour to reduce the risk of a negative encounter can be effective. This management approach typically takes the form of education whereby agencies inform people how to reduce the risk of conflict by reducing bear access to attractants (eg garbage, fruit trees), carrying bear spray or keeping dogs on leash. While education is a form of managing people, it implies voluntary actions and is considered the first step of managing people to achieve coexistence. Some agencies also have enforcement programs in place to increase compliance with attractant management associated regulations and penalties.

Management agencies are influenced by people living in and using the landscape they manage, and local attitudes towards carnivores strongly influence policies put in place that prioritise coexistence (Woodroffe 2000). Education can be used to increase tolerance of grizzly bears on public and private lands outside of the national parks. Interagency management is not only about managing bears and human activity, but also managing educational messaging and awareness. It is important that human behaviour in this complex landscape is similar across jurisdictional boundaries. Joint education between federal and provincial management agencies can work collaboratively to target recreationists and people using bear habitat. People who engage in forms of recreation supported in the national parks (eg hiking, mountain biking, climbing) should have the same kind of information at their disposal when enjoying recreational activities in bear habitat outside of these protected areas. Tourists commonly want to behave in ways that ensure the least damage possible; informing them of the biologically related appropriate behaviours and the reasoning behind them can reduce negative impacts of recreationists on wildlife (Granquist *et al* 2016). This can be accomplished through joint educational programmes and materials created and distributed by federal (eg Parks Canada) and provincial or state agencies (eg Alberta Parks, State Parks). Emphasis should be placed on how to prevent a negative encounter, such as portable electric fencing around clean camps, how to behave during an encounter, how to use bear spray (McLellan 2015) and having dogs on leash or leaving the area (Penteriani *et al* 2016). Part of the objective of this recommendation is to communicate to people that bears are crossing inter-jurisdictional boundaries and potentially being treated differently on either side of a human-created line on a map. This increased public awareness may lead to an increased understanding of the complexities associated with grizzly bear management inside and outside of protected areas, which may in turn lead to increased public support for various difficult management decisions.

Another way to manage people to reduce the challenge associated with uncertainty is to provide some predictability in human use patterns on the landscape. Bears are more likely to use high quality habitat during times when people are inactive (Gibeau *et al* 2002), and human traffic can reduce habitat effectiveness, rendering prime habitat suboptimal (Hood and Parker 2001). In this context, reducing the volume of people on a trail or the times of day when people are active can reduce the risk of conflict and allow bears access to high quality habitat without having to deal with people. This is a form of temporal coexistence where people and bears have access to the same place, but not at exactly the same time (Nevin and Gilbert 2005a, b).

Changes in temporal habitat use were not found to impact overall resource use in Alaska (Rode *et al* 2007), but changes in spatial habitat use can only occur if there are alternative food resources available. Rode *et al* (2006, 2007) found that bears compensated for increased human presence by either increasing foraging efficiency at alternative times and/or locations, consuming other foods, or decreasing energy expended on other activities. In less productive habitats, such as parts of the British Columbia northwest coast or interior, alternative habitat away from people may not be available. Bears in these areas may be able to sustain temporal changes in habitat use, but may be more likely to experience reduced fitness (due to increased travelling and decreased foraging) if forced to seek alternative foraging locations. Using a precautionary approach, researchers have recommended that management plans provide specific temporal or seasonal limitations on human use to provide refuge for bears that were more likely to be displaced from the habitat by people (Elmeligi and Shultis 2015; Nevin 2003; Nevin and Gilbert 2005a, b). This is one of the management tactics that provide predictability in human use.

Predictability in human use spatially can be managed through designated trail systems or landscape development permits. When considering a grizzly bear's home range scale, the importance of spatial predictable human use allows for some areas of the bear home range to be free of people. This provides the bear with a refuge from human disturbance. Predictability of human use temporally can also be used to decrease the magnitude of human disturbance. These management actions can entail seasonal closures of areas and restrictions of human use during certain times of day or night. Increasing predictability and consistency of human activity can allow less tolerant bears to adjust their behaviour patterns temporally or spatially to exploit habitats in the absence of people (Chi and Gilbert 1999; Gibeau *et al* 2001; Nevin and Gilbert 2005a, b). This predictability of human use is a central tenet to managing bear-viewing in coastal areas and could have success in the interior as well.

Predictability of human use is an indirect way of managing bears in the face of uncertainty as it provides certainty in human use. This certainty provides less tolerant bears with more opportunity to access important resources without encountering people. Reducing the risk of encounter reduces the likelihood of needing to manage bears directly. Thus, it reduces the need to address biological uncertainty because less management is required. This whole premise is based, however, on the assumption that bears are being managed to reduce risk to people or their property. While that is usually the case, there are instances where bears are managed away from human development.

LOOKING TO THE FUTURE: MANAGEMENT RECOMMENDATIONS

Taking a conservative and adaptive management approach is one way to cope with a high level of complexity and uncertainty. This can involve catering to the lowest common denominator, in this case the least tolerant bear. That approach, however, may not be feasible as it could entail preventing human use in grizzly bear habitat at all. Adaptive management in the form of diverse policies and practices and applying interdisciplinary approaches to research also reduce uncertainty. Grizzly bears in Alberta are threatened and recovery is a provincial goal, but both male and female grizzly bears disperse gradually (McLellan and Hovey 2001) and population recovery will be slow.

Having local people involved in defining their values associated with management dilemmas is important as they are the ones most heavily affected by policy development (Plummer and

Fennell 2009). Managing agencies should openly work with various stakeholders to implement tactics that will work to ensure grizzly bear habitat security and human use requirements are met. Workshops with stakeholders and agencies should aim to find common ground in grizzly bear management between jurisdictions. These processes should embrace adaptive management, monitoring the effectiveness of applications, recognizing that sometimes mistakes will be made and actions will require improvement. Adaptive management is the answer to the inherent uncertainty of managing complex systems as it focuses on experimentation and learning from feedback (Plummer and Fennell 2009); it is also more proactive in using research, best practices and other resources, and can be more assertive in learning about, developing and implementing solutions (Madden 2004).

Research efforts can confront the uncertainty of the biological data by taking an interdisciplinary approach and incorporating the human dimension. This can lead to a diversification in management recommendations and options (Ludwig *et al* 1993; Elmeligi 2008, 2017). Diversifying policies and practices, especially where uncertainties are high, is a way to spread and reduce the risk of large failures (Bormann and Kiester 2004). In coastal British Columbia, diversification is also reflected in the K'tzim-a-deen Conservancies management plan that manages the conservancies through a series of zones, each of which permits different levels of human activity depending on grizzly bear habitat quality and viewing opportunities combined. Similar approaches are applied in national and provincial parks in western Canada. Diversifying policies, all aimed at a single set of goals, allows more people to find their views applied in at least one approach.

BIBLIOGRAPHY AND REFERENCES

Alberta Environment and Parks, 2009 *Grizzly Bear Response Guide* [online], available from: https://open.alberta.ca/dataset/34f0b200-0df7-4b3c-8752-cdca6fcbe560/resource/88d799e6-c8c9-412d-81ed-7c53583deaca/download/2009-grizzlybearresponseguide-2009.pdf [8 March 2019]

Ascher, W, 2001 Coping with complexity and organizational interests in natural resource management, *Ecosystems* 4, 742–57

Benn, B, and Herrero, S, 2002 Grizzly bear mortality and human access in Banff and Yoho National Parks, 1971–98, *Ursus* 13, 213–21

Bormann, B T, and Kiester, A R, 2004 Options forestry: acting on uncertainty, *Journal of Forestry* 102 (4), 22–7

Bourbonnais, M L, Nelson, T A, Cattet, M R, Darimont, C T, and Stenhouse, G B, 2013 Spatial analysis of factors influencing long-term stress in the grizzly bear (*Ursus arctos*) population of Alberta, Canada, *PLoS One* 8 (12), e83768. doi: 10.1371/journal.pone.0083768

British Columbia Ministry of Forests, Lands, and Natural Resource Operations, 2016 *Preventing and Responding to Conflicts with Large Carnivores Procedure Manual* [online], available from: https://www2.gov.bc.ca/assets/gov/environment/natural-resource-policy-legislation/fish-and-wildlife-policy/4-7-04011__preventing_and_responding_to_conflicts_with_large_carnivores_-_procedures.pdf [8 March 2019]

Chi, D K, and Gilbert, B, 1999 Habitat security for Alaskan Brown Bears at key foraging sites: Are there thresholds for human disturbance? *Ursus* 11, 225–38

COSEWIC 2018 *Bear, Grizzly. Status* [online], available from: http://www.cosewic.gc.ca/eng/sct1/searchdetail_e.cfm?id=1195&StartRow=11&boxStatus=All&boxTaxonomic=All&lo-

cation=1&change=All&board=All&commonName=&scienceName=&returnFlag=0&Page=2   [8   March 2019]

Drechsler, M, 2004 Model-based conservation decision aiding in the presence of goal conflicts and uncertainty, *Biodiversity and Conservation* 13, 141–64

Elmeligi, S, and Shultis, J, 2015 Impacts of boat-based wildlife viewing in the K'tzim-a-Deen Inlet on grizzly bear (*Ursus arctos*) behavior, *Natural Areas Journal* 35 (3), 404–15

Elmeligi, S, 2008 Bear viewing the K'tzim-a-deen Inlet: Effects on grizzly bear behaviour and visitor perceptions of impact, unpublished Masters of Natural Resources and Environmental Studies thesis, University of British Columbia, Prince George, British Columbia, Canada

——, 2017 Grizzly Bear Habitat Management in Canada's Rocky Mountain Parks: Balancing visitor expectation with bear habitat requirements, unpublished PhD thesis, Central Queensland University, Gladstone, Queensland, Australia

Gibeau, M L, Clevenger, A P, Herrero, S, and Wierzcowski, J, 2002 Grizzly bear response to human development and activities in the Bow River Watershed, Alberta, Canada, *Biological Conservation* 103, 227–36

Gibeau, M L, Herrero, S, McLellan, B N, and Woods, J G, 2001 Managing for grizzly bear security areas in Banff National Park and the central Canadian Rocky Mountains, *Ursus* 12, 121–9

Government of Alberta, 2008 *Alberta grizzly bear recovery plan 2008–2013*, Alberta Sustainable Resource Development, Fish and Wildlife Division, Alberta Species at Risk Recovery Plan No 15, Edmonton, Alberta

Granquist, S M, and Nilsson, P, 2016 Who's watching whom? – An interdisciplinary approach to the study of seal-watching tourism in Iceland, *Journal of Cleaner Production* 111, 471–8

Hood, G A, and Parker, K L, 2001 Impact of human activities on grizzly bear habitat in Jasper National Park, *Wildlife Society Bulletin* 29, 624–38

Interagency Grizzly Bear Committee, 2018 *About* [online], available from: http://igbconline.org/about-us/ [8 March 2019]

Kite, R, Nelson, T, Stenhouse, G, and Darimont, C, 2016 A movement-driven approach to quantifying grizzly bear (*Ursus arctos*) near-road movement patterns in west-central Alberta, Canada, *Biological Conservation* 195, 24–32

Ludwig, D, Hilborn, R, and Walters, C, 1993 Uncertainty, resource exploitation, and conservation: lessons from history, *Science* 260, 17, 36

Madden, F, 2004 Creating coexistence between humans and wildlife: Global perspectives on local efforts to address human–wildlife conflict, *Human Dimensions of Wildlife: An International Journal* 9 (4), 247–57

McCracken, H, 1957 *The beast that walks like a man: the story of the grizzly bear*, Oldbourne Press, Londo

McLellan, B N, 2015 Some mechanisms underlying variation in vital rates of grizzly bears on a multiple use landscape, *The Journal of Wildlife Management* 79 (5), 749–65

McLellan, B N, Hovey, F W, Mace, R D, Woods, J G, Carney, D W, Gibeau, M L, and Kasworm, W F, 1999 Rate and causes of grizzly bear mortality in the interior mountains of British Columbia, Alberta, Montana, Washington, and Idaho, *Journal of Wildlife Management* 63 (3), 911–20

Minister of Justice, 2015 *Canada National Parks Act*, Ottawa, Ontario

Moore, S A, Wallington, T J, Hobbs, R J, Ehrlich, P R, Holling, C S, Levin, S, and Westoby, M, 2009 Diversity in current ecological thinking: implications for environmental management, *Environmental Management* 43, 17–27

Nevin, O T, 2003 Towards a theory of carnivore density: the influence of prey abundance and risk-sensitive behavioral change on individual access to high-energy food (salmon): impacts on the density and viability of bear populations, PhD dissertation, Utah State University, Logan, Utah

Nevin, O T, and Gilbert, B K, 2005a Measuring the cost of risk avoidance in brown bears: further evidence of positive impacts of ecotourism, *Biological Conservation* 123, 453–60

——, 2005b Perceived risk, displacement and refuging in brown bears: positive impacts of ecotourism? *Biological Conservation* 121, 611–22

Nielsen, S E, Stenhouse, G B, and Boyce, M S, 2006 A habitat-based framework for grizzly bear conservation in Alberta, *Biological Conservation* 130, 217–29

Parks Canada, 2002 *Parks Canada Charter* [online], available from: http://www.pc.gc.ca/eng/agen/chart/chartr.aspx. [8 March 2019]

Penteriani, V, Delgado, M M, Pinchera, F, Naves, J, Fernandez-Gil, A, Kojola, I, and Lopez-Bao, J V, 2016 Human behaviour can trigger large carnivore attacks in developed countries, *Scientific Reports* 6, 20552. doi: 10.1038/srep20552

Petersen, D, 2000 Grizzly bears as a filter for human use management in the Canadian Rocky Mountain National Parks, *USDA Forest Service Proceedings* 5, 354–61

Plummer, R, and Fennell, D A, 2009 Managing protected areas for sustainable tourism: prospects for adaptive co-management, *Journal of Sustainable Tourism* 17 (2), 149–68

Regan, H M, Ben-Haim, Y, Langford, B, Wilson, W G, Lundberg, P, Andelman, S J, and Burgman, M A, 2005 Robust decision-making under severe uncertainty for conservation management, *Ecological Applications* 15, 1471–7

Rode, K D, Darley, S D, Fortin, J K, and Robbins, C T, 2007 Nutritional consequences of experimentally introduced tourism in brown bears, *Journal of Wildlife Management* 71 (3), 929–39

Rutherford, M B, Gibeau, M L, Clark, S G, and Chamberlain, E C, 2009 Interdisciplinary problem solving workshops for grizzly bear conservation in Banff National Park, Canada, *Policy Sciences* 42 (2), 163–87

Shanley, C S, Kofinas, G P, and Pyare, S, 2013 Balancing the conservation of wildlife habitat with subsistence hunting access: A geospatial-scenario planning framework, *Landscape and Urban Planning* 115, 10–17

Shelton, J G, 2001 *Bear attacks II: myth and reality*, Pallister Publishing, Hagensborg, BC

Sorensen, A A, Stenhouse, G B, Bourbonnais, M L, and Nelson, T A, 2015 Effects of habitat quality and anthropogenic disturbance on grizzly bear (*Ursus arctos horribilis*) home-range fidelity, *Canadian Journal of Zoology* 93, 857–65

United States Fish and Wildlife Service *ECOS/Species Profile for Grizzly Bear* [online], available from: http://ecos.fws.gov/tess_public/profile/speciesProfile?spcode=A001. [13 May 2018]

Wielgus, R B, 2002 Minimum viable population and reserve sizes for naturally regulated grizzly bears in BC, *Biological Conservation* 106, 381–88

Woodroffe, R, 2000 Predators and people: using human densities to interpret declines of large carnivores, *Animal Conservation* 2, 165–73

Living with Bears in Europe

Miha Krofel

Europe is densely populated and extensive wilderness areas are almost non-existent. Nevertheless, we share the continent with roughly 17,000 brown bears (*Ursus arctos*) in what is considered an example of the coexistence model. In contrast to the separation model, where bears and people are kept apart, the coexistence model promotes sharing of the same landscape. However, coexistence between people and bears is challenging and often results in a variety of conflicts: from damage caused to human property to direct threats to human safety that lead to the killing of bears. Several factors affect the probability of these human-bear conflicts and a good understanding of the drivers behind the development of 'problem bear' behaviour is essential when designing effective management measures. The toolbox of human-bear conflict management includes practices such as livestock guarding dogs, electric fences and aversive conditioning of problem bears. Largely unique to Europe is the use of artificial diversionary feeding of brown bears, whereby food is placed in remote areas in order to keep bears away from human settlements. Despite being practised for a long time in many countries, it is only recently that the broader spectrum of positive and negative consequences of this controversial measure has been understood. Public opinion is an important issue in the use of some conflict prevention measures; in some cases, local people react against lethal methods, especially where bears occur in small numbers. Recent advances in the science of human-bear conflicts offer a promise of continuing coexistence between people and brown bears, which are making a slow but steady return to many parts of Europe where they have been exterminated in the past. This also brings potential benefits that are associated with bear presence, such as ecotourism and ecosystem services provided by the bears.

Decline and Recovery of the Largest Carnivore in Europe

After the extinction of the cave bear (*Ursus spelaeus* s. lat.) and retreat of the polar bear (*Ursus maritimus*) to the north, brown bears remained the only bear species extant in Europe since the end of the last glaciation. In historic times, brown bears roamed throughout the European continent, including Britain, but with the increase in human population and growing pressure on the environment and wildlife populations, brown bear range also gradually decreased. This decline of the brown bear population started several thousands of years ago in some parts of western and northern Europe. For example, in Denmark, bears were reported to have disappeared 3500 years ago and during the Middle Ages bears were driven to extinction in Britain and most of the German lowlands (Breitenmoser 1998).

During recent centuries, killing of bears was promoted, often by bounties paid by the state or local authorities. Due to their low reproduction rates, this effectively reduced bear populations in the remaining parts of its range (Zedrosser *et al* 2001). This was facilitated by the development of firearms and increasing deforestation of the once widespread European primeval forests. The latter peaked at the end of the 19th and beginning of the 20th century; as a result, once large bear populations, like those found in Scandinavia and the Dinaric mountains, came close to extinction. The turn of the 20th century also marked the time of the first serious conservation efforts to protect European brown bears. For example, in 1889 the landlords that managed large parts of the Dinaric forests in southern Slovenia became concerned about the bear decline on their estates and initiated several protection measures. These included strict limitation of bear hunting, establishment of artificial feeding sites and a ban on the use of poison baits for wolves, lures that could be accidentally ingested by bears. One landlord went even as far as providing compensation payments for any damage that bears caused on his neighbours' lands (Simonič 1994).

Such initiatives and hunting restrictions became more common after World War I (Swenson *et al* 1995) and helped bears to survive in some of the most remote parts of Europe. During World War II, there was also an attempt to reintroduce bears to eastern Poland, which however failed soon afterwards (Zedrosser *et al* 2001). Since bears were regarded as valuable hunting species, hunting associations in several countries supported bear conservation and hunting regulations. Regulated hunting, as well as the recovery of European forests, helped the larger bear populations to increase again in areas like the Carpathian, Dinaric and Pindos mountains, the eastern Balkans, Scandinavia and northeastern Europe. On the other hand, the smaller populations in the Alps, Apennines, Pyrenees and Spanish Cantabrian mountains continued to struggle on the brink of extinction. To improve the situation in these areas, several population reinforcement actions were conducted at the turn of the 21st century, when bears from Slovenia and Croatia were translocated to Austria, Italy, France and Spain (Swenson *et al* 2000).

THE COEXISTENCE MODEL

Nowadays it is estimated that about 17,000 brown bears live in Europe (excluding Russia). They occur permanently in 22 countries spread over roughly 485,400km^2 (Chapron *et al* 2014). At the same time, Europe is home to approximately 700 million people, who have strongly modified the landscape. In contrast to most other continents, there are almost no large wilderness areas left in Europe. This precludes the establishment of extensive nature reserves where large carnivores are conserved by being kept apart from people. This so-called 'separation model' of conservation was derived from the North American wilderness model and is often used across Asia, Africa and South America. In Europe, the only option for bears to survive is to live side-by-side with people and share the same landscape in what was termed the 'coexistence model' (Chapron *et al* 2014).

One would imagine that survival of viable brown bear populations in high human density areas would be difficult to achieve because of the potential for conflict between humans and bears. However, the current situation in Europe demonstrates that, with appropriate management, the coexistence model can work. This is indicated by the fact that the brown bear is today the most numerous large carnivore species in Europe, with several increasing populations living mainly outside protected areas in human-dominated landscapes. It is significant that Europe has a brown bear population about ten times larger than that of the contiguous United States, despite being half the size and more than twice as densely populated.

However, coexistence between people and bears is challenging and often results in a variety of conflicts. Therefore, a proactive management approach is needed to prevent conflicts from escalating to non-tolerable levels. The critical first step towards successful bear management is good understanding of the human-bear conflicts and the factors affecting them, as well as knowing the effectiveness of various conflict prevention measures.

UNDERSTANDING THE HUMAN-BEAR CONFLICTS

Living with bears is not always easy. Bears can cause damage to human property, but even more problematic is that in some situations bears can be directly dangerous to people. This sets bears apart from other European large carnivores, like grey wolves (*Canis lupus*) and Eurasian lynx (*Lynx lynx*), which are normally no threat to humans. Another peculiarity of human-bear conflicts is that bears do not cause damage only through depredation of livestock, as is common for other predators; because of bears' omnivore feeding habits and opportunistic foraging behaviour, they also frequently raid various food storage areas and can cause damage to crops, beehives, orchards and even vineyards.

Brown bears are large animals that require large amounts of food on a daily basis. During their evolution they developed superb capabilities, both anatomical and behavioural, to find food anywhere in the landscape. In the past, this made them a very successful species and enabled their colonisation of most of the Northern Hemisphere. But, in today's human-dominated world these abilities often lead them into trouble. From the reports of human-bear conflicts throughout their range it is evident that most of these conflicts are connected with bears' foraging activities (Can *et al* 2014; Majić Skrbinšek and Krofel 2015).

Today, an enormous amount of food is discarded each year by people; estimates suggest that 30–40 per cent of all food produced on Earth is wasted (Oro *et al* 2013). Such high calorific anthropogenic food is ideal for bears, which quickly learn where and how to find it. Easy access to anthropogenic food is often cited as the main cause of conflicts with brown bears both in Europe and elsewhere, since it regularly attracts bears close to human settlements (Majić Skrbinšek and Krofel 2015; Swenson *et al* 2000; Wilson *et al* 2006). Especially problematic seems to be the intentional feeding of bears when people throw fruit or sweets to them. Bears that regularly receive food directly from people or find it in the vicinity of human settlements often change their behaviour and become so-called 'problem bears'. These food-conditioned bears often cause the greatest proportion of all the human-bear conflicts in a given area, although they represent only a small part of the bear population. Understanding the occurrence of problem bears and dealing with them is therefore central to any successful human-bear conflict management.

Two behavioural processes characterise the change in bear behaviour leading to the development of a problem bear. These are 'habituation to human presence' and 'conditioning to anthropogenic food' (Majić Skrbinšek and Krofel 2015). Habituation is a process involving a reduction in response over time as bears learn that there are neither adverse nor beneficial consequences of the occurrence of the stimulus, in this case the presence of a human. Operant conditioning is a learning process in which behaviour is strengthened or weakened by reward or punishment. Food conditioning is a type of operant conditioning, in which an animal learns to associate a given neutral stimulus (eg the presence of people) with a high calorific reward in the form of discarded food. Once a bear has undergone such behavioural changes, it is very difficult to reverse them (although see below for methods using aversive conditioning) and in many cases such bears need to be removed in order to prevent excessive conflicts.

Not all bears that approach human settlements are seeking anthropogenic food, however. Studies from Scandinavia (Elfström *et al* 2014) have shown that social interactions among the bears can also play an important role. Large males, which can be a danger to other bears in the population, especially to sub-adults and females with cubs, often occupy the best bear habitats and can displace other bears to the marginal habitats, which include areas close to human settlements. This increases the probability for these bears to become habituated to human presence or food conditioned. It is therefore not surprising that young bears and females with cubs are the categories causing most conflicts with people and that they are also most frequently removed as problem bears (Krofel *et al* 2012). Additional factors that likely explain the higher proportion of young bears among the problem individuals is their inexperience in avoiding humans and in obtaining natural foods (Elfström *et al* 2014).

Other factors that affect the probability of occurrence of human-bear conflicts include season, natural food availability and availability of cover. Often two peaks in occurrence of human-bear conflicts are recorded, one in spring, soon after the emergence of bears from winter dens, and the second during autumn in time of hyperphagia, when bears are building fat reserves for hibernation (Krofel and Jerina 2012). Spring is bear mating season, when avoidance of male bears by the sub-adults and females with cubs is most pronounced and can bring them closer to humans (Elfström *et al* 2014). The autumn peak coincides with the ripening of fruits and crops, which can attract bears closer to people. Besides seasonal differences, several studies have noted considerable change in the conflict frequency from year to year. This is most typical in areas with variable inter-annual masting of locally abundant tree species like beech, oak and white-bark pine, as an increase in bear incidents consistently occurs in years with poor natural food availability (Majić Skrbinšek and Krofel 2015). Natural vegetation is an additional driver of human-bear conflicts as it provides bears with cover, which is especially important in a human-dominated landscape, because it facilitates bear use of areas near human settlements (Ordiz *et al* 2011). Several authors have also noted that dense vegetation around livestock pastures, crop fields, roads, villages and other developed areas increases the risk of bear incidents (Bereczky *et al* 2011; Kaczensky 1999).

The Danger of Bear Attack

Although bear attacks on humans are rare, bears can be a serious danger for a person in certain situations, sometimes with fatal consequences. Besides being dangerous to people, bear attacks are often widely publicised by the media, so even single events can have profound effects on public opinion and tolerance of bears and can jeopardize conservation efforts. Therefore, preventing attacks on people always plays a prominent role in bear management, especially given their increasing trends in Europe (Bombieri *et al* 2019; Penteriani *et al* 2016).

As with agonistic interactions between bears, most negative interactions between bears and people are so-called 'false attacks' or 'bluff charges' which finish without physical contact between the bear and person. Analyses of 818 human-bear encounters reported by Swenson *et al* (1999) showed that false attacks occurred in only 1.5% of these encounters. Real attacks are even rarer, yet Naves *et al* (2016) registered almost 300 brown bear attacks with human injuries in Europe during 2000–15, which included 19 fatalities. Most of the latter (14) occurred in the Carpathians, especially in Romania.

In Europe, bear attacks on people are almost never connected with predation (attacking humans as prey for food); instead the aggressive response is mostly connected to bears feeling threatened by an approaching human. Although most bears react by fleeing, some decide to defend themselves or their offspring (Herrero 2002). Several factors were shown to increase the risk of bear attack, including a bear being wounded (eg during hunting), the presence of cubs, the presence of an animal carcass, proximity to a bear den and the presence of dogs (Herrero 2002; Swenson *et al* 1999). In Scandinavia, the highest risk of bear attack was associated with hunting with dogs and sudden unexpected close encounters between hunters and bears (Sahlén 2013). In general, European brown bears are less aggressive towards people compared to brown bears in North America and Asia. It has been suggested that this is a result of long-term intensive persecution of European bears by humans (Herrero 2002; Penteriani *et al* 2016; Swenson 1999).

An additional factor affecting probability of attack is the habituation of bears to human presence. Although habituated bears are generally less likely to attack people *per encounter* (Smith *et al* 2005), because such bears come into contact with people considerably more frequently compared to non-habituated bears, overall they usually still present a higher risk for human injuries and deaths compared to non-habituated bears (Majić Skrbinšek and Krofel 2015). The exception to this might be well-managed bear-watching areas, where experienced guides supervise visitors constantly. Several such sites have excellent records of zero human injuries despite high frequency of close human-bear encounters (Penteriani *et al* 2017; Smith *et al* 2005).

The Toolbox of Human-Bear Conflict Management

Managers try to reduce human-bear conflicts using a variety of methods. Not all of the measures are effective, however. It is the duty of science to conduct objective testing and provide recommendations regarding which approach will give best results in any given situation. Although many of the conflict prevention methods remain untested (Treves *et al* 2016; van Eeden *et al* 2018), there is an increasing amount of data and experience that can guide decision-making.

In the past, the most common response to bear incidents was killing of the bear. Removing an entire bear population is, of course, a very effective method for preventing further conflicts. However, by modern standards, the practice of exterminating bear populations has become largely unacceptable to society and for some populations even limited removal of individual bears can have strong negative effects. Lethal removal of bears is most effective when focused on problem individuals, which usually cause the majority of human-bear conflicts, as noted above. For individual bears strongly habituated to human presence, or conditioned to anthropogenic food, lethal removal is often the most effective short-term solution (Gunther *et al* 2004). For such removals, it must be ensured that the correct bear is humanely dispatched and this measure must be coupled with effective measures to prevent development of new problem bears, otherwise repeated removals can create a local population sink.

Another way of removing a problem bear is capturing, transporting and releasing it at another location. Such translocations are generally more acceptable to the public than lethal removals. While this measure can sometimes bring temporary good results, it is largely ineffective in the long term (Linnell *et al* 1997). Translocated bears experience high mortality rates, often return to the capture site even from several hundreds of kilometres away, or they can start causing problems in the new area. Translocations are also costly and labour intensive, and it is advisable that large wilderness areas are available for releases. Therefore, this measure is impracticable for most European countries.

While removal of a problem bear can be an important measure to prevent further conflicts with a given individual, it is a 'reactive intervention', ie the conflict has already happened. Because of this, 'proactive interventions' are more desirable in that they prevent the conflicts before they happen. In this case, measures need to be taken that would prevent bears from becoming problem individuals in the first place. This is a more difficult task than simply removing problem bears, but with good understanding of how problem behaviour develops managers can effectively tackle this issue. As described above, habituation to human presence and conditioning to anthropogenic food are the main processes leading to development of problem bears. Therefore, limiting access to human food sources is generally regarded as the most effective proactive way to prevent human-bear conflicts (Majić Skrbinšek and Krofel 2015). In this way, bears are no longer rewarded for approaching humans or developed areas and consequently food-conditioning is considerably less likely.

Methods to limit bears' access to anthropogenic food were initially developed and first put into practice in North America, following numerous attacks on people by food-conditioned bears in several national parks in the USA and Canada (Herrero 2002). This proactive approach has been very successful and helped reverse the trend in human-bear conflicts both inside the parks and in residential areas (Wilson 2007). With increasing bear numbers in Europe and improved international collaboration, these experiences are now being put into practice increasingly in several European countries (eg the LIFE DinAlp Bear Project; see www.dinalpbear.eu). There are numerous approaches about how to effectively prevent bears from accessing anthropogenic food sources (for a detailed review see Sowka 2009). Bear-proof containers prevent bears from using garbage or composts, while at the same time enabling easy access for people. Electric fences and other electric-shocking devices are effective to deter bears from beehives, orchards, bird feeders, food storages and other human property. Electric fences can be used also as night enclosures to protect livestock, which can be further protected with the use of livestock guarding dogs or shepherds. Special attention needs to be given to preventing direct bear feeding by people, as this is the fastest pathway to the development of a problem bear. Strict legislation and its enforcement with timely response is crucial, as well as accompanying public education. Experiences suggest that measures preventing access to anthropogenic foods are more successful when local communities and individual inhabitants are actively involved and empowered (Primm and Wilson 2004).

Generally, these measures are less effective once a bear has already become food-conditioned and habituated to human presence. In such cases much greater efforts are needed to prevent access to anthropogenic food, as such bears can overcome obstacles and deterrents that would prevent access to most non-problem bears. Another measure that is used in parallel in such cases is 'aversive conditioning' (Majić Skrbinšek and Krofel 2015). This method relies on learning through operant conditioning (similar to the food conditioning process described above) and denotes a procedure whereby a negative stimulus prevents unwanted behaviour and reinstates the bear's avoidance of people or human settlements. There are several options of negative stimuli that can be used, although the pain stimuli, like shooting with rubber bullets, generally proved to be the most successful. Effectiveness of aversive conditioning depends on several factors, such as the context in which the learning process took place, the immediacy of a consequence of given behavioural response, and the consistency and magnitude of these consequences. Use of this measure is, in general, met with mixed results, because it is usually effective only in the short term. However, in specific situations some of the aversive stimuli can achieve long-term changes in bear behaviour when applied properly. A crucial aspect of successful application of aversive conditioning is well-established monitoring that quickly detects problem bears in the early stages of development of undesired behaviour. Once the bears have become conditioned to anthropogenic food, the effectiveness of aversive conditioning decreases and many more repetitions are needed to achieve the same effect. Application of aversive conditioning can be very costly and demand considerable effort and consequently this measure is applied more often in cases of threatened bear populations and when possibilities for lethal removal are limited (Majić Skrbinšek and Krofel 2015).

Another method that originates from North America, but is today increasingly used in Europe (although still to a much lower extent), is the use of bear sprays for self-protection in close encounters with bears. Capsaicin-based spray repellents have proved to be very effective in deterring bears from attacking (Smith *et al* 2008). But, more important for preventing attacks on humans is educating residents and visitors to bear areas about proper behaviour, which can considerably reduce the probability of finding oneself in a dangerous situation. Such education is achieved through media, public talks and training programmes or production of various informative materials. These should include general recommendations like making oneself known to the bears as soon as possible by making noise, staying calm in close encounters, keeping dogs on a leash, not approaching animal carcasses, dens or bear cubs and sealing food or other organic material with a strong smell that could attract bears (Herrero 2002).

Further ways to reduce human-bear conflicts are connected to changes in land-use practices. This approach is not always feasible, as it depends on local traditions and interests, but in some situations it can help in avoiding problems with bears. Limiting human encroachment, certain activities or general human access to most crucial bear habitats can give positive results by allowing unhindered foraging opportunities for bears, decreasing the risk of habituation to humans, and providing safety for hikers (Coleman *et al* 2013). Since cover is an important parameter affecting the space used by bears, maintaining open habitats in the vicinity of human settlements could deter bears from approaching settlements and also limit opportunities for habituation to human presence. Some authors therefore recommend removing dense vegetation near crops and around human settlements (Elfström *et al* 2014; Sato *et al* 2005). Also, changes in agriculture from livestock breeding to other land uses such as arable farming and forestry, or growing crops less attractive to bears, can reduce the probability of bear damage (Majić Skrbinšek and Krofel 2015). However, generating a will for such changes among stakeholders is often a considerable challenge (Linnell *et al* 2013).

The Benefits and Problems of Artificial Feeding of Brown Bears

Artificial feeding of brown bears to divert them from human settlements or prevent livestock depredations is a controversial method whose use has been mostly limited to Europe. Here it has a long tradition and has been used for over a century in some areas (Kavčič *et al* 2015). The rationale behind this method is that providing bears with artificial food (most often corn or animal carcasses) in remote areas will prevent them from approaching human settlements or attacking livestock on the pastures. In some parts of Europe such artificial feeding is very intense; for example, in Slovenia every year 12,500kg of corn per 100km^2 is provided to wildlife through a dense system of artificial feeding sites (one feeding site every 2.7km^2) (Krofel and Jerina 2016).

For a long time, this practice was believed to be successful but until recently there were almost no studies that looked into its effects. The first systematic studies conducted during recent years indicate that artificial feeding of bears may not be as effective for preventing conflicts as was first thought. Results from Slovenia and Scandinavia could not find any connection between bears' use of artificial feeding sites and their diversion from human settlements at the annual level (Steyaert *et al* 2014). Further analysis of Slovenian data that took into account seasonal variation also did not detect any effects for most seasons, except for autumn, when negative correlation between the frequency of use of feeding sites and bear occurrence near settlements was confirmed (Garshelis *et al* 2017). Another study in Slovenia looked into the effectiveness of providing bears with animal carcasses in order to prevent attacks on livestock. The ban of this practice due to European Union regulations created an opportunity to test its effects, but the results of these experiments did not indicate any effect on the level of livestock depredations (Kavčič *et al* 2013).

While the effectiveness of artificial feeding of bears to prevent human-bear conflicts is generally low, there is an increasing amount of evidence that this practice can have strong side-effects on several aspects of bear biology and management. Some of these impacts are positive, others negative. Positive consequences include the ability to monitor and hunt bears at feeding sites, which reduces the probability of mistakes in hunting or the chance of wounding the bear. Artificial feeding sites also provide opportunities for reliable bear watching as part of ecotourism initiatives or for monitoring of bear population dynamics (Penteriani *et al* 2017).

On the other hand, artificial feeding of bears considerably changes their diet, which could have further consequences, including reducing the ecological functions that bears perform in the ecosystem, including seed dispersal (Kavčič *et al* 2015). Artificial feeding also considerably reduces the time bears are spending inside dens in winter (Krofel *et al* 2017). In this way, the potential for human-bear conflicts is extended to the part of the year when bears are normally hibernating. Perturbations of bear activity patterns and changes in their local abundance due to artificial feeding can also impact on other species that coexist with bears. For example, a study in Slovenia demonstrated that the artificial feeding of bears locally increased bear scavenging of remains of ungulates killed by the Eurasian lynx, which suffered considerable losses of their prey (Krofel and Jerina 2016). Because bear feeding sites are also regularly used by other wildlife, this could have additional ecological side-effects, which currently remain largely unstudied (Fležar *et al* 2019). Little is also known about the impacts of artificial feeding sites on interactions among the bears and the effects of artificial food on bear health, although several potential deleterious effects have been suggested (Penteriani *et al* 2010, 2017). Because of these documented or potential negative side-effects, it has been suggested that artificial feeding sites may in certain settings represent an ecological trap for the bears (Penteriani *et al* 2018).

Concerns have been raised that artificial feeding promotes habituation to human presence and conditioning to anthropogenic food. While there have indeed been reports of a few individual bears that showed such behavioural changes in response to artificial feeding at bear feeding sites, in general the bears that frequently use feeding sites do not show increased nuisance behaviour (Steyaert *et al* 2014). More likely mechanisms that could link this practice with increased human-bear conflicts are effects of artificial feeding on bear reproduction and their local densities. The main factor influencing bear reproduction is food availability. Since food obtained from artificial feeding can represent a major food source, this practice could increase reproduction, bear abundance and the potential for more human-bear conflicts (Jerina *et al* 2013; Krofel *et al* 2017).

The Benefits of Living with Bears

While living with bears is often challenging, it can also bring benefits to local communities or visitors coming to the bear range. From an economic perspective, the most obvious benefit is income generated through trophy hunting and ecotourism. Brown bears are an attractive species for trophy hunting, which can represent a substantial component of a hunting organisation's income in some regions (Knott *et al* 2014). At the same time, the bear is among the most targeted species for ecotourism, which is a rapidly growing industry in Europe and provides economic benefits to ecotourism companies and other businesses that profit from the tourists attracted to an area for bear viewing (Penteriani *et al* 2017). However, among modern European societies, the most important motivations for bear conservation are aesthetic and ethical, ie their intrinsic value (Linnell *et al* 2005). Simply knowing that bears are present in a forest can make an outdoor experience much more fulfilling and enjoyable, even if the actual animal is never seen. In many parts of Europe bears also represent an important natural and cultural heritage, as is described in detail in other chapters in this volume.

Besides direct benefits for people, bears have been recognized for having an important ecological role in some ecosystems. Perhaps the most frequently reported function performed by bears in nature is seed dispersal. Seed dispersal results from the interaction between bears and fruit-bearing plants, which starts with bears feeding on a fruit, digesting it over couple of hours and then defecating at another place, often several kilometres from the mother plant (Willson and Gende 2004). The fleshy part of the fruit is digested, but the seeds typically pass through the bear's digestive system unharmed and can later germinate. For most fruits that pass through the bear, the germination success of seeds is unharmed or can even increase (Szczutkowska *et al* 2009). However, probably the most important role played by bears in seed dispersal is the transport they provide. Due to the large distances travelled every day, as well as large volume of fruits ingested, bears are unique among mammalian seed dispersers and as such they assist in plant dispersal at a greater spatial scale than is typical. Although fruits and other plant material are usually the most important food source for bears, they are also successful predators. Hunting a variety of prey, from small insects to large ungulates up to the size of a moose (Dahle *et al* 2013), they have an important effect on animal communities and help to maintain balance in the ecosystems by preventing population irruptions (Wallach *et al* 2015). Even more common than predation is the consumption of meat through scavenging. Bears are the largest terrestrial scavengers and have superb olfactory abilities, which make them very efficient in searching for animal carcasses. Because of their size they are able to remove large amounts of carrion in a short period, which is an important ecosystem service provided by scavengers, as it accelerates nutrient recycling and limits disease transmission (Ćirović *et al* 2016).

Living with brown bears in highly populated regions like Europe can be challenging, but coexistence also brings opportunities such as ecotourism. So far, the coexistence model championed by wildlife managers of this continent appears to be working and public opinion surveys indicate that in several countries the majority of the rural population is in favour of living with bears in their surroundings (Kaczensky *et al* 2004; Majić *et al* 2011). Recent advances in the science of human-bear conflicts offer possibilities to further reduce the negative impacts of bears on local communities, while at the same time retaining the benefits associated with this species. Further development of new non-lethal methods to ensure relatively peaceful coexistence is becoming ever more important because public opinion is becoming increasingly unsupportive of lethal methods (Treves and Karanth 2003). Nevertheless, removal of certain individuals, whose behaviour has changed through the processes of habituation and food conditioning, will likely remain an important tool in the foreseeable future to retain the tolerance of local communities towards the largest carnivore of Europe.

Bibliography and References

Bereczky, L, Pop, M, and Chirac, S, 2011 Trouble making brown bears *Ursus arctos* Linnaeus, 1758 (Mammalia: Carnivora): Behavioral pattern analysis of the specialized individuals, *Travaux du Muséum National d'Histoire Naturelle Grigore Antipa* 2, 541–54

Bombieri, G, Naves, J, Penteriani, V, Selva, N, et al, 2019 Brown bear attacks on humans: a worldwide perspective *Scientific Reports* 9: 8573 https://doi.org/10.1038/s41598-019-44341-w

Breitenmoser, U, 1998 Large predators in the Alps: The fall and rise of man's competitors, *Biological Conservation* 83, 279–89

Can, Ö E, D'Cruze, N, Garshelis, D L, Beecham, J, and Macdonald, D W, 2014 Resolving Human-Bear Conflict: A Global Survey of Countries, Experts, and Key Factors, *Conservation Letters* 7, 501–13

Chapron, G, Kaczensky, P, Linnell, J D C, von Arx, M, *et al*, 2014 Recovery of large carnivores in Europe's modern human-dominated landscapes, *Science* 346, 1517–19

Ćirović, D, Penezić, A, and Krofel, M, 2016 Jackals as cleaners: Ecosystem services provided by a mesocarnivore in human-dominated landscapes, *Biological Conservation* 199, 51–5

Coleman, T H, Schwartz, C C, Gunther, K A, and Creel, S, 2013 Grizzly bear and human interaction in Yellowstone National Park: An evaluation of bear management areas, *The Journal of Wildlife Management* 77, 1311–20

Dahle, B, Wallin, K, Cederlund, G, Persson, I L, Selvaag, L S, and Swenson, J E, 2013 Predation on adult moose *Alces alces* by European brown bears *Ursus arctos*, *Wildlife Biology* 19, 165–9

Elfström, M, Zedrosser, A, Jerina, K, Stoen, O G, Kindberg, J, Budic, L, Jonozovič, M, and Swenson, J E, 2014 Does despotic behavior or food search explain the occurrence of problem brown bears in Europe? *Journal of Wildlife Management* 78, 881–93

Elfström, M, Zedrosser, A, Støen, O-G, and Swenson, J E, 2014 Ultimate and proximate mechanisms underlying the occurrence of bears close to human settlements: review and management implications, *Mammal Review* 44, 5–18

Fležar, U, Costa Oliveira, B, Bordjan, D, Jerina, K, and Krofel, M, 2019 Free food for everyone: artificial feeding of brown bears provides food for many non-target species, *European Journal of Wildlife Research*, doi: 10.1007/s10344-018-1237-3

Garshelis, D L, Baruch-Mordo, S, Bryant, A, Gunther, K A, and Jerina, K, 2017 Is diversionary feeding an effective tool for reducing human-bear conflicts? Case studies from North America and Europe, *Ursus* 28, 31–55

Gunther, K A, Haroldson, M A, Frey, K, Cain, S L, Copeland, J, and Schwartz, C C, 2004 Grizzly bear-human conflicts in the Greater Yellowstone ecosystem, 1992–2000, *Ursus* 15, 10–22

Herrero, S, 2002 *Bear attacks: Their causes and avoidance*, 2 edn, Nick Lyons Books, New York

Jerina, K, Jonozovič, M, Krofel, M, and Skrbinšek, T, 2013 Range and local population densities of brown bear *Ursus arctos* in Slovenia, *European Journal of Wildlife Research* 59, 459–67

Kaczensky, P, 1999 Large Carnivore Depredation on Livestock in Europe, *Ursus* 11, 59–72

Kaczensky, P, Blažič, M, and Gossow, H, 2004 Public attitudes towards brown bears (*Ursus arctos*) in Slovenia, *Biological Conservation* 118, 661–74

Kavčič, I, Adamič, M, Kaczensky, P, Krofel, M, and Jerina, K, 2013 Supplemental feeding with carrion is not reducing brown bear depredations on sheep in Slovenia, *Ursus* 24, 111–19

Kavčič, I, Adamič, M, Kaczensky, P, Krofel, M, Kobal, M, and Jerina, K, 2015 Fast food bears: brown bear diet in a human-dominated landscape with intensive supplemental feeding, *Wildlife Biology* 21, 1–8

Knott, E J, Bunnefeld, N, Huber, D, Reljič, S, Kereži, V, and Milner-Gulland, E J, 2014 The potential impacts of changes in bear hunting policy for hunting organisations in Croatia, *European Journal of Wildlife Research* 60, 85–97

Krofel, M, and Jerina, K, 2012 Review of human-bear conflicts: causes and possible solutions, *Gozdarski vestnik (Professional Journal of Forestry)* 70, 235–53

———, 2016 Mind the cat: Conservation management of a protected dominant scavenger indirectly affects an endangered apex predator, *Biological Conservation* 197, 40–6

Krofel, M, Jonozovič, M, and Jerina, K, 2012 Demography and mortality patterns of removed browṇ bears in a heavily exploited population, *Ursus* 23, 91–103

Krofel, M, Špacapan, M, and Jerina, K, 2017 Winter sleep with room service: denning behaviour of brown bears with access to anthropogenic food, *Journal of Zoology* 302, 8–14

Linnell, J D C, Aanes, R, Swenson, J E, Odden, J, and Smith, M E, 1997 Translocation of carnivores as a method for managing problem animals: a review, *Biodiversity and Conservation* 6, 1245–57

Linnell, J D C, Lescureux, N, Majić, A, von Arx, M, and Salvatori, V, 2013 *From conflict to coexistence: Results from a stakeholder workshop on large carnivores in Brussels, January 2013,* Istituto di Ecologia Applicata, Norwegian Institute for Nature Research and IUCN/SSC Large Carnivore Initiative for Europe

Linnell, J D C, Promberger, C, Boitani, L, Swenson, J E, Breitenmoser, U, and Andersen, R, 2005 The linkage between conservation strategies for large carnivores and biodiversity: the view from the 'half-full' forests of Europe, in *Carnivorous animals and biodiversity: does conserving one save the other?* (eds J C Ray, K H Redford, R S Steneck, J Berger), Island Press, Washington, 381–98

Majić, A, Marino Taussig de Bodonia, A, Huber, Đ and Bunnefeld, N, 2011 Dynamics of public attitudes toward bears and the role of bear hunting in Croatia, *Biological Conservation* 144, 3018–27

Majić Skrbinšek, A, and Krofel, M, 2015 *Defining, preventing, and reacting to problem bear behaviour in Europe,* European Commission, Brussels

Ordiz, A, Støen, O G, Delibes, M, and Swenson, J E, 2011 Predators or prey? Spatio-temporal discrimination of human-derived risk by brown bears, *Oecologia* 166, 59–67

Oro, D, Genovart, M, Tavecchia, G, Fowler, M S, and Martínez-Abraín, A, 2013 Ecological and evolutionary implications of food subsidies from humans, *Ecology Letters* 16, 1501–14

Penteriani, V, Delgado, M D M, and Melletti, M, 2010 Don't feed the bears! *Oryx* 44, 169–70

Penteriani, V, Delgado, M D M, Pinchera, F, Naves, J, *et al*, 2016 Human behaviour can trigger large carnivore attacks in developed countries, *Scientific Reports* 6, 20552

Penteriani, V, López-Bao, J V, Bettega, C, Dalerum, F, Delgado, M D M, Jerina, K, Kojola, I, Krofel, M, and Ordiz, A, 2017 Consequences of brown bear viewing tourism: A review, *Biological Conservation* 206, 169–80

Penteriani, V, Delgado, M D M, Krofel, M, Jerina, K, Ordiz, A, Dalerum, F, Zarzo-Arias, A, and Bombieri, G, 2018 Evolutionary and ecological traps for brown bears *Ursus arctos* in human-modified landscapes, *Mammal Review* 48, 180–93

Primm, S, and Wilson, S M, 2004 Re-connecting grizzly bear populations: Prospects for participatory projects, *Ursus* 15, 104–14

Sahlén, V, 2013 *Encounters between brown bears and humans in Scandinavia – contributing factors, bear behavior and management perspectives,* Norwegian University of Life Sciences, Department of Natural Resource Management, Ås

Sato, Y, Mano, T, and Takatsuki, S, 2005 Stomach contents of brown bears *Ursus arctos* in Hokkaido, Japan, *Wildlife Biology* 11, 133–44

Simonič, A, 1994 The legal protection of the brown bear in Slovene territory – Past and present, and some suggestions for the future, in *Rjavi medved v deželah Alpe-Adria: Zbornik posvetovanja* (ed M. Adamič), Ministrstvo za Kmetijstvo & Gozdarstvo RS and Gozdarski inštitut Slovenije, Ljubljana, 11–75

Smith, T S, Herrero, S, and DeBruyn, T D, 2005 Alaskan brown bears, humans, and habituation, *Ursus* 16, 1–10

Smith, T S, Herrero, S, Debruyn, T D, and Wilder, J M, 2008 Efficacy of bear deterrent spray in Alaska, *Journal of Wildlife Management* 72, 640–5

Sowka, P, 2009 *Techniques and refuse management options for residential areas, campgrounds, and group-use area,* Living with Wildlife Foundation and Montana Fish, Wildlife and Parks, Living with Black Bears, Grizzly Bears and Lions Project, 3 edn, Swan Valley, Montana

Steyaert, S M J G, Kindberg, J, Jerina, K, Krofel, M, Stergar, M, Swenson, J E, and Zedrosser, A, 2014 Behavioral correlates of supplementary feeding of wildlife: Can general conclusions be drawn? *Basic and Applied Ecology* 15, 669–76

Swenson, J E, 1999 Does hunting affect the behavior of brown bears in Eurasia? *Ursus* 11, 157–62

Swenson, J E, Gerstl, N, Dahle, B, and Zedrosser, A, 2000 *Action plan for the conservation of the brown bear (*Ursus arctos*) in Europe,* Council of Europe, Strasbourg

Swenson, J E, Sandegren, F, Söderberg, A, Heim, M, Sørensen, O J, Bjärvall, A, Franzén, R, Wikan, S, and Wabakken, P, 1999 Interactions between brown bears and humans in Scandinavia, *Biosphere Conservation* 2, 1–9

Swenson, J E, Wabakken, P, Sandegren, F, Bjarvall, A, Franzen, R, and Soderberg, A, 1995 The near extinction and recovery of brown bears in Scandinavia in relation to the bear management policies of Norway and Sweden, *Wildlife Biology* 1, 11–25

Szczutkowska, S, Selva, N, Bojarska, K, and Valido, A, 2009 The role of the brown bear as a seed disperser, paper presented at the *2nd European Congress of Conservation Biology,* Prague, Czech Republic

Treves, A, and Karanth, K U, 2003 Human-carnivore conflict and perspectives on carnivore management worldwide, *Conservation Biology* 17, 1491–99

Treves, A, Krofel, M, and McManus, J, 2016 Predator control should not be a shot in the dark, *Frontiers in Ecology and the Environment* 14, 380–8

van Eeden, L M, Eklund, A, Miller, J R B, López-Bao, J V, *et al*, 2018 Carnivore conservation needs evidence-based livestock protection, *Plos Biology* 16, e2005577

Wallach, A D, Ripple, W J, and Carroll, S P, 2015 Novel trophic cascades: apex predators enable coexistence, *Trends in Ecology & Evolution* 30, 146–53

Willson, M F, and Gende, S M, 2004 Seed dispersal by Brown Bears, *Ursus arctos,* in southeastern Alaska, *Canadian Field-Naturalist* 118, 499–503

Wilson, S M, 2007 *Community-supported conservation of grizzly bears on private agricultural lands. Final close-out report for conservation innovation grant,* US Department of Agriculture – Natural Resources Conservation Service, Portland, OR

Wilson, S M, Madel, M J, Mattson, D J, Graham, J M, and Merrill, T, 2006 Landscape conditions predisposing grizzly bears to conflicts on private agricultural lands in the western USA, *Biological Conservation* 130, 47–59

Zedrosser, A, Dahle, B, Swenson, J E, and Gerstl, N, 2001 Status and management of the brown bear in Europe, *Ursus* 12, 9–20

16

Citizen Science and Bears

Sarah Elmeligi, Owen T. Nevin and Ian Convery

History and Development of Citizen Science

Bears and other large carnivores excite pubic interest and as such might seem like natural candidates for citizen science projects. In reality, however, these charismatic carnivores often live in remote, rugged, difficult terrain; they are often widely dispersed, living at low densities and are cryptic in their habits. Even though public interest in this species is high, the logistics of citizen science projects sometimes render programmes ineffective or too challenging to manage. With thoughtful planning, however, citizen science projects focusing on grizzly bear research can be a positive experience for participants and increase the scope of research databases. As a recent example of this, a 2018 project developed by the Cornell University-based New York Cooperative Fish and Wildlife Research Unit is using data collected by citizen scientists to better understand New York's black bear population size and distribution, and how that distribution relates to forest, agricultural, and urban/suburban landscapes and communities (https://iseemammals. org/). In this chapter, we report on an earlier 'bear citizen science' project – Grizzly Research in the Rockies (Elmeligi 2016) – and another more established citizen science programme hosted by Alberta Parks, but first we consider the growth of citizen science.

Put simply, citizen science is the involvement of the public in scientific research; recentlywith smartphones and apps, but amateur naturalists have always played an important role in developing our understanding of nature. Before the emergence of the professional scientist it was provincial naturalists, men such as Gilbert White, who made enormous contributions to natural history (1993). White's 1789 book *The Natural History and Antiquities of Selborne* was a pioneering work of natural history and place, and remains one of the most frequently published titles in the English language (see also David Allen's *The Naturalist in Britain* (1976) for an excellent account of the evolution of natural history from the 17th to the early 20th century). Today, the term 'citizen science' is increasingly used to describe the involvement of 'non-expert/non-professional' scientists in research-related activities. Citizen science is a form of research collaboration where data acquisition is performed by 'non-expert' individuals who are often members of the public (Catlin-Groves 2012). Typically, this approach is used for large scale scientific studies (Hart *et al* 2012) and projects that encourage the public to participate by acting as voluntary field assistants, gathering information to greatly increase datasets (Fowler *et al* 2013). These projects, however, can also be designed to recognise and incorporate culture and policy contexts surrounding conservation science (Freitag and Pfeffer 2013) and are thus part of the way in which perceptions of the natural world may change over time.

Beyond simply collecting data, citizen science projects usually incorporate an element of public education (Catlin-Groves 2012) and can dramatically improve public scientific literacy, encouraging more serious consideration of other relevant complex scientific issues (Hart *et al* 2012). Depending on the research project, citizen science can, and ideally should, be beneficial to both the scientific community and the participants themselves. Participants can provide a solution to the limited funding and capacity to collect data while gaining valuable experience in scientific research, as well as educational and health benefits (Fowler *et al* 2013).

There are several ways in which researchers can employ a citizen science programme to assist with research activities, each one becoming progressively more involved and intensive:

1. *Ad hoc* involvement is exemplified by the UK's network of Local Biological Records Centres; these centres collect and collate sightings and observation data submitted by the public which are fed into the national records system. Although the local centres become involved in particular campaigns and initiatives and may be associated with active interest groups (eg The Cumbria Natural History Society; Hewitt 2016), they also provide a baseline data collection facility to receive *ad hoc*, essentially unsolicited, sightings data.

2. Using volunteers to assist with data collection can increase research capacity by creating a large team of people to gather large amounts of data in a short period of time (Catlin-Groves 2012). This is particularly relevant for research projects that involve large datasets (eg BirdTrack: http://www.bto.org/volunteer-surveys/birdtrack/about).

3. Participants can also be involved in data analysis as well as collection. In these projects, analyses are typically time-consuming without being too technically demanding. The Zoological Society of London's (ZSL) InstantWild app (http://www.edgeofexistence.org/instantwild/) provides an excellent example of crowd source data analysis of camera trap images, an extremely time-intensive task.

4. Working collaboratively with scientists, participants can contribute to defining research questions and implications of results, even contributing to publications and presentations where research results are shared with target audiences (eg politicians, public, non-profit organisations, others in the scientific community). Gallo and Waitt (2011) describe a project where volunteers help to identify invasive species and enter them into a public database that is accessed by managers to plan and implement programmes for weed management.

Successes and Criticisms

The scientific benefits of citizen science include expanding projects across larger spatial or temporal scales, obtaining data from private land and increased data collection capacity; the social benefits include educating the public in the scientific process and scientific thinking, inspiring a different appreciation of nature and even promoting support for conservation initiatives (Freitag and Pfeffer 2013), delivering an overall increase in social and cultural capital. This knowledge sharing between interested volunteers and scientists can lead to co-production or even co-management in creating distributive justice and legitimate outcomes (ibid). It is through this process that some researchers refer to citizen science as 'democratising science' in that it enables public citizens to actively participate in scientific programmes, allowing them to access and use both their own data and the collective data generated by others (ibid; Hunter *et al* 2013).

Arguably one of the most recognised successful citizen science efforts has been the Audubon Christmas Bird Count, launched in North America in 1900 (http://birds.audubon.org/christmas-bird-count). From a small beginning (27 birders completed 25 surveys and recorded 90 species in the first year) prompted by Frank Chapman's simple, one-page proposal in *Bird Lore* (Chapman 1900) this project has grown on a truly continental scale engaging more than 60,000 participants annually. The massive datasets resulting from data collection on this large spatial and temporal scale have provided a long-term comprehensive dataset for many bird species over the past 100 years. These data have informed conservation actions, management plans and strategic direction for various environmental organisations (Catlin-Groves 2012). In this context, success depends not only on the quality of the product but also the process. For a citizen science programme to be successful participants need to have a positive and meaningful experience and the data gathered needs to be of sufficient quality to be used in scientific analyses (Fowler *et al* 2013). Globally, the recreational birdwatching community has supported some of the most established, long-term citizen science projects, with examples including the Common Bird Census (1962–2000) and its successor the Breeding Bird Survey (1994–present) in the United Kingdom, and the North American Breeding Bird Survey (1966–present) in the United States of America and Canada.

While some groups, especially birds, have pre-established enthusiast groups and others, for example large carnivores, offer opportunities for community involvement which are perceived as attractive or exciting, others do not. This leads to uneven engagement and concerns about representative coverage. Even within the same class (Insecta), reporting rates and identification success for lepidoptera (butterflies and moths) and odonata (dragonflies and damselflies) may differ greatly from that for diptera (true flies) and homoptera (aphids, hoppers etc).

The main concern from the scientific community, however, centres around the credibility and reliability of datasets gathered by citizen scientists and the validity of associated assessments (Catlin-Groves 2012; Gollan *et al* 2012). For example, in a study of leaf damage in crops on Australian farmland, data collected by volunteers showed greater variation from benchmark values than those collected by scientists. This higher level of variability was present even though the volunteers were landowners with previous experience of assessing crops and so would be considered knowledgeable. The level of variability also varied with habitat attributes, suggesting that some attributes are more difficult to estimate or are more subjective than others (Gollan *et al* 2012). Most researchers believe this concern can be alleviated through rigorous training of volunteers, targeted volunteer recruitment (Fowler *et al* 2013) and, as with any scientific research, investing time in developing a robust sampling design and methodology that reduces the chances of potential bias and ensures that analyses are shaped by the data, not the ability or judgement of the observer (Catlin-Groves 2012). When sound design is combined with rigorous but straight-forward volunteer training, all outcomes may be enhanced (Gollan *et al* 2012; Hunter *et al* 2013).

Some researchers have suggested that volunteers ought to be more involved in the collection of as many objective data elements as possible and that there should be a reduction in the number of subjective interpretations a volunteer has to make in the field (eg counts rather than estimates; Gollan *et al* 2012). It could be argued, however, that this is true of any scientific research project, regardless of whether volunteers are used. Protocols designed for volunteers should attempt to standardise survey efforts while balancing this need with maintaining public interest and involvement (Holt *et al* 2013). In our examples below, volunteer training and clearly defined roles and responsibilities between researchers and citizen scientists helps to reduce variability and ensure standardised data collection. The research projects focus on assessing habitat use and management options for brown bears in the Canadian Rocky Mountain Protected Areas, and work with volunteers in multiple ways based on their interest and experience. For example, volunteers were engaged in remote camera placement or data entry, but professional scientists created the protocols for both and often did the data analysis. There is a risk this approach could leave volunteer participants feeling dissatisfied or less engaged in the project if they perceived that the researchers only involved volunteers in 'low grade' activities while keeping the 'interesting' aspects of data analysis and defining recommendations for themselves. Addressing these limitations directly and devising ways around them that enhance the science without diminishing the role of the citizen is critical to the success of citizen science-related projects (Hart *et al* 2012).

Planning for Success

Successful citizen science programmes are not simply about the science or gathering more data; they also provide participants with a meaningful research experience and a deeper understanding of nature. These programmes require a more specialised and organised process for quality data collection and successful volunteer engagement (Fowler *et al* 2013). The project aims and objectives should include measurable outcomes pertaining not only to the gathering of scientific data but also to public education, restoration, stewardship or community engagement (Freitag and Pfeffer 2013). People participate in citizen science projects often because of a general curiosity in nature (and sometimes a specific interest in the research topic) but also because of an interest in the research process. In addition, participants become involved in projects because of a sense of ownership or geographic relationship to the place to be studied. This is clearly demonstrated by the WildWatch North Pennines (WWNP) programme (WildWatch 2019). Since 2012 citizen scientists have logged more than 20,000 sightings of wildlife in the North Pennines, attended 127 workshops in wildlife identification, shared over 10,000 bird sightings (both common and rare), recorded 71 ring ouzel (*Turdus torquatus*) sightings (informing a North Pennines upland bird atlas) and input over 2,000 moth and butterfly records.

The data collected in this project are fed into a national biological records system through a well-established system of regional record centres. By providing local context, training and identity, WWNP has effectively engaged a large and active body of citizen science volunteers and, by virtue of the engagement with established records systems, a legacy of biological recording which will outlive the WWNP project.

Providing systems where people can see, or be involved in, the data analysis or results is key to maintaining volunteers' interest and engagement in the project. Where it is difficult for volunteers to visualise the data or results, which is often the case until publication of findings, negative impacts on continued project participation have been observed (Catlin-Groves 2012). Technical barriers to the sharing of data and data visualisation are not insurmountable and can be addressed through either bespoke or 'off the peg' web-based solutions (see Prestopnik and Crowston 2012). Some citizen science projects have used these tools to good effect. For example, eBird.org, a collaboration between the Cornell Lab of Ornithology and the National Audubon Society, makes extensive use of real-time graphing and mapping tools to allow visitors to explore submitted data and has developed a dedicated following, submitting approximately two million observations per month (Prestopnik and Crowston 2012).

In a series of interviews with project coordinators, Freitag and Pfeffer (2013) found that the top recommendations for programme improvements were to (1) collaborate with experts; (2) have consistent methods; and (3) present data to policymakers. The aforementioned project on invasive species in Texas worked with citizen scientists to collect data into a public database that was accessible by resource managers for weed management, scientists to track the spread of invasive species, and policymakers to understand the scope of the invasive species problem (Gallo and Waitt 2011). A review of the literature concurred with those three recommendations and added the need for a standardised training programme (Freitag and Pfeffer 2013).

Training citizen scientist volunteers should be thorough, but also simple. Researchers should clearly and concisely convey the right information (Catlin-Groves 2012), but it is often helpful for participants to attend a pre-research workshop providing intensive training on, for example, species identification, data collection protocol and field safety measures (Gallo and Waitt 2011; Holt *et al* 2013). Other training methods have entailed a volunteer accompanying a researcher to a field site and going through the data collection protocol with the opportunity to ask questions and engage in dialogue with the researcher (Gollan *et al* 2012).

During data checking and cleaning it is possible to compare the data generated by volunteers to that of data generated by experts. In these analyses, data generated by citizen scientists have been shown to be in strong agreement with those made by trained scientists (Fowler *et al* 2013). Quality assurance and quality control measures should be embedded within data processing protocols and should contribute to an overall data quality improvement process (Hunter *et al* 2013). This entails identifying the data quality dimensions, performing data quality measures, analysing the results and identifying discrepancies, and implementing tools that provide necessary actions to improve the quality of data (Hunter *et al* 2013).

The internet can be used to market, advertise, brand, recruit and train citizen scientists, thus increasing the reach of the programme (Catlin-Groves 2012). Online training programmes have been found to reduce variability for potentially subjective measures, such as estimating percentage plant cover, between trained volunteers and professionals (Gollan *et al* 2012). Gollan *et al* (2012) suggest that combining an online training programme with in-person, hands-on training is a successful approach to ensure consistency in data collection. Website development is also important in terms of reducing potential errors. For example, Hunter *et al* (2013) found that through the use of pull-down menus, controlled vocabularies, range checking and XML schema compliance (eg defining limited character ranges for valid date entry), they were able to reduce data entry errors by over 70 per cent.

Mobile phones and downloadable apps are also starting to be used in citizen science (eg The Grizzly Scat App: http://www.grizzlyscatapp.ca/; or ZSL InstantWild: http://www.edgeofexistence.org/instantwild/). These apps allow users to contribute to the project immediately and while on-site. The Grizzly Scat App asks users to collect bear scat (in assigned containers) and use the app to mark the location of the scat or any bear sightings. Alberta Parks, Kananaskis Region, uses several apps to engage volunteers in data collection. One app focused on ecologically significant features (ESFs) asks volunteers to record GPS locations of sensitive or rare species, such as whitebark pine trees or mountain goats. Volunteers can use the app when they are enjoying recreational activities on their own without adhering to a pre-determined schedule. These data then form a large database that park ecologists and managers can use in planning and research across a broad protected area landscape. This format can allow participants to submit data in a consistent manner at any time on any day, such as with the Open Air Laboratories (OpAL) Climate Survey where participants submitted photos of specific cloud systems (discussed in Fowler *et al* 2013). Similar apps are being used to mark locations and sightings of birds. This data can be useful in plotting distributions, migration patterns and movements of individuals or species (Catlin-Groves 2012).

Alberta Parks has another app designed specifically for bears that is used by both staff and volunteers. This app records all bear sightings, telemetry locations and aversive conditioning incidences (when a staff member actively hazes or chases a bear out of a high human use area like a campground). This app is an effort by Alberta Parks ecologists to consolidate multiple data sources into one main database as well as increase the database's reliability through increased sample size. The app generates approximately 1500 data points per year and acts as a central depository that is easily accessible. With all of the data in one location, quality control is also improved through standardised review. The volunteers who use the app love it because of its utility, ease of use, and lack of paperwork. Alberta Parks ecologists appreciate that the resulting data is in one centralised location, is updated in real time, and expands their understanding of where bears are on the landscape and where management efforts may be most urgently required.

Alberta Parks, Kananaskis Region, also engages a dedicated team of volunteers to assist with carnivore research in multiple ways across its protected area landscape. This established citizen scientist programme has been running for over 15 years and engages a dedicated team of 50 volunteers. In 2018, volunteers worked over 8000 hours to contribute an enormous amount of data to several research projects. Volunteers are engaged in a variety of research projects, including remote camera instalment and servicing, data entry, bear telemetry, trail counters instalment and servicing, bear den searches and bear population assessments. With a diverse programme like this, standardised protocols for data collection and volunteer safety are critical. Alberta Parks ecologists create the field work and data entry protocols; Alberta Parks' longest-standing and most experienced volunteer is now the volunteer coordinator of this multi-faceted programme.

Maintaining a safe work environment that aligns with Government of Alberta Occupational Health and Safety (OH&S) standards is essential. All volunteers are thoroughly trained once they become part of the team. A specific team of volunteers is dedicated to training new volunteers in these standards by reviewing existing policy and field protocols. Volunteers are also trained in first aid, radio communications and must meet or exceed Government of Alberta standards for working in bear country. Once volunteers are ready for field work, they accompany other experienced volunteer team leads for their first two shifts, which ensures their safety and consistent data collection. All volunteers also review a daily OH&S bulletin before they go into the field.

Schedules for all activities are managed by a volunteer. People are encouraged to sign up based on their schedule and interests. This ensures volunteer satisfaction. However, volunteers are only allowed to sign up for projects if they have completed the associated training as different projects require different skills or knowledge of specialised equipment. For example, all volunteers are permitted to work on remote camera servicing and data entry, but only experienced and trained volunteers are permitted to work with bear telemetry or trail counter servicing.

Most volunteers work with remote cameras. These cameras measure human and wildlife trail use, as well as wildlife habitat use. Some cameras are placed on human use trails to measure human and bear use of these movement corridors, whereas others have been placed on known bear-rub trees to examine bear habitat use and behavioural patterns. Volunteers are trained in camera locations and placement and work closely with Alberta Parks ecologists. Volunteers also work on the camera data entry, contributing thousands of hours to creating the massive dataset that ecologists use in analysis.

While most volunteers work on data collection-related efforts, some volunteers also execute statistical analyses and write reports. The majority of these volunteers are undergraduate students and retired professionals who come to Alberta Parks seeking experience through an internship.

In these cases, the volunteers examine data with an Alberta Parks ecologist and discuss potential research questions and approaches. Park ecologists provide a general framework for a final report based on the scientific method and direct the volunteer to other professionals for assistance as required. The volunteers work independently to address their research question and submit a final report to the Alberta Parks ecology team. These reports are typically for internal consumption only; portions of them are sometimes used by park ecologists in presentations or other reports. These reports can also be distributed to prospective graduate students as a starting point to define more detailed research initiatives.

Quality control remains a challenge for this programme, particularly when volunteers leave the programme and new ones come on board. Ensuring training for data continuity is crucial. Another challenge can arise from inability to discipline a volunteer if their performance is not at a sufficiently high level and begins to affect data quality. These challenges are minor, however, when compared to the gains of this programme.

This extensive research programme has not only increased capacity of the Kananaskis Region ecology team, but it has enabled some research projects to happen. For example, several years ago, a comprehensive project examining grizzly bear population size and density using DNA analysis would not have happened without the help of this dedicated volunteer team. Another massive benefit of this programme is to the volunteers themselves, who develop a deep, meaningful connection to these Protected Areas and become important stewards for bear conservation. This active base of citizen scientists with a high level of knowledge has worked to influence social norms in surrounding small communities and has made a big difference. Our experience is that volunteers like to know they are involved in real science that influences management.

CASE STUDY: GRIZZLY RESEARCH IN THE ROCKIES

The Canadian Rocky Mountains are a vast landscape, home to a very low-density grizzly bear population, which is the focus of various scientific research projects. Fieldwork for these research projects is challenging, due partly to the large landscape that needs to be covered for data collection.

Alberta's grizzly bears are listed as threatened under the Alberta Wildlife Act. Engaging the public in grizzly bear recovery is an essential component of the Alberta Grizzly Bear Recovery Plan (Alberta Grizzly Bear Recovery Team 2008) and is also a fundamental element of successful management in areas where people and these large carnivores co-exist. With the increased capacity required for successful data collection and the public interest, grizzly bear research projects in Alberta and interior British Columbia naturally lend themselves to citizen science programmes.

This interdisciplinary study examined grizzly bear habitat use around hiking trails in the Rocky Mountain National Parks (Banff, Jasper, Kootenay and Yoho) in Alberta and British Columbia, Canada. Ecological data pertaining to bear habitat use was gathered through GPS collars on 10–12 grizzly bears in the parks and a series of remote cameras on hiking trails of various human-use levels, and social data was collected through a trail user survey assessing support for various grizzly bear-related management strategies. Data from these various sources were integrated in analysis to create holistic management recommendations that aimed to reduce human impact on grizzly bear habitat and meet visitor expectations. As with the Alberta Parks programme mentioned above, volunteers helped with remote camera placement and data entry; they also assisted with the trail user survey.

The involvement of the local community in this project, from research design through methodology and analysis, was integral to project success for two key reasons: (1) it was physically impossible for the research team to conduct all data collection in the same timeframe; and (2) public support for grizzly bear research and management is essential for population recovery programmes to be successful.

Before research began, Grizzly Research in the Rockies (GRR), a newly created non-profit organisation, hosted a fundraising event with the main goal of involving the local community in the research. Local businesses donated dozens of raffle prizes, which were promoted on social media in the weeks prior to the event. Over 200 community members attended, over CDN $2500 were raised, an article was published in the local newspaper and the event was talked about around the town of Canmore for months. This initial effort was also used to start volunteer recruitment, which continued through effective partnerships with other local environmental organisations, through a GRR blog (www.grizzlyresearchrockies.wordpress.com) and the Parks Canada volunteer network.

Volunteers were asked to participate in one or more 'teams' based on their interest and ability. One team was responsible for setting up and taking down remote cameras, another for disseminating visitor surveys at trailheads and a third for helping with data entry (classifying images from the remote cameras). Each of these teams involved a different level of physical fitness and time commitment; the variety of work available attracted a variety of people. Some were most interested in hiking all summer while others were more interested in chatting with tourists about bears. By offering a range of volunteer options we were able to attract 97 volunteers who worked for varying lengths of time from May to October over a three-year period. In all, over 900 full days were contributed by this volunteer network, which equated to 1.5 full-time positions for each year of the project.

All volunteers attended an annual mandatory day-long training session that described project objectives, safety protocols and methodological steps required to ensure consistency in data collection and entry. The workshop also discussed a strict protocol for working with remote cameras in the national parks, as required by Parks Canada research permit. The training sessions included a bear safety video and discussed all safety protocols associated with field work. Remote camera training included a hands-on session where volunteers put up and took down cameras as if in the field. Survey training included a session where volunteers practised survey delivery and the associated preamble to other volunteers as if in the field. Training for data entry volunteers was done one on one for an hour; training focused on the project's data entry protocol and application of the computer program used. Given that there were many photographs of people, all data entry volunteers were also required to sign a confidentiality agreement to ensure privacy of people captured with remote cameras. To ensure privacy, no images of people's faces were used in presentations or research materials. All images of people were deleted once all data was entered.

Keeping in regular contact with our volunteers was important so that all participants could feel part of the project, regardless of their time commitment. Weekly project emails were used to update volunteers regarding project progress, as well as sharing 'interesting' or 'exceptional' images from the camera traps. This helped volunteers feel like they were a part of the larger research project. A total of eight people volunteered all three years of field work, and 21 people volunteered for two years. The large proportion of repeat volunteers helped to ensure a transfer of knowledge from experienced to new volunteers, which contributed to data collection consistency and accuracy.

At the end of the field season, all volunteers received an online survey asking them about their experience: what they learned, what they liked/disliked and whether they would return the following year. All volunteers were given an opportunity to debrief and their feedback was instrumental in shaping the volunteer programme for the following season. Most volunteers rated their experience highly, commenting that it was rewarding to be part of a team working towards larger project objectives, they liked learning about bears and their habitats, and enjoyed meeting new like-minded people.

Inherent recognition and communicating gratefulness for volunteer involvement is also a cornerstone of interaction with citizen scientists. Ensuring they are happy with their experience is essential. Researchers continually thanked volunteers for their time. At the end of each field season, we hosted a volunteer appreciation event that involved a short hike and some food to share stories of the summer gone by.

For this project, working with citizen scientists not only dramatically increased the volume of data collected, but it also helped the project to maintain public support and a presence in local media. In turn, this helped the project to raise additional funds and to grow the volunteer programme each year. Volunteers who have participated in this project have increased their direct experience with grizzly bear research programmes and their understanding of how research efforts such as this feed into bear management.

ENSURING MEANINGFUL OUTCOMES

Clear, well-articulated outcomes are an important factor determining project success. In some instances, project coordinators have recommended that raw data be in such a format that it can be given to the relevant government agency for inclusion in a larger database, whereas in other cases the coordinator wanted results that could be used for advocacy work and presented at public meetings (Freitag and Pfeffer 2013). Where final results are presented should not impact the robustness of the scientific research and methodology, but it should be considered in the project's planning stages to ensure that the approach will render results that are applicable to the contextual challenges requiring research and citizen participation in the first place. Project planners should continually ask themselves two key questions: (1) why am I doing this work?; and (2) why do I need to engage the public to increase and ensure project success? Simplified research findings should be presented to the citizen scientist participants and publicly online to demonstrate the usefulness and applicability of what volunteers are doing, thus providing an important feedback loop to encourage further participation (Hart *et al* 2012). In the case study above, research results were shared on the GRR blog, through a final, large volunteer appreciation event hosted in partnership with Parks Canada, and a public lecture hosted in partnership with WildSmart (a local environmental organisation).

As stated earlier, amateur naturalists have played an important role in shaping our understanding of natural heritage, and we would argue that in the 21st century the role of the citizen scientist is as important as ever. They can provide valuable support to research programmes where funding might be limited (an increasing problem in conservation research), often extending the scope and/or duration of data collection. Moreover, in a conservation landscape saturated with multimedia information, citizen scientists provide additional 'eyes and ears' to cope with the sheer volume and range of data available. When citizen scientists can be engaged on projects focused on species at risk, there is also potential to increase public support for research and conservation efforts. This can translate to increased public interest and funding, which can have far-reaching benefits. As the editors indicate in the introduction to this book, people's interpretations of nature and wilderness have shifted over time, yet the importance of culture to the ways we identify, create, manage and think about 'nature as heritage' remains as significant as ever. Citizen scientists have a rich and illustrious heritage, and they will doubtless continue to play an important role in our shifting interpretations of natural heritage in the future.

BIBLIOGRAPHY AND REFERENCES

Alberta Grizzly Bear Recovery Team, 2008 *Alberta Grizzly Bear Recovery Plan 2008–2013*, Alberta Sustainable Resource Development Fish and Wildlife Division, Alberta Species at Risk Recovery Plan No 15, Edmonton

Allen, D E, 1976 *The Naturalist in Britain: a Social History*, Allen Lane, London

Catlin-Groves, C L, 2012 The Citizen Science Landscape: From Volunteers to Citizen Sensors and Beyond, *International Journal of Zoology* 2012, Article ID 349630, doi:10.1155/2012/349630

Chapman, F M, 1900 A Christmas Bird-Census, *Bird Lore* 2 (192), available from: https://archive.org/stream/birdlore21900nati#page/192/mode/2up [8 April 2015]

Elmeligi, S, 2016 Grizzly bear habitat management in Canada's Rocky Mountain Parks: balancing visitor expectations with bear habitat requirements, PhD, Central Queensland University, Australia

Elmeligi, S, Finn, S, Nevin, O T, and Convery, I, 2016 Citizen Science and the Perception of Nature, in *Changing Perceptions of Nature* (eds I Convery and P Davis), The Boydell Press, Woodbridge, 253–64

Finn, S, 2015 *WildWatch North Pennines Final Project Report* [online], available from: http://www.northpennines.org.uk/Pages/WildWatch.aspx [1 July 2015]

Fowler, A, Whyatt, J D, Davies, G, and Ellis, R, 2013 How Reliable are Citizen-Derived Scientific Data? Assessing the Quality of Contrail Observations Made by the General Public, *Transactions in GIS* 17, 488–506

Freitag, A, and Pfeffer, M J, 2013 Process, Not Product: Investigating Recommendations for Improving Citizen Science 'Success', *PLoS ONE* 8 (5), e64079, doi:10.1371/journal.pone.0064079

Gallo, T, and Waitt, D, 2011 Creating a successful citizen science model to detect and report invasive species, *BioScience* 61 (6), 459–65

Gollan, J, Lobry de Bruyn, L, Reid, N, and Wilkie, L, 2012 Can Volunteers Collect Data that are Comparable to Professional Scientists? A Study of Variables Used in Monitoring the Outcomes of Ecosystem Rehabilitation, *Environmental Management* 50 (5), doi:10.1007/s00267-012-9924-4

Hart, A, Stafford, R, Goodenough, A, and Morgan, S, 2012 The role of citizen science and volunteer data collection in zoological research, *International Journal of Zoology* 2012, Article ID 105345, 3 pages, doi:10.1155/2012/105345

Hewitt, S, 2016 The Significance of Natural History Collections in the Twenty-first Century, *Changing Perceptions of Nature* (eds I Convery and P Davis), The Boydell Press, Woodbridge, 111–22

Holt, B G, Rioja-Nieto, R, MacNeil, M A, Lupton, J, and Rahbek, C, 2013 Comparing Diversity Data Collected Using a Protocol Designed for Volunteers with Results from a Professional Alternative, *Methods in Ecology and Evolution* 4, 383–92

Hunter, J, Alabri, A, and van Ingen, C, 2013 Assessing the quality and trustworthiness of citizen science data, *Concurrency and Computation: Practice and Experience* 25 (4), 454–66

Prestopnik, N R, and Crowston, K, 2012 Citizen science system assemblages: understanding the technologies that support crowdsourced science, *Proceedings of the 2012 iConference*, doi:10.1145/2132176.2132198, 168–76

White, G, 1993 *The Natural History of Selborne* (ed R Mabey), Everyman, London

WildWatch, 2019 *WildWatch Findings* [online], available from: http://www.northpennines.org.uk/our-work/wildwatch/wildwatch-findings/ [23 March 2019]

17

Understanding Local Folklore and Attitudes in Apennine Brown Bear Conservation

JENNY ANNE GLIKMAN AND BEATRICE FRANK

Folklore, myths and symbols can influence the way people perceive different species, especially when societies associate multiple and differing meanings to animals. Throughout history and across geographic distribution bears have been portrayed and valued for their beauty, power and strength, their ecological significance, or their kinship to people. However, bears have been disliked and feared for their ferocity and for the negative economic impacts they can inflict on people and their livelihoods. The way bears are portrayed still affects people's attitudes and willingness to support bear conservation. Using a research project from central Italy as example, we highlight how local narratives, attitudes and behaviours towards bears are important considerations for achieving conservation success.

BEAR CONSERVATION AND MANAGEMENT

The conservation and management of large carnivores often occurs in highly contested and complex environments where diverse and opposing dispositions toward predators can lead to conflict or coexistence situations (Mattson *et al* 2006; Redpath *et al* 2015; Frank *et al* 2019). How individuals and societies live with these species, in both conflict or coexistence, is influenced by values, beliefs, cognitions, emotions and feelings. These factors influence our perceptions of a species as much as economic loss, risk to safety, human fatality, the historical presence or absence of the species and communities' livelihoods (Kaczensky *et al* 2004; Glikman *et al* 2012; McFarlane *et al* 2007). Understanding the reasons behind people's disposition toward predators can be even more complex when large carnivores have entrenched cultural and historical meanings (Mattson *et al* 2006) and evoke mythical symbolisms (Harker and Bates 2007). The symbolic status of large carnivores is so significant that biologists have suggested that beliefs about these predators can be more important than the objective biological truth of a species in shaping people's attitudes (Fritts *et al* 2003). Popular culture and identities associated to large carnivores, positive or negative, can indeed influence whether a human-carnivore encounter will turn into a conflict or coexistence situation, making the difference between failing or succeeding in carnivore conservation (Hazzah *et al* 2014; Young *et al* 2015).

Popular culture, including local narratives, folklore and myths, can undermine carnivore conservation efforts by perpetuating negative discourse and behavioural norms, thus jeopardizing the outcome of any management action (Mattson *et al* 2006). Alternatively, it can generate support through iconic use of species imagery (de Pinho *et al* 2014; Matejova 2015). Bears are a perfect example of this challenge. In this chapter, we explore bear folklore, myths and stories around the world to understand better how popular culture influences people's dispositions toward coexisting with them. We then focus on the local cultural context surrounding Apennine brown bear conservation in Italy's Abruzzo, Lazio and Molise National Park (PNALM) and its buffer zone. We use this example to illustrate the importance of including popular culture in bear conservation. We conclude by offering insight into how deep-rooted and longstanding cultural beliefs drive people's attitudes.

BEAR POPULAR CULTURE

The most common representations of animals in literature occur in fables, legends, stories and myths. In most cases, humans use their imagination and cultural stereotypes to anthropomorphise animals (Harel 2009; Foltz 2010). Large carnivores are used often as metaphors for human traits, behaviours or abstract values. This is true for bears, which some societies regard as being spiritual entities, they are used as symbols of wilderness, or to embody immorality and negative human traits (Lumsden 1998; Brunner 2007; Ratamäki 2008). While an in-depth discussion of bear folklore and myths is beyond the scope of this chapter, we discuss below some of the positive and negative ways bears have been portrayed in human imagery.

The way bears have been conceptualised differs across cultures, yet there are common positive traits that societies have used to narrate the relationships between humans and bears. Often the bear is portrayed as a spiritual bridge between people and divinity (Shepard and Sanders 1985; Black 1998). In classical Greece, for example, Zeus fell in love with the nymph Calisto. Hera, Zeus' wife, assuming that Calisto had an affair with her husband and her child was Zeus' son, transformed Calisto into a bear. The child, separated from his mother and raised by other humans, became a hunter. Years later, the child – now grown up – was going to kill a bear, not knowing it was his mother Calisto. To save both from this terrible destiny, Zeus transported Calisto and the son to the heavens, creating the constellations known as the Great and Little Bear (*Ursa major and Ursa minor*) (Bieder 2007). Gibbon (1964, 236) notes, 'when a name is applied to a star group, that name itself becomes a common denominator of whatever legends may be attached thereto.' Consequently, *Ursa major* and *minor* are 'seen' as bears by many distinct civilizations in the Northern Hemisphere (Gibbon 1964).

In other cases, bears were the protectors of people, represented as invincible warriors for their strength and ferocity (Shepard and Sanders 1985; Clark and Slocombe 2009; Pastoureau 2011). In northern Europe, early legends exist about living beings that were half-bear/half-human, symbolising strength and demonstrating how people had great respect for carnivores that could stand upright and enjoy a diverse diet like humans (Werness 2004; Schwartz *et al* 2003). The Vikings believed that wearing bear fur during battle guaranteed protection. Some Norwegian warriors, the Berserkers (*ber* – bear and *serkr* – coat), were feared because it was believed that they could transform themselves into bears and use the animal's wild ferocity during battle (Bieder 2007). Bears' humanlike resemblance and power resulted in different cultures worshipping the species in totems, ceremonies and rituals. The bear became a symbol of royalty (eg King Arthur – Arthur derived from the Celtic word for bear, *artos*) and symbolised cities (eg Berlin and Bern) (Shepard and Sanders 1985; Schwartz *et al* 2003; Benson 2004; Riabov and De Lazari 2009).

Bears have also had negative connotations in popular culture. With the increased influence of the Church across Europe, carnivores became a symbol of an untamed, wild nature, portraying the evil and immoral traits of humans. Bears specifically were seen as strong animals, yet lazy, clumsy and lustful (Rowland 1973; Black 1998). These animals feature in stories, paintings and sculptures, mainly to provide moral lessons for a chaste life. The legend of the half-human and half-bear, for example, changed in meaning in medieval stories, as the bear-man became a symbol of male sexuality typifying fornication and sexual congress by seducing women or kidnapping and raping them (Rowland 1973; Black 1998; Lumsden 1998; Brunner 2007).

Popular culture about bears, as shown above, can shift from reverential to depicting carnivores as unruly and fearsome – an entity to be mastered (Botkin 2004; Shepard and Sanders 1985). In some cases, this perspective persists today, especially where bears are regarded as hazards, pests or problem animals and are persecuted accordingly (McLellan *et al* 2017). The oral traditions of many cultures contain stories of people being attacked – and sometimes killed – by large carnivores. In Prince Edward Island, Canada, a local tale describes how, during a journey through the woods, an islander climbed a tree to escape a bear. The tale narrates how the bear climbed up the tree too and gnawed the flesh from the islander's heels (Hornby 1988). Few stories of bears eating humans have supporting documentation, yet they fuel perceptions of risk and phobias across societies (Ratamäki 2008).

Stories about humans conquering ferocious bears to tame wilderness, and of man's primal quest to conquer fear and prove bravery by killing predators, are widespread (Child and Darimont 2015; Gelo 1987). In Bulgarian folklore, for example, St Andrew, while fasting and praying in the mountains, tamed a bear and rode the predator back to the monastery. According to another tale, the same saint was ploughing his field with an ox when a bear came and ate the ox. The saint battled and overpowered the bear, harnessed the predator to the yoke and continued to plough his field (Stefansen 2013).

It is evident that different species of bear occupy a range of symbolic meaning to people across the world, from magnificent to dreadful, divine to fearsome, useful to repugnant (Ingold 1994; Janoušková 2007). While the meanings associated with bears are rooted in the specific cultural contexts in which the species are found, we can see how across human imagery the bear has gained both positive and negative connotations. Stories based on worldviews and associated meanings have deeply influenced attitudes and behaviours towards bears over the centuries, often determining whether a human-bear interaction turns to conflict or coexistence (Kellert 1994; Mattson *et al* 2006). Because of popular culture and symbolic idealisations, human reactions to bears can range from persecuting the species and opposing conservation initiatives to proactively mitigating conflict, managing attractants and supporting habitat management. As such, knowing what stories societies tell about bears provides insight to understand the reasons behind human-carnivores conflict or coexistence. To better grasp the power of cultural narratives and how they drive people's attitudes toward bears, we use the example of the Apennine brown bears (*Ursus arctos marsicanus*) in central Italy's Abruzzo, Lazio and Molise National Park (PNALM) and its buffer zone.

Bear Conservation in Abruzzo, Lazio and Molise National Park (PNALM), Italy

In Italy, Apennine brown bears are critically endangered, with their core distribution in the PNALM and its buffer zone (1294km^2) (Ciucci *et al* 2017; Fig 17.1). The PNALM territory extends across three different administrative districts, Abruzzo, Lazio and Molise. Within the buffer zone, where most of the local communities exist, year-round hunting is allowed and development and exploitation of natural resources are less rigorously regulated and monitored than in the park itself (Ciucci and Boitani 2008).

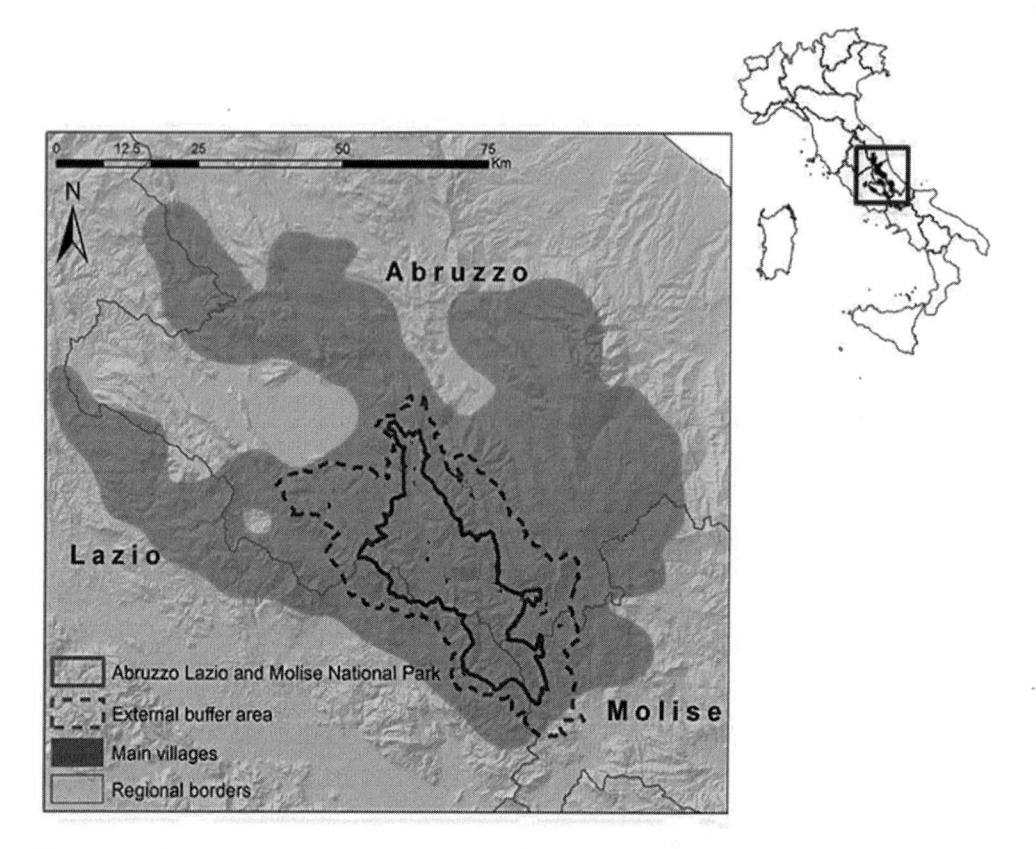

FIGURE 17.1. APENNINE BROWN BEAR RANGE IN CENTRAL ITALY (INSET), WITH REFERENCE TO PNALM (CIUCCI *ET AL* 2017).

In Italy, bears are fully protected by national legislation, but continue to be illegally killed by poachers (Falcucci *et al* 2009). Development for housing, industry and communications also threatens habitats and the bear population, and policy differences across the three administrative regions contribute to conservation problems (Anonymous 2011).

A snowball sampling approach was used to recruit participants with diverse backgrounds (eg agriculture, natural resource sector, local government staff, non-government organisations) (Hay 2005; Newing 2011). Participants were recruited with the aim of reflecting variation in human experiences, attitudes and behaviours related to bears (Biernacki and Waldorf 1981). Forty-four interviews were conducted in the area. A semi-structured interview guide, informed by other relevant research, was used to collect the data (Kellert 1994; McFarlane *et al* 2007). Analysis followed an iterative process, where a coding scheme was developed that reflected saturation of key concepts and patterns in themes across each dataset (Fusch and Ness 2015; Newing 2011). Relevant quotes were also extracted to illustrate findings.

Across PNALM, the majority of respondents (83 per cent) held positive attitudes towards bears and were of the opinion that bears should remain completely protected (88 per cent): 'The bear is really beautiful and deserves protection' (p 18). The Camosciara area – a valley within the PNALM – was designated as a royal hunting reserve in 1872 to protect rare species including the Apennine brown bear (Sievert 1999), so perhaps it is no surprise that deep-rooted hunting lifestyles and local cultural traditions were recorded. Interviewees expressed pride in their popular culture and in sharing the landscape with bears: 'local hunters [from Abruzzo] made the park because they understood that the bear was facing extinction' (p 42). Such feelings were clarified through locals' lengthy description of their attachment to the species; by sharing stories, they had learned about the bears from their ancestors and by stressing that the bears have always been part of their landscape and cultural background.

An interesting finding related to local popular culture was the widespread perception that, similar to local communities, bear behaviour and bear stories were changing. Locals believed that the shift from a pastoral life to a more urban one they were experiencing was experienced also by bears. A participant suggested: 'the bear is similar to shepherds because it lives isolated in the mountains [...] but now all agricultural land is abandoned and people have their orchards next to their homes' (p 12). The participant hinted at the fact that in the past shepherds used to live in isolation with their flocks for a long time in the mountains (ie from spring to autumn). Bears were perceived as conducting a similar life to the shepherds by being on their own in wilderness. However, this is no longer the case for shepherds or bears, with locals spending decreasing time in the mountains and bears coming into villages to search for food. Furthermore, while in the past residents believed bears had no fear of humans, this was no longer the case. Old local legends about bears described this animal as fierce because of its human-like behaviour: 'the bear used to come into the orchards, and it was not afraid of humans. Sometimes he [the bear] ate the corn, when some kids saw and disturbed him, the bear followed them and threw rocks at them' (p 456). Current stories about bears, especially the ones fitted with collars for ecological studies, describe the animals as weak: 'you scream at a bear with a collar and he [the bear] escapes' (p 27) and 'they have the collar around their neck and are not wild anymore' (p 33). These beliefs contradict the historical memories of the species as being fierce and strong.

While attitudes toward bears were positive among local people, they did not feel the same about the park administrators. Distrust of the park administration was evident, with locals challenging the park policy towards bears and their ecology (Ciucci *et al* 2014). Some residents, for example, alleged that park staff had food-conditioned bears to eat chickens, causing bears to venture into town and, in turn, imposing economic hardships on people. Others suggested the park managers should reignite a 1980s World Wildlife Fund (WWF) campaign of planting apple trees to help feed bears: 'why do I need to feed their animals with my food [agricultural produce]?' (p 12). Such a strategy is in conflict with the park's stated policy to manage the use of attractants in the PNALM. Some participants expressed frustrations about the park administration: 'this was the land of my family from generations, and from one day to another it was park territory. [Now] I need to ask [permission] to cut a tree in my yard' (p 31). This frustration was related to animosity around economic development in the park, which was perceived as harmless to bears: 'bears are not affected by a ski resort. We saw a bear crossing the ski resort without any issues. They [the park] do not allow any new development. People want a new ski resort for jobs and tourism' (p 14). The perception that bears are a higher priority than locals' livelihood influences people's negative dispositions toward the park authorities.

To conclude, by asking participants about their cultural beliefs about the bear, we have discovered that the problem is not the Apennine brown bear *per se*, but the administrative and political context around the species – a key understanding to develop future strategies for bear conservation and foster a positive popular culture around bears. Attitudes to bears, while still positive, are changing as human-human relations over resources and land uses are becoming more conflict-laden. A perceived emphasis on protecting bears above human wellbeing has ignited negative interactions between local communities and the park administration: 'We don't see anything that the park does [...] We need to change the park administration here. Change the director. Give more power to the communities' (p 8). These human-human conflicts are leading to changes in narratives about bears across the PNALM, which can influence local people's attitudes towards the species over time.

Culturally shared stories, along with first-hand experiences, influence people's dispositions towards bears (Clark and Rutherford 2014; Camino *et al* 2016; Waylen *et al* 2009). This has been widely demonstrated in the literature and popular culture, and through the examples presented here. Across cultures, folklore, myth and stories bears are depicted in dualistic manners. Positive narratives about the species describe this animal as magnificent, one to be respected for its strength and power, while negative stories criticised this predator for its wildness, unpredictability and ferociousness. In PNALM, these opposing attitudes towards bears are evident. On one side, people are proud to share the landscape with Apennine brown bears and want the species to persist across the landscape since it is part of this area's cultural identity. On the other side, bears evoke fear in people, are perceived to cause economic hardships and are viewed as barriers to livelihood improvement (Mattson *et al* 2006; Glikman *et al* 2012). Furthermore, communities believe that the conservation of bears has become more important than safeguarding local culture and livelihoods, with consequent changes to their identity. Linked to this is the strong desire for people to retain autonomy and power over private land management and development (Morzillo *et al* 2007; Ciucci and Boitani 2008; Campbell and Lancaster 2010). As a result, bear conservation interventions in PNALM are being partially effective or failing due to local resistance and mistrust – or human-human conflicts over bear management.

Considerations for Bear Conservation

Lack of community support for the park's administrators in PNALM has resulted in observable, negative effects on bear conservation efforts in the area. As shown by Mattson *et al* (2006), conflicts between parks administration and local communities around conservation/use values can lead to contentious management contexts where power dynamics between humans jeopardise conservation success, and create barriers toward coexisting with wildlife (Young *et al* 2010; Madden and McQuinn 2017; Frank *et al* 2019). Indeed, a sense of impotence about decisions taken by authorities about wildlife conservation may result in local communities feeling they have to endure all the cost of conservation. They then redirect their anger to wild species rather than to addressing the power issues they experience with other players (Barua *et al* 2013; Nyhus 2016; Frank *et al* 2019). Opposition toward conservation can indeed become even more severe when local communities perceive that their own needs are regarded as subordinate to those of wildlife (Madden 2008; Songhurst 2017). As a result of the failure to build trust and transparency between groups interested in the human-wildlife interactions, conservation interventions can face local resistance and fail. Deep-rooted reasons behind human-wildlife conflicts must be addressed for conservation measures to succeed (Madden and McQuinn 2014, 2017; Dayer *et al* 2017; Hill 2017).

Positive narratives and interrelated attitudes are not necessarily enough to garner conservation support. Equally important is the *context* in which attitudes toward bears are built, as clearly shown throughout the PNALM example. While it is clear that cultural beliefs and attitudes about bears influence the willingness to coexist with the species – as denoted by shared stories of where bears belong or how they should be managed – the root issues are often about human-human conflicts (HHC), particularly when they relate to people's wellbeing. As such, we recommend starting any conservation project by exploring and distinguishing where the frictions lie between different stakeholders. What are the different interests or the social drivers and root causes of HHC? Discussion of the interactions between, and stories about, humans and wildlife – or human-wildlife conflict to coexistence situations – is essential. Understanding popular culture can help to unpack the reasons why opposition to conservation action persists and the remedial actions that are required.

Understanding how dispositions vary across cultural and administrative contexts can help map areas of support and opposition toward carnivore conservation and management. Such knowledge can represent the turning point between failing and succeeding in conservation when efforts are focused on places where public participation and engagement is most needed. We suggest going beyond bio-physical research, and starting to integrate social and humanities sciences in order to develop projects that use collaborative approaches and unite people through shared narratives about carnivores (Blicharska and Mikusinski 2014; Clark 2002; Rust *et al* 2017). Bringing together people with different views can encourage building positive relationships by identifying and acknowledging commonalities between those engaged. This does not mean avoiding any undesired disposition toward bears and their management. It is important to identify negative attitudes, as they are the key to designing interventions that address conflicts. Having a shared understanding of both negative and positive dispositions toward carnivores is the first step toward building socially driven management plans – or plans that include human-human as well as human-wildlife issues and aim at increasing social acceptance, tolerance and positive behaviour among groups and species.

It is important to understand what meanings carnivores have for local communities in order not only to highlight synergies between social and biological values and needs, but also to explicitly acknowledge the importance of local culture in achieving success (Blicharska and Mikusinski 2014; Waylen *et al* 2009; Wondolleck and Yaffee 2000). Engaging with communities to understand their beliefs, for example those beliefs communicated through folklore, can be insightful when designing conservation efforts that are culturally sensitive and meaningful for both people and carnivores (McLennan and Hill 2012). Doing so will enable dialogue that explicitly acknowledges the importance of local culture and its role in achieving conservation success (Clark and Rutherford 2014). Such an approach enables the development of more effective conservation interventions that are respectful of local livelihood necessities and are culturally relevant.

BIBLIOGRAPHY AND REFERENCES

Anon, 2011 *Piano d'azione nazionale per la tutela dell'orso bruno marsicano (PATOM)*, Quad Cons Nat 37, Ministero dell'Ambiente – ISPRA, Roma, Italy [in Italian]

Benson, K, 2014 *Gwich'in Knowledge of Grizzly Bears*, Gwich'in Social and Cultural Institute/Gwich'in Renewable Resources Board [online], available from: http://www.grrb.nt.ca/pdf/wildlife/grizzly/Gwichin%20 TK%20of%20SAR%20Grizzly%20report_Final.pdf [10 October 2016]

Bieder, R E, 2007 *Orso (Bear)*, Urra-Apogeo s.r.l., Milan, Italy

Biernacki, P, and Waldorf, D, 1981 Snowball Sampling: Problems and Techniques of Chain Referral Sampling, *Sociological Methods Research* 10 (2), 141–63

Black, L T, 1998 Bear in Human Imagination and Ritual, *Ursus* 10, 343–7

Blicharska, M, and Mikusinski, G, 2014 Incorporating social and cultural significance of large old trees in conservation policy, *Conservation Biology* 28 (6), 1558–67

Botkin, D B, 2004 *Our Natural History: The Lessons of Lewis and Clark*, 2 edn, Oxford University Press, Oxford, UK

Brunner, B, 2007 *Bears: A Brief History*, Yale University Press, New Haven, USA

Camino, M, Cortez, S, Cerezo, A, and Altrichter, M, 2016 Wildlife conservation, perceptions of different co-existing cultures, *International Journal of Conservation Science* 7 (1), 109–22

Campbell, M, and Lancaster, B, 2010 Public attitudes toward black bears (*Ursus americanus*) and cougars (*Puma concolor*) on Vancouver Island, *Society and Animals* 18, 40–57

Child, K R, and Darimont, C T, 2015 Hunting for trophies: online hunting photographs reveal achievement satisfaction with large and dangerous prey, *Human Dimensions of Wildlife Journal* 20 (6), 531–41

Ciucci, P, and Boitani, L, 2008 The Apennine brown bear: A critical review of its status and conservation problems, *Ursus* 19, 130–45

Ciucci, P, Tosoni, E, Di Domenico, G, Quattrociocchi, F, and Boitani, L, 2014 Seasonal and annual variation in the food habits of the remnant Apennine bear (*Ursus arctos marsicanus*) population, central Italy, *Journal of Mammalogy* 95, 572–86

Ciucci, P, Altea, T, Antonucci, A, Chiaverini, L, Di Croce, A, Fabrizio, M, Forconi, P, Latini, R, Maiorano, L, Monaco, A, Morini, P, Ricci, F, Sammarone, L, Striglioni, F, and Tosoni, E, RLBMN, 2017 Distribution of the brown bear (*Ursus arctos marsicanus*) in the Central Apennines, Italy, 2005–2014, *Hystrix*, 28 (1), 86–91

Clark, D A, and Slocombe, D S, 2009 Respect for grizzly bear: an Aboriginal approach for co-existence and resilience, *Ecology and Society* 14 (1), 42, available from: www.ecologyandsociety.org/vol14/iss1/art42/ [17 October 2016]

Clark, S G, and Rutherford, M B, 2014 *Large carnivore conservation: Integrating science and policy in the North American West*, The University of Chicago Press, Chicago, USA

Clark, T W, 2002 *The Policy Process: A Practical Guide for Natural Resource Professionals*, Yale University Press, New Haven, USA

Dayer, A A, Williams, A, Cosbar, E, and Racey, M, 2017 Blaming threatened species: media portrayal of human-wildlife conflict, *Oryx*, 1–8

de Pinho, J R, Grilo, C, Boone, R B, Galvin, K A, and Snodgrass, J G, 2014 Influence of Aesthetic Appreciation of Wildlife Species on Attitudes towards Their Conservation in Kenyan Agropastoralist Communities, *PLoS ONE*, 9 (2), e88842

Falcucci, A, Ciucci, P, Maiorano, L, Gentile, L, and Boitani, L, 2009 Assessing habitat quality for conservation using an integrated occurrence mortality model, *Journal of Applied Ecology* 46, 600–9

Foltz, R, 2010 Zoroastrian attitudes toward animals, *Society and Animals* 18, 367–78

Frank, B F, Glikman J A, and Marchini, S, 2018 *Human-wildlife interactions: turning conflict into coexistence*, Cambridge University Press (in press)

Fritts, S H, Stephenson, R O, Hayes, R D, and Boitani, L, 2003 Wolves and humans, in *Wolves: behavior, ecology and conservation* (eds L D Mech and L Boitani), The University of Chicago, Chicago, 289–316

Fusch, P I, and Ness, L R, 2015 Are we there yet? Data saturation in qualitative research, *The Qualitative Report* 20 (9), 1408

Gelo, D, 1987 The Bear, in *American Wildlife in Symbol and Story* (eds A K Gillespie and J Mechling), University of Tennessee Press, Knoxville

Gibbon, W, 1964 Asiatic Parallels in North American Star Lore: Ursa Major, *The Journal of American Folklore* 77 (305), 236–50

Glikman, J A, Vaske, J J, Bath, A J, Ciucci, P, and Boitani, L, 2012 Residents' support for wolf and bear conservation: the moderating influence of knowledge, *European Journal of Wildlife Research* 58, 295–302

Harel, N, 2009 The animal voice behind the animal fable, *Journal of critical animal studies* 7 (2), 9–21

Harker, D, and Bates, D C, 2007 The Black Bear Hunt in New Jersey: A constructionist Analysis of an Intractable Conflict, *Society and Animals* 15, 329–52

Hay, I, 2005 *Qualitative research methods in Human Geography*, 2nd edn, Oxford University Press, Australia

Hazzah, L, Dolrenry, S, Naughton, L, Edwards, C T T, Mwebi, O, Kearney, F, and Frank, L, 2014 Efficacy of two lion conservation programs in Maasailand, Kenya, *Conservation Biology* 28, 851–60

Hill, C, 2017 Introduction. Complex problems: Using a biosocial approach to understanding human-wildlife interactions, in *Understanding Conflicts About Wildlife: A Biosocial Approach* (eds C M Hill, A D Webber and N E C Priston), Berghahn, Oxford, 1–14

Ingold, T, 1994 From trust to domination: an alternative history of human–animal relations, in *Animals and Human Society: Changing Perspectives* (eds A Manning and J Serpell), Routledge, London, 1–22

Janoušková, Z, 2007 Conservation and Bears in Canadian Literature, unpublished BA thesis, Masaryk University, Brno, Czech Republic

Kaczensky, P, Blazic, M, and Gossow, H, 2004 Public attitudes towards brown bears (*Ursus arctos*) in Slovenia, *Biological Conservation* 118, 661–74

Kellert, S R, 1994 Public attitudes toward bears and their conservation, *International Conference on Bear Research and Management* 9, 43–50

Lumsden, P L, 1998 The bear in selected American, Canadian, and Native literature: A pedagogical symbol linking humanity and nature, unpublished PhD thesis, University of Alberta, Edmonton, Canada

Madden, F, 2008 The growing conflict between humans and wildlife: Law and policy as contributing and mitigating factors, *Journal of International Wildlife Law & Policy* 11, 189–206

Madden, F, and McQuinn, B, 2017 Conservation Conflict Transformation: Addressing the Missing Link in Wildlife Conservation, in *Understanding Conflicts About Wildlife: A Biosocial Approach* (eds C M Hill, A D Webber and N E C Priston), Berghahn, Oxford, 148–69

Matejova, M, 2015 Is global activism saving the polar bear? *Environment: Science and Policy for Sustainable Development* 57 (5), 14–23

Mattson, D J, Byrd, K L, Rutherford, M B, Brown, S R, and Clark, T W, 2006 Finding common ground in large carnivore conservation: Mapping contending perspectives, *Environmental Science and Policy* 9, 392–405

McFarlane, B L, Watson, D O, and Stumpf-Allen, R C G, 2007 *Public perceptions of conservation of grizzly bears in the Foothills Model Forest: a survey of local and Edmonton residents*, Natural Resources Canada, Canadian Forest Service, Northern Forestry Centre, Edmonton, Alberta, Canada and Foothills Model Forest, Hinton, Alberta, Information Report NOR-X-413

McLellan, B N, Proctor, M F, Huber D, and Michel, S, 2017 *Ursus arctos* (amended version published in 2016), The IUCN Red List of Threatened Species 2017: e.T41688A114261661. http://dx.doi.org/10.2305/IUCN.UK.2017-1.RLTS.T41688A114261661.en (21 November 2017)

McLennan, M R, and Hill, C M, 2012 Troublesome neighbours: changing attitudes towards chimpanzees (*Pan troglodytes*) in a human-dominated landscape in Uganda, *Journal of Nature Conservation* 20, 219–27

Morzillo, A T, Mertig, A G, Garner, N, and Liu, J, 2007 Spatial distribution of attitudes toward proposed management strategies for wildlife recovery, *Human Dimension of Wildlife* 12, 15–29

Newing, H, Eagle, C, Puri, R, and Watson, C, 2011 *Conducting research in conservation: Social science methods and practice*, Routledge, Abingdon, UK

Pastoureau, M, 2011 *The Bear: History of a Fallen King*, Belknap Press

Ratamäki, O, 2008 Finland's wolf policy and new governance, *The Journal of Environment Development* 17 (3), 316–39

Redpath, S M, Bhatia, S, and Young, J, 2015 Tilting at wildlife: reconsidering human-wildlife conflict, *Oryx* 49 (2), 222–5

Riabov, O, and De Lazari, A, 2009 Misha and the bear: the bear in metaphor for Russia in representations of the "Five Day War", *Russian Politics and Law* 47 (5), 26–39

Rowland, B, 1973 *Animals with Human faces: a guide to animal symbolism*, The University of Tennessee Press, Knoxville, USA

Rust, N A, Abrams, A, Challender, D W S, Chapron, G, Ghoddousi, A, Glikman, J A, Gowan, C H, Hughes, C, Rastogi, A, Said, A, Sutton, A, Taylor, N, Thomas, S, Unnikrishnan, H, Webber, A D, Wordingham, G, and Hill, C M, 2017 Quantity does not always mean quality: the importance of qualitative social science in conservation research, *Society and Natural Resources* 30 (10), 1304–10

Schwartz, C C, Swenson, J E, and Miller, S D, 2003 Large carnivores, moose, and humans: a changing paradigm of predator management in the 21st century, *Alces* 39, 41–63

Shepard, P, and Sanders, B, 1985 *The Sacred Paw: The Bear in Nature, Myth and Literature*, Viking Penguin Inc., New York, USA

Songhurst, A, 2017 Measuring human-wildlife conflicts: Comparing insights from different monitoring approaches, *Wildlife Society Bulletin* 41 (2), 351–61

Stefansen, S, 2013 *Førkristne tradisjoner i bulgarsk folkeliv Transformasjon og opptak i den kristne tro*, available from: https://brage.bibsys.no/xmlui/bitstream/handle/11250/242931/687759_FULLTEXT01.pdf?sequence=1&isAllowed=y [16 October 2018]

Waylen, K A, Fisher, A, McGowan, P K, Thirgood, S J, and Milner-Gulland, E J, 2009 Effect of local cultural context on the success of community-based conservation interventions, *Conservation Biology* 24 (4), 1119–29

Werness, H B, 2004 *The Continuum Encyclopedia of Animal Symbolism in Art*, Continuum, New York, USA

Wondolleck, J J M, and Yaffee, S L, 2000 *Making Collaboration Work: Lessons From Innovation In Natural Resource Management*, Island Press, Washington, USA

Young, J C, Marzano, M, White, R M, McCracken, D I, Redpath, S M, Carss, D N, Quine, C P, and Watt, A D, 2010 The emergence of biodiversity conflicts from biodiversity impacts: Characteristics and management strategies, *Biodiversity and Conservation* 19, 3973–90

Young, J K, Ma, Z, Laudati, A, and Berger, J, 2015 Human-carnivore interactions: Lessons learned from communities in the American West, *Human Dimensions of Wildlife* 20 (4), 349–66

18

Reducing Human Impacts on Andean Bears in NW Peru Through Community-based Conservation

Samantha A Young, Russell C Van Horn
and Jenny Anne Glikman

Andean bears (*Tremarctos ornatus*) are the last remaining bears in South America. They live throughout the tropical Andes in a large latitudinal (~11°N–22°S) and elevational gradient (~200–4700m above sea level (masl)) across diverse habitats. They are threatened throughout their range by habitat loss, habitat fragmentation and hunting, and in many places they overlap with human settlements and agricultural fields, creating competition or conflict for resources. Using a case study in northwestern Peru, we discuss how human activities affect the landscape and, in turn, the ecology of Andean bears, which have been identified as keystone actors in their environment. We then illustrate strategies that have been used to mitigate human impacts through community-based conservation (ie fuel-efficient stoves and environmental education), and how we have come to understand and address the needs of both bears and people through research in both the human and bear dimensions of conservation. We discuss the results of programme evaluations and their effectiveness, and conclude with implications for wildlife management and lessons from collaborating with local communities, governments and non-governmental organisations (NGOs).

Andean Bears

Andean bears, sometimes called spectacled bears, are declining in numbers due to habitat degradation, habitat fragmentation and unsustainable poaching (Velez-Liendo and García-Rangel 2017), making them globally vulnerable to extinction and endangered in Peru (MINAGRI 2014). Efforts to conserve Andean bears, and other large carnivores, can only succeed if the anthropogenic factors that underlie their endangerment are addressed (eg Peyton 1994).

Andean bears survive in a variety of habitats, including the seasonally dry tropical forests of northwest Peru (Figueroa 2013a), as at our core study area of Cerro Venado (Lambayeque, Peru, 6°26'S, 79°33'W). Because the seasonally dry tropical forest occurs at low elevations, in relatively gentle topography, with a climate that is more conducive to agricultural development than that of this bear's other habitats, most of this habitat has long been subject to strong human impacts, meaning that most Andean bears are now found in other habitats. The pressures that have reduced most lowland tropical dry forests continue to be a risk to the remaining patches and their bears.

Andean bears persist in this habitat partly because they are opportunistic omnivores; throughout their range they consume stems, leaves or fruits from at least 305 plant species, and prey or scav-

FIGURE 18.1. SAPOTE FRUIT, *COLICODENDRON SCABRIDUM*.

enge on at least 40 animal species (Figueroa 2013a; Gonzales *et al* 2016)1825. Near Cerro Venado they eat at least 26 species of plants, including sapote (*Colicodendron scabridum* (Fig 18.1), previously *Capparis scabrida*; Cornejo and Iltis 2008) and pasallo (*Eriotheca ruizii*; Figueroa 2013b). Although meat appears to be a small part of the Andean bears' nutrition, most information on their diet has come from scat analyses (eg Figueroa 2013a; Gonzales *et al* 2016)1825, which are potentially misleading (eg Klare *et al* 2011); we don't know how well scat contents reflect the nutritional importance of items consumed by Andean bears.

Various bear species adjust when and where they forage according to the availability of nutritional resources (eg American black bear, *Ursus americanus*; Noyce and Garshelis 2011). Although the foraging ecology of Andean bears has not been well studied, they may focus their foraging efforts on key resources, for example bromeliads in alpine grasslands (Peyton 1980), clusters of fruiting aguacatillo (*Nectandra acutifolia*) in the Ecuadorian cloud forest (Molina Proaño 2012), and perhaps sapote in the dry forests of northwest Peru (Osgood 1914; Peyton 1981; Amanzo *et al* 2013).

Bear foraging, body condition and reproductive rates have been empirically linked in other bear species, as reviewed for polar bears (*Ursus maritimus*) by Rode *et al* (2010). The body condition of Andean bears at Cerro Venado improves during the sapote fruiting season and declines when sapote fruit is unavailable and the resident adult bears forage primarily on the wood of pasallo (Amanzo *et al* 2013). In addition to affecting bear body condition and perhaps reproductive success, the availability of sapote fruit appears to influence even the seasonality of dry forest bear reproduction. Timing of bear mating at Cerro Venado appears linked to female body condition and thus the availability of sapote fruit (Appleton *et al* 2018). It's likely, then, that reproduction by these dry forest bears depends on the availability of sapote fruit.

Unfortunately, sapote is considered endangered in Peru (MINAGRI 2016) and it is rare and localised at Cerro Venado. Across 40 randomly located sites there, from 200–1153 masl, we have identified 30 species of woody plants and cacti. Very few of these woody plants were sapote (0.9% of 1314 individuals), all from below 737 masl. In contrast, pasallo was much more common (11.3 per cent of woody plants) and widespread, from 375–1151 masl.

HUMANS IN THE ANDEAN BEAR LANDSCAPE

Since prehistory, humans have used and modified the Andean landscape and have reduced bear numbers through habitat degradation, habitat fragmentation and unsustainable poaching (Bonacic *et al* 2017; Velez-Liendo and García-Rangel 2017). In recent decades, the overlap between humans and wildlife has intensified in and near the study area, resulting in negative consequences for both sides. Although our goal as scientists with San Diego Zoo Global is the conservation of bears and their habitats, the central underlying issue is humans, either because they perceive themselves as the victim in a conflict, or because they are actively causing harm to wildlife or wildlife habitat.

Humans have actively altered the environment near Cerro Venado for at least 7000 years (Ancajima Salvatierra 2010). However, the rate and magnitude of change from human activities has increased in the last several decades at Cerro Venado and elsewhere in northwest Peru, possibly due to the agrarian land reforms of the 1960s, in which large privately-held estates became cooperative farms, and due to the overall increase in human population (Peyton 1981; Ancajima Salvatierra 2010; Ektvedt *et al* 2012). All human settlements and major intensive agriculture developments near the core study area are in valley bottoms, primarily next to the flood plain of the Río La Leche (Ancajima Salvatierra 2010), so the most intense human activities are near the most valuable nutritional resource for bears: sapote. Indeed, the low elevation distribution of sapote trees makes this resource vulnerable to human impact. Although sapote fruit appears to be rarely consumed by people in the study area, people eat the fruit elsewhere (Cornejo and Iltis 2008) and wherever the tree has been studied its wood is harvested for a variety of uses, including as fuel (Rodríguez Rodríguez *et al* 2007; Cornejo and Iltis 2008). While monitoring sapote phenology in our collaborative research, we have observed that human-caused mortality of sapote within the study area is approximately three times the rate of natural mortality. We've observed land clearing that's removed some groves of sapote close to human settlements, adjacent to our core study area, and we've frequently observed trees from which some limbs have been removed, probably reducing fruit production. Human actions may also reduce the availability of other resources for bears in this area; free-ranging cattle and goats drink and wallow at lower-elevation waterholes, which we believe precludes their use by wild Andean bears. Other bears adjust the times and locations when they use resources in response to human activities and infrastructure (eg Martin *et al* 2010), so although local people may not often directly interact with Andean bears, they may indirectly impact them.

Thus, to tackle the issue of diminishing resources for bear populations, there is a need to involve the local people in conservation. Humans are the drivers and the solution to all conservation challenges. However, all too often, few opportunities are provided for communities living with and depending on threatened species to participate in conservation, voice concerns about the ecosystem or livelihoods, or engage in discourse. Because human communities are part of the natural landscape, and it is their own natural and cultural heritage that is threatened, excluding them from conservation initiatives can stand in the way of successful, long-term actions.

A growing field of study that draws from several of the social sciences (eg social psychology, anthropology and sociology) is the Human Dimensions of Wildlife (HDW; see Decker *et al* 2012). This area of investigation attempts to describe, predict, understand and influence human thought and action toward natural environments. Within HDW there are diverse methods with different levels of community involvement that attempt to understand the motivations driving specific behaviours: from standard surveys, where participants give input by answering specific questions, to in-depth interviews, where interviewers engage in conversations with respondents to understand their perceptions from a cultural perspective. There can also be added layers of engagement using focus groups and workshops, where participants interact with one another and exchange ideas on specific topics with the interviewer and with other community members. These facilitated techniques allow direct participation in the decision-making process, which has been shown to increase ownership over the issue and reduce conflict (Madden and McQuinn 2014).

In the foothills of our study site of Cerro Venado, the NGO Spectacled Bear Conservation Society (SBC) has worked for several years to establish a conservation presence in the local communities of the Leche River watershed, hiring local staff and working with landowners. In 2009, San Diego Zoo Global joined forces with SBC to conduct ecological research and later establish an ongoing community-based conservation programme. Since then, we've worked closely with SBC staff, local institutions and rural communities to identify and implement several strategies to directly or indirectly relieve negative environmental impacts caused by human activities; we've done so by gaining trust within the communities and facilitating the adoption of a suite of sustainable behaviours. Our strategies in working with the community included: (1) *Building capacity* for sustainable activities by training local programme coordinators and field technicians, and promoting fuel-efficient cooking; (2) *Environmental education*, where we trained teachers, developed curricula, and provided material and subject matter support; (3) *Economic development*, where we hired local community members to run field programmes and diversified the economy in a sustainable manner; and (4) *Evaluation and adaptation*, to ensure that the activities and the overall programme remained locally appropriate and effective. Although visibility is relatively good in the dry forest and there may be the potential for ecotourism focused on endemic birds, opportunities for bear-viewing are probably limited to the brief fruiting season of the sapote (Amanzo *et al* 2013). What follows is an account of the environmental education and fuel-efficient cookstove programmes, with assessments of their success.

Forest Guardians

San Diego Zoo Global (SDZG) and SBC developed an environmental education programme, called Forest Guardians (FG), focused on training and supporting local teachers. A Peruvian coordinator, who was part of the SBC staff, and trained by SDZG staff in advance of workshops, and who was in regular communication with SDZG staff, ran the programme. Together, we conducted teacher training workshops that integrated information about natural and cultural heritage and introduced novel curricula, progressive teaching approaches and practical applications for behavioural changes. Teachers that committed to Forest Guardians were required to carry out school-based projects designed by themselves and their students; some examples include recycling campaigns, medicinal plant gardens and environmental awareness marches. We facilitated community festivals where projects, food and heritage were celebrated and conducted an international exchange where Peruvian teachers travelled to a sister programme in Hawaii, and Hawaiian teachers travelled to Peru.

To assess the effectiveness of the FG programme, we surveyed a total of 35 participant and non-participant teachers on their environmental knowledge, attitudes and behaviour. We found significant differences between the two groups of teachers, with a higher occurrence of steward-ship-oriented attitudes in FG teachers; These teachers reported teaching a significantly larger breadth of environmental topics and activities. Participating in FG was also positively correlated with teaching a greater breadth of environmental subjects [Spearman's r=523, n=32, p=0.001]. Almost all FG teachers reported a change in classroom practices after participating in a training workshop, and we found a positive correlation between participation in FG and attitudes towards conservation (Spearman's r=686, n=31, p< 0.001), as well as knowledge of conservation programmes in the region (Spearman's r=431, n=32, p=0.007). Additionally, 77 per cent of 27 FG teachers stated they talked about these topics outside of the classroom, indicating that they were engaging their broader community in environmental topics. We also briefly measured similar characteristics of the students of FG teachers and found that students exposed to a great breadth of environmental topics in class had high frequencies of high composite scores of the following: Attitudes towards environmental education (83 per cent of 203 students); attitudes towards environmental stewardship (90 per cent of 213 students); attitudes towards bears (71 per cent of 210 students); behaviours towards conservation activities (77 per cent of 220 students); knowledge of conservation programmes (63 per cent of 210 students); and knowledge of conservation institutions in the region (84 per cent of 205 students).

Fuel-Efficient Cookstoves

We began exploring alternative cooking methods as a result of data and observations from SBC indicating that communities were impacting bear habitat by entering the forest to collect fuel wood and cutting sapote trees for fuel or construction. The majority of households in the upper watershed communities surrounding Cerro Venado cook via traditional open fires (Fig 18.2, the *fogon*), utilising little more than rocks and wood as a stove. This method is relatively inefficient at cooking and burning wood due to the quick loss of heat (Wathore *et al* 2017). It is also harsh on the health of the cook – almost always a woman – as the stove provides the cook no protection from the heat and smoke. A high occurrence of health concerns, such as respiratory illness and burns as a result of cooking have been observed in developing countries that use open wood fire stoves such as the *Fogon* (Grieshop *et al* 2011).

To address the above concerns, fuel-efficient cookstoves, known in Peru as *cocinas mejoradas* (CM), were selected for a small scale programme in 2014 and 2015. These were chosen due to their familiarity in the region (leading to easy acceptance of the technology), the availability of the materials, and the simple and modifiable design (Fig 18.2). The stoves were built in 12 homes in 2014 and in another ten homes in 2015, with participants selected by local leaders, who identified families most in need. To increase investment in programme success, participants were required to engage in pre-construction meetings with SBC and principal investigators, assist in the construction of the stove and attend post-construction focus groups. A local resident with experience in building CM was contracted to construct all 22 stoves.

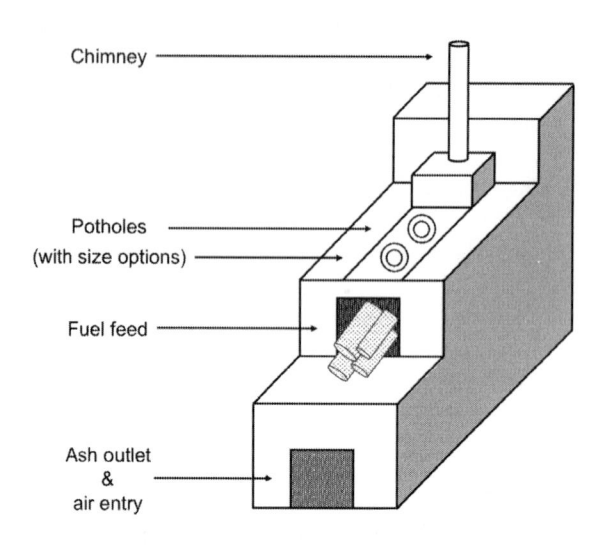

Chimney

Potholes
(with size options)

Fuel feed

Ash outlet
&
air entry

FIGURE 18.2 DIAGRAM OF A *COCINA MEJORADA*.

To gain an understanding of perceptions of change, two focus groups were conducted with men and women separately one year after the 2014 stove construction, and then semi-structured interviews were conducted one year after the 2015 construction. Results indicated almost exclusively positive feelings towards the CM, which had entirely replaced the use of the *fogon* in participant households. Discussion responses spanned four categories of perceived benefits to the family: (1) *Reduction in time and resources*, with 50 per cent less firewood needed to cook throughout the day, a 50 per cent reduction in trips to collect wood, and significantly reduced time spent cooking; (2) *Health*, where the CM was reported to eliminate ailments, with six out of seven men (86 per cent) and seven out of eight women (88 per cent) stating that there was no longer smoke in the cooking area, while eye-tearing, coughing, sore throats and flu-like symptoms were reduced or eliminated, with no more topical burns and less danger to the family; (3) *Convenience*, where three out of seven men (43 per cent) and five out of eight women (63 per cent) stated that the stove stays lit, items can cook simultaneously, food heats up faster and remains hot longer, the stove gets hotter, they can leave it unsupervised and there's more time for other things; and (4) *Aesthetics*, where ten out of 18 people (66.7 per cent) stated that they thought the stove looked nice in their home, pots and the stove remain unstained, the cook (almost always the woman) did not get dirty and other people liked their stove.

Additionally, a simple quantitative test was conducted to verify participant perceptions of the differences between the *fogon* and the CM. Two households, the first with a traditional *fogon* and the second with a CM, were given an equivalent weight and type of firewood and asked to cook with that exclusively for three days. Results showed a 25 per cent reduction in time spent cooking and a 56 per cent reduction in fuel wood used in the household using the CM.

PROGRAMME EFFECTIVENESS AND IMPLICATIONS FOR THE CONSERVATION OF ANDEAN BEARS AND THEIR HABITAT

Seasonally dry tropical forest remains primarily in fragments inaccessible to humans (Linares-Pal-omino *et al* 2010) and that inaccessibility protects much of the Andean bears' habitats, for now. By incorporating indices of human impacts into analyses, Wallace *et al* (2014) identified a priority conservation unit for Andean bears that included Cerro Venado. Only about 4.25% of this conservation unit is currently under legal protection, so bear conservation there will obviously depend on coexistence between bears and humans. In the challenges encountered during the five years of working with the SBC field team and local communities near Cerro Venado, we have been able to create expectations that are more realistic, devise strategies to obtain more results, and come away with lessons that can be used for future work in these communities or other regions altogether.

To begin with, the authors did not live at the field site but visited in short durations for training, workshops, presentations and evaluation of HDW research. Over time, we learned that a well-trained, independent and confident local coordinator is essential to oversee day-to-day activities and proper and long-term programme function. In identifying coordinators and other local staff, cultural differences between Peruvian and non-Peruvian collaborators led to assumptions of abilities or communications practices being taken for granted (eg understanding of the use of 'Track Changes' in editing documents or methodology for interaction with a community). Initially, staff did not voice misunderstandings, lack of knowledge or unexpected programme outcomes, etc. This was exacerbated by the long distance between countries and initially inconsistent and infrequent communication.

Over the course of time spent working with in-country staff, the following actions helped secure more reliable behaviour and results: more frequent trips to the field site, frequent progress reports in writing or verbally through in-person/virtual meetings (eg Skype), repetition of requests and responsibilities (including communicating challenges), confirmation and repetition of understanding of concepts, goals, actions and tools (including computer programs or field equipment), modelling desired behaviours for local staff either by us or by experienced Peruvian individuals or staff, and clear, small, digestible sets of instructions given at a time.

In working with teachers, we found too much curriculum given at once was overwhelming and less likely to be used. Participatory methods of learning were somewhat novel and slow to be accepted but were valued in the end. Teachers required frequent reminders to complete tasks and attend events, as well as consistent check-ins regarding progress in implementing projects. Teachers within a school often preferred to work together on a single project, maximising manpower and resources. Support materials for the completion of projects were best loaned out on a temporary basis at the specific request of a teacher for a specific project, rather than be permanently 'gifted' to schools as a complete toolkit; gifts often went unused or were lost. Surveys were best completed during in-person interactions, otherwise they would not be returned, and focus groups were successful with teachers, who enjoyed interacting with one another.

Based on previous research with teachers in the study area, we've come to understand some overarching themes, which have reaffirmed the programme design of working with teachers. We've confirmed that teachers are leaders in their community and agents of community change. They work and often live in the communities where they are respected and entrusted with future generations, they instigate community-wide events, and are sought after by families for advice. Our intention was to target the teacher as a community pillar and create a multiplier effect, as a teacher connects with many individuals within the community. Our research has also confirmed that teachers and the community value environmental stewardship, and participants are proud to discuss the conservation actions that they themselves carried out. The programme builds upon the concept that teachers and schools are models for the residents in the ways in which they can manage their own resources, address current issues, and become informed and active citizens who protect their natural heritage. A teacher reported the following to us: 'Children of the Forest Guardians programme are becoming more aware of the problems facing our environment and ...

in our community, where desertification is most notable, with consequences such as drought and increased heat. Children are planting native trees to address this problem.'

Our efforts have had positive impacts on the environment: schools now have edible gardens, fruit orchards and green spaces where children harvest food to eat in school and take home, there is increased greenery and shade in the hot and dusty school grounds and in communal areas of town, and garbage is collected and reused or recycled for various purposes; all of these illustrate the direct benefits of natural spaces and cultivate a respect for nature. Building on our experiences thus far, future plans include continuing to engage teachers currently in the programme, building upon initially successful efforts for experiential and nature-based learning, as well as expanding to schools in more remote rural communities further up the watershed where support resources are scarcer and impact on bears is potentially even stronger.

The implications of the fuel-efficient cookstove programme are numerous. Use of the stoves showed a clear reduction in respiratory illness and safety and hygiene concerns, along with an opportunity for health education in general. With more time for women outside of the kitchen, there are opportunities for increased independence, education and empowerment. Families were engaged in the conservation programme, grateful for the technology and open to other opportunities for collaboration. By providing clear individual and familial benefits from this conservation programme, we've earned the communities' trust for future programme participation and directly changed their behaviour to reduce impact on the ecosystem.

Based on participant self-reporting, the impact on the environment is cut in half due to fewer trips into the forest and less wood use, leading to fewer trees cut and a reduction in potential encounters with bears. Everyone we talked to was eager to obtain a fuel-efficient stove, and those that received one explicitly stated wanting the rest of their community to receive a stove. Due to limited project funds and the need to first test the viability of the programme, we could only provide a subset with the stoves and opted to ask local community leaders to select recipients based on household need, ensuring that the programme worked through local governance procedures. In the future, we would like to extend this effort to all families and communities in the Leche River watershed. There was also willingness for certain community members to be trained in stove design and construction, leading us to investigate the viability of building capacity for a local stove-making business. Further research is needed to understand which trees are the most fuel-efficient to further reduce firewood use, and to map forest access points relative to sapote and pasallo, to further reduce human impact on vital bear foods. Additionally, a broader study to quantitatively compare firewood in fuel-efficient versus traditional stoves would be beneficial, but given limited staff time and motivation on the part of participant families, that has been difficult to accomplish.

Working with a local community has numerous benefits and challenges. Our programme was designed to be comprehensive to mutually benefit the community and the ecosystem, including not only environmental education and fuel-efficient cooking, but also diversifying the economy through alternative livelihoods, and artisanal training and awareness-building through traditional craft products.

However, working with entire communities of people, from a different culture, likely with different priorities and experiences, comes with a host of challenges. Examples include people agreeing to participate in a programme or meeting but not showing up for many reasons, including difficulties travelling, personal scheduling conflicts, or distrust in the true motivations for the event, among other things. Additionally, despite several confirmations for focus groups, participants failed to arrive and participation was only achieved through door to door petitions at the start of the meeting. We believe this is due to communities not being accustomed to providing feedback, having their voices heard, or involvement in an iterative process. Ultimately though, frequent visits and reminders, usually on the day of the programme, helped increase attendance. Gaining the confidence of a trusted community member or leader, who served as a liaison to the programme, increased programme participation. Clearly illustrated benefits to the community of a particular programme or event were also important in garnering support. Participatory decision-making and meeting the needs of the community based on data was shown to result in higher success. While our goal for programmes was to ultimately benefit Andean bear conservation, the advertised purpose of a programme was geared towards the priorities of the community: highlighting job opportunities, where work is particularly scarce for women, offering professional development credits for teachers, who are already overworked, and the gift of cooking technology, as traditional stoves are generally agreed to be inconvenient and not ideal.

There is still much to learn about Andean bears, their habitats and their conservation, but it is clear that their greatest threats are human-generated activities. Human communities impact the ecosystem and share the surrounding environment with bears and will undoubtedly affect and be affected by management decisions. Humans must be considered an equal player to prevent a long-term imbalance in the landscape but are, unfortunately, often the least addressed element in conservation programmes.

The conservation issues outlined here illustrate positive change in the environment resulting from eliciting the participation of local people. Our multi-pronged programmes, including environmental education and fuel-efficient cooking, are evidence-based and adaptable and can be applied in many contexts. Though community-based conservation programmes are long-term efforts and require patience and cultural sensitivity, we have planted seeds for attitudes and behaviours to establish a sentiment of environmental stewardship; an important piece in effective conservation. Ultimately, humans have the last word in conservation and the rural communities of Lambayeque, Peru, determine the fates of Andean bears and other species within the tropical dry forests.

BIBLIOGRAPHY AND REFERENCES

Amanzo, J, Appleton, R, and Van Horn, R, 2013 Andean bear (*Tremarctos ornatus*) body condition and the effect of seasonal availability of sapote fruit (*Colicodendron scabridum*, Capparaceae) in the tropical dry forest of Lambayeque, Peru, *Proceedings of the 22nd International Conference on Bear Research and Management* 75

Ancajima Salvatierra, E A, 2010 *Panorama histórico de Batán Grande*, Editora SRL 955, Chiclayo, Peru

Appleton, R D, Van Horn, R C, Noyce, K V, Spady, T J, Swaisgood, R R, and Arcese, P, 2018 Phenotypic plasticity in the timing of reproduction in Andean bears, *Journal of Zoology* (in press)

Bonacic, C, Amaya-Epinel, J D, and Ibarra, J T, 2017 Human-wildlife conflicts: An overview of cases and lessons from the Andean region, in *Tropical conservation: Perspectives on local and global priorities* (eds A A Aguirre and S Sukumar), Oxford University Press, New York, 109–25

Cornejo, X, and Iltis, H H, 2008 A revision of *Colicodendron* (Capparaceae), *Journal of the Botanical Research Institute of Texas* 2, 75–93

Decker, D J, Riley, S J, and Siemer, W F, 2012 *Human Dimensions of Wildlife Management*, 2 edn, Johns Hopkins University Press, Baltimore, Maryland

DRYFLOR *et al*, 2016 Plant diversity patterns in neotropical dry forests and their conservation implications, *Science* 353, 1383–7

Ektvedt, T M, Vetaas, O R, and Lundberg, A, 2012 Land-cover changes during the past 50 years in the semi-arid tropical forest region of northern Peru, *Erdkunde* 66, 57–75

Figueroa, J, 2013a Revisión de la dieta del oso andino *Tremarctos ornatus* (Carnivora: Ursidae) en América del Sur y nuevos registros para el Perú, *Revista del Museo Argentino de las Ciencias Naturales* 15, 1–27

———, 2013b Composición de la dieta del oso andino *Tremarctos ornatus* (Carnivora: Ursidae) en nueve áreas naturales protegidas del Perú, *THERYA* 4, 327–59

Gonzales, F N, Neira-Llerena, J, Llerena, G, and Zeballos, H, 2016 Pequeños vertebrados en la dieta del oso andino (*Tremarctos ornatus* Cuvier, 1825) en el norte del Perú, *Revista Peruana de Biología* 23, 61–6

Grieshop, A P, Marshall, J D, and Kandlikar, M, 2011 Health and climate benefits of cookstove replacement options, *Energy Policy* 39, 7530–42

Klare, U, Kamler, J F, and Macdonald, D W, 2011 A comparison and critique of different scat-analysis methods for determining carnivore diet, *Mammal Review* 41, 294–312

Linares-Palomino, R, Kvist, L P, Aguirre-Mendoza, Z, and Gonzales-Inca, C, 2010 Diversity and endemism of woody plant species in the Equatorial Pacific seasonally dry forests, *Biodiversity and Conservation* 19, 169–85

Madden, F, and McQuinn, B, 2014 Conservation's blind spot: The case for conflict transformation in wildlife conservation, *Biological Conservation* 178, 97–106

Martin, J, Basille, M, Van Moorter, B, Kindberg, J, Allainé, D, and Swenson, J E, 2010 Coping with human disturbance: spatial and temporal tactics of the brown bear (*Ursus arctos*), *Canadian Journal of Zoology* 88, 875–83

MINAGRI, 2014 Decreto Supremo No 004-2014-MINAGRI Decreto Supremo que aprueba la actualización de la lista de clasificación y categorización de las especies amenazadas de fauna silvestre legalmente protegidas, *El Peruano* 520497–520504, Lima, Peru

———, 2016 Resolución Ministerial 0505-2016-MINAGRI Decreto Supremo que aprueba la clasificación oficial de especies de flora silvestre categorizadas como amenazadas, Servicio Nacional Forestal y de Fauna Silvestre (SERFOR), Lima, Peru

Molina Proaño, S, 2012 *Análisis preliminar de la dinámica poblacional y amenazas del oso andino (Tremarctos ornatus) al nor-occidente del Distrito Metropolitano de Quito (DMQ) - Ecuador*, unpublished Msc thesis, Universidad San Francisco de Quito, Quito, Ecuador

Noyce, K V, and Garshelis, D L, 2011 Seasonal migrations of Minnesota black bears (*Ursus americanus*): causes and consequences, *Behavioral Ecology and Sociobiology* 65, 823–35

Osgood, W H, 1914 Mammals of an expedition across northern Peru, *Fieldiana: zoology* 10, 143–85

Peyton, B, 1980 Ecology, distribution, and food habits of spectacled bears, *Tremarctos ornatus*, in Peru, *Journal of Mammalogy* 61, 639–52

———, 1981 Spectacled bears in Peru, *Oryx* 16, 48–56

———, 1994 Conservation in the developing world: ideas on how to proceed, *International Conference on Bear Research and Management* 9, 115–27

Rode, K D, Amstrup, S C, and Regehr, E V, 2010 Reduced body size and cub recruitment in polar bears associated with sea ice decline, *Ecological Applications* 20, 768–82

Rodríguez Rodríguez, E F, Bussman, R W, Arroyo Alfaro, S J, López Medina, S E, and Briceño Rosario, J,

2007 *Capparis scabrida* (Capparaceae) una especie del Perú y Ecuador que necesita planes de conservación urgente, *Arnaldoa* 14, 269–82

Velez-Liendo, X, and García-Rangel, S, 2017 *Tremarctos ornatus, IUCN Red List of Endangered Species*, Gland, Switzerland

Wallace, R B *et al*, 2014 *Andean Bear Priority Conservation Units in Bolivia & Peru*, Wildlife Conservation Society, Centro de Biodiversidad y Genética de la Universidad Mayor de San Simón de Bolivia, Universidad Cayetano Heredia de Perú and Antwerp University, La Paz, Bolivia

Wathore, R, Mortimer, K, and Grieshop, A P, 2017 In-use emissions and estimated impacts of traditional, natural, and forced-draft cookstoves in rural Malawi, *Environmental Science and Technology* 51, 1921–38

Afterword

'It's Me Bear': Reflections on a Unique Career Working with Bears

Lynn Rogers

'When I first started studying bears in 1965 they had varmint status, like a rat'

I remember vividly my first encounter with a bear. It was spring and some friends and I had decided to head out camping. We were teenagers and off on a great adventure. Having set up our camp site and with the evening settling into night, everyone started to head to bed. I remember thinking to myself that as the weather was so nice it would be a great night to sleep under the stars. As I was slowly drifting off to sleep I heard something moving toward me; immediately I was alert, my body had tensed. I lay there with the hair on my neck standing. Slowly, out of the darkness emerged a black bear. Terrified, I lay there still; it sniffed my feet and continued to sniff up my body; eventually satisfied that I was not a threat it moved over me to access the garbage bag we had left hanging on a tree. As I lay, following the bear's every movement with my eyes, I was as mesmerised by this animal as I was scared. This encounter was the starting point of my fascination with bears and, whilst my exposure to bears was, beyond that moment, limited, it would influence many of my decisions over the next few years.

It was some years later when I was studying at Michigan State University that my next major bear experience would come into place. In my junior year, the Research Director for the Michigan Department of Conservation selected me for a summer internship capturing and ear tagging black bears. As it turns out I was particularly good at it; in fact, in one month I had captured and tagged more bears than the project had in the previous year. Within two years I trapped and tagged 191 bears. At this point we were using conventional methods of trapping, either darting or leg snares, and the data we collected in the study was at the forefront of informing so much of the understanding we have today. It was an extraordinary project to be involved in and I remember being so inspired and excited by the programme.

Word of my performance in the capture and tag programme reached a world pioneer in bear field research, Professor Albert W Erickson from the University of Minnesota, and he was so intrigued he came to Michigan to meet me. Within a week of that meeting he offered me a major opportunity – to become his graduate student and conduct Minnesota's first black bear field study. So, at the completion of my undergraduate studies in 1968, I moved to Minnesota to work with Prof Erickson. My PhD studies created another exciting opportunity as I became one of the first people to use radio collars, a technology that would go on to revolutionise wildlife research. I was also afforded the opportunity to work with renowned physiologist Dr Ulysses S Seal and physicist Robert Maxwell, two of the best minds in their fields, as we looked at hibernation physiology of black bears.

It was during this time as I reflected on my interactions with bears to date, from that teenage camping trip, through the capture and tag programme in Michigan, to my current work with Erickson, that I realised at no time had a bear tried to attack me. In fact, they only wanted to escape, running from me, climbing higher in trees; even when I held screaming cubs, mothers only bluff charged. My personal experience was nothing like the public portrayal or even my original perception.

It was then that I began to question the rationale behind human interactions with bears and realised that the current management was flawed and required change. In particular, I was struck by the fact that all of the documentation was geared toward 'fearful management' of bears. At this point Minnesota had the longest running bounty on bears in the United States of America. In fact, at the time, bears were classified as varmints to be eliminated year-round by trapping, shooting and poison. In 1965 fewer than 6000 black bears remained, most of them in one protected area in northeastern Minnesota.

Making the changes to bear management I thought were necessary was going to be a massive step change. It required change in legislation; that requires a political appetite for change and that political appetite is fed and informed by the desires and opinion of the general populace. Public perception of bears was reinforced by the media hype surrounding a limited number of negative encounters with bears and I could understand the fear; I had grown up with it, influenced by hunting magazines, government warnings and media sensationalism; I had shared it. I teamed up with hunting leader Richard Anderson, State Representative Cal Larson and State Senator Cliff Ukkelberg to develop legislation that would give Minnesota bears the respect and protection of big game status. In 1971, the legislation was passed and the next twist in my career began.

In response to the legislation the Department of Natural Resources asked me to outline a new direction for Minnesota's black bear management. Within this management plan I focused on a cultural change within the hunting fraternity. The plan proposed a shift in bear hunting from a year-round activity, essentially pest management, to a restricted season of six weeks annually. These seasonal restrictions were befitting of the bears' new status as a game species and were designed to protect cubs from being orphaned and ensure populations were at optimal sizes for growth and maintenance. It also focused on reducing wounding loss and limited methods for hunting. These changes saw the population of Minnesota's black bears quadruple over the next 25 years.

However, the initial implementation of the bear management strategy was under intense scrutiny. I had altered decades of accepted practices and, in the process, created a significant amount of angst within Minnesota. For long-term success public opinion of black bears needed to be changed. Capitalising on the media coverage that these changes created, and using my research to date, we started to slowly change public opinion, but there were still too many unanswered questions about black bear behaviour, which prompted me to start my next line of research: if I was going to convert fear to trust then I needed to provide a more holistic insight into bears and I needed to develop my trust with the animals as well. I wanted to do what Jane Goodall and Dian Fossey were doing (with chimpanzees and mountain gorillas respectively); this necessitated getting closer to the bears, to build trust, to communicate with them. Maybe this is where 'hey bear, it's me bear' started, but you know, talking to bears is not new; in many ways it is a continuation of native people's traditions and respect towards bears. Pacific coast peoples who come across bears in the forest will talk to them, explain the situation and sometimes ask the bear to respect their space or apologise for disturbing them (Clark and Slocombe 2009).

An opportunity presented itself in 1984 for me to develop this research approach. There were a number of 'problem bear' episodes at the Kawishiwi Campground in the Superior National Forest, Michigan. Bears were turning up at the campground, attracted by the food on offer. I filled a large box with beef fat and placed this a half-mile away from the campground, close to a Forest Service field lab. The bears ate as much as they wanted and moved on. I would throw food 30 feet away from me, and then gradually I would throw it closer and closer until a few of the bears would eventually even take food from my hand. It was easy. No problems.

To explore the possibility of accompanying wild black bears on their daily routines, I undertook a study into their aggressive-looking behaviours and personalities at a supplemental feeding site which I established which was visited repeatedly by 18 males and eight females. I would follow a single bear for up to a day at a time, monitoring every movement, every gesture. We wandered off into the woods together. I could hear them breathing. I could hear their movements, but I couldn't see them. They were like shadows. What I observed was that the bears displayed the lunges, slaps to the ground and explosive blowing that had traditionally been considered threats, but none of the bears attacked. There was the occasional nip or swipe, but it was worth it. These actions or interactions were more displays of anxiety than aggression and these behaviours declined as the bears grew accustomed to my presence. Within four bear visits, each bear became accustomed to the presence of a reclining person within 30m. Within eight visits, most readily took food from, or within 5m of, an immobile or slowly moving person. Very few became accustomed to being touched while all became accustomed to talking. Personalities differed; some were more nervous and blustery while others were calm and quicker to trust, but each bear was predictable once its personality was known.

Earlier in my career, when I had first started questioning our management strategies, I had reviewed nationwide records of killings by black bears. Only one black bear in about a million had killed a human; this data combined with my feeding station research highlighted that observers would have extremely low risk of a serious problem with black bears. To continue building trust I placed radio collars on the most trusting bears and developed routines by which these bears could recognise me and accept my presence outside of the feeding area and eventually anywhere they encountered me. After 50–100 hours of accompanying them, the bears seldom looked at me; in fact they behaved as if I was simply not there: not a danger and unimportant to their agenda. Most people are afraid of what a bear is going to do instead of what a bear actually ends up doing, which is usually to run away from human contact.

I recruited field assistants and, working in shifts, we used our new-found trust to record the bears' activities and habitat use, including when the bears bedded down at night, cub care, sleep patterns, and responses to weather, wolves and other wildlife. Observers followed less than 10m behind foraging bears. At greater distances, the bears sometimes lost track of observers and became wary of their rustlings. Bears also sometimes became wary when observers approached to within a few metres, although this wariness waned as bears became more habituated. An intense look from a bear indicated its concern over an observer's proximity or actions. The bears which we followed sometimes gave 'threat' displays (lunging, slapping vegetation, blowing) when observers got in their way in unusually food-rich areas. Most startled or defensive reactions (jumping away, whirling around, starting up trees) were due to sudden, seemingly aggressive acts by observers (sneezing, tripping, falling, accidentally hitting the bear) or by the sudden appearance of an extra observer in dense brush or on an overhead ledge. For this reason, data collecting sessions were conducted by lone observers.

With time (100–150 hours), mutual trust developed, 'threats' all but disappeared, and the fully habituated bears foraged, slept and appeared to be comfortable with a single observer 1–5m behind or occasionally closer to see certain foods. Sensitive, experienced observers saw less than one 'threat' per 100 hours of observation, with most of the threats occurring in dusk or darkness when it was more difficult to anticipate bears' movements. Observers used dim flashlights to aid observations and computer entries at night. The bears typically slept or nursed from one to two hours after sundown to 0.5 hours before sunrise. Observers spent nights in sleeping bags 1–8m from the sleeping bears.

To begin a new year of observations, researchers reinforced the previous year's habituation by resting near dens and day beds before extensive movement began. This presence was especially important with new-born litters because cubs developed wariness of strangers in late March and early April around the time of emergence. Prolonged handling of cubs during that time (the third month of life) further habituated them to people, making them less likely to distract their mothers with distress calls when observers accompanied them later.

The artificial feeding site was essentially discontinued in 1988 and 1989; bear use of the feeding site had waned by then and observers were concentrating on obtaining data from habituated bears rather than on habituating new ones. However, when we finished the study, the results were startling. In the six years that we used diversionary feeding at Kawishiwi, nuisance complaints fell by 88 per cent. Instead of digging in garbage cans, the bears were ignoring them completely. This in turn had a positive effect on local attitudes about bears. Residents, with a reduction in issues and greater exposure to bear behaviour, became willing to coexist with bears and were protective of them. The use of diversionary feeding is explored in more detail by Miha Krofel elsewhere in this volume (Chapter 15: Living with Bears in Europe).

The study had gained national recognition by this stage and my methods were demonstrated to be safe. As such, I attracted further funding for the study and was authorised for participation by volunteers, furthering my objective of removing the stigma attached to bears. I had nearly 200 volunteers safely accompany bear families over the next several years, continuing to challenge the conventional wisdom with no injuries or issues for the participants or the bears. Nuisance behaviour is not because bears get habituated or food-conditioned, it's because of hunger. All data say that black bears become less likely to attack when they lose their fear of people.

The habitat use data we collected in this study became the core information for management models that enabled foresters to protect important black bear habitats. Our observations of bear-human interactions continue to improve the management of situations in which bears had traditionally been killed. This observational approach also identified, for the first time, that bears often foraged in clear cuts – openings in which all trees and most shrubs had been cut. These sunlit areas had an abundance of berries and other foods enjoyed by bears, including ants. This discovery had significant implications for forestry management as clear cuts had become controversial and environmental groups wanted clear cutting stopped while the Congressional Appropriations Committee wanted National Forests to produce more income.

In 1996, I decided to take the work I started in 1984 to the next level and I added touch, the universal language, to build deeper trust. The first step was to develop enough trust that I could fit a radio collar without the need of a tranquiliser or other inhibitors. For some resident bears, bears that I've known since they were cubs, touch involves touching tongues, as this is how bears develop scent memories. This process then developed to the point that I was able to film close proximity footage of bear foraging and den construction activities while being ignored, so much so that the bears sometimes bumped into me. This work culminated in the ability to place den cams in occupied dens, creating the ability to explore hibernation without the traditional 'observer effects' and den abandonment.

There were two results of my touch experiment; the first was a deeper understanding of black bear ecology, behaviour and bear-human relations than ever before; the second was an increased level of public interest, providing a further positive media discussion on the behaviour of bears. While achieving the above, my method was not without criticism and required constant justification to both regulators and funders that this was a sound practice. This included working closely with the Minnesota Department of Natural Resources to alleviate regulatory concerns.

The overall focus and aim of my work was to better understand black bears, their behaviour and their lives and with that information reduce the fear and misunderstanding of these creatures in our world. This is work and a focus I continue to support through the not-for-profit North American Bear Center (NABC).

At the crux of my research the turning point came when I finally began interpreting bear behaviour in terms of their fear rather than my fear. In fact, looking back, I'm embarrassed at how long it took me to get over my fear. I'd spend time with bears, and then over the winter I'd have nightmares about them turning on me. But getting closer opened the door to everything: learning their language, the details of their social organisation, how they use the forest. Over time I found I could build trusting relationships with these intelligent, wild animals and this central philosophy has afforded me not only the opportunity to grow my understanding of these wonderful creatures but has also allowed me tools to change the state's and the public's perception of these animals. In doing so, I believe we have advanced the long-term survival of bears worldwide by replacing misconceptions with scientific facts about bears, their roles in ecosystems and their relations with humans. *I wish the rest of the world could see bears the way I do.*

FIGURE 19.1. THE AUTHOR WITH A BLACK BEAR.

Bibliography and References

Brooks, R T, McRoberts, R E, and Rogers L L, 1998 Predictive relationships between age and size and front foot pad width of northeastern Minnesota black bears, *Ursus americanus*, *Canadian Field-Naturalist* 112 (1), 82–5

Clark, D A, and Slocombe, D S, 2009 Respect for Grizzly Bears: an Aboriginal Approach for Co-existence and Resilience, *Ecology and Society* 14 (1), 42–60

DelGiudice, G D, Rogers, L L, Allen, A W, and Seal, U S, 1991 Weights and hematology of wild black bears during hibernation, *Journal of Wildlife Diseases* 27 (4), 637–42

Hellgren, E C, Rogers, L L, and Seal, U S, 1993 Serum chemistry and hematology of black bears: physiological indices of habitat quality or seasonal patterns? *Journal of Mammalogy* 74 (2), 304–15

Maxwell, R, Thorkelson, J, Rogers, L L, and Brander, R B, 1988 The field energetics of winter-dormant black bear (*Ursus americanus*) in northeastern Minnesota, *Canadian Journal of Zoology* 66, 2095–2103

McMillin, J M, Seal, U S, Rogers, L L, and Erickson, A W, 1976 Annual testosterone rhythm in the black bear (*Ursus americanus*), *Biology of Reproduction* 15, 163–7

McRoberts, R E, Brooks, R T, and Rogers, L L, 1998 Using nonlinear mixed effects models to estimate size-age relationships for black bears, *Canadian Journal of Zoology* 76, 1098–1106

Moen, A N, and Rogers, L L, 1985 Radiant surface temperatures and hair depths of a black bear, *Ursus americanus*, *Canadian Field-Naturalist* 99 (1), 47–50

Peters, G, Owen, M, and Rogers, L, 2007 Humming in bears: a peculiar sustained mammalian vocalization, *Acta Theriologica* 52, 379–89

Rogers, L L, 1974 Shedding of foot pads by black bears during denning, *Journal of Mammalogy* 55 (3), 672–4

——, 1975 Parasites of black bears (*Ursus americanus* Pallas) of the Lake Superior Region, *Journal of Wildlife Diseases* 11, 189–92

——, 1985 Aiding the wild survival of orphaned bear cubs, *Wildlife Rehabilitation* 4, 104–11

——, 1986 Homing by black bears in Minnesota, *Canadian Field-Naturalist* 100 (3), 350–3

——, 1987 Effects of food supply and kinship on social behavior, movements, and population dynamics of black bears in northeastern Minnesota, *Wildlife Monograph* 97, 72

——, 1987 Navigation by adult black bears, *Journal of Mammalogy* 68 (1), 185–8

——, 2011 Does diversionary feeding create nuisance bears and jeopardize public safety? *Human-Wildlife Interactions* 5 (2), 287–95

Rogers, L L, and Applegate, R, 1983 Dispersal of fruit seeds by black bears, *Journal of Mammalogy* 64 (2), 310–11

Rogers, L L, and Durst, S C, 1987 Evidence that black bears reduce peripheral blood flow during hibernation, *Journal of Mammalogy* 68 (4), 872–5

Rogers, L L, and Mansfield, S, 2011 Misconceptions about black bears: a response to Geist (2011), *Human-Wildlife Interactions* 5 (2), 173–6

Rogers, L L, and Mech, L D, 1981 Interactions of wolves and black bears in northeastern Minnesota, *Journal of Mammalogy* 62 (2), 434–6

Rogers, L L, and Rogers, S M, 1976 Parasites of bears: a review, *International Conference on Bear Research and Management* 3, 411–30

Rogers, L L, and Wilker, G W, 1990 How to obtain behavioral and ecological information from free-ranging, researcher-habituated black bears, *International Conference on Bear Research and Management* 8, 321–8

Rogers, L L, Kuehn, D W, Erickson, A W, Harger, E M, Verme, L J, and Ozoga, J J, 1976 Characteristics and management of black bears that feed in garbage dumps, campgrounds, or residential areas, *International Conference on Bear Research and Management* 3, 169–75

Rogers, L L, Mansfield, S A, Hornby, K, Hornby, S, Debruyn, T D, Mize, M, Clark, R, and Burghardt, G M, 2014 Black Bear Reactions to Venomous and Non-venomous Snakes in Eastern North America, *Ethology* 120, 641–51, doi: 10.1111/eth.12236

Rogers, L L, Stowe, C M, and Erickson, A W, 1976 Succinylcholine chloride immobilization of black bear, *International Conference on Bear Research and Management* 3, 431–6

Rogers, L L, Wilker, G A, and Scott, S S, 1991 Reactions of black bears to human menstrual odors, *Journal of Wildlife Management* 55 (4), 632–4

Stringham, S F, and Rogers, L L, 2017 Fear of Humans by Bears and Other Animals (Anthropophobia): How Much is Natural? *Journal of Behavior* 2 (2), 1009–25

Stringham, S F, Rogers, L L, and Bryant, A, 2017 Semantic vs. Empirical Issues in the Bear Diversionary Baiting Controversy, *Environment and Ecology Research* 5, 436–42, doi: 10.13189/eer.2017.050604

Contributors

Philip Charles grew up in Suffolk, where his childhood passion for wildlife and the natural world led him to Otley College, Ipswich, to study for a diploma in Animal Management. He then completed a degree in Animal Conservation Science at the University of Cumbria. After graduating in 2011, he took the opportunity to study bear populations in coastal British Columbia. He worked as a lead bear guide for six years at the Spirit Bear Lodge, where he established summer internship programmes for Kitasoo/Xai'xais youth. Following cultural adoption, he became a fully integrated member of this First Nations society. He founded and manages Spirit of Suffolk, a conservation-based tour operator, and teaches in the animal studies department at Otley College.

Melanie Clapham is a Postdoctoral Research Fellow at the University of Victoria, Canada. She serves as a Director and Conservation Scientist for the BearID Project, a non-profit research organisation that develops non-invasive technologies to identify and monitor bears and other wildlife. She is interested in how social and environmental factors influence bear behaviour and the implications of this for management and conservation. Her research has primarily focused on chemical signalling in bears, and its relevance to mating and establishing dominance. As part of her postdoctoral research, she is co-directing a project developing facial recognition technology for bear identification. Through her work, she works with First Nations to help facilitate science-based management decisions. She also works closely with ecotourism companies in British Columbia to assess and reduce the impacts of commercial viewing on wildlife.

Ian Convery is Professor of Environment and Society at the University of Cumbria. He has spent the last 20 years or so working on understanding societal interactions with, connections to, and perceptions of, the 'natural world'. His current interests focus on public engagement with species reintroductions and rewilding, and he is co-chair of the IUCN Rewilding Task Force. His children, on the other hand, think that he ought to spend less time thinking up terrible bear puns and more time doing important stuff, like making marmalade sandwiches.

Koen Cuyten studied bears in the Bear Forest at Ouwehand Zoo in the Netherlands during his studies of Animal Management; in 2004, he joined Bears in Mind, where he has been working as Project Coordinator ever since. Cuyten's work at the foundation is highly inspiring and motivating, but also challenging, because of the continual need to help captive bears in distress and protect wild bears in their natural environment. He also works for the Rewilding Foundation on projects advocating the safeguarding and restoration of interconnected ecosystems, where large carnivores such as leopard, bear and wolf play a vital role as a keystone species.

Elizabeth O Davis is a Postdoctoral Associate at the San Diego Zoo's Institute for Conservation Research. She is part of a team that aims to halt the decline of bears throughout Asia, due to the trade in bear bile and bear parts for traditional medicine. Specific goals of this work include understanding which groups are buying bear bile and other bear parts, and how researchers may open lines of communication with these groups to begin effective behaviour change.

Peter Davis is Emeritus Professor of Museology in the International Centre for Cultural and Heritage Studies at Newcastle University, UK. He is the author of several books, including *Museums and the Natural Environment* (1996), *Ecomuseums: a sense of place* (1999; 2nd edition 2011) and (with Christine Jackson) *Sir William Jardine: a life in natural history* (2001). He has co-edited several books in the *Heritage Matters* series, including *Making Sense of Place* (2012), *Safeguarding Intangible Cultural Heritage* (2012), *Displaced Heritage* (2014), *Changing Perceptions of Nature* (2016) and *Heritage and Peacebuilding* (2017). With Michelle Stefano he edited *The Routledge Companion to Intangible Cultural Heritage* (2017). He is currently President of the Society for the History of Natural History.

Sarah Elmeligi is an interdisciplinary ecologist who integrates biological and social data to inform human use of protected areas and bear management in western Canada. Her Masters degree from the University of Northern British Columbia investigated the impacts of bear-viewing tourism on grizzly bear behaviour and visitor satisfaction/perceptions of the viewing encounter. Her PhD from Central Queensland University focused on the relationship between grizzly bears and hikers in the Canadian Rocky Mountain National Parks. She has extensive experience of working with a broad network of stakeholders within the environmental non-profit sector, including government authorities and First Nations communities, campaigning for the creation and improved management of protected areas. Currently, Elmeligi works as a Park Development Planner with Alberta Parks, where she integrates her research and work experience to create management plans that provide quality recreation experiences and protect wildlife habitats.

Beatrice Frank is the Social Science Specialist for Capital Regional District Regional Parks, Canada, and an adjunct professor at the University of Victoria. In the last ten years, she has focused on better defining tolerance and coexistence and developed the conflict-to-coexistence concept, which she is furthering in her most recent research and publications on wildlife and protected areas.

Barrie K. Gilbert gained a degree in biology at Queen's University, followed by graduate studies at Duke University on fallow deer and dolphin communication. He joined the faculty of Utah State University in 1976 specialising in behavioural observation of all three species of North American bears in the Rocky Mountains, Alaska and coastal British Columbia. However, his career almost ended before it began when one of the first wild grizzlies he encountered tore off most of his face and scalp. After recovery, he returned to grizzly research, gaining new insights into these often-maligned giants. Dr Gilbert's work centred on ways to keep both humans and bears safe, convinced that bears are another culture to be understood and protected. He leads ethical bear-viewing trips to coastal British Columbia, to help people appreciate wild grizzlies and the habitat they require. In his new book he explodes myths about grizzlies, and shows the intelligent, adaptable side of these astonishingly social animals, how they help ecosystems function and restore ecological integrity.

Jenny Anne Glikman is Associate Director of Community Engagement at the San Diego Zoo's

Institute for Conservation Research, and board member of the IUCN Task Force on Human-Wildlife Conflict as well as the IUCN Bear Specialist Group (Human-Bear Conflict Expert Team). As a social scientist, she focuses on understanding the relationships between humans and wildlife. Her work ranges from studying and addressing human-wildlife interactions to exploring various aspects of local consumers of wildlife products in several countries.

Tracy Ann Hayes is a lecturer in the Institute of Health at the University of Cumbria. She embraces transdisciplinary methodologies that utilise creative and narrative approaches to research and teaching. Her research explores young people's relationship with the natural environment, building on her practical experience of working with children, families and adults, and her realisation that some young people may be excluded from opportunities to experience and understand nature. A qualified youth worker and community development professional, she is a Fellow of the Higher Education Academy, and co-convener of the Nature, Outdoor Learning and Play special interest group for the British Educational Research Association.

Mike Jeffries is an ecologist at Northumbria University, Newcastle upon Tyne. His research focuses on ponds and wetlands. The work mixes the natural history of pond invertebrates and plants, and how their distributions change over time, plus the significance of ponds as a source and sink of greenhouse gases. Ponds are not just of scientific importance. They are portals to other worlds of magical folk and mysterious creatures, not least in the wilds of Northumberland. A menagerie of teddy bears, barghasts and natural history TV favourites all stalk through Jeffries' research, and help students understand the strangeness and delight of the natural world.

Jón Jónsson is a folklorist and project manager at the University of Iceland's Research Centre in Strandir, which is located in the Westfjords of Iceland, and focuses on folklore research. U-Iceland's Research Centres are located in rural areas throughout the country and provide a venue for collaboration with local authorities, institutions, businesses and individuals. Jónsson's field of study is applied and public folklore and scholarly collaboration with tourism, museums and artists. He has also studied diaries and daily life in Iceland in the 19th and 20th centuries and recently published a book on beggars and vagabonds in Iceland's old rural society. Jónsson participates in the research project 'Visitations: Polar bears out of place', with an emphasis on legends and folk belief in connection with polar bear encounters in Iceland.

John Kitchin is a post-graduate researcher at the University of Cumbria. He is particularly interested in exploring our relationships with nature and collecting stories from people who live and work with bears.

Miha Krofel is Assistant Professor and wildlife researcher at the Biotechnical Faculty, University of Ljubljana (Slovenia). He serves as external adviser for the World Wide Fund for Nature (Switzerland). His research focus is on large carnivore ecology, management and conservation in Eurasia and Africa. Most of his studies on bears centre on improving our understanding of basic ecology and effects of bear management measures. He has explored topics such as human-bear conflicts, interactions between bears and other carnivores, effects of artificial feeding on bear denning behaviour and the influence of bear-watching tourism. In addition to bears, Krofel is currently involved in projects dealing with Eurasian lynx, grey wolves and golden jackals in Europe, snow leopards in Mongolia, cheetahs and leopards in Namibia, and lizards in the Canary Islands.

Gareth Longstaff is a lecturer in media and cultural studies at Newcastle University, UK. Both his teaching and research interests are primarily concerned with queer history and heritage, queer theory, gender and sexuality, celebrity, discourses of self-representation, pornography and psychoanalysis. In his forthcoming monograph 'Celebrity and Pornography: The Psychoanalysis of Self Representation' he engages and applies queer theory to Freudian and Lacanian psychoanalysis, the celebrification of desire, and the mediated screening of subjectivity and jouissance in self-representational photography, pornography and digital/networked media in celebrity culture. He is a queer activist and chairs the staff LGBTQ+ network at Newcastle. As well as this, he also works at the intersections of queer history, culture and heritage and is currently working towards an AHRC/Arts Council bid to create and sustain a Queer Creative Archive and Hub of the North-East of England.

Henry McGhie has had a lifelong fascination with nature, especially birds. He heads up Curating Tomorrow, a consultancy for museums and the heritage sector, helping them draw on their unique resources to enhance their contributions to society and the natural environment, the Sustainable Development Goals, climate action and nature conservation. This involves curating collections, research, ideas, partnerships, exhibitions, events, consultations, policies and/or strategies together to address key challenges and questions. Henry was involved in getting museums recognised in the Workplan for the Paris Agreement, and has edited two books on climate change communication, and another on 19th century ornithology. He previously worked at Manchester Museum (University of Manchester) as Head of Collections and Curator of Zoology. His work is directed towards supporting a future where people and nature flourish together.

Jeff Meldrum is a Full Professor of Anatomy and Anthropology at Idaho State University. His research centres on the evolution of hominin bipedalism. His interests in the footprints attributed to *sasquatch* came into focus when he personally examined a line of 15-inch tracks in the Blue Mountains of southeastern Washington, in 1996. His lab now houses well over 300 footprint casts attributed to relict hominoids around the world. He conducts collaborative laboratory and field research throughout North America and internationally. He is author of *Sasquatch: Legend Meets Science* (2006), which explores the contemporary scientific evidence for the reality of this legendary species and acknowledges tribal people's traditional knowledge of this subject. In addition, he has published two field guides, one focusing on *sasquatch*, the second considering the potential of relict hominoid species around the world (2013, 2016). He is editor-in-chief of the scholarly-refereed journal, *The Relict Hominoid Inquiry* (www.isu.edu/rhi), now in its seventh year.

Owen T. Nevin is Associate Vice-Chancellor, Gladstone Region, CQUniversity, Australia. He holds a BSc (Hons) in Biology and Ecology from the University of East Anglia (UK) and a PhD in Wildlife Ecology from Utah State University (USA). He is a population and behavioural ecologist specialising in large carnivores. Much of his research work focuses around advancing the conservation of bears and their habitats through developing better management and understanding of bears, bear-viewing ecotourism and resource exploitation (fisheries and forestry). He held the prestigious position of 'Stokes-Leopold Memorial Scholar' at Utah State University from

2002 to 2003. In 2003, he was elected to the Society for Conservation Biology's European Board, where he served for six years; he later served on the Global Board of Governors from 2010 to 2013. In 2017, he was appointed as an Anniversary Visiting Professor of Conservation Biology at the University of Cumbria. His expertise is called upon by industry as an expert witness on bear viewing safety, on the Conservation Advisory Panel for the Ministry of Defense, and the Biodiversity Assessment Panel for the Center for Alpine Ecology. He is currently Independent Chair of the Port Curtis Integrated Monitoring Program.

Heather Prince is Associate Professor of Outdoor and Environmental Education and Principal Lecturer in Collaborative and Experiential Learning at the University of Cumbria, UK. She designs, develops and teaches on undergraduate and postgraduate courses in outdoor studies, and is interested in creative pedagogic practice of outdoor learning in schools and higher education, adventure, ecology and sustainability. She is co-editor of the *Routledge International Handbook of Outdoor Studies* and *Research Methods in Outdoor Studies*, associate editor of the *Journal of Adventure Education and Outdoor Learning* and Principal Fellow of the Higher Education Academy, UK.

Lynn Rogers has spent more than 50 years studying wildlife behaviour and ecology, specialising in bears, focusing in particular on the American black bear in northeastern Minnesota, USA. Although in his early work he applied the traditional tools of wildlife management, and in fact pioneered the use of radio telemetry to study bears, he later turned to the trust-based research methods epitomised by the work of ethologists like Jane Goodall. He has combined these direct observational approaches with the use of modern technologies, including GPS telemetry, camera traps and remote video, to study behaviour, ecology, hibernation, vocalisations, body language, social organisation, physiology and bear-human relations. He is the founder and principal biologist of the Wildlife Research Institute (WRI) near Ely, Minnesota.

Kristinn Schram is Associate Professor of Folkloristics/Ethnology at the University of Iceland. His field of study ranges from oral narrative to food and festivals, ironic performances to media representations, in a variety of cultural spaces such as Arctic shores and city streets. He lectures on the dynamics of identity, national images and tradition, folk narrative and urban folklore. Among current research topics are the exoticism of the North, transnational performances of the West-Nordic region and sociocultural aspects of climate change and mobility in the North Atlantic. He participates in the research project 'Visitations: Polar bears out of place', concerning human/non-human relations in the context of climate change and environmental behaviour; historic, current and future.

Bryndís Snæbjörnsdóttir and Mark Wilson are a collaborative art partnership. Bryndís Snæbjörnsdóttir is Professor of Fine Art at the Icelandic University of the Arts, Reykjavík; Mark Wilson is Professor in Fine Art at the Institute of the Arts, University of Cumbria, UK. Their interdisciplinary art practice is research-based and socially-engaged, exploring issues of history, culture and environment in relation to both humans and non-human species. Working very often in close consultation with experts and amateurs in the field, their work tests cultural constructs and tropes, and human behaviour in respect of ecologies, extinction, conservation and the environment. Underpinning much of their practice are issues of psychological and physical displacement and realignment in respect of land and environment and the effect of these positions on cultural perspectives. Their artworks have been exhibited throughout the UK and internationally. They are frequent speakers at international conferences on issues related to their practice. Their works have been widely discussed in texts across many disciplinary fields and regularly cited as contributive to knowledge in the expanded field of research-based art practice. They conduct their collaborative practice from bases in Iceland and the north of England. More information on Snæbjörnsdóttir/Wilson's practice is available at: www.snaebjornsdottirwilson.com

Russ Van Horn serves San Diego Zoo Global as a Scientist in Population Sustainability. He integrates behavioural and ecological theory into conservation research and practice, using direct and indirect methods to seek effective and sustainable solutions to conservation challenges. He leads a programme focused on collaborative research for the conservation of Andean bears, especially in Peru. He is also involved with integrative analyses of data from captive bears to inform zoo husbandry, provide additional perspectives for field data, and facilitate field research. He has been involved in research ranging from savannah baboons and spotted hyenas to small mammals, neotropical migrant songbirds, elk and bison. An Associate Wildlife Biologist for The Wildlife Society (USA), he also serves as co-chair of the IUCN's Andean Bear Expert Team.

Samantha Young worked for seven years on the community engagement team at the San Diego Zoo Institute for Conservation Research, creating community-based conservation programmes in Peru and Mexico. Fluent in Spanish, she worked with local communities on conservation education, livelihood improvement and teaching sustainable practices, and carried out research in human perceptions of the natural world. Working in rural and urban settings, she trained education supervisors, teachers, community liaisons and citizen scientists to conduct programming, helping to reduce human impacts on the environment. She also carried out sociological research on environmental issues using face-to-face interviews and other survey methods. She currently lectures on biology and anthropology at Southwestern College and Grossmont College in San Diego.

Index

HERITAGE MATTERS

Printed in the United States
by Baker & Taylor Publisher Services